The Limits of Sisterhood

The Limits of Sisterhood

The Beecher Sisters on Women's Rights and Woman's Sphere

Jeanne Boydston

Mary Kelley

Anne Margolis

The University of North Carolina Press

Chapel Hill and London

Manufactured in the United States of America

Library of Congress Cataloging-in-Publication Data

Boydston, Jeanne.
  The limits of sisterhood.

  (Gender and American culture)
  Includes index.
    1. Women's rights—United States—History—19th
century—Sources. 2. Feminism—United States—History—
19th century—Sources. 3. Beecher, Catharine Esther,
1800–1878. 4. Stowe, Harriet Beecher, 1811–1896.
5. Hooker, Isabella Beecher, 1822–1907. I. Kelley,
Mary, 1943– . II. Margolis, Anne Throne.
III. Title. IV. Series.
HQ1236.5.U6B69 1988   305.4′2′0973   87-19771
ISBN 0-8078-1768-6
ISBN 0-8078-4207-9 (pbk.)

To Our Mothers

Juanita Laymance Boydston

June Viel Bremer

Janice Weingarten Throne

Contents

Illustrations

Acknowledgments

We began this project in 1983 as three individual scholars with different interests in Catharine Beecher, Harriet Beecher Stowe, and Isabella Beecher Hooker. Anne Margolis had been engaged in extensive research on Hooker and the postbellum women's rights movement. Originally projecting an article on the Beecher-Tilton scandal, Margolis became convinced that the three sisters merited a book-length study. Jeanne Boydston's research on the history of housework had led her to recognize the contradictions within Catharine Beecher's life and work and to wrestle with the implications of Beecher's vision of domesticity for women of other races and classes. In her study of twelve nineteenth-century American women writers, Mary Kelley had come to understand the significance of Harriet Beecher Stowe for illustrating key themes and tensions within the nineteenth-century debate on woman's sphere.

In a sense, then, the process of melding these separate interests into a single volume has amounted to an extended "conversation among ourselves"—a conversation about the nineteenth century and the roles of white middle-class women within it, but also about the implications of that earlier period for the lives of women in the present. We hope the spirit of that conversation has informed the pages that follow.

Research on the sisters' roles in the Beecher-Tilton scandal, begun in 1982 with the support of a Grant-in-Aid from the American Council of Learned Societies, was continued under grants from the Division One Research Funding Committee of Williams College. Generous funding for the ongoing work on Catharine Beecher was provided by the Research Council of Rutgers University and a Henry Rutgers Research Fellowship. A Dartmouth College Faculty Fellowship and the Committee on Research made possible more extensive research on Harriet Beecher Stowe. We have all benefited from the assistance of former and present students, including in particular Dina Esposito, Terry Flemming, Marion Halliday, Christine Harrington, Michael Kolster, Katherine Monteiro, and Kathleen Waters. Virginia Close and Patricia Carter, librarians at Dartmouth College, and Peggy Hilbert, secretary at Throne International Metals, lightened many a task. Each of us wishes to thank Gail Patten, the administrative assistant in the Department of History, Dartmouth College, for her commitment to this project.

We were fortunate to be able to draw upon the archival expertise of the following repositories, all of which have preserved and made accessible the extraordinarily rich papers of the Beechers. Particularly indebted as we are to the Stowe-Day Foundation, we thank Joseph Van Why, Elise Thall, Dorothy Mills, and especially Diana Royce and Bill Staples. We also acknowledge the late Joseph K. Hooker for permission to publish his grandmother's papers. We are grateful for the support of the Alderman Library, University of Virginia; the Beinecke Rare Book and Manuscript Library and the Sterling Memorial Library, Yale University; the Connecticut Historical Society; the Connecticut State Library; the Henry E. Huntington Library; the Houghton Library, Harvard University; the Massachusetts Historical Society; the Mount Holyoke College Library/ Archives, Mount Holyoke College; the Arthur and and Elizabeth Schlesinger Library, Radcliffe College; the Sophia Smith Collection, Smith College; and the Vassar College Library, Vassar College.

Iris Tillman Hill, Editor-in-Chief at the University of North Carolina Press, strongly supported the project from the outset. Linda Kerber and Nell Painter, the editors of the series that this volume inaugurates, encouraged our work and offered generous suggestions on the manuscript. We thank David Leverenz and Brenda Silver for reading sections of the materials on Harriet Beecher Stowe, and the members of the Social and Cultural History Seminar at Rutgers-Camden for their comments on an earlier draft of the essays on Catharine Beecher. The late Sydney Ahlstrom's respect for the varieties of religious experience made him an invaluable resource in studying Isabella Beecher Hooker.

The character of this collaboration has also been shaped by the experiences of our individual lives. Sidney Throne provided his daughter with access to the resources of his office. We stand indebted to Ann Bremer for providing a model of sisterhood, to Annette Kolodny for sharing the wisdom of her own experience, and to Lori Ginzberg for caring deeply about the ideas and the words of this manuscript. Manual Ayala, Kirsten Harvey, Todd Harvey, Brooke Karlsen, Jennifer Bernadette Margolis, Natalie Rose Margolis, and Joel Steiker have lived on closer terms with the Beecher family than they might have wished—in the case of Jennifer and Natalie, for virtually their entire lives. We thank them all for their patience.

Language cannot adequately express appreciation for the continuing sensitivity and support of Brian Margolis, Carol Karlsen, and Robert Kelley. Their being here for the duration has meant everything.

May 1987   J. B.
                                                                                 M. K.
                                                                                 A. M.

Chronology

1800	Catharine Esther Beecher is born to Lyman Beecher and Roxana Foote Beecher in East Hampton, Long Island.
1805	Mary Foote Beecher is born to Lyman Beecher and Roxana Foote Beecher in East Hampton, Long Island.
1810	The Beecher family moves to Litchfield, Connecticut.
1811	Harriet Elizabeth Beecher is born to Lyman Beecher and Roxana Foote Beecher in Litchfield, Connecticut.
1816	Roxana Foote Beecher, mother of Catharine and Harriet, dies in Litchfield, Connecticut.
1822	Isabella Holmes Beecher is born to Lyman Beecher and Harriet Porter Beecher, his second wife, in Litchfield, Connecticut. Alexander Fisher, Catharine's fiancé, dies at sea.
1823	Catharine founds the Hartford Female Seminary. Mary joins Catharine as a teacher in the Seminary.
1824	Harriet attends the Hartford Female Seminary.
1827	Mary marries Thomas Clap Perkins.
1828	Mary gives birth to Frederick Beecher Perkins. Three more children are born to Mary Beecher Perkins and Thomas Clap Perkins during the next eight years.
1829	Catharine publishes *Suggestions Respecting Improvements in Education*. Failing to raise an endowment for her Hartford Seminary, Catharine moves in with Mary.
1832	The Beecher family moves to Walnut Hills, Cincinnati, Ohio, where Lyman Beecher becomes president of the Lane Theological Seminary.

1833   Catharine establishes the Western Female Institute in Cincinnati, Ohio.

1834   Harriet publishes "A New England Sketch" in *Western Monthly Magazine*.

1835   Isabella's mother, Harriet Porter Beecher, dies in Cincinnati, Ohio. Isabella moves to Hartford, Connecticut, to live with her half sister, Mary, and attend the Hartford Female Seminary.

1836   Catharine publishes *Letters on the Difficulties of Religion*.
        Harriet marries Calvin Stowe. Their twin daughters, Harriet and Eliza Stowe, are born.

1836–37?   Isabella returns to Cincinnati, Ohio, where she attends the Western Female Institute.

1837   Catharine's Western Female Institute fails. Catharine publishes *An Essay on Slavery and Abolitionism*.

1838   Harriet gives birth to Henry Ellis Stowe. Two years later, her second son, Frederick William Stowe, is born. Isabella returns to live with Mary and attends the Hartford Female Seminary.

1841   Catharine publishes *A Treatise on Domestic Economy*. Isabella marries John Hooker.

1842   Isabella gives birth to Thomas Beecher Hooker, who dies later that year. Three more children are born to Isabella Beecher Hooker and John Hooker in the next thirteen years.

1843   Harriet publishes *The Mayflower: or, Sketches of Scenes and Characters among the Descendants of the Puritans*. Georgiana May Stowe is born.

1844   Catharine organizes the Central Committee for Promoting National Education and begins touring the East to raise money for educating women to go to the West as teachers.

1846	Harriet spends fifteen months at a water cure in Brattleboro, Vermont. Two years later Calvin spends more than a year at the same water cure.
1848	Harriet gives birth to Samuel Charles Stowe. He dies from cholera during an epidemic the next year.
1850	Catharine founds the Milwaukee Female Seminary. Catharine publishes *Truth Stranger than Fiction.* Harriet and Calvin move to Brunswick, Maine, where he has accepted an appointment at Bowdoin College. Harriet's seventh child, Charles Edward Stowe, is born.
1851	Catharine publishes *The True Remedy for the Wrongs of Woman.* Catharine lives with Harriet Beecher Stowe and Calvin Stowe while Harriet completes *Uncle Tom's Cabin.* Harriet publishes *Uncle Tom's Cabin* serially in the *National Era.* A two-volume edition appears in 1852.
1852	Catharine founds the American Women's Educational Association.
1854	Harriet publishes an "Appeal to the Women of the Free States."
1855	Catharine publishes *Letters to the People on Health and Happiness.*
1860	Isabella writes her first prosuffrage document, "Shall Women Vote? A Matrimonial Dialogue." From April through August Isabella seeks medical treatment from Mrs. R. B. Gleason at the Elmira, New York, water cure.
1863	Lyman Beecher dies in Brooklyn, New York.
1865	Harriet publishes *House and Home Papers.*
1868	Isabella publishes "A Mother's Letters to a Daughter on Woman Suffrage" anonymously in *Putnam's Magazine.*

1869   Catharine and Harriet publish *The American Woman's Home.*

Isabella sponsors and organizes Hartford's first woman suffrage convention and presides over the founding of the Connecticut Woman Suffrage Association.

1871   Catharine publishes *Woman Suffrage and Woman's Profession.*

Harriet publishes *My Wife and I.*

Isabella meets Victoria Woodhull in Washington, D.C., on the opening day of the woman suffrage convention that Isabella has organized.

1872   In November *Woodhull and Claflin's Weekly* accuses Henry Ward Beecher of committing adultery with Elizabeth Tilton.

1873   Isabella publishes *Womanhood: Its Sanctities and Fidelities.*

1874   Catharine publishes *Educational Reminiscences and Suggestions.*

1874–75   Isabella joins John Hooker in Europe in order to escape the growing controversy generated by the Beecher-Tilton scandal and the resulting trials.

1878   Catharine Esther Beecher dies in Elmira, New York.

Harriet publishes her last novel, *Poganuc People.*

1886   Calvin Stowe dies.

1888   Isabella delivers a speech before the International Council of Women entitled "The Constitutional Rights of the Women of the United States" (published two years later).

1893   Isabella serves on the Board of Lady Managers of the Columbian Exposition in Chicago, Illinois.

1896   Harriet Beecher Stowe dies in Hartford, Connecticut.

1898   Isabella publishes "Are Women Too Ignorant?"

1900   Mary Beecher Perkins dies in Hartford, Connecticut.

1901   John Hooker dies.

1902   Isabella publishes *An Argument on United States Citizenship*.

1907   Isabella Beecher Hooker dies in Hartford, Connecticut.

Abbreviations

Abbreviations for Archives Cited in Notes and Documents:

AL	Alderman Library, University of Virginia, Charlottesville, Va. Harriet Beecher Stowe Collection
BL	Beinecke Rare Book and Manuscript Library, Yale University, New Haven, Conn. American Literature Collection
CHS	Connecticut Historical Society, Hartford, Conn. Isabella Beecher Hooker Papers
AH&G/CSL	Connecticut State Library Archives, History and Genealogy Unit, Hartford, Conn. Elizabeth Lyman Collection
HL	Henry E. Huntington Library, San Marino, Calif. Clara Colby Papers James T. Fields Papers
HOU	Houghton Library, Harvard University, Cambridge, Mass. Houghton Mifflin Papers
MHS	Massachusetts Historical Society, Boston, Mass. Follen Papers
MHCL	Mount Holyoke College Library/Archives, South Hadley, Mass. Beecher Family Papers, 1822–1903
SchL	Arthur and Elizabeth Schlesinger Library on the History of Women in America, Radcliffe College, Cambridge, Mass. Beecher-Stowe Family Papers Olympia Brown Papers Alma Lutz Papers

SD   Stowe-Day Foundation, Hartford, Conn.
              Acquisitions
              Foote Collection
              Isabella Beecher Hooker Collection
              Joseph K. Hooker Collection
              Katharine S. Day Collection
              Langdon Collection
              White Collection

SML   Sterling Memorial Library, Yale University,
              New Haven, Conn.
              Beecher Family Papers

SSC   Sophia Smith Collection, Smith College,
              Northampton, Mass.
              Garrison Family Papers
              Sara Payson Parton Papers

VCL   Vassar College Library, Poughkeepsie, N.Y.
              Susan B. Anthony Papers

              Abbreviations for Published Works Cited
              as Sources for Documents:

Autobiography Barbara M. Cross, ed., *The Autobiography of Lyman
              Beecher*, 2 vols. (Cambridge, Mass.: Harvard
              University Press, Belknap Press, 1961).

AWH   Catharine E. Beecher and Harriet Beecher Stowe, *The
              American Woman's Home or, Principles of Domestic
              Science* (New York: J. B. Ford, 1869).

CEB Appeal Catharine E. Beecher, *An Appeal to the People in
              Behalf of Their Rights as Authorized Interpreters of the
              Bible* (New York: Harper and Brothers, 1860).

CEB ESA   Catharine E. Beecher, *An Essay on Slavery and
              Abolitionism, with Reference to the Duty of American
              Females* (Philadelphia: Henry Perkins, 1837).

CEB ER   Catharine E. Beecher, *Educational Reminiscences and
              Suggestions* (New York: J. B. Ford, 1874).

CEB *LDR* Catharine E. Beecher, *Letters on the Difficulties of Religion* (Hartford: Belknap and Hamersley, 1836).

CEB *LPHH* Catharine E. Beecher, *Letters to the People on Health and Happiness* (New York: Harper and Brothers, 1855).

CEB *Suggestions* Catharine E. Beecher, *Suggestions Respecting Improvements in Education, Presented to the Trustees of the Hartford Female Seminary* (Hartford: Packard and Butler, 1829).

CEB *TDE* Catharine E. Beecher, *A Treatise on Domestic Economy, for the Use of Young Ladies at Home, and at School* (Boston: Marsh, Capen, Lyon, and Webb, 1841).

CEB *TR* Catharine E. Beecher, *The True Remedy for the Wrongs of Woman* (Boston: Phillips, Sampson, and Company, 1851).

CEB *TSF* Catharine E. Beecher, *Truth Stranger than Fiction* (New York: printed for the author, 1850).

CEB *WSWP* Catharine E. Beecher, *Woman Suffrage and Woman's Profession* (Hartford: Brown and Gross, 1871).

HBS *MWI* Harriet Beecher Stowe, *My Wife and I; or Harry Henderson's History* (Boston: Houghton, Mifflin and Co., 1896).

HBS *UTC* Harriet Beecher Stowe, *Uncle Tom's Cabin; or, Life among the Lowly*, 2 vols. (Boston: John P. Jewett and Co., 1852).

IBH *Argument* Isabella Beecher Hooker, *An Argument on United States Citizenship before the Constitutional Convention of the State of Connecticut, January 1, 1902* (Hartford: Plimpton, Mfg., printers, 1902).

IBH *CRW* Isabella Beecher Hooker, *The Constitutional Rights of the Women of the United States: An Address before the International Council of Women, Washington, D.C., March 30, 1888* (Hartford: Case, Lockwood and Brainard, 1900).

IBH *ML*   Isabella Beecher Hooker, *A Mother's Letters to a Daughter on Woman Suffrage* (Hartford: Press of Case, Lockwood and Brainard, 1870).

IBH *W*   Isabella Beecher Hooker, *Womanhood: Its Sanctities and Fidelities* (Boston: Lee and Shepard Publishers, 1873).

LHBS   Charles Edward Stowe, *Life of Harriet Beecher Stowe* (Boston: Houghton Mifflin and Co., 1889).

Editors' note: For convenience of reading, in the following documents the ampersand has been silently changed to "and."

The Limits of Sisterhood

I.

Introduction

THIS is a book about three nineteenth-century American women—three females in a society dominated by males, three sisters and daughters in one of the nation's most illustrious (and controversial) families, and three children of an old religious elite that was struggling to extend its dominance into a new epoch. Together, the lives of Catharine Esther Beecher, Harriet Beecher Stowe, and Isabella Beecher Hooker spanned the entire nineteenth century, chronicling the astonishing range of activities that engaged the energies and loyalties of white, middle-class women and demonstrating how those interests changed over time. Separately, they suggest the private experiences, the relationships, and the individual successes and conflicts that helped shape a century of women's history.

These would be reasons enough for a book—but there is another. During a century when people were almost continuously at odds over the proper place of females, Beecher, Stowe, and Hooker shared a commitment to women's power. Each in her own way—Catharine as an educator and writer of advice literature, Harriet as an author of novels, tales, and sketches, Isabella as a women's rights activist—devoted much of her adult life to elevating women's status and expanding women's influence in American society. Moreover, each ultimately achieved a position from which to make her views heard, and each contributed to the ideas of womanhood that have been carried into the twentieth century. These three women were certainly not the only Victorians to influence America's ideas of gender. And yet the white middle class of which they were a part exerted a significant influence over larger cultural norms, and white middle-class women in the Northeast played particularly visible roles in the nineteenth-century debate over woman's sphere. Catharine Beecher, Harriet Beecher Stowe, and Isabella Beecher Hooker were among the most prominent of these. How they understood their experiences, how they generalized from them to the experiences of American women as a group, and how they formulated their goals registered in the lives of women across the country. Thus, this is a book about three visions of female power, and the implications of those visions for American women.

Catharine Beecher, Harriet Beecher Stowe, and Isabella Beecher Hooker formed their perspectives on womanhood in a society aflame with the zeal of reform. Early nineteenth-century religious disestablishment had opened the way for a flowering of sects, cults, and denominations. In the antebellum decades, the religious millennialism of the second Great Awakening gave rise to an extended network of benevolent reform associations and, only slightly later, to the abolition and temperance movements that in turn became training grounds for the women's rights movement. During the same period, utopian communities tested alternative forms of economic and social organization, and dietary reformers, mesmerists, hydropathists, and animal magnetists offered new treatments for America's health.

Catharine, Harriet, and Isabella were all participants in this era of reform. Born in 1800, Catharine pioneered the expansion of educational opportunities for women early in the century, not only enhancing the academic curriculum for students at her three seminaries, but also insisting that women head such institutions. Particularly in the field of teaching, Catharine played an important role in the development of increased professional opportunities for women. Meanwhile, she wrote extensively on health, dietary, and dress reform, on the proper design and operation of the American home, and on the shaping of American culture.

Harriet, eleven years Catharine's junior, shared her elder sister's interest in women's education, women's health, and, most importantly, women's role in the family. Unlike Catharine, she supported the postbellum demand for female enfranchisement in an effort to broaden women's influence in society. But it was as a writer that Harriet made her most important contributions to nineteenth-century reform. In *Uncle Tom's Cabin* she mounted a singularly powerful assault upon the scourge of nineteenth-century America, the institution of slavery. Her intense opposition, which found eloquent expression in the novel, was fueled by what she recognized to be slavery's destructive impact upon the family. In both *Uncle Tom's Cabin* and subsequent essays, she especially sought to rally the nation's women into becoming a force for the eradication of slavery's evils. Harriet continued to elaborate in later novels, tales, and sketches upon the idea of woman as the redemptive force in American society.

Virtually a generation younger than Catharine, Isabella eventually became the most outspoken advocate of woman suffrage among the Beecher clan as well as an exponent of spiritualism, an increasingly popular alternative to traditional Protestantism. After years of immersion in domesticity, she emerged as a national leader in the agitation for women's rights during the postbellum period. Isabella soon earned widespread recognition as a result of her keen abilities as an organizer and as a constitutional debater in print and at the podium. However, she gained unwanted notoriety as a result of her defense of controversial fellow suffragists, most notably Elizabeth Cady Stanton, Susan B. Anthony, and Victoria Woodhull.

The Beecher sisters' involvement in the reform movements of the nineteenth century came to them almost as an inheritance from their father, Lyman Beecher, one of antebellum America's most prominent ministers. In an autobiography compiled a few years before his death in 1863, Lyman recalled that six decades earlier he had found himself "harnessed to the Chariot of Christ, whose wheels of fire have rolled onward, high and dreadful to his foes, and glorious to his friends. I could not stop."[1] His words provided an appropriate epitaph not only for himself and his seven sons, all of whom became ministers, but for three of his four daughters as well. Like their father, Catharine, Harriet, and Isabella remained harnessed to the chariot. Not simply witnesses to the social and cultural transformations that characterized their century, the Beecher siblings were engaged and influential participants.

Lyman Beecher's career as a reformer emerged in the context of his deep involvement in revivalism.[2] Like other evangelical Protestants, Beecher joined the sacred and secular. Considering human beings responsible for their individual salvation, he insisted that they also hold themselves responsible for the salvation of society. In the first two decades of the nineteenth century, he matched deed to word when he rallied his flocks and New England's clergy to oppose dueling and then to support the fledgling cause of temperance. The next crusade took Beecher and most of his family to Cincinnati's Lane Theological Seminary early in the 1830s. Shortly after he assumed the presidency of Lane, Beecher found himself caught between the school's abolitionist students and the outraged board of trustees, who demanded that all antislavery discussion cease. Lyman aligned himself with the trustees, informing the students late in 1834 that they must submit to the regulations or leave the seminary. Beecher retained his presidency—and nearly lost his institution. The "Lane rebels," who included almost all of the students, abandoned Lane for Oberlin College, leaving the sixty-year-old Beecher struggling to keep Lane's doors open until his retirement fifteen years later in 1851.

Although Lyman Beecher had declared that a cause should be advocated "only in so far as the community will sustain the reformer," his own career was enmeshed in controversy.[3] In this respect, too, Catharine,

Harriet, and Isabella followed in his footsteps. In 1850 Catharine published *Truth Stranger than Fiction*. Offered as a defense of her former student, Delia Bacon, who was said to have encouraged an improper relationship with Congregational minister Alexander MacWhorter, the volume amounted to a sustained assault upon the integrity of New England's Congregational clergy. The resulting criticism of Catharine was intense, but it paled before the reponse to Harriet's "The True Story of Lady Byron's Life," published by the *Atlantic Monthly* in 1869, and *Lady Byron Vindicated*, issued a year later. Vilified on both sides of the Atlantic because her article made public the speculations about Lord Byron's incestuous relationship with a half sister, Harriet remained committed to vindicating Lady Byron *and* herself. Only two years later, Isabella was caught between loyalty to another suffragist and to her family. In November 1872, Victoria Woodhull, a women's rights activist notorious for her advocacy of free love, publicly charged Reverend Henry Ward Beecher with having committed adultery with Elizabeth Tilton, his parishioner and wife of his closest friend. The resulting ecclesiastical and civil trials generated national headlines on an almost daily basis. Alone among the Beecher siblings, Isabella openly questioned her brother's innocence.[4]

Catharine, Harriet, and Isabella's prominence in the reforms as well as the controversies of nineteenth-century America cannot be ascribed solely to their family legacy, however. They were also actors in one of the most profound shifts in gender relations in the course of American history—the influx of white middle-class women into organized social reform. Even prior to the Revolution, Americans had begun to associate women's traditional domestic role with particular attributes, the most important of which was piety. In the early nineteenth century, that association was elaborated into a set of gender conventions identifying woman with her duties to the family in the home. The "cult of domesticity," as historians have termed this perspective on womanhood,[5] was not in fact a single belief system, but rather a malleable group of ideas that ascribed to women, as wives and especially as mothers, a special capacity for nurturance and benevolence.

The ideology of domesticity functioned in part as a rationale for segregating women in their own "separate sphere" and as a rebuttal to those who were attempting to extend equal rights arguments to women. Yet domesticity turned out to have unexpected implications. By attributing to women precisely those values that seemed most endangered by the dislocations of early industrialization, domesticity provided the framework within which Catharine, Harriet, and Isabella, as well as countless other nineteenth-century women, organized to reform American society. Convinced that the values they upheld in the home uniquely qualified them to become both the conservators and the final arbiters of morality in society generally, large numbers of antebellum women began to move into organized benevolent work, establishing maternal associations and tract societies; founding orphanages and homes for the aged and widowed and unwanted; and raising money for direct relief—food, fuel, and clothing—for the urban poor. Some immersed themselves in the great reform movements of the nineteenth century, including abolitionism and temperance. Implicit in such activism was the conviction that the female experience represented a cultural alternative to the materialism and competitive individualism of industrial capitalism.

Domestic ideology thus offered one rationale for expanding woman's sphere and increasing female influence. Indeed, by encouraging women to see themselves as a separate group and by providing the aegis under which women learned organizational skills and assumed an enlarged role in social reform, domesticity may well have functioned as a precondition for nineteenth-century feminism. Certainly, at least one argument for the expansion of women's legal and political rights was that effective moral guardianship required these tools. But domesticity was not the only philosophical framework within which nineteenth-century women sought power within American society. The women's rights movement itself was rooted as well in an alternative analysis, natural rights theory, the belief that all citizens had legal and political rights *as individuals*. As it was applied to women, this equal justice argument emphasized women's personhood, instead of imputing any special mission to their gender.

Domesticity and natural rights theory were based on logically opposed premises about the nature of women, and over the course of the nineteenth century, they appeared to vie as competing rationales among those who sought to improve women's social, economic, legal, and political status. Yet the two approaches to women's struggle for self-determination were seldom kept entirely distinct. Although the organized women's rights movement is generally dated from the 1848 convention in Seneca Falls, New York, nineteenth-century feminism emerged at least a decade earlier, when abolitionists like Angelina and Sarah Grimké insisted upon their right as moral beings to stand before audiences of men and women and address them on the subject of slavery.[6] Castigated for stepping out of woman's proper sphere, the Grimkés justified their actions by invoking both egalitarian and domestic principles. They insisted that women had the same rights as men to speak out publicly, and yet they also argued that, as women, white females bore a special obligation to their black sisters to oppose the desecration of family life and womanhood under slavery.

In differing ways, each of the Beecher sisters also illustrated this blending of seemingly contradictory premises. Catharine was an early advocate of domesticity with its emphasis upon the shared experiences of womanhood. Yet she opposed female suffrage in part because she believed that all women were not the same—and certainly *not* equally qualified to vote. Harriet based her demand for women's legal and political rights on the grounds of woman's distinctive mission as the reformer of her society—but she buttressed that demand with the insistence that women were individuals with the same rights and responsibilities as men. The combination of natural rights theory, with its definition of women as citizens, and domestic ideology, especially the emphasis upon sexual solidarity among women, reached its culmination in Isabella. She meshed legal and constitutional arguments for women's social and political equality with a profound conviction that, because of the power inherent in motherhood, woman alone embodied the higher morality through which American society was to be purified and reordered.

As they frequently coexisted in a single analysis, so versions of domesticity and natural rights theory shared some important limitations. Neither fully addressed the diversity of experience and circumstance of nineteenth-century American women. Emphasizing a shared experience, domesticity obscured the individuality of women's lives. As Catharine, Harriet, and Isabella demonstrated so well in their respective positions on woman suffrage, even women who shared a common class, race, and family affiliation could reach very different conclusions about the same issue. On the other hand, a singular focus on women's natural rights as political beings ignored much that women did hold in common, and especially the structural inequities in American society between men and women. As Catharine recognized in her repeated warnings about female vulnerability, women and men did not compete for power as equal individuals, but as heirs of a system of dominance and subordination based upon gender. Finally, neither of these frameworks *necessarily* addressed the creation of a more just or humane society for all its members. The exclusive focus upon gender entailed in domesticity helped to conceal the significance of the sharp conflicts of interest and condition fostered by nineteenth-century economic expansion. Especially, it helped to hide the meaning of class and race in American society. Similarly, the movement for women's rights and woman suffrage repeatedly compromised its avowed commitment to the rights of all individuals. In their factional struggles and in their search for widespread social support, some suffragists narrowed their vision from the empowerment of all women to that of white, native-born women of the middle and upper classes. The degree to which and in what ways the activism of nineteenth-century white middle-class women (proceeding from domestic or natural rights premises or a combination of the two) brought lasting change to American society is a question we must each answer for ourselves. In this book, we have sought to offer a context in which a part of that evaluation can occur.

In an effort to preserve the integrity of Catharine's, Harriet's, and Isabella's lives and writings while also establishing a common framework to facilitate comparison and analysis, we have divided the material on each of the sisters into three parallel sections. In "Shaping Experience," we not only describe the experiences that fashioned the adult but also suggest how each woman perceived these experiences and attempted to form them into a mature perspective on what it meant to be female in nineteenth-century America. The sections on "The Power of Womanhood," then, are intended to present those perspectives. We have chosen the word "power" because they did—because at the core of each sister's thinking was a commitment to the idea that womanhood carried with it a particular and unique agency for shaping American society. We have used the word "womanhood" because all of these sisters articulated their beliefs in the context of all females, arguing in effect for the existence of a transcending bond among all women. In "The Politics of Sisterhood," we test those bonds, examining the implications of their perspectives for the sisters themselves, as individuals and as sisters, and exploring the ramifications for women of other classes and races.

We have not included a separate section on the fourth Beecher sister, Mary Beecher Perkins (born in 1805), and that decision warrants some explanation. Our interest has been in tracing, not only individual lives, but the tension between individual lives and certain general ideas of womanhood as they evolved and changed over the century. To that end, Catharine, Harriet, and Isabella offered particular advantages, since all three participated actively in the public debate over those ideas *and* experienced the personal implications of the gender system. Perkins did not participate in that debate. Indeed, she passed her life in almost deliberate obscurity; as she wrote to Isabella in 1841, "I could not perform any of my duties if I gave way to my feelings and allowed myself to attend meetings and become as much interested as I easily could."[7]

And yet Mary Beecher Perkins was an important figure in Beecher family history. She contributed to the success of Catharine's first school, provided boarding for both Catharine and Harriet, helped to raise Isabella, and carried on correspondence with her various sisters throughout her lifetime. Her life came closest to approximating the ideal of woman-hood about which her sisters spoke and wrote so widely. For these rea-sons, we have touched upon Mary's role in her sisters' lives throughout the essays and, especially, have included excerpts from several of her letters in the final section of the book, "Conversations among Our-selves." There, Catharine Beecher, Harriet Beecher Stowe, Isabella Bee-cher Hooker, and Mary Beecher Perkins speak simply as sisters—siblings who teased and fought with and protected each other, women whose very different lives sometimes drew them far apart and whose shared identity as Beechers was sometimes strong enough to bind them together again.

NOTES

1. Barbara M. Cross, ed., *The Autobiography of Lyman Beecher*, 2 vols. (Cambridge, Mass.: Harvard University Press, Belknap Press, 1961), 1:46. In these two volumes of recollections to which father and children contributed, the Beechers told much about themselves and about how they wished to be remem-bered. Historians with a less personal stake have found the family a rich and important source for study of the nineteenth century. Milton Rugoff's *The Beechers: An American Family in the Nineteenth Century* (New York: Harper and Row, 1981) is the most recent example. Marie Caskey has also examined the Beechers in the context of nineteenth-century Protestantism. See *Chariot of Fire: Religion and the Beecher Family* (New Haven, Conn.: Yale University Press, 1978).

2. The relationship between evangelical Protestantism and reform has been examined in Whitney R. Cross, *The Burned-over District: The Social and Intel-lectual History of Enthusiasm in Western New York, 1800–1850* (Ithaca, N.Y.: Cornell University Press, 1950); Timothy L. Smith, *Revivalism and Social Re-form in Mid-Nineteenth-Century America* (New York: Abingdon Press, 1957); Carroll Smith-Rosenberg, *Religion and the Rise of the American City: The New York City Mission Movement, 1812–1820* (Ithaca, N.Y.: Cornell University Press, 1971); Paul E. Johnson, *A Shopkeeper's Millennium: Society and Revivals in Rochester, New York, 1815–1837* (New York: Hill and Wang, 1978).

3. Quoted in Rugoff, *American Family*, p. 273.

4. Although the scandal has been treated merely as an amusing or quaint Victorian episode by some historians, there are two good book-length accounts: Robert Shaplen's *Free Love and Heavenly Sinners: The Story of the Great Henry Ward Beecher Scandal* (New York: Alfred A. Knopf, 1954) and Altina L. Waller's *Reverend Beecher and Mrs. Tilton: Sex and Class in Victorian America* (Am-herst: University of Massachusetts Press, 1982). There is, as yet, no fully reliable and satisfactory account of Victoria Woodhull's life. The best biography to date

is Emanie Sachs, *The Terrible Siren* (New York: Harper and Brothers, 1928).

5. There is now a rich literature on the nature and meaning of domesicity for nineteenth-century women. The first of these studies was Barbara Welter's "The Cult of True Womanhood," *American Quarterly* 18 (Summer 1966): 151–74. It was followed by Kathryn Kish Sklar's *Catharine Beecher: A Study in American Domesticity* (New Haven, Conn.: Yale University Press, 1973)—a biography that has illuminated the present volume and set the standard of excellence for all subsequent work on the Beecher sisters—and Nancy F. Cott's now classic *The Bonds of Womanhood: "Woman's Sphere" in New England, 1780–1835* (New Haven, Conn.: Yale University Press, 1977). Recent additions to this literature include Mary P. Ryan, *Cradle of the Middle Class: The Family in Oneida County, New York, 1790–1865* (New York: Cambridge University Press, 1981); Nancy A. Hewitt, *Women's Activism and Social Change: Rochester, New York, 1822–1872* (Ithaca, N.Y.: Cornell University Press, 1984); and Carroll Smith-Rosenberg, *Disorderly Conduct: Visions of Gender in Nineteenth-Century America* (New York: Alfred A. Knopf, 1985). In a subsequent article, Welter suggested the possible connections between domesticity and the rise of nineteenth-century feminism, a subject that Nancy Cott developed at the end of her study. See Barbara Welter, *Dimity Convictions: The American Woman in the Nineteenth Century* (Athens: Ohio University Press, 1976), pp. 83–102.

6. Feminism and abolitionism are the subject of Blanche Glassman Hersh's *The Slavery of Sex: Feminist-Abolitionists in America* (Urbana: University of Illinois Press, 1978). See also Gerda Lerner, *The Grimké Sisters from South Carolina: Pioneers for Woman's Rights and Abolition* (New York: Schocken Books, 1967). The major accounts of the movement include: Eleanor Flexner, *Century of Struggle: The Woman's Rights Movement in the United States*, rev. ed. (Cambridge, Mass.: Harvard University Press, Belknap Press, 1975); Anne F. and Andrew M. Scott, *One Half The People: The Fight for Woman Suffrage* (New York: J. B. Lippincott and Co., 1975); Ellen DuBois, *Feminism and Suffrage: The Emergence of an Independent Movement in America, 1848–1869* (Ithaca, N.Y.: Cornell University Press, 1978); and Ellen DuBois, ed., *Elizabeth Cady Stanton/ Susan B. Anthony: Correspondence, Writings, Speeches* (New York: Schocken Books, 1981). Other primary sources can be found in the six-volume *History of Woman Suffrage*, ed. Elizabeth Cady Stanton, Susan B. Anthony, et al. (New York: Fowler and Welles, 1881–1922), and the more accessible abridged version in one volume, *The Concise History of Woman Suffrage: Selections from the Classic Work of Stanton, Anthony, Gage, and Harper*, ed. Mari Jo and Paul Buhle (Chicago: University of Illinois Press, 1978).

7. Mary Beecher Perkins to Isabella Beecher Hooker, January 13, 1841, SD. See Document 104.

I.   Shaping Experience

2.

Catharine Esther Beecher: "The Distinguishing Characteristics of My Own Mind"

Aᴛ the height of her career in the mid-nineteenth century, Catharine Esther Beecher was one of the most famous women in America. She had first gained prominence as a teacher and a staunch advocate of improved education for women. Over the course of her lifetime, Beecher founded three academies for young women;[1] authored textbooks on domestic science, arithmetic, physical education, and moral philosophy; and worked tirelessly to promote the entry of females into the teaching profession.

Early on, Beecher's work in women's education led her to a second career. Writing on subjects as diverse as religion, health, family life, abolitionism, and women's rights, she emerged as an influential voice in reflecting and shaping how middle-class Americans in the nineteenth century thought about themselves and their world. Beecher helped form the vision of the American home as a refuge from society. She opposed Calvinism and aided in creating the Victorian ethos that replaced it. She presided over the birth of a gender ideology that has survived into the late twentieth century. In all this, her impact on American cultural and social history extended far beyond the perhaps several thousand women who were her students.[2]

Beecher's two careers were but dual aspects of a single life project—to promote the independent power and status of women, or, as she put it more pragmatically seven years before her death, "to *train* woman for her true business and then pay her so liberally that she can have a house of her own whether married or single."[3] It was a formulation full of paradox. For Beecher, at the core of the concept of woman's "true business" was the traditional notion of a world divided by gender. To men, she assigned the rough and tumble arenas of politics and business; to women, the retirement of family life where, as mothers, they would preside over "the gentler charities of life."[4] But in antebellum America, "woman's place" implied women's dependence. Elevating women's domestic work to "a *profession*, offering influence, respectability and independance"[5] meant pushing hard against the tradition itself.

The paradoxes of Beecher's work reflected the paradoxes of her life. Catharine Beecher identified true womanhood with the family and motherhood; yet she never married, never bore children, and never established a permanent home, cautioning her sister Isabella, "It is not best for any of my friends to calculate upon me as a fixture *anywhere* for any *given* time."[6] Beecher counseled women to effect change only by gentle influence—while, like a runaway coach, she circled the northern half of the nation, chiding her enemies and exhausting her relatives and friends. It was a cowed Calvin Stowe who wrote to Harriet Beecher Stowe in 1848: "Cate has neither conscience nor sense—if you consent to take half a pound, she will throw a ton on to your shoulders, and run off and leave you, saying—*it isn't heavy—it isn't heavy at all, you can carry it with perfect ease.* I will have nothing to do with her in the way of business, any more than I would with the Devil." He added: "She would kill off a whole regiment like you and me in three days."[7] And even as she argued that women should rely on men as their natural protectors, Beecher herself remained skeptical, claiming that the day when most males would be motivated by benevolence was "a millennial point far beyond our present ken."[8]

Such contradictions may suggest falsity—the manipulation of cultural norms to personal ends. Certainly, Beecher was ambitious; from very early on in her life, she meant to "be head"[9]—to assert power and to have that power felt. Moreover, her vision for American womanhood remained narrow. Premised on the experiences of white, middle-class Protestant women like herself, it never challenged the class or racial divisions that tore at nineteenth-century America. To the contrary, by limiting difference to the matter of gender, Beecher helped to create a rhetoric that veiled many of the forms of privilege and deprivation in her world.[10]

But her need to "be head" points as well to other dimensions of Beecher's character. For leadership was a decidedly masculine ambition in mid-nineteenth-century America and one which she learned early from her father. Indeed, a passion for authority ran in the veins of the Beecher clan, and its presence in Catharine reminds us that, as well as a public figure, "Cate" was both a sister and a daughter—an individual enmeshed in a family history. She was also a female in a society that viewed women as creatures of limited abilities. Beecher spent her adult life trying to reconcile these identities.

Catharine Esther Beecher was born September 6, 1800, in East Hampton, Long Island. She was the first child of Roxana Foote Beecher and Lyman Beecher. In family legend, but also, apparently, in life, Roxana approached the model of Puritan womanhood—a pious, unassuming wife who rose at daybreak to pray[11] and accepted God's providence without complaint. It had not always been so. During her courtship with Lyman, Roxana had resisted the harsh doctrines of Calvinism: "When I pray for a new heart and a right spirit," she had asked, "must I be willing to be denied, and rejoice that my prayer is not heard?"[12] But in eventually yielding to Lyman, Roxana had also yielded to his faith. Even at the death of a child, Lyman recalled, Roxana "showed . . . an entire acquiescence in the Divine will."[13]

To piety, Roxana joined the industriousness of the eighteenth-century "notable housewife." Lyman was proud of her skill in furnishing the East Hampton home, spinning and painting the carpet, and refinishing chairs with paint and varnished patterns cut from gilt paper. Roxana also took in boarders, taught school, and designed her own stove for more efficient heating.[14]

Catharine later credited her mother with teaching her a "*high ideal* of excellence,"[15] but she may also have learned from her something of the dissatisfactions of the largely private female life. Roxana's early letters from East Hampton are marked by a sense of isolation and of hard work in a household perennially short of money and quickly filling up with children. Lyman was often gone; Roxana wrote her sister, Harriet Foote, that, "Catherine's prattle and the smiles of my little boy contribute to enliven many a gloomy moment."[16]

These feelings may have been transmitted to her daughter, who showed an early aversion to domestic work. Certainly, it was Lyman who captured Catharine's deepest devotion. She once described him as a man with a "passionate love of children." As the first born, Catharine received this affection in extra measure, traveling with her father on his rounds, romping with him at home, sharing with him a love of adventure and a dislike of "hard study." In contrast to Roxana, whom Catharine remembered as having a "shrinking nature," Lyman was outgoing and relished the exercise of power, both within his congregation and as a member of the clerical profession. These qualities thrilled his eldest child. As a young adult she wrote to her brother Edward, "The fact is I never hear any body preach that makes me *feel* as Papa does—perhaps it may be, because he is *Papa*—but I cannot hear him without its making my *face burn* and my heart beat."[17]

Isolated though it was, East Hampton reflected something of the economic and racial diversity of American society. Struggling to support a growing family, the Beechers themselves faced recurrent financial insecurity. Nearby lived the last of the Montauk Indians, "despised, abused, [and] degraded" and eking out a survival "by whaling and the petty trade of broom and basket making." Within the immediate household were two black servants, bound to the family as girls to care for the children, and Catharine's beloved Aunt Mary, whose experiences in the West Indies had taught her a lifelong "horror and loathing" of slavery.[18]

But these influences paled beside the intense sense of family destiny that infused the Beecher household. Both Lyman and Roxana were fond of tracing their ancestry to the oldest and most distinguished families of New England. Both valued respectability and rank. Roxana's carpet had been the first in East Hampton, and she taught her daughter "to draw and paint in water colors" and to ornament fine woods "with landscapes, fruits and flowers"—accomplishments suited to young women of refined society.[19] Lyman's aspirations took a different form. Convinced he was called by God to his work, he preached throughout Long Island, and occasionally in New England. In 1800 and again in 1807, he led revivals in his parish. In the meantime, he began to publish his sermons and became involved in synod politics.

In 1810, Lyman's efforts were rewarded when he was called to the prominent ministry of Litchfield, Connecticut. Catharine later described the first five years in Litchfield as a period of "sunshine, love, and busy activity, without any memory of a jar or cloud."[20] They were important years for her. Litchfield was a prosperous community, where "no appearance of poverty" marred the neat, white houses.[21] The Beechers counted among their friends some of the most distinguished families of the state, and Catharine was enrolled in Sarah Pierce's Female Academy to learn "those rules of delicacy and propriety" appropriate to the town's "singularly good" society.[22] When the Beechers arrived, politically conservative Litchfield was girding itself against attempts to overthrow both the Federalist party and the state-established Congregational church. Flourishing in Litchfield's society, and watching as her father became its champion, Catharine learned the prerogatives of a class long accustomed to religious and social leadership.

When Catharine was sixteen, these years of "unalloyed happiness"[23] came to an end with her mother's death. At Lyman's encouragement, she responded to the loss by attempting to fill Roxana's place, caring for her seven younger siblings and helping to manage the daily affairs of domestic life.[24] The experience may have provided Catharine with an early insight into the uses of domesticity to enhance her own status. Her new role was short-lived, however, for a year later, in 1817, she was displaced by Lyman's second wife, Harriet Porter. Catharine's reactions to the marriage were mixed. She would recall Harriet Porter Beecher as a woman who "sometimes failed in manifesting pleasure and words of approval at the well-doing of subordinates." Yet Catharine valued her stepmother's connections with elite society, and would seek to emulate the "refined style of house-keeping" that she introduced into the Beecher home.[25]

Roxana Beecher's death marked the end of Catharine's childhood world. By the spring of 1819, Lyman began to urge his eldest to think more seriously about religion. On and off for six years, he strove to bring Catharine to submission to the Calvinist God, exhorting her to put aside her "rebellious" heart and accept both her own utter unworthiness and the majesty of God's supreme power.

For young women in the Puritan tradition, the meaning of conversion was complex. A man might submit himself to God and yet retain the full scope of the world on which to imprint his character. For Beecher boys, this would mean careers in the ministry, the profession most prized by their father and the one to which, at Roxana's death, he had pledged his sons.[26] But for women, religious submission was linked to civil and social submission in marriage, which commonly followed it as the second step toward adulthood.[27] Her years at Miss Pierce's academy notwithstanding, Catharine's youth—and especially her close identification with her father—left her ill-suited for this act of womanly self-abnegation. She had been raised to take pride in her own competence. Her father, she remembered years later, had called her "the *best boy* he had"[28]—and like a Beecher boy, she relished autonomy.

As the surviving correspondence makes clear, at stake for her was not only her soul but her relationship with Lyman. After 1822, the conflicts grew sharper. In April of that year, Catharine's fiancé, Alexander Metcalf Fisher, drowned at sea. Although deeply religious, Fisher died unconverted—and so, within Calvinist beliefs, damned. The pain of Fisher's death would remain with Beecher throughout her life.[29] The injustice of his possible damnation appalled her and gave focus to her own disputes with Calvinist theology. "Oh, Edward," she wrote to her brother, "where is he now? Are the noble faculties of such a mind doomed to everlasting woe. . . ?" She could not believe it. God had created humans fallible, she reasoned. If even such a man as Fisher must be damned—a man who had lived an evidently blameless life and whose diaries revealed an agonizing search for salvation—then God must be brutal and justice meaningless. Surely Fisher was "with our dear mother in the mansions of the blessed," she concluded, explaining to Lyman, "Dear father, I *must* believe this; it is the only way in which I can perceive or realize that God is merciful and good. . . ."[30]

In the end, Catharine rejected Lyman's religion, but the act of independence cost her, both at the time and later. Even after the crisis had passed, she remained depressed; for her, as she later explained to Edward, religion remained "mostly a way of darkness and heaviness"—a painful reminder of the distance that now separated her from her father and his world.[31] Still unresolved, moreover, was the question of her future.

In the spring of 1823, Catharine moved to Hartford, Connecticut, where she founded the Hartford Female Seminary, choosing, as she wrote to her father, the only "sphere of usefulness" available to women outside of the home.[32] This was not an entirely accurate assessment. First, in the 1820s many Americans still doubted that women belonged in the classroom—at least beyond the dame schools that taught children the rudiments of numbers and reading. Much less was woman's place at the *head* of an academy![33] Opposing that prejudice was part of Catharine Beecher's lifework. But she was wrong on a second count. Women found other occupations—as domestic servants and seamstresses, as factory operatives and street vendors. The eldest daughter of Lyman Beecher had more numerous options, however, and she intended to exercise them. Convinced of her own abilities and reared to savor reputation and influence, she wanted a profession—as a Beecher, a profession as nearly like the ministry as she could make it.

Catharine Beecher's Hartford Seminary would become a milestone in the history of women's education. Insisting that intellectually rigorous subjects be included in the curriculum and fighting for the financial security of a permanent endowment, Beecher would help to open up for young women of the middle class alternatives to the dame schools and finishing schools that had before characterized their educational opportunities.

The seminary was also a milestone for Beecher personally, and it foreshadowed the strategies that would guide her public reform activities thereafter. She would always be an institution-builder. It was not for the woman who would "be head" to throw her energies into the abyss of anonymity offered by tract societies and prayer groups. Moreover, whatever their potential as agents for change, Beecher's institutions would

always be premised on ideas acceptable to the more prosperous classes—
as the idea of "a good female school" had become attractive to Hartford's elite by the 1820s.[34] Indeed, although Catharine's own frustrations
often led her beyond what the community was willing to accept, her
father's social pragmatism would remain the hallmark of her own organizing efforts. Finally, in Hartford Catharine discovered the value of
sisterhood. As she recalled in her later *Educational Reminiscences*, when
she had sought to expand the school, "the leading gentlemen of Hartford" had balked, declaring the scheme " 'visionary and impracticable.'
. . . But the more intelligent and influential women came to my aid, and
soon all I sought was granted." She added, "It has ever been housekeepers, mothers, and school-teachers who aided in planning and executing, while inexperienced business and professional men, acting on
committees and as trustees, have been the chief obstacles to success."[35]

Beecher's reliance on Hartford women did indeed pay off. Although
she never achieved an endowment, her school grew from seven to several
hundred students and from a room over a harness shop to a new building with a large study hall, a lecture room, and six recitation chambers.
She drew students from throughout the region and supervised an instruc-
tional staff of eight women. Among these were her sisters Mary and
Harriet, the latter coming to the seminary as a student and then staying
on to become a teacher.

Cultivating as her school's patrons women whose friendship might
enhance her personal status was not unimportant to Beecher, who
yearned in Hartford for the special community standing that she had
enjoyed as the pastor's daughter in both East Hampton and Litchfield.
Yet Catharine's lifelong affinity for elite society had other roots as well.
Still operating within the worldview of her father's Calvinism, she saw
social relations as a series of hierarchies; "the wealthier classes," she was
convinced, "will be followed by all the rest."[36]

In 1829, after six years in Hartford, Beecher published *Suggestions
Respecting Improvements in Education*. Offered as a treatise on education, *Suggestions* was also Beecher's first full-scale statement of the social
philosophy to which—with strikingly few alterations—she would remain
committed for the rest of her life. In it, she attempted to pull together the
threads of her experience. She identified her chosen career as teacher
with women's traditional domestic work; at the same time, and undoubtedly remembering her struggle to find her own voice in her religious
debates with Lyman and Edward, she recast both the teacher and the
mother as female counterparts of the minister, charged, not only with the
education of the mind, but with the perfection of the soul. But the soul as

it concerned Catharine in *Suggestions* was changed from the one for which Lyman struggled: rather than in spiritual redemption, she looked for salvation in social conduct, in the rules of decorum and moral rectitude that had defined her own childhood world in Litchfield.

In framing this philosophy, Beecher was seeking to reclaim her father through the model of her mother. Yet her vision was not a simple transcription from life. For Roxana Beecher, as for most middle-class wives, the work of married life had been carried out largely anonymously. In *Suggestions*, Catharine began to rewrite that experience, transforming Roxana's discouragement and isolation into a public mission fired with the passion and preeminence of the ministry. Ironically, it was not a mission likely to please Lyman, who believed that women assumed public religious roles only at the cost "of that female delicacy, which is above all price."[37] Indeed, the maternal legacy that Catharine created ignored the central difference between mother and daughter: Roxana had achieved womanly submission; Catharine, who even in *Suggestions* revealed her dissatisfaction with the superior social prerogatives of men, never would.[38]

NOTES

1. The best known of these were the Hartford Female Seminary (established in 1823 in Hartford, Connecticut), the Western Female Institute (established in 1833 in Cincinnati, Ohio), and the Milwaukee Female Seminary (established in 1850 in Milwaukee, Wisconsin). In addition, in 1848 Catharine established a short-lived school in Burlington, Iowa, and she and her sister Harriet Beecher Stowe opened a school together in Brunswick, Maine, in 1851. For additional information on Beecher as an educator, see Kathryn Kish Sklar, *Catharine Beecher: A Study in American Domesticity* (New Haven, Conn.: Yale University Press, 1973); Willystine Goodsell, *Pioneers of Women's Education in the United States* (New York: AMS Press, 1970); and Mae Elizabeth Harveson, *Catharine Esther Beecher, Pioneer Educator* (Philadelphia: Science Press Printing Company, 1932).

2. Historians differ on the long-term impact of Beecher's work. In *Century of Struggle: The Woman's Rights Movement in the United States*, Eleanor Flexner grouped Beecher with "the women educators who accepted the status quo for women." She noted, however, that Beecher was a defender of the status quo "with a difference," since Beecher fought for higher standards in women's education (rev. ed., Cambridge, Mass.: Harvard University Press, Belknap Press, 1975), pp. 30–31. In *Catharine Beecher*, biographer Sklar disagreed, focusing on the "strong female role-identity" implicit in a separation of spheres (p. 270).

Recent studies have examined the class interests that domesticity served. For example, Christine Stansell has explored the use of the domestic ideal to justify middle-class intrusion into antebellum working-class homes. See Christine Stansell, "Women, Children, and the Uses of the Streets: Class and Gender Conflicts in New York City, 1850–1860," *Feminist Studies* 8, no. 2 (Summer 1982): 309–35.

3. Catharine Beecher to "My dear Lizzie," July 24, 1867, SchL.

4. Catharine E. Beecher, *An Essay on Slavery and Abolitionism, with Reference to the Duty of American Females* (Philadelphia: Henry Perkins, 1837), p. 128. See Document 50.

5. Catharine E. Beecher, *Suggestions Respecting Improvements in Education, Presented to the Trustees of the Hartford Female Seminary* (Hartford: Packard and Butler, 1829), p. 51. See Document 21.

6. Catharine Esther Beecher to Isabella Beecher Hooker, April 24, 1860, SD.

7. Calvin E. Stowe to Harriet Beecher Stowe, August 8, 1848, SD. See also Calvin E. Stowe to Harriet Beecher Stowe, November 22, 1846, SD, excerpted in Document 35.

8. Catharine Beecher, "An Appeal to American Women," in Catharine E. Beecher and Harriet Beecher Stowe, *The American Woman's Home, or Principles of Domestic Science* (New York: J.B. Ford, 1869), p. 468. See Document 75.

9. Catharine Esther Beecher to Edward Beecher, n.d. [March 3, 1827], SD. See Document 19.

10. One version of this analysis is found in Ann Douglas, *The Feminization of American Culture* (New York: Alfred A. Knopf, 1977). For an overview of Douglas's argument, see pp. 3–16.

11. William Henry Beecher discovered this while sorting through some of his mother's papers a decade after her death. He mentions it in a letter to his (and Catharine's) maternal grandmother, Roxanna Ward Foote, August 27, 1826, SD.

12. Roxana Foote to Lyman Beecher, September 1, 1798, in Barbara M. Cross, ed., *The Autobiography of Lyman Beecher*, 2 vols. (Cambridge, Mass.: Harvard University Press, Belknap Press, 1961), 1:57.

13. Ibid., 1:127.

14. Ibid., 1:86; Catharine E. Beecher, *Educational Reminiscences and Suggestions* (New York: J. B. Ford, 1874), pp. 10–12. See Documents 1 and 5.

15. CEB *ER*, p. 10. See Document 5.

16. Roxana Foote Beecher to Harriet Foote, May 8, 1802, SD. Spelling was not yet standardized at the beginning of the nineteenth century. Roxana sometimes spelled Catharine's name with an "a"—often, as here, with an "e." Catharine herself always spelled it with an "a." Roxana's letters are reminiscent of those of an earlier eighteenth-century woman and wife of a minister, Esther Edwards Burr. See Carol F. Karlsen and Laurie Crumpacker, eds., *The Journal of Esther Edwards Burr, 1754–1757* (New Haven, Conn.: Yale University Press, 1984).

17. CEB *ER*, pp. 15–16 (see Document 5). Catharine Esther Beecher to Edward Beecher, n.d. [October 18, 1824?], SD.

18. *Autobiography*, 1:128, 64, 87, 94. For reference to the Beechers' two indentured servants, see Document 1.

19. CEB *ER*, p. 10. See Document 5.

20. Catharine Esther Beecher, "Reminiscences of Litchfield" in *Autobiography*, 1:159.

21. Harriet Porter Beecher to Nathaniel Coffin, December 4, 1817, SD.

22. CEB *ER*, p. 25; Harriet Porter Beecher to Nathaniel Coffin, December 4, 1817, SD.

23. Beecher, "Reminiscences of Litchfield" in *Autobiography*, 1:159.

24. CEB *ER*, pp. 19–20. Catharine described her domestic role in a letter to her aunt, Harriet Foote, [February 1, 1817], SD. See Document 6.

25. CEB *ER*, pp. 23–25.

26. William Henry Beecher to Roxanna Ward Foote, August 27, 1826, SD. See n. 11 above.

27. For additional discussion of this point, see Sklar, *Catharine Beecher*, pp. 28–42.

28. Memorial by "R," n.d., MHCL.

29. See, for example, Beecher's oblique reference to Fisher's death in *Letters to the People on Health and Happiness* (New York: Harper and Brothers, 1855), p. 114.

30. Catharine Esther Beecher to Edward Beecher, June 4, 1822 in *Autobiography*, 1:356, and Catharine Esther Beecher to Lyman Beecher, New Year, 1823, in *Autobiography*, 1:370. See Documents 8 and 12.

31. Catharine Esther Beecher to Edward Beecher, March 26, 1825, MHCL. See Document 15.

32. Catharine Esther Beecher to Lyman Beecher, February 15, 1823, SD. See Document 13.

33. Some female academies had survived from the eighteenth century, but the significant expansion of women's education, with women in leadership roles, may be dated from 1819, when Emma Willard opened the Middlebury (Vermont) Female Seminary. That was followed by Beecher's Hartford Female Seminary in 1823, Zilpah Grant's Ipswich (Massachusetts) Female Seminary in 1828, and Mary Lyon's Mount Holyoke Seminary in South Hadley, Massachusetts, in 1837.

34. Catharine Esther Beecher to Lyman Beecher, February 15, 1823, SD. See Document 13.

35. CEB *ER*, pp. 33, 78–79.

36. Catharine E. Beecher, *A Treatise on Domestic Economy, for the Use of Young Ladies at Home, and in School* (Boston: Marsh, Capen, Lyon, and Webb, 1841), p. 27. See Document 51.

37. Quoted in Milton Rugoff, *The Beechers: An American Family in the Nineteenth Century* (New York: Harper and Row, 1981), p. 74.

38. In *Private Woman, Public Stage: Literary Domesticity in Nineteenth-Century America* (New York: Oxford University Press, 1984), Mary Kelley discovers

that a search for female forebears—involving, often, a revision of actual family history—was common to early nineteenth-century female writers, who were grappling with their own sense of illegitimacy as thinkers and public figures. See especially pp. 37–55.

In his Autobiography *(written in the 1850s), Lyman Beecher reminisced about the East Hampton household, Roxana's skill as a homemaker, and Catharine's birth on September 6, 1800.*

1   There was not a store in town, and all our purchases were made in New York by a small schooner that ran once a week.

We had no carpets; there was not a carpet from end to end of the town. All had sanded floors, some of them worn through. Your mother introduced the first carpet. Uncle Lot gave me some money, and I had an itch to spend it. Went to a vendue [auction], and bought a bale of cotton. She spun it, and had it woven; then she laid it down, sized it, and painted it in oils, with a border all around it, and bunches of roses and other flowers over the centre. She sent to New York for her colors, and ground and mixed them herself. The carpet was nailed down on the garret floor, and she used to go up there and paint. She also took some common wooden chairs and painted them, and cut out figures of gilt paper, and glued them on and varnished them. . . .

Well, we got nestled down in our new house, Grandmother Foote, Roxana, Mary, and I[1] . . . and when we sat down at our own table for the first time, I felt strong emotion, very much like crying.

Soon after, our first child was born. I shall never forget my feelings when Grandma Foote put her in my arms. "Thou little immortal!" was all I could say. We called her Catharine Esther, the first from Aunt Benton, my foster-mother, the second from my own mother.

Soon after, your mother took Drusilla Crook, a colored girl, about five years old, to take care of the baby. We called her Zillah. She was bound to us till she was eighteen. When Mary was born, we took a sister of Zillah's named Rachel.[2] . . . When I moved to Litchfield they accompanied us, and staid till their time was out. . . .

[*Autobiography*, 1:86–87]

---

1. Roxana's mother and sister Mary joined the East Hampton household at the time of Catharine's birth. Her mother returned to the family home, Nutplains, near Guilford, Connecticut, shortly thereafter. Mary Foote remained with the Beechers until her brief and disastrous marriage to a West Indian slave-owner, after which she rejoined the Beechers and lived with them until her death in 1813.

2. Drusilla and Rachel Crook were indentured servants, not slaves.

Even with bound servants, life in East Hampton was busy—and often lonely—for Roxana Beecher. Excerpts from her letters, and from an early one from Catharine to her aunt, provide glimpses of the work and education of turn-of-the-century middle-class females.

2   April 29, 1801

My dear Sister [Harriet Foote]

I have this moment heard of an opportunity of sending to Killingsworth[.] I have therefore seated myself with my breakfast table half cleared and Catherine[3] in my lap who is quite ill since yesterday to write. . . . We enjoy very good [health] Mr[.] B[.] and myself[.] Catherine has considerable fever but I hope she will not be sick very long[.] I have not yet called in a Physician but shall if she grows any worse today—If I had a mother or a sister Where I could get to them without as much fuss as would be sufficient to prepare for an India Voyage it [seems] as if it would be a great comfort and as it is I should be glad if I could hear from my friends a little oftener[.] I have not had any letters from Guilford since those you sent on when you went to Newburgh. . . . [C]ome and see me as soon as you can. . . .

        adieu your

        RB

Love to Mama and Mary and all[4]

        [Roxana Foote Beecher to Harriet Foote, SD]

3   Oct[obe]r 4, 1809

Dear Aunt [Harriet Foote]

[W]e arrived at home safe and sound[.] I was very sea sick[.] I had a very sore throat[.] Aunt Mary is keeping school and will for a week or more[.] Mama has got so mutch worke to do that she cannot attend to her school[. T]he ladies have just begun to parse and I have just begun

---

3. On Roxana's spelling of Catharine's name, see above, "The Distinguishing Characteristics of My Own Mind," n. 16.

4. The version of this letter included in Lyman Beecher's *Autobiography* includes an additional final line: "Tell Mama folks say Catharine looks just like her." See *Autobiography*, 1:88.

to[.] I don[']t know but that I shall go back whith you when you come over next spring if I can leav my school[.] I wish you would write to me[.] [Y]ou never wrote to me in the worlde[.] [G]ive my love to Mary[.][5] [W]ill you be so good as to read Mary[']s letter to her[?]

I am your affectionate niece
Catharine Beecher

[CEB to Harriet Foote, SD]

---

4 Feb[ruar]y 23, 1810

My dear Friend [Lyman Beecher]

. . . Our family are in usual health and matters go in a comfortable manner[. T]he boys cut their cedars and their fingers much as usual. . . . I think I shall send them to school to Mr[.] Parsons next week else I fear they will make no proficiency at all in your absence. . . . Your friends make affectionate enquiries after you . . . but I have not seen many persons. . . . The children send all the love to papa that I can put in my [letter]—Catherine is so very desirous of writing to you that it was with difficulty I could persuade her it was not worth while to put you to the expence of postage for her little letters—she is busily engaged in painting some flowers for her work-basket[. S]he learns her geography in the morning and finishes her knitting in the evening in order to save time in the afternoon for painting[. S]he is [I] hope improving in diligence and knowledge, but I fear [I] cannot say the same of the boys. . . . May you be guided in all your ways preserved from evil and returned in safety to

your ever affectionate—
R Beecher

[Roxana Foote Beecher to Lyman Beecher, SD]

When she was seventy-four years old, Catharine Beecher published her Educational Reminiscences and Suggestions. *Largely devoted to an examination of her public career, the volume opened with memories of her childhood and of her parents.*

---

5. Probably Catharine's younger sister Mary (later Mary Beecher Perkins), born in 1805, who may have been visiting at Nutplains.

5   It was my good fortune to be born in humble circumstances, the eldest of thirteen children, all but two trained to maturity, and most of them in a good degree under my care through infancy and childhood.

My mother . . . and her sisters taught me to read, write and spell, with a few lessons in geography. They also gave me a little instruction in arithmetic which was soon forgotten.

They also taught me to sew neatly, to knit, to perform properly many kinds of domestic labor, and to aid in the care and training of the younger children. My mother taught me to draw and paint in water colors, and then to varnish with a fine white varnish she learned how to prepare from a small English Encyclopedia. When about fourteen I thus painted and varnished a chamber set of fine white wood. . . . These were ornamented with landscapes, fruits and flowers, and at that time were a great novelty.

Much of my success in after life has been owing to certain traits in my mother's character and their influence on my early training. These were a *high ideal* of excellence in whatever she attempted, a habit of regarding all knowledge with reference to its *practical* usefulness, and remarkable *perseverance* in holding on persistently till the object sought was attained. . . .

. . . [H]er beautiful specimens of needlework, her remarkable paintings. . . , her miniature likenesses of friends on ivory, accomplished when the mother of four and five young children, a housekeeper and a teacher of a boarding school, are all illustrations of her high ideals and her perseverance. . . .

. . . In some book of travels she had read of the Russian stove, and so with only her Encyclopedia and a common mason, she had one constructed which warmed six rooms with no more fuel than many of her neighbors used for one fire. . . .

Some of my own natural traits were decidedly the opposite of those of my mother, and what I accomplished in after life was in a good degree owing to her early training which modified these defects. But oh, the mournful, despairing hours when I saw the children at their sports, and I was confined till I had picked out the bad stitches. . . !

But I was trained to perfect and uncomplaining obedience. . . . But my good educators all had a hard task; for it seemed as if I had a decided genius for nothing but play and merriment. . . .

I think that my mother's natural and acquired traits tend to prove that there is in mind no distinction of sex, and that much that passes for natural talent is mainly the result of culture.

For my father had that passionate love of children which makes it a pleasure to nurse and tend them, and which is generally deemed a distinctive element of the woman. But my mother, though eminently benevolent, tender, and sympathising, had very little of it. I cannot remember that I ever saw her fondle or caress her little ones as my father did; but her devotion to them seemed more like the pitying tenderness of a gentle angel.

Then, again, my father was imaginative, impulsive, and averse to hard study; while my mother was calm and self-possessed, and solved mathematical problems, not only for practical purposes, but because she enjoyed that kind of mental effort. . . .

My father was trained as a dialectician, and felt that he excelled in argumentation; and yet my mother, without any such training, he remarked, was the only person he had met that he felt was fully his equal in an argument. Thus my father seemed, by natural organization, to have what one usually deemed the natural traits of a woman, while my mother had some of those which often are claimed to be the distinctive attributes of man.

My mother had the refined and shrinking nature which made her unable to take the lead in general gatherings as ministers' wives are expected to do. . . . But at the same time, in sudden emergencies she had more strength and self-possession than my father.

At sixteen, I lost this lovely mother. . . .

[CEB *ER*, pp. 9–16]

Following Roxana Beecher's death in 1816, Catharine not only took on an enlarged share of household labor but also attempted, as she later said, "to supply my mother's place" to the younger children.[6]

6   [February 1, 1817]
Dear Aunt Harriet [Foote]—

It seems a very long time since we have heard from Nutplains and we begin to feel very anxious to hear from all our dear friends there especially how aunt Jane does—we have not heard a word from Guilford

---

6. Catharine Esther Beecher to Harriet Porter, n.d. [1817?], *Autobiography*, 1:264. See Document 7.

since you wrote. . . . Is Harriet[7] well and a good girl and does she re-member all her brothers and sisters and good friends here—How is our dear grandmother[']s health this winter and how do you do? I hope you will answer these enquiries as soon as you recieve [*sic*] this letter. The family here are all in as good health as usual. [W]e have but three boarders and get along as well as we can desire. We have done all our winter sewing and knitting and find we have more leisure than we could have expected. Edward still continues at South Farms[.] William is in Mr[.] Collins['] store for the present but boards at home—Mary goes to school to Miss Pierce—and George to Miss Collins. Henry is a very good boy and we think him a remarkably interesting child and he grows dearer to us every day. [H]e is very affectionate and seems to love his father with all his heart—His constant prattle is a great amusement to us tho' some-times it is tiresome. He often speaks of his sister Harriet and wishes Spring would come so that she might come home and go to school with him. Charles is as fat as ever tho' he is much less trouble as he can take more care of himself—He can speak a few words to express his wants but does not begin to talk. . . .

The children I suppose would all send their love if they knew I was writing[. P]resent mine to Grandmama[,] Aunt Jane[,] Uncle George[,] Harriet[,] and her little cousin and believe me to be

your very affectionate niece
Catharine

[CEB to Harriet Foote, SD]

When she learned of her father's intention to remarry, seventeen-year-old Catharine wrote to welcome Harriet Porter to the family.

7   [1817?]

Dear Madam,—The prospect of the connection to take place between my father and yourself, and the tender alliance so soon to subsist be-tween you and this family, give me the liberty and pleasure of address-ing you, though I have never enjoyed the satisfaction of personal ac-quaintance.

---

7. Her younger sister, later Harriet Beecher Stowe, who was sent to Nutplains to visit her grandmother following Roxana Beecher's death.

As the oldest child and daughter, I feel it my duty to express to you my feelings on this occasion. . . .

It pleased God to deprive me of a kind and tender mother at an age when I had just begun to realize her uncommon worth, and at a time when I particularly felt the need of the watchful care and kind advice of a mother. It was at an age when I knew my character was forming in the eyes of the world—when I was expected to throw off the character of a girl and assume that of a woman—when every action of my life would be regarded, not as the impulse of an uninformed child, but as springing from the fixed principles of an established character.

With these feelings, dear madam, imagine how terrible was the stroke that deprived me of my guide, my adviser, and my best earthly friend; that left me comparatively alone to grope my own way through the dangers and vicissitudes of early life; for who can fill a *mother's* place but *a mother*. But this was not my only misfortune. It was not for my own loss alone that I mourned; the stroke fell heavily upon my dear remaining parent. It left him solitary, comfortless, and afflicted, and it was a loss which I felt it utterly out of my power to repair or alleviate. I also felt bitterly for my dear brothers and sisters, thus with myself deprived of a tender and affectionate parent; and, above all, I realized the heavy care and responsibility which rested upon me, as their eldest sister, to supply my mother's place to them.

I have at times, though naturally of a cheerful disposition, felt almost wretched when reflecting upon my father's, my brothers' and sisters', and my own unhappy situation. Think, then, dear madam, how great must be my joy and relief, and how unbounded ought to be my gratitude to God, our heavenly Father, for His sudden and unforeseen mercy in thus providing one so competent, and who, I doubt not, will so kindly fill all the tender relations of my dear departed parent—one who will prove a kind and affectionate companion to my father, and relieve his mind from heavy domestic cares—a tender and watchful mother to my dear brothers and sisters, and who will be to me a guide, a pattern, and friend, to whom I may look up for assistance and advice, so necessary and desirable.

I speak for myself, and for all my brothers and sisters who are capable of considering the extent of their obligation to you, when we promise to make it our constant study to render you the affection, obedience, and all the kind offices which we should wish to pay our own mother were she now restored to us from the grave. The sacred name of *mother*, so bound up in our hearts, would alone entitle you to the most undeviating affection and respect.

My brothers and sisters desire to be remembered to her who, they trust, will soon be their dear protector and friend, and join their affectionate salutations with those of one who hopes ere long to be truly your dutiful and affectionate daughter.

[Catharine Beecher]

[CEB to Harriet Porter Beecher in *Autobiography*, 1:264–65]

The following excerpts trace the religious crisis of Catharine's young adulthood—both her rejection of basic tenets of her father's faith and her efforts to claim an intellectual equality with her father and her brother Edward, who was preparing for the ministry at Yale. The selections begin with the death of Alexander Fisher, Catharine's fiancé, and end with Catharine's choice of a career.

8   June 4, 1822
[Catharine to Edward Beecher]

Your letter came at a time when no sympathy could soothe a grief "that knows not consolation's name." Yet it was not so much the ruined hopes of future life, it was dismay and apprehension for his immortal spirit. Oh, Edward, where is he now? Are the noble faculties of such a mind doomed to everlasting woe, or is he now with our dear mother in the mansions of the blessed? . . .

Could I but be assured that he was now forever safe, I would not repine. . . .

I feel that my affliction is what I justly deserve. Oh that God would take possession of the heart that He has made desolate, for this world can never comfort me. . . .

But I am discouraged, and at a loss what to do. I feel no realizing sense of my sinfulness, no love to the Redeemer, nothing but that I am unhappy and need religion; but where or how to find it I know not. . . .

[Catharine Beecher]

[CEB to Edward Beecher in *Autobiography*, 1:356–57]

9   July, 1822

Dear Brother,

When I began to write to you on the subject which now occupies my thoughts, it was with a secret feeling that you could do something to remove my difficulties. But this feeling is all gone now. I have turned to you, and to father, . . . and have again and again felt to my very soul that it is a case in which "the help of man faileth."

It is the feeling of entire guilt, willful and inexcusable, which gives all the consistency and excellency to the Gospel. . . .

This feeling I can not awaken in my heart, nor is my understanding entirely convinced that it ought to exist. . . .

The difficulty in my mind originates in my views of the doctrine of original sin, such views as seem to me sanctioned not only by my own experience, but by the language of the Bible. . . .

. . . I see that I am guilty, very guilty, . . . but not guilty as if I had received a nature pure and uncontaminated. . . .

When I have confessed my sins to God, there has always been a lurking feeling . . . that, as God had formed me with this perverted inclination, he was, as a merciful being, obligated to grant some counteracting aid. . . .

. . . I am most unhappy in the view which this doctrine presents of my own state and that of my fellow-creatures, except the few who are redeemed from the curse. When I look at little Isabella,[8] it seems a pity that she ever was born, and that it would be a mercy if she was taken away. . . .

[CEB to Edward Beecher in
Autobiography, 1:357–59]

10   [circa August, 1822]

[Catharine to Lyman Beecher[9]]

I am like a helpless being placed in a frail bark, with only a slender reed to guide its way on the surface of a swift current that no mortal

8. Catharine's younger sister, the eldest surviving child of Lyman and Harriet Porter Beecher.

9. A note that Catharine left for Lyman in his study in Litchfield. Lyman's response, written on the back, follows.

power could ever stem, which is ever bearing to a tremendous precipice, where is inevitable destruction and despair.

If I attempt to turn the swift course of my skiff, it is only to feel how powerful is the stream that bears it along. If I dip my frail oar in the wave, it is only to see it bend to its resistless force.

There is One standing upon the shore who can relieve my distress, who is all powerful to save; but He regards me not. I struggle only to learn my own weakness, and supplicate only to perceive how unavailing are my cries, and to complain that He is unmindful of my distress.

[CEB to Lyman Beecher in
Autobiography, 1:360]

---

11   [circa August, 1822]
[Lyman Beecher to Catharine]

I saw that frail boat with feeble oar, and that rapid current bearing onward to destruction an immortal mind, and hastened from above to save. Traveling in the greatness of my strength, I have pressed on through tears and blood to her rescue.

It is many days, many years, I have stood on the bank unnoticed. I have called, and she refused; I stretched out my hand, and she would not regard. At length I sunk the bark in which all her earthly treasure was contained,[10] and, having removed the attraction that made her heedless, again I called, and still I call unheard. My rod has been stretched out and my staff offered in vain. While the stream prevails and her oar bends, within her reach is My hand, mighty to save, and she refuses its aid.

What shall I do? Yet a little longer will I wait, and if she accept my proffered aid, then shall her feet be planted on a rock, and a new song be put into her mouth. If she refuse, the stream will roll on, and the bark, the oar, and the voyager be seen no more.

[Lyman Beecher to CEB in
Autobiography, 1:361]

10. A reference to Fisher's death.

12   New Year, 1823
[Catharine to Lyman Beecher]

... I had all along looked forward to the time of my arrival in Franklin[11] as the period when (if I was to be brought into the kingdom by suffering and sorrow) my heart would find in God that comfort and peace which was nowhere else to be found; and if I did not then obtain religion, I felt that my heart would, almost from *necessity*, return to the world to receive its dregs of happiness for a portion; an unsatisfying portion, indeed; but the heart must have *something* to rest upon, and if it is not God it will be the world. ...

Day after day I went, mourning and distressed, to pour out my sorrows to God ... and each succeeding day I felt that the act of love and submission which he required, in order that my prayers might find acceptance, was what I could never perform. ...

But such dreadful feelings did not continue long. Soon the conviction that God was just and merciful, and would ever do right, which I scarcely ever before questioned, returned, and I resolved I would not *believe any thing* that obscured these perfections, and gradually my feelings were brought to be something of this kind.

The Savior has dwelt in our nature; he knows what my weakness is. ... I will go to him every day and ask for his aid, resolving to *strive* to regulate my thoughts, and words, and actions by his word; and that, if I can not *be* a Christian, I will try to be as near *like* one as I can. ...

Dear father, I must believe this; it is the only way in which I can perceive or realize that God is merciful and good. ... I must believe ... that in due time we shall find that he *is* a rewarder of those who diligently seek him. ...

When I think of Mr. Fisher, and remember his blameless and useful life, his unexampled and persevering efforts to do his duty both to God and man, I believe that a merciful Savior has not left him to perish at last; ... and that in the Day of Judgment we shall find that God is influenced in bestowing his grace by the efforts of men; that he does make the needful distinction between virtue and vice; and that there was

11. Fisher's home, where Catharine went to share her grief with his family and to sort through various of his papers and diaries.

more reason to hope for one whose whole life had been an example of
excellence, than for one who had spent all his days in guilt and sin. . . .

          [Catharine Beecher]

                          [CEB to Lyman Beecher in

                      Autobiography, 1:368–70, 373]

---

13   Feb[ruary] 15, 1823

My dear Papa,

Your letter arrived a few days since and is filled with just such arguments and exhortations as I expected and has produced the same effect, as all human efforts have and probably always will when unassisted by the Holy Spirit.

. . . Should arguments equally powerful with those advanced by you and Mr[.] Fisher,[12] and ten thousand times more so, be advanced to prove that I had physical strength to remove the everlasting hills . . . it would all be to no purpose; *consciousness* would be that brow of iron that would resist them all. . . .

As to my future employments after leaving here, I am uncertain and wish I could talk with you, that my mind may be settled on this point; but as this cannot be I will state some of my thoughts of the subject for your consideration. I should wish in future to follow, that course in which I could be most extensively useful and at the same time consult my own and the happiness of my friends. Generally speaking there seems to be no very extensive sphere of usefulness for a single woman but that which can be found in the limits of a school room; but there have been instances, in which women of superior mind and acquirements have risen to a more enlarged and comprehensive boundary of exertion and by their talents and influence have accomplished what in a more circumscribed sphere of action would have been impossible—My employments this winter which have been chiefly mental, and the observations which I have made upon the relative character of the talents which God has given me, have led to the inquiry whether there is not a course which

---

12. Alexander Metcalf Fisher's father. Catharine was visiting with the Fisher family when this letter was written. In the version of this letter included in Lyman Beecher's *Autobiography*, "Mr Fisher" is changed to "Edward." See *Autobiography*, 1:377.

might be pursued, which would lead to a different and more extended field of usefulness, than is attained by the generality of females. . . .

I have always supposed that the distinguishing characteristics of my own mind, were an active and inventive imagination, and quick perceptions in matters of taste and literature, yet I think there is reason to believe that in those pursuits which require more solid and powerful operations of mind there is no deficiency of ability. . . . I have abridged Mrs. B's Chemistry. . . . I also abridged in the same manner her work on Philosophy and also a good part of Logic. . . . In order to recover my knowledge of Arithmetic I went over with it all, beginning at Addition. I then began Day[']s Algebra, and . . . finished it in five weeks. . . . I have also gone far enough in Geometry to perceive I can go farther without more labour than I should be willing to bestow were it desirable.

I believe that my memory is quick and retentive . . . and I believe the only reason why my mind is not stored with an abundance of useful knowledge is entirely owing to the careless indolence of past years—All the knowledge that I have has as it were, *walked into my head*, without any exertion to acquire or any care to arrange it.

In consideration of the above, is there not reason to believe that if there is a place where female intellect and influence can be extensively and beneficially exerted, that at some future time should my life be prolonged, I might render myself more extensively useful by strengthening and increasing my own intellectual resources than I should be by devoting my time to the drudgery of communicating the first rudiments of knowledge to a few, which perhaps might be better performed by others?—Circumstances at present seem to be such, that it does not seem necessary on pecuniary accounts that I should make any immediate exertion. The family here seem to love me. . . . Mr[.] Fisher, thinks my income[13] if properly managed will not be less than 130 dollars, half of which *after this year* I believe will supply my wants and the rest I should wish to employ in charitable purposes or in increasing the comfort of my friends, as I have no fancy for laying up money. As to my own gratification . . . when I am at home I should wish to assist Mama in household affairs tho' not to do much in the kitchen—I feel anxious that Harriet[']s mind should not be left to run to waste as mine has and should feel a pleasure in taking care of her education which things I might accomplish with suitable attention to regularity, and economy of time—

There is one thing however which I have thought of which perhaps

13. Alexander Fisher had left Catharine $2,000 in his will.

would be better and as agreeable—When I was in Hartford, Mr[.] Hawes[14] lamented the want of a good female school there. Now if it is the case that they need a good school in Hartford and if matters could be so arranged that Mary and I could commence one there, it might be so contrived that Mary might do the most that required to be done that occupies time and receive the most of the profits also and, I might take the general care and superintendence and in this way I might have considerable time for my own improvement and also secure the benefit of Edward[']s assistance[.]

These things I [have] thought of and suggest them for your consideration. . . .

> yours affectionately
> Catharine
>
> [CEB to Lyman Beecher, SD]

> *The Hartford Female Seminary opened in May 1823,*
> *but Catharine found the first term a financial disap-*
> *pointment. Reviewing the school's accounts for her fa-*
> *ther, she revealed her new role as family head to the*
> *group of Beecher siblings living in Hartford, including*
> *her sister Mary, who had joined her in the school.*

14   October [1823]

Dear Papa

I have this morng been making up our accounts for the summer and find that we shall only just clear our expences for the season; I had anticipated some thing more than this tho' I knew we should have more expences at the commencement than at any future time—Our board and necessary expences such as washing[,] candles[,] etc[.] amount to about 3,25 per week—our school room rent to 14 dollars for this summer and the expences of benches[,] table[,] chairs[,] etc[.] for the school room to 20 dollars more[.] Mrs[.] Hawes says she thinks we have done well for the first term (as there is 2 of us) to come out even but I was in hopes of something over so that you would need to be at no more expence for Mary—

As it is, however[,] she will have to come to you for some of her winter

14. Reverend Joel Hawes, pastor of the First Congregational Church in Hartford, Connecticut.

cloathing—she feel[s] very loath to do [it but] I don[']t see any other way—she needs a new great coat[,] a frock and a bonnet which will amount to 20 dollars. . . .

I hope to see you on you[r] way to Worcester. . . . I hope you will be able to bring the money for George[']s board then as Dr[.] Strong[15] needs it much—I don[']t know how your pocket is furnished with money just now but if you can furnish the demands here this fall, I hope by next Spring we shall some of us be able to contribute to your comfort in money matters—I am sure it is the greatest wish I have in this world, to see you above the vexatious cares of this *mammon of unrighteousness.* . . .

Mary is well and my eyes are better—Edward also is well. . . . My school is to be out the saturday forenoon of the week after the ordination in W[orchester]. . . . Love to Mama[,] Aunt E[sther] and all at home. . . .

>your affectionate daughter.
>Catharine

>>[CEB to Lyman Beecher, SD]

Watching as her younger brother William struggled with conversion, Catharine remembered her own religious crisis three years earlier.

15   March 26, 1825

Dear Edward

. . . It makes me feel sorrowful when I talk with W[illia]m or read his letters for his feelings are so much as mine were and I am afraid his experience will be too much like mine. . . .

It is much easier f[or] those to persevere in religion who find the way easy and delightful that [*sic*] for those who find it mostly a way of darkness and heaviness. And for my part I cannot say that I ever found it much otherwise, tho' I would not cease to walk in it for all the pleasures the world can afford. . . .

>I am ever your affectionate sister
>Catharine

>>[CEB to Edward Beecher, MHCL]

15. Catharine, Edward, Mary, and George Beecher all boarded in the Strong home.

In 1826, Catharine led a revival among her students. It was a role of uncertain propriety for a woman—and as close as she would come to actually being a minister.

16   June 1, 1826

My dear Brother [Edward]

... I must write to tell you the good news in our family—Cousin Dorcas after a long season of deep distress has I trust become a child of God—Her case seems to be a very decided one and just such an one as I should desire and I trust that she is to be a burning and shining light. ... Four other of my scholars I trust have also been renewed in the temper of their minds. ... I trust this is only the beginning, but I have been greatly tried by the absence of Mr[.] Hawes. He was aware of all the circumstances of my school, and seemed to think as I did that the state of feeling preparatory to a revival was begun—yet he thought best to go to Northampton to spend a week or ten days—tho' he had just been absent for that period—

His reason for going was to assist in the great revival there and to gain *the spirit of a revival*—He was conscientious I believe but greatly misjudged and did not rightly feel the importance of a minister[']s presence among his people at this time—

I felt like crying all day after he went away and I and my little church in school have been laboring *all alone* this fortnight past—But God has been with us so that we have had no cause for fear or discouragement— Pray for us—and write soon

Your aff[ection]ate sister

Catharine

[CEB to Edward Beecher, MHCL]

17   [between June 1 and August 1, 1826]

Dear Brother Edward

... The state of things in my school still continues interesting. I have hope for 15 or more.

There are 8 or 10 in town who have lately as I trust become pious. ... We have a little meeting every day after school for scholars in my room. From 20 to 30 usually attend. ...

Your affectionate sister

Catharine

[CEB to Edward Beecher, MHCL]

18   "To those who profess or have the hope of Piety in Miss Beecher[']s School"

My dear young ladies. It has given me great joy to observe how much the spirit of our dear Saviour has dwelt among you and how ready you have been to use your influence among your companions, in promoting the honour of his blessed name by prayers and labours for their salvation. He has been pleased to smile upon our efforts . . . to encourage us to persever[e] in seeking higher attainments. . . .

. . . It has begun to be known that some religious attention is awakened in our school—Christians in this place, are beginning to be interested and encouraged by the news . . . and now seems to be the all important time—This week I feel as if it would probably *be decided* whether the good work begun so auspiciously should be extended in the school—and from the school to the churches in this place—or whether the excitement shall be transcient [*sic*] and the world and the church should turn aside a little moment to see what [God] is doing for us, and then *pass away*—I feel that it almost entirely rests with *us* my dear young ladies, and I wish you should know and feel this responsibility—If we are faithful in devotedness, in prayer and in labours *this week* I believe . . . that by the blessing of God, the current of feeling will set the right way. . . . Now I do not wish, that you should talk about the situation of our school, at all, except among yourselves[.] Try to keep every thing as *still* and *secret* as possible—but oh my dear fellow christians be faithful in prayers[,] in labours and in interest for the school. . . .

Remember you are "the called" of Jesus Christ—a holy nation—a peculiar people—that ye should show forth the glory of him who called you from darkness into marvellous light—

. . . I beseech you by the pangs you felt when your own feet were in the horrid pit and mirey clay—by the hopes and peace ye have tasted in communion with God and the hope of Heaven; by the great love of him who hath washed you in his own blood and sent you forth as his dear children—by the ineffable blessedness of the heavenly mansions you hope to inhabit, by the weeping and woe of that hell from which you are redeemed, by all that is glorious in our hopes and dreadful in our fears for the future destinies of the dear immortal around us—*be faithful in interest in labours and prayers*[.] And when he who is the chief Shepherd shall appear then shall ye appear with him—and those also redeemed by you[r] faithfulness, shall rejoice with you to enter the joy of our Lord—

With prayers and fervent affection
your friend
CE Beecher

[CEB, "To those who profess . . . ," SD]

---

*Her new school nearly completed, in 1827 Catharine
was bursting with confidence. At the same time, as her
August 23, 1828, letter to Edward suggests, her outward successes continued to exact a private price.*

19   [March 3, 1827]
Dear Edward
   I send with this letter a newspaper containing the prospectus of my
school. . . .
   . . . Say to Papa and other friends that I am not going into *partnership*
with any one—I shall be head and pay salaries and I *mean to make
money by it.*
   Mary will try keeping house 5 or 6 weeks and if she can get along and
likes it better than school I shall look for some one to take her place in
school—Folks say they think after trial she will like school best[.]
   I hope the building will be done in two or three weeks after my term
commences—I hope mama and aunt Homes will look about for a housekeeper for me in case Mary should conclude to go into school. . . .
   We are all well—Love to all
          Your aff[ection]ate Sister
          C—

[CEB to Edward Beecher, SD]

---

20   August 23, 1828
My Dear Brother [Edward]
   . . . I hope your *inward man* will soon be taught how to behave himself
in all circumstances and emergencies. I wish I could catch my *inward
woman*, and give her such an inspection and exposition, but she is such a
restless being that I cannot hold her still long enough to see her true form
and outline.
   I am so much engaged in moulding, correcting, and inspecting the

character of *others* that I sometimes fear my own will be a "cast away," but then I comfort myself with the reflection that "he that watereth, shall himself be watered," and I cannot say but the promise has in a measure been verified to me.

My school is not yet what I intend to make a school before I stop.—I must make *one more step* and that as great an one as stepping from my private school of 30 or 40 to the charge of an endowed seminary of 130 or 40. I have many plans. . . .

> Aff[ectionate]ly yours
> CE Beecher
>
> [CEB to Edward Beecher, MHCL]

In 1829, Beecher published Suggestions Respecting Improvements in Education, *detailing her arguments for women's education and justifying her own career. Complaining of the low status of women's work, she broached what would become the central theme of her life's work: that women, in their roles as mothers and teachers, were the world's true ministers.*

21   . . . Most of the defects which are continually discovered and lamented in present systems of education may be traced, either directly or indirectly to the fact, that the *formation of the minds of children has not been made a profession securing wealth, influence, or honour*, to those who enter it.

The three professions of law, divinity, and medicine, present a reasonable prospect of reputation, influence and emolument to active and cultivated minds. The mercantile, manufacturing and mechanical professions, present a hope of gaining at least that *wealth* which can so readily purchase estimation and influence. But the profession of a *teacher* has not offered any such stimulous [*sic*].

It has been looked upon as the resource of poverty, or as a drudgery suited only to inferior minds and far beneath the aims of the intellectual aspirant for fame and influence, or of the active competitor for wealth and distinction. . . .

In all other professions, we find *bodies of men* united by a common professional interest. . . . The duties of all other professions are deemed of so much consequence that *years* must be spent, even after a liberal education, in preparing for these *peculiar* duties. . . .

But to *form the mind of man* is deemed so simple and easy an affair, that no such preparation or precautions are required. *Any person* may become a teacher without any definite preparation, and without any test of skill or experience. . . .

It is to *mothers*, and to *teachers*, that the world is to look for the character which is to be enstamped on each succeeding generation, for it is to them that the great business of education is almost exclusively committed. And will it not appear by examination that neither mothers nor teachers have ever been properly educated for their profession[?] What is *the profession of a Woman?* Is it not to form immortal minds, and to watch, to nurse, and to rear the bodily system. . . ?

But let most of our sex upon whom these arduous duties devolve, be asked; have you ever devoted any time and study, in the course of your education, to any preparation for these duties? . . . Were you ever taught to understand the operation of diet, air, exercise and modes of dress upon the human frame? . . . Perhaps almost every voice would respond, no. . . .

Again let our sex be asked respecting the instruction they have received in the course of their education, on that still more arduous and difficult department of their profession, which relates to the *intellect* and the *moral susceptibilities*. Have you been taught the powers and faculties of the human mind, and the laws by which it is regulated? . . . Have you learned the best mode of correcting bad *moral* habits and forming good ones? . . . Has any woman studied her profession in this respect? It is feared the same answer must be returned. . . .

. . . There is no dispute on the point that some minds naturally have a strong *bias* for certain pursuits . . . but this does not decide that if extra stimulus were applied to exercise and improve the *other* faculties, they might not advance in nearly equal proportion. . . .

If it be claimed that it is necessary to the *improvement of the several arts and sciences*, that *man* should turn his attention exclusively to some one particular department, and thus prevent the equilibrium of character desired, it may be granted to *one* sex, but it is not necessary for *woman*. On the contrary, *a well balanced mind* is the greatest and best preparative for her varied and complicated duties. Woman, in her sphere of usefulness, has an almost equal need of all the several faculties. She needs the discrimination, the solidity, and the force of character which the cultivation of the reasoning powers confers; she needs the refinement of taste, the chastened glow of imagination, the powers of quick perception, and of ready invention. Which of these shall we say a woman may dispense with in preparing herself for future duties[?]

May we not ascribe to this defect in education, the not unreasonable prejudice which has existed against *learned ladies*[?] Those who have been ambitious to maintain that character, by following the bias of a literary taste, too often have cultivated certain powers of mind in a disproportionate extent, and destroyed that true balance of mind which is so necessary for a woman, in forming a just estimate of her relative duties, as well as for the faithful discharge of them. . . .

But the most important and most neglected department in education still remains unfilled, and unsustained in all our institutions for education. We have yet to learn what could be effected, were the cultivation of the social feelings, and the formation and correction of the moral character and habits, the distinct department of one person, who should by talents and experience be suitably qualified. To fill such a station, it would indeed task to their utmost limit all the powers of intellect, the resources of knowledge and the affections of the heart. . . .

. . . Let a teacher have sufficient time and facilities afforded, let her make this a definite and express object, let her seek to learn from the experience of others the various operations of the human mind, let her study the various methods of controling [*sic*] the understanding, the conscience, and the natural affections, and there is scarce any thing she may not hope to effect. . . .

. . . The Author of our being has so regulated the dispensations of his Providence, and the constitution of our moral, intellectual, and physical natures, that *doing right*, on the whole, does tend to promote the happiness of every individual in all cases, even in this world, and doing wrong, does eventually lead to a diminution of enjoyment. Whenever, then, the human mind can, by reason or persuasion, be brought to feel that the path of rectitude is the path of happiness, no other motives can operate so powerfully; for happiness will be sought wherever it is believed that it can be found. . . .

. . . [I]t seems of great importance that the formation of the female character should be committed to the female hand. It will be long, if ever, before the female mind can boast of the accurate knowledge, the sound judgment, and ready discrimination which the other sex may claim. But if the mind is to be guided chiefly by means of the affections; if the regulation of the disposition, the manners, the social habits and the moral feelings, are to be regarded before the mere acquisition of knowledge, is not *woman* best fitted to accomplish these important objects[?] Beside this, . . . it is necessary that a degree of familiarity of intercourse, at all times and places, an intimate knowledge of feelings; affections, and weaknesses be sought by a teacher, which is not practicable or proper for one of the other sex to attain.

It may be said, and said truly, that women are not prepared by *sufficient knowledge* to become teachers in many branches. But they *can be prepared*, and where they are not so well qualified as one of the other sex, they so often excel in patience and persevering interest, as to more than counter-balance the deficiency.

The writer cannot but believe, that all female institutions . . . ought to be conducted exclusively by females, *so soon as suitable teachers of their own sex can be prepared.* And is it not an indication that such is the will of Providence, when we see a *profession*, offering influence, respectability and independance [*sic*], thrown open to woman? Until this day no other profession could with propriety admit the female aspirant, nor till this day has the profession of a teacher been the road to honour, influence, and emolument. But the feelings of enlightened society are fast changing on this momentous subject. . . . The time is not far distant when it will become an honourable profession, and beneath its liberal portal, woman is gladly welcomed to lawful and unsullied honours. Here, all that stimulus of motive which animates the other sex in their several professions, may be applied to quicken and animate her energies. *She* also, can discern before her the road to honourable independance [*sic*], and extensive usefulness, where she need not outstep the proscribed boundaries of feminine modesty, nor diminish one of those retiring graces that must ever constitute her most attractive charms. . . .

. . . Here then is the only lawful field for the ambition of our sex. Woman in all her relations is bound to "honour and obey" those on whom she depends for protection and support, nor does the truly feminine mind desire to exceed this limitation of Heaven. But where the dictates of authority may never controul [*sic*], the voice of reason and affection, may ever convince and persuade; and while others govern by motives that mankind are ashamed to own, the dominion of woman may be based on influence that the heart is proud to acknowledge. . . .

Woman has never wakened to her highest destinies and holiest hopes. She has yet to learn the purifying and blessed influence she may gain and maintain over the intellect and affections of the human mind. Though she may not teach from the portico, nor thunder from the forum, in her secret retirements she may form and send forth the sages that shall govern and renovate the world. . . . Though she may not be cloathed as the ambassador of Heaven, nor minister at the altar of God; as a secret angel of mercy she may teach its will, and cause to ascend the humble, but most accepted sacrifice. . . .

Another defect in regard to *female* education is, inattention to those habits and employments which relate to a woman's *domestic* pursuits. There was a time when the only object of woman's education seemed to be, to prepare her for an active, economical and accomplished *house-wife*, and no intellectual refinement or erudition was esteemed of any value, but rather a disadvantage. Mankind, perhaps, are now urging to the other extreme; and in regarding the *intellect* are beginning to over-look the future duties and employments of domestic life. It is true a well cultivated and well regulated mind is the *best* preparative for such duties, but it is not the *only* one. A woman needs to form habits of method, regularity, order and economy in *youth*, or she probably will not be prepared for the proper discharge of future duties. The comfort and respectability of every family depend upon the existence of these qualities in that female mind which directs its domestic arrangements. . . .

The observation of the writer on this subject has led her to feel that there is a lamentable neglect of these particulars, in regard to female education. It is not so often the case, as could be desired, that young ladies are found, who have formed habits of neatness, order and regu-larity in the care of their person, room and employments. Many of those who fall under the observation of the writer, are deficient in the art of using the needle with neatness and despatch [*sic*], and very seldom is it the case, that young ladies have either sufficient ingenuity or experience to cut and make those articles of dress usually made by the female hand.

This is a subject to which the writer thus alludes, from the belief that *teachers*, as well as parents, need to direct more attention to a remedy of evils which already are the consequences of such neglect. There is no doubt but that if suitable attention is given to this subject, teachers can accomplish much in the formation of such habits, and preparation for such duties, as are indispensable to domestic order and comfort. . . .

[CEB *Suggestions*, pp. 4–9, 41–42, 44–45, 50–51, 53–54, 58–59]

3.

Harriet Beecher Stowe: "Changing to Nobody Knows Who"

IN the year 1850 Harriet Beecher Stowe was astonished to discover that the world had begun to notice
her existence. Asked by Sarah Josepha Hale, the editor of *Godey's Lady's
Book*, to provide an autobiographical sketch for inclusion in a volume
entitled *Woman's Record*, Stowe declined, "wholly innocent as I am of
any pretensions to rank among 'distinguished women.'" Rather, she suggested that her eldest sister would be a more appropriate selection.
Catharine, she insisted, had "lived much more of a life—and done more
that can be told of than I whose course and employments have always
been retired and domestic." However, in shielding herself, Stowe inadver-
tently opened a window to her life, telling Hale that she had read her
letter "to my tribe of little folks assembled around the evening centre
table to let them know what an unexpected honour had befallen their
Mama." Hale's request for a daguerreotype had provided the wife and
mother with an amusing diversion as she imagined the response "of the
children should the well known visage of their mother loom out of the
pages of a book before their astonished eyes." Stowe's self-portrait barely
mentioned the fiction she had been contributing to magazines including
Godey's for the past fifteen years. Instead, she described herself as engaged in "the necessary but unpoetic duties of the family." And noting
that which she considered obvious, Stowe concluded that such a life had
been "so thoroughly uneventful and uninteresting that I do not see how
anything can be done for me in the way of a sketch."[1]

Less than two years later, the publication of *Uncle Tom's Cabin*
changed that life irrevocably. Initially serialized in Gamaliel Bailey's antislavery weekly, the *National Era*, beginning in early June 1851, *Uncle
Tom's Cabin* made both the relatively obscure weekly and the author
famous before the final installment was published ten months later. Issued in two volumes on March 20, 1852, and purchased by 3,000 read-

ers on that day alone, the novel reached a sale of 150,000 within six months. Sales were followed by admiring letters from the already notable. Henry Wadsworth Longfellow congratulated the author on the success she had achieved and praised the novel as "one of the greatest triumphs recorded in literary history."[2] John Greenleaf Whittier sent "ten thousand thanks for thy immortal book."[3]

The fame of the wife and mother who had become a public figure was pervasive. Never again would a request such as Hale's prove unexpected and never again would Stowe so readily reject the adjective "distinguished." Prominence spurred her literary productivity. Within a year after the novel was finished, she completed its supplement, *A Key To Uncle Tom's Cabin*, and three years later she published her second antislavery novel, *Dred*. In a career that spanned another quarter of a century, the woman who turned forty the year she began *Uncle Tom's Cabin* published eight more novels, more than a hundred tales and sketches, and a steady stream of articles. Stowe characterized four of those novels as comprising a "Domestic Series," a characterization that is equally applicable to nearly everything she wrote.[4] Whatever the vehicle, whether novel, story, or article, Stowe addressed contemporary issues concerning women, and whatever the specific topic, whether suffrage, household management, or marriage, she made the printed page the lectern from which she sought to persuade her readers.

Fame notwithstanding, Stowe's orientation remained largely unchanged from the sentiments expressed in her letter to Hale. Shaping both her fiction and her conception of her literary vocation, the "necessary but unpoetic duties of the family" remained integral to a career that transformed Stowe into a public figure whose influence extended far beyond the boundaries of her home. Precisely because domesticity constituted the experiential and ideological core of her existence, it provided both the context in which she pursued her career as a writer and the substance of her writings. Indeed, Stowe considered her domestic and literary vocations so intertwined that she made them one. In response to an inquiry about the origins of *Uncle Tom's Cabin*, Stowe highlighted the relationship between these vocations, declaring, "I wrote what I did because as a woman, as a mother, I was oppressed and heartbroken, with the sorrows and injustice I saw."[5] Having been appalled by the impact of slavery upon the family, she believed she could do no other. During the next three decades, that same woman continued to choose her subjects and to persuade her readers on the basis of her allegiance to domesticity. Enveloped by the perspective, the language, the metaphor, and the meaning of wifehood and motherhood for woman, Stowe's prose constituted a compelling chapter in the history of literary domesticity.[6]

Born in Litchfield, Connecticut, on June 14, 1811, Harriet Beecher, the sixth child and third daughter of Lyman and Roxana Beecher, could not have ignored domesticity as an obvious choice during a century in which nine out of ten women married. It was also the vocation celebrated by an increasingly popular ideology that presumed basic differences between the sexes and made those differences a basis for designating separate, albeit complementary, roles for women and men. Domesticity was said to be the locus of a woman's identity and the sphere for which she was destined. In dividing the world on the basis of gender and mandating marriage and motherhood as the sole occupations for the female, this ideology simultaneously exalted the woman as morally superior and circumscribed the boundaries of her life. The celebration of distinctions based upon gender also served to obscure differences in race and class, both of which were becoming more visible in antebellum America.[7]

The young and impressionable Harriet also had a personal model as the daughter of Roxana Foote Beecher. Because her mother died shortly after Harriet's fifth birthday, it was Roxana's memory that was venerated by her daughter. The idealized memory, Harriet said, "had more influence in moulding her family, in deterring from evil and exciting to good, than the living presence of many mothers."[8] Having married Lyman Beecher in September 1799 and borne seven children before her death in the same month seventeen years later, Roxana was a woman whose existence was defined totally by domesticity. Nevertheless, it was the eldest daughter, Catharine, who provided a living model that proved more crucial in her younger sister's initial search for a vocation.

At the age of seventy-six, Harriet recalled "somewhere between my twelfth and thirteenth year I was placed under the care of my elder sister Catharine, in the school she had just started in Hartford, Connecticut." Having assumed responsiblity for the adolescent, Catharine supervised Harriet's education—much to the younger sister's consternation. "It was my dream to be a poet," Harriet remembered, and, at the time, she had begun composing a drama in blank verse, filling "blank book after blank book with this drama." But Catharine demanded that she concentrate instead upon texts such as Joseph Butler's *Analogy of Religion, Natural and Revealed, to the Constitution and Course of Nature*. Although the imposing title suggested that the contents would prove daunting for an aspiring poet, Catharine's second demand insured Harriet's attention to

Butler's theological discourse. The student was to become her sister's apprentice, instructing "a class of girls as old as myself, being compelled to master each chapter just ahead of the class I was teaching."[9] Harriet found herself involved in similar preparation for a host of subjects, including such requisite female accomplishments as painting and drawing. Soon she was able to inform her friend Mary Swift that she was a "*real school ma'am.*" The satisfactions notwithstanding, Harriet admitted that her obligations left time for nothing else: "my school duties take up *all* my time—so that I cannot visit much nor read for amusement or write half what I wish to."[10] Harriet's "dream to be a poet" had been set aside, at least temporarily, as she joined the ranks of an increasingly popular vocation for unmarried women.[11]

Catharine continued to be an indirect influence for nearly another decade. When Lyman became president of Lane Theological Seminary in the fall of 1832, Catharine, Harriet, and Isabella accompanied him to Cincinnati, Ohio. Shortly after their arrival, Catharine proposed that some of her former colleagues at Hartford Female Seminary join her in establishing another institution. "The ladies of this place," she wrote to Mary Dutton, "are all exceeding anxious to have a school got up under my auspices."[12] Harriet, who had joined the undertaking, regarded the matter as a collaborative effort. Writing to her friend Georgiana May, she declared, "We mean to turn over the West by means of *model schools* in this, its capital." Women, Harriet added, were to be educated for the same vocation as she had ostensibly chosen, and she and Catharine were determined "ourselves to set an example of what females can do in this way."[13]

Both Catharine and Harriet intended to act as the school's principals, recruiting others for the classroom. Catharine had declared, "I cannot teach myself," but her younger sister soon yielded to the need for more teachers.[14] In a letter written by their sister-in-law, Katherine Edes Beecher, shortly after the founding of the Western Female Institute, both sisters were described as doing "well"—Harriet was "keeping school as assiduously as if she liked it," while her sister kept "the world going busily, as usual."[15] Simultaneously with the establishment of the institute, there was another supposed collaboration in which Catharine benefitted from her sibling's labor. Published in the spring of 1833, *Geography for Children* had the names of both sisters on the title page despite the fact that the volume was completely written by Harriet.

Although the publication of *Geography for Children* suggested that Harriet had begun to search for an alternative to teaching, the volume itself did not suggest a rebirth of her "dream to be a poet." Nonetheless, she was engaged in other literary efforts more akin to that ambition. Shortly after her arrival in Cincinnati, Harriet, along with Catharine, joined the Semi-Colon Club, a literary society that met weekly and read compositions submitted by the members. In a letter to her friend Georgiana May, Harriet provided "a history of my campaign in this circle." Written in the form of "a letter from Bishop Butler," Harriet's initial volley amusingly recalled Catharine's insistence that she study Joseph Butler's *Analogy*. Although the satire of Butler's "outrageous style of parentheses and foggification" might well have signaled Harriet's growing independence from her former teacher, the younger sister's second literary effort for the Semi-Colon Club, an essay on the "Modern Uses of Language," underlined Catharine's continuing presence. The club's members had been impressed and, as Harriet told Georgiana, they had "requested leave to put it in the 'Western Magazine,' and so it is in print." The modest author hastened to add that "it is ascribed to *Catharine*." Anonymity was crucial, at least for Harriet, who informed Georgiana that she had "no notion of appearing in *propia personae*."[16] Actually, the essay appeared under "B" in the *Western Monthly Magazine*, edited by Judge James Hall. However, in another letter to her brother George, Harriet revealed that only modesty lingered. Her latest effort, "rather a contemptible little affair," she told George, nonetheless would be appearing in Hall's *Monthly* signed by "Miss Harriet Beecher."[17] Published in April of 1834, Harriet's tale of romance, entitled "A New England Sketch," also garnered a prize of fifty dollars for its author. In spite of herself, the world was beginning to notice Miss Beecher's literary efforts. Still, Harriet remained in the classroom for nearly two more years, and when she did resign from the institute, her reasons had nothing to do with the tales and sketches she had been publishing in various periodicals. Instead, the resignation stemmed from a more conventional, albeit momentous, decision. She had decided to marry Calvin Stowe, a member of Lane's faculty. That is, she told Georgiana, she would soon "cease to be Hatty Beecher and change to nobody knows who." But if Harriet could not foretell the future of Hatty, she could tell Georgiana that "Sister Katy is not here, so she will not witness my departure from her care and guidance to that of another."[18]

Little more than two years after her marriage on January 6, 1836, Harriet offered two seemingly contradictory portraits of herself in letters written to Georgiana May and Mary Dutton. After telling Georgiana about a typical day in which she had been completely immersed in the demands of domesticity, she concluded ruefully, "I am but a mere drudge with few ideas beyond babies and housekeeping."[19] And yet the letter to Mary suggested otherwise. Determined "not to be a mere domestic slave, without even the leisure to *excell* in my duties," she informed Mary that she had already made an income sufficient to employ a second servant and thereby to set aside three hours a day for her tales and sketches. "If you see my name coming out everywhere—you may be sure of one thing," she declared, "that I do it for *the pay*."[20] Actually, the two portraits were not contradictory, revealing instead that Harriet had already established the pattern that she would maintain throughout the pursuit of her dual vocation. "*The pay*" received constituted a receipt for the broadened "duties" of a wife and mother. With "hand, heart, and head full," as she told Georgiana, Harriet had exchanged the two portraits for one.

Indeed she had. Six years after her marriage, Stowe had given birth to four children and had also composed a sufficient number of tales and sketches for publication in a collection. And in the latter endeavor, Calvin *and* Catharine shared in care and guidance. It was Catharine who made the initial contacts with prospective publishers in New York City before Harriet traveled east for the negotiations. (Catharine's involvement did not end here: she would also write the preface for the first edition of the collection.) Calvin's contribution was less tangible but at least as crucial. In an exchange of letters, Calvin informed his wife that she "must be a *literary woman*."[21] On her part, Harriet made it clear that the woman was simultaneously and always the wife and mother. Emphasizing that their children were "just coming to the age when everything depends on my efforts," she queried Calvin: "Can I lawfully divide my attention by literary efforts?"[22] Apparently, the answer was yes. *The Mayflower: or, Sketches of Scenes and Characters among the Descendants of the Puritans* was published by Harper and Brothers in 1843.

But being "literary" and being a "woman," especially a woman who was a wife and mother, were not necessarily complementary circumstances. The demands of domesticity persistently came into conflict with the completion of a tale or sketch; indeed, there were times when the domestic vocation appeared to preclude the literary. Invariably, Stowe gave a higher priority to guiding and restraining a husband who was a self-admitted "creature of impulse" and to rearing and supporting children who received "all [her] life and strength and almost [her] separate consciousness."[23] The endless litany of household duties to be performed echoed through Harriet's letters during the decade after publication of *The Mayflower*. Always there was "the cleaning—the children's clothes, and the baby." Always too there was concern for her health. The demands of domesticity were partly responsible. There were times, Harriet told Calvin, when it seemed "as if anxious thought [had] become a disease with me from which I could not be free."[24] Equally important, Harriet's health was also adversely affected by successive pregnancies, at least two of which ended in miscarriages. Writing to his wife after she had sought recovery at a water cure in Brattleboro, Vermont, Calvin recalled Harriet's being "so feeble, and the prospect of permanent paralysis [being] so threatening" that he had resigned himself to their separation. Nevertheless, he informed her that he too had been in "a sad state physically and mentally." But the cure he proposed for himself required the end of their separation and perhaps posed a further threat to Harriet's health: "If your health were so far restored that you could take me again to your *bed and board*, that would be the surest and safest, and indeed the only infallible way."[25] Harriet and Calvin continued to face an irresolvable dilemma: one's needs clashed with the other's; one's cure threatened the other's health.

Despite Calvin's reflections on the source of his maladies, he himself spent more than a year at the same water cure shortly after Harriet's return. Harriet also had two more children, both of whom were sons. The first, described by Harriet as "my beautiful, loving, gladsome baby," died at eighteen months from cholera during the summer of 1849.[26] The second was born the following summer shortly after Calvin had accepted an appointment at Bowdoin College. Three months before his birth, Harriet brought three of their five children east and began renovations on the house in Brunswick, Maine. Recalling that summer in a letter to her sister-in-law, Sarah Buckingham Beecher, Harriet said it had "seemed as if I could scarcely breathe, I was so pressed with care." Nonetheless, the wife and mother had managed to continue the pursuit of her other vocation. Her "leisure hours," as she ironically referred to them, had been spent "in making up my engagements with newspaper editors." She had "written more than anybody, or I myself, would have thought."[27]

Harriet Beecher Stowe's experience had been shaped by both the social and cultural milieu of the early nineteenth century and the individual circumstances of her life. Coming to maturity in a society that presumed a female's commitment to domesticity alone, Stowe fulfilled this expectation in her role as the wife of Calvin Stowe and the mother of their seven children. The home provided the locus of her existence. But Stowe, in turn, shaped experience. The novels, the stories, the articles, in sum, the literary career spanning nearly half a century, signified that she had traversed the boundaries separating home from the world beyond. Having made her two vocations one, she created her legacy of literary domesticity.

NOTES

1. Harriet Beecher Stowe to Sarah Josepha Hale, November 10, [1850], HL.

2. Henry Wadsworth Longfellow to Harriet Beecher Stowe, undated, in Charles Edward Stowe, *Life of Harriet Beecher Stowe* (Boston: Houghton Mifflin and Co., 1889), p. 161. Annie Fields also edited a collection of Stowe's letters. See *Life and Letters of Harriet Beecher Stowe* (Boston: Houghton Mifflin and Co., 1898). Originally published by J. B. Lippincott in 1941, Forrest Wilson's *Crusader in Crinoline: The Life of Harriet Beecher Stowe* is still the most extended biography. Wilson's study was reissued by Greenwood Press in 1972. See also John R. Adams, *Harriet Beecher Stowe* (New York: Twayne Publishers, 1963).

3. John Greenleaf Whittier to Harriet Beecher Stowe, undated, in *LHBS*, p. 162.

4. Harriet Beecher Stowe to [Henry Oscar] Houghton, August 11, 1884, HOU. The four novels cited by Stowe were *My Wife and I*, *We and Our Neighbors*, *Pink and White Tyranny*, and *Poganuc People*. Stowe also noted that the first two "treat of the 'woman question,'" as indeed they do. See excerpt from HBS *MWI* in Document 82.

5. Harriet Beecher Stowe to Lord Denman, January 20, 1853, AL.

6. Literary domesticity is the subject of a recent study based upon the private papers and published prose of twelve nineteenth-century American women writers, including Stowe. See Mary Kelley, *Private Woman, Public Stage: Literary Domesticity in Nineteenth-Century America* (New York: Oxford University Press, 1984).

7. The significance of domesticity, ideologically and experientially, has been explored in an impressive body of scholarship. The earliest examination of the ideology is found in Barbara Welter's "The Cult of True Womanhood," *American Quarterly* 18 (Summer 1966): 151–74. Studies that examine ideology and experience include Kathryn Kish Sklar, *Catharine Beecher: A Study in American Domesticity* (New Haven, Conn.: Yale University Press, 1973); Nancy F. Cott, *The Bonds of Womanhood: "Woman's Sphere" in New England, 1780–1835* (New Haven, Conn.: Yale University Press, 1977); Carl Degler, *At Odds: Women and the Family in America From the Revolution to the Present* (New York: Oxford University Press, 1980); and Mary Ryan, *Cradle of the Middle Class:*

The Family in Oneida County, New York, 1790–1865 (New York: Cambridge University Press, 1981).

8. Barbara M. Cross, ed., *The Autobiography of Lyman Beecher*, 2 vols. (Cambridge, Mass.: Harvard University Press, Belknap Press, 1961), 1:224. Stowe also drew upon her memory of Roxana for her portrayal of Harry Henderson's mother in HBS *MWI*.

9. Harriet Beecher Stowe to Charles Edward Stowe, [1886], in *LHBS*, pp. 29–32. See Document 22. The Hartford Female Seminary is described in the first essay on Catharine Beecher titled "The Distinguishing Characteristics of My Own Mind."

10. Harriet Beecher to Mary Swift, [1828], AL.

11. Women's entrance into the classroom as students as well as teachers is examined in Sklar, *Catharine Beecher*; Anne Firor Scott, "What, Then, Is the American: This New Woman?" *Journal of American History* 65 (December 1978): 679–703; Anne Firor Scott, "That Ever Widening Circle: The Diffusion of Feminist Values from the Troy Female Seminary, 1822–1872," *History of Education Quarterly* 19 (1979): 3–27; Maris Vinovski and Richard Bernard, "Beyond Catharine Beecher: Female Education in the Antebellum Period," *Signs: Journal of Women in Culture and Society* 3 (Summer 1978): 856–69; and Maris Vinovski and Richard Bernard, "The Female Schoolteacher in Antebellum Massachusetts," *Journal of Social History* 10 (March 1977): 332–45.

12. Catharine Beecher to Mary Dutton, February 3, 1833, quoted in Sklar, *Catharine Beecher*, p. 111.

13. Harriet Beecher to Georgiana May, [1833], in *LHBS*, pp. 72–73. See Document 25.

14. Catharine Beecher to Mary Dutton, February 3, 1833, quoted in Sklar, *Catharine Beecher*, p. 111.

15. Katherine Edes Beecher to Mary Beecher Perkins and Thomas Perkins, November 4, 1834, quoted in Sklar, *Catharine Beecher*, p. 112.

16. Harriet Beecher to Georgiana May, [Fall 1833], in *LHBS*, pp. 69–71. See Document 26.

17. Harriet Beecher to George Beecher, January 3, 1834, SD. See Document 27. "A New England Sketch" was preceded by the appearance of "Modern Uses of Language" and "Isabelle and her Sister Kate," both of which were published anonymously in the *Western Monthly Magazine*.

18. Harriet Beecher Stowe to Georgiana May, January 6, 1836, in *LHBS*, pp. 76–79. See Document 28.

19. Harriet Beecher Stowe to Georgiana May, June 21, 1838, in *LHBS*, pp. 90–93. See Document 30.

20. Harriet Beecher Stowe to Mary Dutton, [December 1838], BL. See Document 31. The tensions engendered by Stowe's pursuit of her dual vocation are elaborated upon in Mary Kelley, "At War With Herself: Harriet Beecher Stowe as Woman in Conflict Within the Home," *American Studies* 19 (Fall 1978): 23–40.

21. Calvin Stowe to Harriet Beecher Stowe, April 30, 1842, SD. See Document 32.

22. Harriet Beecher Stowe to Calvin Stowe, [1842], in *LHBS*, pp. 103–5. See Document 33.

23. Calvin Stowe to Harriet Beecher Stowe, October 16, 1836, SD.; undated memorandum, quoted in Edward Wagenknecht, *Harriet Beecher Stowe: The Known and the Unknown* (New York: Oxford University Press, 1965), p. 63.

24. Harriet Beecher Stowe to Calvin Stowe, [May 1844], SchL.

25. Calvin Stowe to Harriet Beecher Stowe, June 30, 1846, SD. Jane Donegan's recent study analyzes hydropathy's appeal to antebellum women. She also notes that this alternative to conventional therapeutics elicited support from men as well as women. See *"Hydropathic Highway to Health"*: *Women and Water-Cure in Antebellum America* (Westport, Conn.: Greenwood Press, 1986).

26. Harriet Beecher Stowe to Calvin Stowe, July 26, [1849], in *LHBS*, pp. 124–25. See Document 39.

27. Harriet Beecher Stowe to Sarah Buckingham Beecher, December 17, 1850, SchL. See Document 40.

In a letter written to her youngest son, Charles Edward, a decade before her death in 1896, Harriet Beecher Stowe recalled her early years at her sister Catharine's Hartford Female Seminary.

22   [1886]
[Harriet to Charles Edward Stowe]

Somewhere between my twelfth and thirteenth year I was placed under the care of my elder sister Catharine, in the school that she had just started in Hartford, Connecticut. When I entered the school there were not more than twenty-five scholars in it, but it afterwards numbered by the hundreds. . . .

In school my two most intimate friends were the leading scholars. They had written to me before I came and I had answered their letters, and on my arrival they gave me the warmest welcome. One was Catherine Ledyard Cogswell, daughter of the leading and best-beloved of Hartford physicians. The other was Georgiana May, daughter of a most lovely Christian woman who was a widow. . . . Georgiana was older and graver, and less fascinating to the other girls, but between her and me there grew up the warmest friendship, which proved lifelong in its constancy.

Catherine and Georgiana were reading 'Virgil' when I came to the school. I began the study of Latin alone, and at the end of the first year made a translation of 'Ovid' in verse, which was read at the final exhibition of the school, and regarded, I believe, as a very creditable performance. I was very much interested in poetry, and it was my dream to be a poet. I began a drama called 'Cleon.' The scene was laid in the court and time of the emperor Nero, and Cleon was a Greek lord residing at Nero's court, who, after much searching and doubting, at last came to the knowledge of Christianity. I filled blank book after blank book with this drama. It filled my thoughts sleeping and waking. One day sister Catharine pounced down upon me, and said that I must not waste my time writing poetry, but discipline my mind by the study of Butler's 'Analogy.' So after this I wrote out abstracts from the 'Analogy,' and instructed a class of girls as old as myself, being compelled to master each chapter just ahead of the class I was teaching. About this time I read Baxter's 'Saint's Rest.' I do not think any book affected me more powerfully. As I walked the pavements I used to wish that they might sink beneath me if only I might find myself in heaven. I was at the same time very much interested in Butler's 'Analogy,' for Mr. Brace used to lecture on such themes when I was at Miss Pierce's school in Litchfield. I also began the study of French and Italian with a Miss Degan, who was born in Italy.

[Harriet]

[HBS to Charles Edward Stowe,
LHBS, pp. 29–32]

Having been enlisted as Catharine's apprentice shortly after her arrival at Hartford Female Seminary, Harriet soon became a full-fledged teacher. In the following letters to her maternal grandmother, Roxana Ward Foote, and her brother, Edward, Harriet told them about her progress in French and Italian (and social accomplishments such as painting). Like the other instructors with whom she became friends, young Harriet's days were filled with teaching and study.

23   January 3, 1828
My Dear Grandmother,

I should have written before to assure you of my remembrance of you, but I have been constantly employed, from nine in the morning till after dark at night, in taking lessons of a painting and drawing master, with only an intermission long enough to swallow a little dinner which was sent to me in the schoolroom. You may easily believe that after spending the day in this manner, I did not feel in a very epistolary humor in the evening, and if I had been, I could not have written, for when I did not go immediately to bed I was obliged to get a long French lesson.

The seminary is finished, and the school going on nicely. Miss Clarissa Brown is assisting Catharine in the school. Besides her, Catharine, and myself, there are two other teachers who both board in the family with us: one is Miss Degan, an Italian lady who teaches French and Italian; she rooms with me, and is very interesting and agreeable. Miss Hawks is rooming with Catharine. In some respects she reminds me very much of my mother. She is gentle, affectionate, modest, and retiring, and much beloved by all the scholars. . . . I am still going on with my French, and carrying two young ladies through Virgil, and if I have time, shall commence Italian.

I am very comfortable and happy.

I propose, my dear grandmamma, to send you by the first opportunity a dish of fruit of my own painting. Pray do not devour it in anticipation, for I cannot promise that you will not find it sadly tasteless in reality. If so, please excuse it, for the sake of the poor young artist. I admire to cultivate a taste for painting, and I wish to improve it; it was what my dear mother admired and loved, and I cherish it for her sake. I have thought more of this dearest of all earthly friends these late years, since I have been old enough to know her character and appreciate her worth. I sometimes think that, had she lived, I might have been both better and happier than I now am, but God is good and wise in all his ways.

[Harriet]

[HBS to Roxana Ward Foote, *LHBS*, pp. 41–42]

---

24   [1829]

[Harriet to Edward]

My situation this winter is in many respects pleasant. I room with three other teachers, Miss Fisher, Miss Mary Dutton, and Miss Brigham. Ann Fisher you know. Miss Dutton is about twenty, has a fine mathematical mind, and has gone as far into that science perhaps as most students at college. She is also, as I am told, quite learned in the languages. . . . Miss Brigham is somewhat older: is possessed of a fine mind and most unconquerable energy and perseverance of character. From early childhood she has been determined to obtain an education, and to attain to a certain standard. Where persons are determined to be anything, they will be. I think, for this reason, she will make a first-rate character. Such are my companions. We spend our time in school during the day, and in studying in the evening. My plan of study is to read rhetoric and prepare exercises for my class the first half hour in the evening; after that the rest of the evening is divided between French and Italian. . . . Little things have great power over me, and if I meet with the least thing that crosses my feelings, I am often rendered unhappy for days and weeks. . . . I wish I could bring myself to feel perfectly indifferent to the opinions of others. I believe that there never was a person more dependent on the good and evil opinions of those around than I am. This desire to be loved forms, I fear, the great motive for all my actions. . . .

[Harriet]

[HBS to Edward Beecher, *LHBS*, pp. 45–49]

When Lyman Beecher became president of Lane Theological Seminary in 1832, Harriet and Catharine accompanied him to Cincinnati, Ohio. The elder sister founded a second school shortly after their arrival, and Harriet, as she told her friend Georgiana May, joined Catharine in establishing the Western Female Institute. Although they served as coprincipals, only Harriet taught at the school.

25   [1833]
[Harriet to Georgiana]

We mean to turn over the West by means of *model schools* in this, its capital. We mean to have a young lady's school of about fifty or sixty, a primary school of little girls to the same amount, and then a primary school for *boys*. We have come to the conclusion that the work of teaching will never be rightly done till it passes into *female* hands. This is especially true with regard to boys. To govern boys by moral influences requires tact and talent and versatility; it requires also the same division of labor that female education does. But men of tact, versatility, talent, and piety will not devote their lives to teaching. They must be ministers and missionaries, and all that, and while there is such a thrilling call for action in this way, every man who is merely teaching feels as if he were a Hercules with a distaff, ready to spring to the first trumpet that calls him away. As for the division of labor, men must have salaries that can support wife and family, and, of course, a revenue would be required to support a requisite number of teachers if they could be found.

Then, if men have more knowledge they have less talent at communicating it, nor have they the patience, the long-suffering, and gentleness necessary to superintend the formation of character. We intend to make these principles understood, and ourselves to set the example of what females can do in this way. You see that first-rate talent is necessary for all that we mean to do, especially for the last, because here we must face down the prejudices of society and we must have exemplary success to be believed. We want original, planning minds, and you do not know how few there are among females, and how few we can command of those that exist.

[Harriet]

[HBS to Georgiana May, *LHBS*, pp. 72–73]

Harriet and Catharine also joined the Semi-Colon Club, a literary society that gathered weekly and read contributions of the members. The "soirées," as Harriet termed them, were generally held at the home of her uncle, Samuel Foote. Harriet's letter to Georgiana described her "campaign in this circle." The essay that was ascribed to Catharine appeared as "Modern Uses of Language" in the third issue of Judge James Hall's Western Monthly Magazine. *"A New England Sketch," described in Harriet's letter to her brother George and published under her name, was also issued by the* Magazine *in April of 1834.*

26   [Fall 1833]
[Harriet to Georgiana]

I am wondering as to what I shall do next. I have been writing a piece to be read next Monday evening at Uncle Sam's *soirée*. It is a letter purporting to be from Dr. Johnson. I have been stilting about in his style so long that it is a relief to me to come down to the jog of common English. Now I think of it I will just give you a history of my campaign in this circle.

My first piece was a letter from Bishop Butler, written in his outrageous style of parentheses and foggification. My second a satirical essay on the modern uses of languages. This I shall send to you, as some of the gentlemen, it seems, took a fancy to it and requested leave to put it in the 'Western Magazine,' and so it is in print. It is ascribed to *Catharine*, or I don't know that I should have let it go. I have no notion of appearing in *propria personae*.

The next piece was a satire on certain members who were getting very much into the way of joking on the worn-out subjects of matrimony and old maid and old bachelorism. I therefore wrote a set of legislative enactments purporting to be from the ladies of the society, forbidding all such allusions in future. It made some sport at the time. I try not to be personal, and to be courteous, even in satire. . . .

   [Harriet]

     [HBS to Georgiana May, *LHBS*, pp. 69–71]

---

27   Jan[uary] 3, 1834
My Dear Brother

Why under the sun have I neglected you? Don't ask me. Vacation came and Monday I had forty calls to make and a party in the evening. . . .

I thought of you too the other evening at Uncle Samuel's soirée—We had a very pleasant time—I wrote a piece—a little bit of a love sketch and sent it in—Thinking it was rather a contemptible little affair—and indeed much hesitating whether I would have it read at all—But somehow or other everybody was mightily taken with it—and I have heard more about it since than about anything I ever did—Judge Hall wants to put it in his Magazine and so I have promised it to him and so you will see it. . . .

> *Very affectionately* yours
> Hatty

> [HBS to George Beecher, SD]

> *On January 6, 1836, Harriet Beecher married Calvin Stowe, a member of Lane's faculty. Less than an hour before the ceremony, she began the following letter to Georgiana. Noting that she would no longer be "Hatty Beecher," she told her friend that she would "change to nobody knows who." Harriet Beecher Stowe concluded the letter seven weeks later, telling Georgiana that she and Calvin were coming east prior to his departure for Europe. Harriet became pregnant and remained in Cincinnati, however. Calvin spent nearly a year abroad purchasing books for Lane's library and collecting information on education for Ohio's legislature.*

28   January 6, 1836
[Harriet to Georgiana]

Well, my dear G., about half an hour more and your old friend, companion, schoolmate, sister, etc., will cease to be Hatty Beecher and change to nobody knows who. My dear, you are engaged, and pledged in a year or two to encounter a similar fate, and do you wish to know how you shall feel? Well, my dear, I have been dreading and dreading the time, and lying awake all last week wondering how I should live through this overwhelming crisis, and lo! it has come and I feel *nothing at all.*

The wedding is to be altogether domestic; nobody present but my own brothers and sisters, and my old colleague, Mary Dutton; and as there is a sufficiency of the ministry in our family we have not even to call in the foreign aid of a minister. Sister Katy is not here, so she will not witness my departure from her care and guidance to that of another. None of my numerous friends and acquaintances who have taken such a deep interest in making the connection for me even know the day, and it will be all done and over before they know anything about it.

Well, it is really a mercy to have this entire stupidity come over one at such a time. I should be crazy to feel as I did yesterday, or indeed to feel anything at all. But I inwardly vowed that my last feelings and reflections on this subject should be yours, and as I have not got any, it is just as well to tell you *that*. Well, here comes Mr. S[towe], so farewell, and for the last time I subscribe

Your own

H.E.B.

Three weeks have passed since writing the above, and my husband and self are now quietly seated by our own fireside, as domestic as any pair of tame fowl you ever saw; he writing to his mother, and I to you. Two days after our marriage we took a wedding excursion, so called, though we would most gladly have been excused this conformity to ordinary custom had not necessity required Mr. Stowe to visit Columbus, and I had too much adhesiveness not to go too. Ohio roads at this season are no joke, I can tell you, though we were, on the whole, wonderfully taken care of, and our expedition included as many pleasures as an expedition at this time of the year *ever* could.

And now, my dear, perhaps the wonder to you, as to me, is how this momentous crisis in the life of such a wisp of nerve as myself has been transacted so quietly. My dear, it is a wonder to myself. I am tranquil, quiet, and happy. I look *only* on the present, and leave the future with Him who has hitherto been so kind to me. 'Take no thought for the morrow' is my motto, and my comfort is to rest on Him in whose house there are many mansions provided when these fleeting earthly ones pass away.

Dear Georgy, naughty girl that I am, it is a month that I have let the above lie by, because I got into a strain of emotion in it that I dreaded to return to. Well, so it shall be no longer. In about five weeks Mr. Stowe and myself start for New England. He sails the first of May. I am going with him to Boston, New York, and other places, and shall stop finally at

Hartford, whence, as soon as he is gone, it is my intention to return westward.

> [Harriet]
>
> [HBS to Georgiana May, *LHBS*, pp. 76–79]

In the following excerpt from one of the letters that the Beechers circulated among themselves, Harriet described herself and her family little more than a year after her marriage. The "lassies" are her twin daughters Hattie and Eliza. (Originally, one of the twins was called Isabella Beecher; however, Calvin insisted that the child's name be changed to Harriet Beecher. The other twin bore the name of Calvin's first wife who had died in 1834).

29   [c.April 16], 1837

Dear Friends All

That the "mistress of two lassies" should put pen to paper at all is something of a circumstance, but that she should do it when there are plenty of others who have no children is more—But my words shall be few—and under regular heads 1st *Myself* my ideas are best expressed by the first line of the 90th psalm short metric in the version of Dr. Watts— 2nd my children—one is fat—the other poor [—]one pretty well the other feeble and sickly and either one of them more than babies of their age in general 3 My husband—Is a very worthy man and tries to do his duty all round that is to say lecturing and attending faculty meetings in the day time and rocking the crib and tending one baby or another nights—in consequence of which he is often tired and sleepy at both periods. Lastly—one of my babies has awakened and crieth wherefore I must go leaving much love.

> [Harriet]
>
> [HBS to other members of
> the Beecher family, SD]

*Shortly before the following letter was written to
Georgiana May, Harriet's third child, Henry, was born.
The presence of a servant notwithstanding, Stowe was
totally consumed by the demands of domesticity. Six
months later, in a letter to another friend and former
colleague, Mary Dutton, Harriet reported that she had
engaged a second servant. Determined to pursue two
vocations simultaneously, Stowe was trying to set aside
time to compose tales and sketches. Her contributions
in the latter regard began to appear regularly in
periodicals such as* Godey's Lady's Book.

30   June 21, 1838
My Dear, Dear Georgiana,

Only think how long it is since I have written to you, and how changed
I am since then—the mother of three children! Well, if I have not kept the
reckoning of old times, let this last circumstance prove my apology, for I
have been hand, heart, and head full since I saw you.

Now, today, for example, I'll tell you what I had on my mind from
dawn to dewy eve. In the first place I waked about half after four and
thought, "Bless me, how light it is! I must get out of bed and rap to wake
up Mina, for breakfast must be had at six o'clock this morning." So out
of bed I jump and seize the tongs and pound, pound, pound over poor
Mina's sleepy head, charitably allowing her about half an hour to get
waked up in,—that being the quantum of time that it takes me,—or used
to. Well, then baby wakes—quâ, quâ, quâ, so I give him his breakfast. . . . I get my frock half on and baby by that time has kicked himself
down off his pillow, and is crying and fisting the bed-clothes in great
order. I stop with one sleeve off and one on to settle matters with him.
Having planted him bolt upright and gone all up and down the chamber
barefoot to get pillows and blankets to prop him up, I finish putting my
frock on and hurry down to satisfy myself by actual observation that the
breakfast is in progress. Then back I come into the nursery, where, remembering that it is washing day and that there is a great deal of work to
be done, I apply myself vigorously to sweeping, dusting, and the setting
to rights so necessary where there are three little mischiefs always pulling
down as fast as one can put up.

Then there are Miss H[attie] and Miss E[liza], concerning whom Mary
[Beecher Perkins] will furnish you with all suitable particulars, who are

chattering, hallooing, or singing at the tops of their voices, as may suit their various states of mind, while the nurse is getting their breakfast ready. This meal being cleared away, Mr. Stowe dispatched to market with various memoranda of provisions, etc., and the baby being washed and dressed, I begin to think what next must be done. I start to cut out some little dresses, have just calculated the length and got one breadth torn off when Master Henry makes a doleful lip and falls to crying with might and main. I catch him up and turning round see one of his sisters flourishing the things out of my workbox in fine style. Moving it away and looking the other side I see the second little mischief seated by the hearth chewing coals and scraping up ashes with great apparent relish. Grandmother lays hold upon her and charitably offers to endeavor to quiet baby while I go on with my work. I set at it again, pick up a dozen pieces, measure them once more to see which is the right one, and proceed to cut out some others, when I see the twins on the point of quarreling with each other. Number one pushes number two over. Number two screams: that frightens the baby and he joins in. I call number one a naughty girl, take the persecuted one in my arms, and endeavor to comfort her. . . . Meanwhile number one makes her way to the slop jar and forthwith proceeds to wash her apron in it. Grandmother catches her by one shoulder, drags her away, and sets the jar out of her reach. By and by the nurse comes up from her sweeping. I commit the children to her, and finish cutting out the frocks.

But let this suffice, for of such details as these are all my days made up. Indeed, my dear, I am but a mere drudge with few ideas beyond babies and housekeeping. As for thoughts, reflections, and sentiments, good lack! good lack!

I suppose I am a dolefully uninteresting person at present, but I hope I shall grow young again one of these days, for it seems to me that matters cannot always stand exactly as they do now.

Well, Georgy, this marriage is—yes, I will speak well of it, after all; for when I can stop and think long enough to discriminate my head from my heels, I must say that I think myself a fortunate woman both in husband and children. My children I would not change for all the ease, leisure, and pleasure that I could have without them. They are money on interest whose value will be constantly increasing.

[Harriet]

[HBS to Georgiana May, *LHBS*, pp. 90–93]

31   [December 1838]

Oh Mary—

You precious good soul you dear friendly kindly cosy warm hearted little body without whom we might all have died forty times over of the blues during the last long winter—I do most humbly and freely confess and acknowledge that I have three letters from you at this present writing lying unanswered—But wherefore? because I love you not—Nay— Why then? Oh Mary ask of all the hundred and forty things which a body finds to do when one is vainly puffing and chasing and panting just to keep in sight of ones duties. . . .

Saturday Evening Dec[ember] 8th The foregoing I wrote when I could not write any better and felt that I must write something. Tonight I feel as if I could put English together in rather better shape—To begin then— Here we are—me and my Professor in the same old house—after all the vision of a house this fall proved a mirage of the desert to us. . . . Well now for particulars—We have our olmsted stove moved into the parlour and use only one part of it and it keeps the room delightfully warm. [H]ere we eat our meals, near enough to the fire to toast our bread as we go along which I think is the ne plus ultra of a sociable cosy breakfast or tea—Mr[.] Stowe reads german books and translates sometimes as he goes along and I'll tell you for your edification that he has read to me the story of "Blue Beard[,]" "Puss in boots" and various others of the kind out of the old mother German to say nothing of Faust, of which by way of routing a fit of the blues the good man undertook a translation—I also have made a new arrangement—I have realized enough by writing one way and another to enable me to add to my establishment a stout German girl who does my housework leaving to Anna[1] fulltime to attend to the children so that by [this] method in disposing of time I have about three hours per day in writing and if you see my name coming out everywhere—you may be sure of one thing, that I *do* it for *the pay*—I have determined not to be a mere domestic slave—without even the leisure to *excell* in my duties—I mean to have money enough to have my house kept in the best manner and yet to have time for reflection and that preparation for the education of my children which every mother needs—I have every prospect of succeeding in this plan and I am certain as yet that I am not only more comfortable but my house affairs and my

1. After becoming Harriet's servant in the late 1830s, Anna remained with the family during their years in Cincinnati and then accompanied them to Brunswick, Maine in 1850.

children are in better keeping than when I was pressed and worried and tested in trying to do more than I could. . . .

Mary—I am *very busy* now what with the superintending my children and house and german girl who is "fresh caught" and needs a deal of shaping so that I scarcely find time to meet my writing engagements. I intend to raise $300 before spring—I have good hopes of doing it. . . .

        Aff[ectionate]ly Yours
        HEBS

                                [HBS to Mary Dutton, BL]

In the following exchange of letters, Calvin and Harriet discussed the latter's vocation as a writer. Accompanied by her daughter Hattie, Stowe had gone east to negotiate the publication of a collection of tales and sketches. Insisting that she "must be a literary woman," Calvin encouraged an uncertain Harriet. Although she was confident about her prospects, Harriet was deeply concerned about meeting the responsibilities entailed in her other vocation. Our children, she told Calvin, "need a mother's whole attention." Nonetheless, The Mayflower *was published by Harper and Brothers in 1843.*

32   April 30, 1842

My dear Wife,

Aunt Esther[2] and Anna were sure of a letter Thursday, but I was not—yet I thought I could not fail to have one this morning—but nothing came! How is this? . . . It is too hard, with all our anxiety to know how you and little Hattie got up the river. As to matters at home, we all get on nicely. Children are all well, and we find all things go smoothly. I don't know how I can endure your absence, for this week has seemed an interminably long one, and I want to see you most prodigiously. My days are heavy and my nights joyless—but I can bear it all if you will come back strong and well, with the prospect of living many years to come. I desire that our days may be long in the land, both for my sake and the children's. I am an uncivil fellow, I know; but a loving one notwithstanding. . . .

---

2. Esther Beecher, Lyman's sister, joined the household, serving as Harriet's substitute during her absence.

You must be a *literary woman*. It is so written in the book of fate. Make all your calculations accordingly, get a good stock of health, brush up your mind, drop the E. out of your name, which only encumbers it and stops the flow and euphony, and write yourself only and always, *Harriet Beecher Stowe*, which is a name euphonious, flowing, and full of meaning; and my word for it, your husband will lift up his head in the gate, and your children will rise up and call you blessed. A kiss for little Hattie and two dozen for yourself from your loving husband. Love to all friends.

> [Calvin]

> [Calvin Stowe to HBS, SD]

---

33   [1842]
[Harriet to Calvin]

I have seen Johnson of the 'Evangelist.'[3] He is very liberally disposed, and I may safely reckon on being paid for all I do there. Who is that Hale, Jr., that sent me the 'Boston Miscellany,' and will he keep his word with me? His offers are very liberal—twenty dollars for three pages, not very close print. Is he to be depended on? If so, it is the best offer I have received yet. I shall get something from the Harpers sometime this winter or spring. Robertson, the publisher here, says the book will sell, and though the terms they offer me are very low, that I shall make something on it. For a second volume I shall be able to make better terms. On the whole, my dear, if I choose to be a literary lady, I have, I think, as good a chance of making a profit by it as any one I know of. But with all this, I have my doubts whether I shall be able to do so.

Our children are just coming to the age when everything depends on my efforts. They are delicate in health, and nervous and excitable, and need a mother's whole attention. Can I lawfully divide my attention by literary efforts?

There is one thing I must suggest. If I am to write, I must have a room to myself, which shall be *my* room. I have in my own mind pitched on Mrs. Whipple's room. I can put the stove in it. I have bought a cheap carpet for it, and I have furniture enough at home to furnish it comfortably, and I only beg in addition that you will let me change the glass door

3. New York's *Evangelist* had been publishing some of Stowe's tales and sketches since the late 1830s.

from the nursery into that room and keep my plants there, and then I shall be quite happy. . . .

[Harriet]

[HBS to Calvin Stowe, *LHBS*, pp. 103–5]

As Harriet's letter to Calvin suggests, domesticity re-mained integral to Stowe's identity and experience. Here she elaborated upon the "dark side of domestic life." Because the family's financial situation was pre-carious during this decade Harriet had to do more of the housekeeping herself. Less than two years before the letter was written, she had also given birth to her fifth child. Harriet gave her daughter the name of her close friend Georgiana May.

34   June 16, 1845

My Dear Husband,

It is a dark, sloppy, rainy, muddy, disagreeable day, and I have been working hard (for me) all day in the kitchen, washing dishes, looking into closets, and seeing a great deal of that dark side of domestic life which a housekeeper may who will investigate too curiously into minu-tiae in warm, damp weather, especially after a girl who keeps all clean on the *outside* of cup and platter, and is very apt to make good the rest of the text in the *inside* of things.

I am sick of the smell of sour milk, and sour meat, and sour every-thing, and then the clothes *will* not dry, and no wet thing does, and everything smells mouldy; and altogether I feel as if I never wanted to eat again.

Your letter, which was neither sour nor mouldy, formed a very agree-able contrast to all these things; the more so for being unexpected. I am much obliged to you for it. As to my health, it gives me very little solicitude, although I am bad enough and daily growing worse. I feel no life, no energy, no appetite, or rather a growing distaste for food; in fact, I am becoming quite ethereal. Upon reflection I perceive that it pleases my Father to keep me in the fire, for my whole situation is excessively harassing and painful. I suffer with sensible distress in the brain, as I have done more or less since my sickness last winter, a distress which some days takes from me all power of planning or executing anything; and you know that, except this poor head, my unfortunate household has no mainspring, for nobody feels any kind of responsibility to do a thing in time, place, or manner, except as I oversee it.

Georgiana is so excessively weak, nervous, cross, and fretful, night and day, that she takes all Anna's strength and time with her; and then the children are, like other little sons and daughters of Adam, full of all kinds of absurdity and folly.

When the brain gives out, as mine often does, and one cannot think or remember anything, then what is to be done? All common fatigue, sickness, and exhaustion is nothing to this distress. Yet do I rejoice in my God and know in whom I believe, and only pray that the fire may consume the dross; as to the gold, that is imperishable. No real evil can happen to me, so I fear nothing for the future, and only suffer in the present tense. . . .

    [Harriet]

             [HBS to Calvin Stowe, *LHBS*, pp. 111–12]

After suffering from invalidism for more than two years, Harriet sought relief at a water cure in Brattleboro, Vermont in May 1846. She stayed there until March of the next year, while Calvin and the children remained in Cincinnati. In the following exchange of letters, Harriet and Calvin candidly acknowledged the serious frictions in their marriage, expressing disappointment in one another while affirming a mutual devotion.

35   Nov[ember] 22, [18]46

My dear Wife,

I promised to write you every Sab[bath] eve, but I feel so tired tonight that I am almost sick of my bargain. Dr. Muzzey thinks you had better by all means stay at B[rattleboro] so long as there is any chance for recovery. Much as I suffer from your absence, I should suffer still more from your presence, unless you can be in a better condition than you have been for a year past. It is now a full year since your last miscarriage, and you well know what has been the state of things both in regard to yourself and me ever since. I am almost a-weary of life, and were it not for the poor little helpless children, should be glad to be gone. . . . My nerves and brain are in poor condition to meet the demands that are continually made upon them—and in addition to all this, here is this matter of Cate's and Gov[ernor] Slade,[4] which threatens to make me no little amount of care and labor. I told Cate from the first that I *could not* and *would not* take any labor or responsibility about it—and wrote her so from N.Y. last Summer. She replied in the most nonchalant, imperious, Devil-may-care style, that she could *not understand what I meant, that I was as much committed as anybody, that nobody was to do more than they could etc. etc. etc.* as if I was after all to be the main spoke in the wheel. Now I was from the beginning apprehensive that she might cut just this caper, as she is very apt to do; and, therefore, I was the more careful to tell her from the first, and repeatedly and earnestly, that I could take no responsibility about the matter,—and *that I shall stick* to whether she *understands* it or not. You know very well that I cannot take any more loading on to my poor brain.

Well, if you are not able by next Spring to come home and stay at home and be a help to me, I am determined to get out of this fix at some rate or other, and find some position where there will be less care and labor and wearing anxiety. I will not try to run away from God, but the state of your health shall be my guiding providence. . . .

[Page has been cut off]

[Calvin Stowe to HBS, SD]

36　　　　　　January 1, 1847

My Dearest Husband

. . . I was at that date of marriage a very different being from what I am now and stood in relation to my Heavenly Father in a very different attitude— My whole desire was to live in love, absorbing passionate devotion to one person— Our separation was my first trial—but then came a note of comfort in the hope of being a mother— No creature ever so longed to see the face of a little one or had such a heart full of love to bestow— Here came in trial again sickness, pain, perplexity, constant discouragement—wearing wasting days and nights—a cross, deceitful, unprincipled nurse—husband gone—no friend but Anna—When you came back you came only to increasing perplexities— Ah, how little comfort I had in being a mother—how was all that I proposed met and

4. Calvin was referring to Catharine Beecher's Central Committee for Promoting National Education: Harriet's sister had enlisted a reluctant Calvin in the establishment of the organization, and she and Calvin had recruited Vermont's governor William Slade to serve as secretary and agent.

crossed and my way ever hedged up! . . . In short—God would teach me that I should make no family be my chief good and portion and bitter as the lesson has been I thank Him for it from my very soul. One might naturally infer that from the union of two both morbidly sensitive and acute, yet in many respects exact opposites[—]one hasty and impulsive—the other sensitive and brooding—one the very personification of exactness and routine and the other to whom everything of the kind was an irksome effort—from all this what should one infer but some painful friction. But all this would not after all have done so very much had not Providence as if intent to try us throws upon the heaviest external pressure . . . but still where you have failed your faults have been to me those of one beloved—of the man who after all would be the choice of my heart still were I to choose—for were I now free I should again love just as I did and again feel that I could give up all to and for you—and if I do not love never can love again with the blind and unwise love with which I married I love quite as truly tho far more wisely. . . . In reflecting upon our future union—our marriage[—]the past obstacles to our happiness[—]it seems to me that they are of two or three kinds—1st those from physical causes both in you and in me—such on your part as hypocondriac morbid instability for which the only remedy is physical care [and] attention to the laws of health—and on my part an excess of sensitiveness and of confusion and want of control of mind and memory—this always increases on my part in proportion as I am blamed and found fault with and I hope will decrease with returning health—I hope that we shall both be impressed with a most solemn sense of the importance of a wise and constant attention to the laws of health. Then in the second place the want of any definite plan of mutual watchfulness, with regard to each other's improvement[,] of a definite time and place for doing it with a firm determination to improve and be improved by each other—to confess our faults one to another and pray one for another that we may be healed. . . .

      Yours with much love

      H

                      [HBS to Calvin Stowe, SchL]

Two years after Harriet's return to Cincinnati, Calvin, who was afflicted with gout, spent fifteen months at the same water cure. Still in Brattleboro during the summer of 1849, Calvin told Harriet that he was deeply worried about her health—"hot weather always affects you so badly, and the season is so sickly." His letter was prophetic: although Harriet survived the cholera that swept Cincinnati, their infant Charley died in the epidemic exactly one month later. In a series of letters to Calvin, Harriet kept her husband informed about the family. Her final letter about the death of their son was written "as though there were no sorrow like my sorrow."

37   June 25, 1849

My dear Wife,

. . . Your letters are the greatest comfort I have, and I want them *as quick* and *as often* as possible. You have no idea of the delight with which I take one of your letters out of the office, and then wander off to one of these beautiful secluded spots, and then read it and read it and read it, and then come home to my room and read it over and over again. . . .

I cannot help feeling anxious about you this hot weather. Hot weather always affects you so badly, and the season is so sickly. It seems very hard that you cannot be here with me, when this is the very thing you need, and we should enjoy it so much together. But our poverty is from the Lord, and we are not to blame for it; and I doubt not it is for the best, but I confess I do not see how. If I could have you all here, little and big, for one summer, no words can tell how delighted, I should be. . . . I thank the good Lord for taking so kind a care of you and Anna and the children. The dear little ones, how my heart goes out after them, for all in general, and for each one in particular. I think exactly how each one looks, and almost see them as I am about on my walks and when alone in my chamber. I commend you all to God, I most earnestly and fervently pray that he may spare you all, and allow me to come and live among you with a healthful body and a cheerful mind. All our trials thus far, have been most mainfully [manifestly?] for our good—they have been richly intermingled with mercies—and we will still hope and trust. Write as often as you can without injury to yourself or others.

> Most affectionately yours,
> C. E. Stowe

[Calvin Stowe to HBS, SD]

---

38 June 29, 1849

My Dear Husband,

This week has been unusually fatal. The disease in the city has been malignant and virulent. Hearse drivers have scarce been allowed to unharness their horses, while furniture carts and common vehicles are often employed for the removal of the dead. The sable trains which pass our windows, the frequent indications of crowding haste, and the absence of reverent decency have, in many cases, been most painful. Of course all these things, whether we will or no, bring very doleful images to the mind.

On Tuesday one hundred and sixteen deaths from cholera were reported, and that night the air was of that peculiarly oppressive, deathly kind that seems to lie like lead on the brain and soul.

As regards your coming home, I am decidedly opposed to it. First, because the chance of your being taken ill is just as great as the chance of your being able to render us any help. To exchange the salubrious air of Brattleboro for the pestilent atmosphere of this place with your system rendered sensitive by water-cure treatment would be extremely dangerous. It is a source of constant gratitude to me that neither you nor father are exposed to the dangers here.

Second, none of us are sick, and it is very uncertain whether we shall be.

Third, if we were sick there are so many of us that it is not at all likely we shall be taken at once. . . .

July 3. We are all in good health and try to maintain a calm and cheerful frame of mind. The doctors are nearly used up. Dr. Bowen and Dr. Peck are sick in bed. Dr. Potter and Dr. Pulte ought, I suppose, to be there also. The younger physicians have no rest night or day. Mr. Fisher is laid up from his incessant visitations with the sick and dying. Our own Dr. Brown is likewise prostrated, but we are all resolute to stand by each other, and there are so many of us that it is not likely we can all be taken sick together. . . .

July 10. Yesterday little Charley was taken ill, not seriously, and at any other season I should not be alarmed. Now, however, a slight illness seems like a death sentence, and I will not dissemble that I feel from the outset very little hope. I still think it best that you should not return. By so doing you might lose all you have gained. You might expose yourself to a fatal incursion of disease. It is decidedly not your duty to do so. . . .

July 15. Since I last wrote our house has been a perfect hospital. Charley apparently recovering, but still weak and feeble, unable to walk or play, and so miserably fretful and unhappy. Sunday Anna and I were fairly stricken down, as many others are, with no particular illness, but with such miserable prostration. I lay on the bed all day reading my hymn-book and thinking over passages of Scripture. . . .

July 23. At last, my dear, the hand of the Lord hath touched us. We have been watching all day by the dying bed of little Charley, who is gradually sinking. After a partial recovery from the attack I described in my last letter he continued for some days very feeble, but still we hoped for recovery. About four days ago he was taken with decided cholera, and now there is no hope of his surviving this night.

Every kindness is shown us by the neighbors. Do not return. All will be over before you could possibly get here, and the epidemic is now said by the physicians to prove fatal to every new case. Bear up. Let us not faint when we are rebuked of Him. I dare not trust myself to say more but shall write again soon.

[Harriet]

[HBS to Calvin Stowe, *LHBS*, pp. 120–24]

---

39   J[u]ly 26, [1849]

My Dear Husband,

At last it is over and our dear little one is gone from us. He is now among the blessed. My Charley—my beautiful, loving, gladsome baby, so loving, so sweet, so full of life and hope and strength—now lies shrouded, pale and cold, in the room below. Never was he anything to me but a comfort. He has been my pride and joy. Many a heartache has he cured for me. Many an anxious night have I held him to my bosom and felt the sorrow and loneliness pass out of me with the touch of his little warm hands. Yet I have just seen him in his death agony, looked on his imploring face when I could not help nor soothe nor do one thing, not one, to mitigate his cruel suffering, do nothing but pray in my anguish that he might die soon. I write as though there were no sorrow like my sorrow, yet there has been in this city, as in the land of Egypt, scarce a house without its dead. This heart-break, this anguish, has been everywhere, and when it will end God alone knows.

[Harriet]

[HBS to Calvin Stowe, *LHBS*, p. 124]

In the spring of 1850, Calvin accepted an appointment at Bowdoin College. Accompanied by three of her children, Harriet preceded him east to begin renovations on a house in Brunswick, Maine. In July Calvin arrived, as did their seventh child who was born on July 8. It was not until Christmas that the family was settled, and Harriet was finally able to write a letter to her sister-in-law Sarah Buckingham Beecher, recounting the simultaneous pursuit of her domestic and literary vocations.

40   December 17, [1850]

[Harriet to Sarah]

Is it really true that snow is on the ground and Christmas coming, and I have not written unto thee, most dear sister? No, I don't believe it! I haven't been so naughty—it's all a mistake—yes, written I must have—and written I have, too,—in the night-watches as I lay on my bed—such beautiful letters— I wish you had only gotten them; but by day it has been hurry, hurry, hurry, and drive, drive, drive! or else the calm of a sick-room, ever since last spring. . . .

Sarah, when I look back, I wonder at myself, not that I forget any one thing that I should remember, but that I have remembered *anything*. From the time that I left Cincinnati with my children to come forth to a country that I knew not of almost unto the present time, it has seemed as if I could scarcely breathe, I was so pressed with care. My head dizzy with the whirl of railroads and steamboats—then ten days' sojourn in Boston and a constant toil and hurry in buying my furniture and equipments and then landing in Brunswick in the midst of a drizzly, inexorable northeast storm, and beginning the work of getting to order a deserted damp old house. All day long running from one thing to another.

Then comes a letter from my husband saying he is sick abed—and all but dead—don't ever expect to see his family again wants to know how I shall manage in case I am left a widow—knows we shall get in debt and never get out—wonders at my courage—thinks I am very sanguine—warns me to be provident as there won't be much to live on, in case of his death etc. etc. I read the letter and poke it into the stove, and proceed.

In all my moving and fussing Mr. Titcomb has been my right-hand man. Whenever a screw was loose—a nail to be driven—a lock mended —a pane of glass set—and these cases were manifold he was always on hand. But my sink was no fancy job—and I believe nothing but a very particular friendship would have moved him to undertake it. So this same sink lingered in a precarious state for some weeks—and when I had *nothing else to do*—I used to call and do what I could in the way of enlisting the good man's sympathies in its behalf.

How many times I have been in and seated myself in one of the old rocking-chairs—talked first of the news of the day—the railroad—the last proceedings in Congress—the probabilities about the millenium and thus brought the conversation by little and little round to my sink!—because, till the sink was done, the pump could not be put up and we couldn't have any rainwater. Sometimes my courage would quite fail me to introduce the delicate subject and I would talk of everything else, turn and get out of the shop and then turn back as if a thought had just struck my mind and say

Oh, Mr. Titcomb! about that sink?

Yes, ma'am, I was thinking about going down street this afternoon to look out stuff for it.

Yes, sir, if you would be good enough to get it done as soon as possible—we are in great need of it.

I think there's no hurry. I believe we are going to have a dry time now so that you could not catch any water and you won't need a pump at present.

These negotiations extended from the first of June to the first of July and at last my sink was completed—and so also was a new house spout, concerning which I had had divers communings with Deacon Dunning of the Baptist church. Also during this time good Mrs. Mitchell and myself made two sofas—or lounges—a barrel chair—divers bedspreads —pillow cases—pillows—bolsters—mattresses; we painted rooms; we revarnished furniture—we—what *didn't* we do?

Then came on Mr. Stowe—and then came the eighth of July and my little Charley. I was really glad for an excuse to lie in bed for I was full tired I can assure you. Well, I was what folks call very comfortable for two weeks, when my nurse had to leave me and the very night she left I had an attack of fever and an ague in my breast—and for six weeks after I was never well—the pain in my breast was incessant—and I was miserably [sic] in every respect—at last I went to Boston to consult Dr. Hoffendahl and then one of my breasts gathered and discharged and after that I began slowly to recover tho very weak.

During this time I have employed my leisure in making up my engagements with newspaper editors. I have written more than anybody, or I myself would have thought. I have taught an hour a day in our school—and I have read two hours every evening to the children. The children study English history in school, and I am reading Scott's historic novels in their order. Tonight I finish the Abbot—shall begin Kenilworth next week—yet I am constantly pursued and haunted by the idea that I don't do anything. Since I began this note I have been called off at least a dozen times—once for the fishman, to buy a codfish; once to see a man who had brought me some barrels of apples—once to see a book-man—then to Mrs. Upham[5] to see about a drawing I promised to make for her—then to nurse the baby—then into the kitchen to make a chowder for dinner and now I am at it again for nothing but deadly determination enables me ever to write—it is rowing against wind and tide. . . .

To tell the truth, dear, I am getting tired; my neck and back ache, and I must come to a close. . . .

Affectionately yours,

H. Stowe

[HBS to Sarah Buckingham Beecher, SchL]

---

5. Phebe Lord Upham was married to Thomas Upham, a member of Bowdoin College's faculty.

4.

Isabella Beecher Hooker:
"A Tread Mill of Self Analysis"

DESPITE the recent intensification of interest, both popular and scholarly, in the female members of the Beecher family, Isabella Beecher Hooker—the only sister to campaign actively for woman suffrage—remains relatively unknown.[1] During her lifetime (1822–1907), Hooker's contemporaries regarded her as a highly effective organizer on both the state and national suffrage fronts, an eloquent public speaker on behalf of the constitutional rights of women, and a pivotal figure in the controversies that distinguished the post-Civil War women's rights movement. Isabella's comparative lack of recognition can be attributed to several factors, the most important of which are the relatively late date (1974) at which much of her suffrage-related correspondence became available to researchers and the damage done to her reputation (both contemporaneous and posthumous) by her largely misunderstood role in the adultery scandal surrounding her brother, Henry Ward Beecher. In light of the latter, the documents themselves were often misread when they were not simply ignored, reinforcing the tendency among women's historians and Beecher family historians to treat Isabella as a lesser figure at best and—at worst—as an anomaly. Yet the time is ripe for a reappraisal of Hooker's career precisely on the grounds that her life and writings can provide us with a new way of approaching the complex interconnections between domestic ideology, especially the celebration of motherhood, and the more overtly political aspects of postbellum feminism.

Isabella's adult life was characterized by ongoing and only partially successful efforts to resolve a series of conflicts. First, she attempted to live up to and embody an ideal of domesticity inherited from her sisters that was often at odds with her daily experience as a wife and mother. She was also torn between the competing and sometimes contradictory demands of her various roles as a wife, mother, and sister. Finally, her commitment to her domestic obligations frequently clashed with her desire to achieve individual impact and recognition as an advocate for women's social and political rights. If her conflicts illuminate the domestic experience of white middle-class Protestant women, Hooker's attempts at resolution constitute an as yet unwritten chapter in the political history of her sex. Moreover, Isabella's response to the Beecher-Tilton scandal, undoubtedly the most controversial aspect of her career, marks the point of intersection between the politics of the suffrage movement and the internal politics of the Beecher clan. Her consistent defense of Victoria Woodhull's right to free speech, coupled with her principled refusal to *assume* that her prestigious brother was innocent, ignited a bitter family feud that would serve as a dramatic illustration of the limits of sisterhood—both literally and figuratively understood.

Born to Lyman Beecher and his second wife, Harriet Porter Beecher, a full twenty-two years after her half sister Catharine, Isabella devoted herself almost exclusively to her domestic responsibilities in the years prior to the Civil War. After her marriage she did serve as an occasional participant in antislavery events under her husband's tutelage; and, like other women of her generation, Hooker joined the Sanitary Commission during the war. Yet in spite of the fact that she had composed a powerful prosuffrage argument in 1860, Isabella held off from active involvement in the women's rights movement until 1868. By that time, the forty-six-year-old wife and mother of three was facing the prospect of what she herself referred to as a "half-forsaken nest."[2] Isabella's eldest daughter Mary had wed two years earlier and Alice would marry John Calvin Day the following summer despite her mother's objections, leaving only fourteen-year-old Edward ("Ned") at home. Thus Isabella found herself for the first time at a stage in her life that permitted and virtually required her to seek a nonfamilial outlet for her pent-up energies, aspirations, and ideas. Only under these circumstances was she able and willing to make the transition from her experience as a relatively isolated and anonymous wife and mother to her career as a well-known women's rights activist.

Until this seemingly sudden transformation occurred, Isabella did little that would distinguish her from her white middle-class peers. After her mother died of consumption in 1835, "Bell" had come under the supervision of a half sister, Mary Beecher Perkins, who lived in Hartford, Connecticut, with her attorney husband. There, after attending the seminary founded by another half sister, Catharine Beecher, the seventeen-year-old Isabella met John Hooker, a law clerk six years her senior who worked in her brother-in-law's office. As his wife would become fond of pointing out, John was the descendant of Thomas Hooker, author of "the first written constitution of the world" and founder of Connecticut colony.[3]

Two years later, in August of 1841, they married—but only after John successfully resisted the pressure jointly exerted by Lyman, Catharine, and Isabella, who wanted him to conform to the Beecher family pattern by leaving the law and devoting himself to the ministry. John's love of the law and his independence of mind soon contributed to a more serious split within the family over the question of slavery and would eventually affect his wife's views regarding the scandal surrounding her half brother Henry. For the moment, however, Isabella was determined to avoid the "radical defect" she had observed in the marriages of several of her Beecher siblings. As she had confided to her fiancé in 1839, "some even of my brothers and sisters . . . did not start rightly." Meditating upon the reciprocal duties of husband and wife, she cited their lack of mutual "self-denial" and "self-sacrifice" and proceeded to warn John that the prospect of compelled submission was "galling to a sensible woman" like herself. Yet she effusively praised her sister Mary's subduing influence on her "wayward spirit," reassuring John that she was ready to render him "the required obedience without being constantly reminded that such is the will of God and the expectation of man."[4]

Isabella's less than conventional ideas regarding the relative positions of husband and wife, most notably her rejection of the "mistaken" view that wives were to have "*no* will of their own—except so far as it coincides with their husband's"—did not prevent her from making marriage and motherhood the main focus of her existence during the next three decades of her life. Beginning in 1842, she gave birth to four infants—three of whom survived—in the next thirteen years. The fact that this was a small family by nineteenth-century standards, when viewed within the context of Isabella's published views on birth control, suggests that the Hookers had made a joint decision on moral and economic grounds to control the size of their family by limiting the frequency of their sexual contact. Isabella's call for male sexual restraint in her 1867 essay on "Motherhood" was part of a specifically feminist demand for birth control that historian Linda Gordon has referred to as the "voluntary motherhood movement." Hooker's postbellum essay is also significant because she argued that fewer children and a higher quality of parenting—especially of mothering—constituted a better indication of a couple's piety than the quantity of children they produced.[5]

Isabella's mature views on motherhood, in turn, had their foundation in the personal experiments in maternal guidance and "governance" that she candidly recorded in the series of bound journals that she kept from August 1845, the month of Mary's birth, through the birth of Ned ten years later. Judging from these journals, Hooker experienced considerable anxiety and frustration as well as intense gratification as she struggled with the responsibilities of living up to her ideal of a good Christian mother. Perhaps because she herself had been left motherless at an early age, Isabella registered acute discomfort at the prospect of having to rely solely upon herself when confronted with the daily dilemmas of child-rearing. Faced with John's tendency not to "assist or advise" her, she tried to compensate by "study[ing] over the subject of government" and seeking guidance from Christ.

Dealing with her daughters' markedly different temperaments proved to be an especially perplexing task. Alice struck her as "a fancy piece to amuse and please," while she regarded Mary as "a solid article for daily use and comfort." Not surprisingly, Isabella attributed the "whole difficulty between them" to "everlasting jealousy," lamenting: "Lately they have taken to hugging and kissing me a great deal—and the rivalry is quite distressing to the unlucky object of their caresses." Quite sensibly, Isabella reasoned that such behavior was probably typical of children who were "so nearly of one age." But she candidly admitted that their rivalry frequently caused her to lose self-control and "sin with my tongue." Observing that her "consciousness of shortcomings as a mother would be materially lessened" if only she could learn to "restrain this unruly member," Isabella pledged "to watch and note progress in the right."

Sounding at times uncannily like a modern mother, Isabella also proved to be as worried about the state of her children's teeth as she was about the state of their souls: "By dint of a penny a day as bribe they are now brushing their teeth after each meal—pretty thoroughly—and I am greatly in hope of securing the habit to them for life." Yet unlike most of her twentieth-century counterparts, Hooker took her maternal shortcomings so seriously that she preferred to "die this day" rather than lead her children "away from happiness and heaven by wrong example or neglect."[6]

These high maternal expectations make it clear why Isabella applied herself so intensely to the never-ending task of perfecting her skills at maternal governance. As a result, she enjoyed precious little leisure time for self-cultivation. During the separations from her husband occasioned by her visits with relatives and his legal business, she openly despaired of "ever improving much in mind or acquirements." Even reading was made "difficult if not impossible" by the combined "cares of housekeeping and children," as she noted plaintively to John. With obvious envy, she went on to cite the educational "acquirements" of a young woman who had offered "to enlist with much zeal in Cath[arine]'s educational effort." In effect disparaging her own efforts, she praised the woman's knowledge of law, medicine, and literature, a knowledge that had accumulated during long years of invalidism.[7]

In another letter Isabella openly vented her mounting frustration, taking John to task for his extended absence: "I find to my astonishment, that there is a tameness and insipidity in my daily life that I never realized before—and which would not now exist to the same extent if you were here." She could not resist describing an innocent flirtation in which she had just engaged, explaining: "You *can have* no idea of the pleasure of being admired and loved—after having been shut out from the world as I have been . . . and filled with care and anxiety and labor. . . . The fact is I was engaged so young—I had little time to know my power—until after my destiny was sealed."[8]

The belief that marriage had indeed "sealed" her destiny helps explain why Isabella pronounced herself "melancholy" while visiting her sister Harriet, whose recent novel *Uncle Tom's Cabin* was becoming an unprecedented best seller. "Seeing the evidences of genius all around me here—my own littleness fairly stared me in the face . . . but I . . . begin to think my . . . order and housekeeping capacity are worth something in this matter of fact world." She tried to compensate John and comfort herself for her "lack of brilliancy," defensively reminding him that "I should not be half so good a *wife* and mother probably as I am now—one cannot do or be forty things at once."[9]

Such compensations formed the keystone of the nineteenth-century advocacy of complete dedication to domesticity, but they failed to satisfy Isabella, whose health—rarely good—had once again begun to suffer. In 1853 she sought treatment at the Florence, Massachusetts, water cure. Once there she confessed to her husband: "I do believe I have less self-reliance, in its best sense too, than I had six or eight years ago. You have more and I seem to lose as you gain."[10] A letter that Isabella penned to John seven years later makes it clear that her acute distress was psychological as well as physiological in nature: "Oh my *soul*—if you would only teach me how to earn money—but there's no use in hoping—I can[']t write a book nor draw pictures—nor do any other productive work—I have always told you, that you overestimated your wife."[11] Hooker's dismay at her inability to perform "work" for which she would receive financial compensation and public recognition derived from two sources: feelings of rivalry with her successful siblings, especially her two well-known sisters, and growing discontent with the ideology of separate spheres. Finding herself immersed in a virtual "tread mill of self analysis" during her stays at the water cure, Isabella came to resent having to "run on the credit" of her relations and trade on her Beecher "family name." Ironically, only at home could she "lay claim to a particle of individuality." Yet her proven domestic abilities no longer satisfied her: she, too, wanted to exert her "great power of personal influence" on a "broad scale." Recognizing that she possessed a "magnetism of heart and eye and voice, that is quite individual," Isabella realized that what she wanted most was to "sweep people along in the right path."[12]

By the late 1850s, Isabella was beginning to perceive her private predicament within the context of the mounting public debate over woman's "proper sphere." Responding to an anonymous article in the *Atlantic Monthly* advocating equal education for women, she confessed to her friend Rachel Burton, "I would rather have written these twelve pages, than any other twelve that ever I read." She added: "There's not a vital thought there, but I have had for my own, and spoken it too, in a whisper and in my blundering way." Hooker angrily attributed her inability to clothe her "bare bones" of thought "in the flesh and drapery of historic literature" to the unequal educational opportunities afforded by Lyman Beecher to his children: "At sixteen and a half, just when my brothers began their mental education, mine was finished. . . . Till twenty three, their father, poor minister as he was could send them to College and Seminary all *six*—cost what it might, but never a daughter cost him a hundred dollars a year, after she was sixteen." Scoffing at a neighbor's suggestion that women were superior to men, she insisted that "they are cut from the same *batch*" and attributed women's apparent "quickness of perception" to the fact that "they have been driven to their wits . . . by this deprivation of all external helps." Isabella concluded by predicting that "when physical and mental training are similar," they would rank as equals.[13]

A subsequent letter praising this article initiated a warm exchange with its author, Thomas Wentworth Higginson, a Boston abolitionist and supporter of women's rights. Higginson noted that "the history of the race has never been written—only of one sex" and encouraged Isabella to follow the example of Lucretia Mott, Lucy Stone, and Antoinette Brown, who defended their sex despite the criticism heaped upon them by "the mass of women, especially educated women."[14] Hooker responded by sending him a copy of her first attempt to express her views in public, "Shall Women Vote? A Matrimonial Dialogue." As its subtitle suggests, she chose a deceptively conventional format in which to present her decidedly unconventional vision of "a very respectable Congress" drawn from the ranks of single women "and all who would be single if they did not fear the loneliness and ennui of such a life, all the widows and childless ones, and then the middle-aged mothers who have reared their brood and started them on their own independent flight." Isabella singled out this last group as having the most to offer in the way of improving the public sphere. As the author's private child-rearing journals testify so eloquently, "middle-aged mothers" like herself had indeed gained their "maturity of thought" as well as their "real wisdom" in the "most motherly" of ways. They had learned to adapt "influence and government" to the characters of each of their children in an effort to insure "a harmonious whole, from so many discordant or at least different elements." Having been previously banned from public places such as the polls and the jury box, mothers would be all the more likely to arrive at "closer discriminations and more righteous judgments," for they had been "self disciplined in the cloister of the home."[15]

It may have been the prospect of a female legislature that caused Higginson to pronounce this essay "radical," despite Isabella's cautious conclusion that she would not open the polls to women "unless public opinion demanded it." He accurately predicted that the article would prove unpalatable to editors and urged Isabella not to be discouraged if it was rejected. It was then that, propelled by growing self-doubt as well as increasingly poor health, Isabella left for her five-month stay at an Elmira, New York, water cure. Once there she expressed her determination "to rove the woods—and do everything that I have no time and strength for at home."[16]

The almost daily letters she wrote home provide a fascinating first-hand account of the local treatment offered at the Gleason Cure as well as valuable insights into Isabella's views of herself, her family, and the relationship between physical and moral traits. Her acute suffering from dysmenorrhea (painful menstruation) and a prolapsed uterus prompted and justified her stay there. But the prolonged nature of her absence—especially in the face of her son Edward's severe illness and John's repeated pleas for her return—suggests that the water cure figured in her life (as it did in the lives of countless other white middle-class women of this period) as a much-needed respite from the unceasing demands of domesticity. It was only a partial respite at best, though. Isabella's voluminous correspondence with her family revolved around domestic matters both urgent and routine, posing and responding to detailed inquiries concerning everything from the proper care and treatment of her ailing five-year-old son to the selection of suitable material for her daughters' new dresses. Nevertheless, the water cure did function as a safe and respectable middle ground, for it enabled Isabella to enjoy new social contacts as well as the enforced leisure that made self-improvement and self-analysis possible. As several historians have recently suggested, some women may even have employed their invalidism as a desperate means of exerting a measure of covert control over their own lives as well as the lives of their families.[17] What is most notable in Isabella's case is her determination to resist her paralyzing fears of inadequacy and reject the social role of delicate invalid (a role satirized so wittily by Harriet in her devastating portrait of Marie St. Clare in *Uncle Tom's Cabin*). Out of Isabella's struggle to achieve personal recognition and public usefulness was emerging a revised definition of the power of womanhood as well as an expanded sense of vocation. Isabella was about to enter the public arena.

NOTES

1. Popular treatments include Doris Faber's chapter on Catharine and Harriet in her book *Love and Rivalry: Three Exceptional Pairs of Sisters* (New York: Viking Press, 1983), pp. 2–63. While there is, as yet, no full-length biography of Isabella, the *Guide/Index* to the microform edition of her papers includes a substantial essay that appraises her career as a reformer. See Anne T. Margolis, "A Tempest Tossed Spirit: Isabella Beecher Hooker and Woman Suffrage" in *The Isabella Beecher Hooker Project* (Hartford, Conn.: SD, 1979), pp. 9–45.

2. Isabella uses this metaphor on the last page of her Diary of 1862–68 and in Isabella Beecher Hooker, *A Mother's Letters to a Daughter on Woman Suffrage* (Hartford, Conn.: Press of Case, Lockwood and Brainard, 1870), pp. 3–4. See Document 59.

3. Believing that Cincinnati was harmful to a young girl of Bell's temperament, Harriet had suggested that her younger sister be sent to live in greater "retirement" with Mary. For her part, Isabella was eager to move to Hartford, professing herself ready to help Mary with housework as a substitute for less "serious and profitable habits." See Harriet Beecher Stowe and Isabella Beecher Hooker to Lyman Beecher, July 3, [1837?], SD, and Isabella Beecher Hooker, "The Last of the Beechers: Memories on My Eighty-Third Birthday," *The Connecticut Magazine* 9 (May 1905): 289. While this article is significant because it contains Isabella's retrospective account of her own career, that account is extremely condensed and highly selective.

4. Isabella Beecher Hooker to John Hooker, August 30, 1839, SD. See Document 41.

5. Linda Gordon, *Woman's Body, Woman's Right: A Social History of Birth Control in America* (New York: Penguin Books, 1975), chap. 5, pp. 95–115.

Isabella's equation of smaller families and a higher quality of parenting in her essay on "Motherhood" can be found in Isabella Beecher Hooker, *Womanhood: Its Sanctitites and Fidelities* (Boston: Lee and Shepard Publishers, 1873), pp. 15, 24–27. See Document 92.

6. Isabella Beecher Hooker, 1845–55 Journals, entries of August 14, 1850; April 18, 1852; March 21, 1851; and March 17, 1852, SD. See Document 43.

7. Isabella Beecher Hooker to John Hooker, February 21, 1847, SD. See Document 42.

8. Isabella Beecher Hooker to John Hooker, January [11], 1849, SD.

9. Isabella Beecher Hooker to John Hooker, June 26 [and 27], [18]52, SD. See Document 110.

10. Isabella Beecher Hooker to John Hooker, October 16, 1853, SD.

11. Isabella Beecher Hooker to John Hooker, January 24, 1860, SD.

12. Isabella Beecher Hooker to John Hooker, June 24, 1860, SD. See Document 47.

13. Isabella Beecher Hooker to Rachel Burton, January 25, 1859, SD. See Document 44. This article, written by Thomas Wentworth Higginson, was entitled "Ought Women to Learn the Alphabet?"

14. Thomas Wentworth Higginson to Isabella Beecher Hooker, February 19, 1859, SD. Although Hooker's letter of praise to Higginson has not been located and may no longer exist, Higginson recalled its contents in a letter he wrote to Isabella on January 15, 1898, now in the Stowe-Day Foundation's collection of her papers.

15. Isabella Beecher Hooker, Manuscript of "Shall Women Vote? A Matrimonial Dialogue," dated February 18, 1860, SD, pp. 2, 6, 12. See Document 49.

16. Thomas Wentworth Higginson to Isabella Beecher Hooker, March 4, 1860, and Isabella Beecher Hooker to John Hooker, April 12, 1860, SD.

17. Isabella Beecher Hooker to John Hooker, April 28, 1860; June 19, 1860; June 24, 1860; and July 15, 1860, SD. See Documents 45–48. This interpretation of the covert power struggles among women patients, their families, and their doctors is elaborated at length in Carroll Smith-Rosenberg's provocative article, "The Hysterical Woman: Sex Roles and Role Conflict in Nineteenth-Century America," *Social Research* 39, no. 4 (Winter 1972): 652–78. Background on the water cure movement can be found in Kathryn Kish Sklar's insightful discussion of female invalidism in *Catharine Beecher*, pp. 204–16; while the controversy among women's historians regarding how to interpret the medical profession's treatment of women can be followed in the articles by Smith-Rosenberg, Ann Douglas Wood, and Regina Morantz in *Clio's Consciousness Raised*, ed. Mary Hartman and Lois W. Banner (New York: Harper Colophon Books, 1974), pp. 1–53.

*Writing from Batavia, New York, where she was visit-
ing relatives, the seventeen-year-old Isabella Beecher
candidly confided her anxieties to her fiancé, John
Hooker, regarding their impending marriage.*

41   Aug[ust] 30, 1839
[Isabella to John Hooker]

Your letter—dearest, just received and still in my hands—only hastens
the performance of my resolution of some days standing—to *commence*
at least a mammoth sheet letter in anticipation of the Hartford mail—
and a few moments more would have found me seated as now—*"uniting
duty with pleasure"*—as fast as pen could scribble. . . . The company
was informed of my new friendship almost immediately—and "Willy"
[her brother William] has taken occasion to remind me thereof sundry
times—during the two days of our visit—so you see I am not likely to
forget my engagements—however much I might wish to do so. He is
sorry with some other of my friends—that is—the first feeling is regret
and fear—regret at *losing*—as it were a young and petted sister—and
fear—which he—alas—has too much reason to indulge—of the happiness of a married life. I have—for some moments in looking at the
families of some even of my brothers and sisters—felt misgivings—many
and great—but then—I feel that there is a radical defect in their plan—
one which can be avoided—they did not start rightly—they did not each
in the commencement of a married life—and before it in the freshness
of affection—resolve upon self-denial—self-sacrifice—a consideration of
the other's feelings as much as their own—besides this—naturally and
palpably unsuitable dispositions, have in the case before me unfitted the
individuals for either happiness or usefulness in this world—[D]earest—
can it be so with us—I cannot believe it possible—if I did I would love
you as a brother—a friend—but never otherwise—if I tho[ugh]t my married life would be such as I have seen exhibited in my own family—I
never could bring myself to fulfill an engagement, otherwise delightful.
But—if we can both live with that constant reference to God—to eternity—that now we theoretically desire—if practically we accomplish this,
I do not fear—I can unreservedly—willingly and happily commit myself
to your love and care—and we may be happy—I know you are willing
and desire to "go with me"—but you must go farther—or I may be a
drawback upon your progress in holiness—we must each urge the other
to exertion and never be contented with an already acquired measure of
piety—Am I not looking forward—too much—too far?—and yet—'Tis

now that our plans unavoid[a]bly are forming—and it does seem to me—that the views we now take of life and of our duties here—will have more effect than those of almost any other period. I am at times completely sobered down—and really seem to be ready for usefulness when the opportunity offers—but I never have been tried as yet—and the event may prove—that resolving is easier than performing. Do not think—dear John—that this is penned—especially for your edification—it is but the expression of hopes and fears—that now Sister Mary's ready ear is denied me must be aimed at your patience and affection—Oh what a sister—she has been to me—and to you—also—for you do owe her much—very much—not only lately—but in the *formation* of the character that now you love. She has in some things been to me a model—and her gentle—perhaps almost imperceptible influence has, softened and subdued—a sometime wayward spirit—and helped to purify a naturally warm heart. I give you full permission to love her with all your heart—for in doing so you do but love me the more. . . .

. . . [W]e had a most labored discussion of the relative position of a wife—to her husband—her duty of submission &c—the Bible doctrine on the subject I always assented to—and admired—the only matter of wonderment is that while ministers and others insist most strenuously—on the duties of a lady—the husband's fulfillment of his obligations is taken for granted—and "husbands *love* your wives—even as Christ loved the church" seems an entirely superfluous command—I acknowledge great cause for thankfulness—that you my dear Sir—are one—to whom I can in all love render the required obedience without being constantly reminded that such is the will of God and the expectation of man—I don't know how it can be otherwise but galling to a sensible woman—especially when she is eminently the one to be consulted as to have her wishes gratified during an engagement and the early part of married life—to find in a few months that one whom she has heretofore looked upon as an equal—a companion and friend[—]wishes to assume the appearance and manner of a superior—a master. I have seen it done—through mistaken notions however—not understanding the feelings of a high minded woman—and it is most unhappy in its effect. I do believe the love of power is i[n]nate—in all minds—and of what use it is I am at a loss to determine—there seems no good to result—to any one—from the possession of this quality—if such it may be called—but—I am wandering—for personally I fear nothing—universally I do regret that so many fine women are made unhappy—by firstly, being petted and spoiled by attention and admiration while young ladies—and then learning all at once that thro' mistaken ideas of propriety they are to have *no*

will of their own—except so far as it coincides with their husband's. . . .
Have I not more than accomplished my promise—this sheet is full—and
I have not moved since commencing it—my head aches instead of my
heart—now—so I must once more leave you—I need not remind you to
write immediately—to your beloved one.

Dearest—I am yours—truly—

Isabel[la]

[IBH to John Hooker, SD]

---

*Six years after her marriage, Isabella vented her domes-
tic frustrations to John while visiting relatives in Hartford. She had borne two children, one of whom died in
infancy, and may have realized that she was in the early
stages of another pregnancy.*

42   Feb[ruar]y 21, 1847
[Isabella to John Hooker]
You may rest assured that I was disappointed last night when ten o'clock
fairly came and went—without bringing my truant husband. . . . Today
has been stupid and uncomfortable—a storm here, is very different from
what it is when you have friends and houses near—you seem so shut in
and shut out from all human society—there is scarce a hope of ever
emerging into life and light again. I don't know why it is—but the care of
little Mary is more irksome to me on the Sabbath than any other day—it
always seems as if she solicited more attention—and my sole companion
being reading—this is more than usually difficult to give. . . .

I have been reading or trying to read today . . . Religio Medico—and
the sequel—Christian Morals—by Sir Thomas Browne M.D. written two
hundred years ago—I like the quaint old style—and the book is
eminently of a religious and highly spiritual cast—if my head were stronger, physically, and my time uninterrupted I should enjoy reading it
through—but it requires close attention—and this it is almost impossible
for me to give with Mary at my elbow and with my brain half asleep
from want of fresh air and company and exercise. I do quite despair of
ever improving much in mind or acquirements—tho' I am no less sorry
for this for your sake, than for my own. But I am satisfied that even with
the best health I can hope to have, I cannot bear steady or severe application—and the cares of housekeeping and children will make any effort at
mental improvement difficult if not impossible. I can never cease to

regret the very early age at which I was compelled to leave off study—it was my intention to have been a school girl till I was twenty at least—yet precious little did I ever study after sixteen—which is just the age to begin with some due appreciation of its value and meaning. I sometimes wonder that I pass muster as well as I do—(insignificant as my acquirements are to my own eyes) when I remember this—and it is the only view, in which I am disposed to murmur or complain of my early loss of health and strength—in all other respects—the loss may have been a blessing—I cannot perceive its use here nor do the benefits *seem* to me equal to this loss.

I was reading today a letter from a young lady—who offers to enlist with much zeal in Cath[arine]'s educational effort—in which she describes as requested her education and capabilities. She mentions that during long continued illnesses—her acquirements in the reading line are said to surpass those of most professional gentlemen—while in the *law* she has studied all that law students do in the first two years of their courses—and has made herself perfectly familiar with the theory of law, from choice—Medicine she has been quite familiar with from necessity—and her right hand being the only part of her body she could move without assistance. She has written a great deal—and published some books for children—I really envied her her acquirements—the letter was well written—exceedingly—and full of christian zeal and a willingness to devote herself to usefulness in any sphere—

Well this [is] quite too long a letter to send to such a naughty husband. But as it is written and has afforded me much pleasure in the writing—besides helping to spend a long evening that would otherwise have hung heavily on my hands I will even send it, in spite of your ill deserts—and will subscribe myself your loving
Wife—

[IBH to John Hooker, SD]

The following entries come from the 1845–55 journals, one devoted to each child, in which Isabella recorded her daily hopes, fears, and observations regarding her three surviving children: Mary (born in 1845), Alice (born in 1847), and baby Edward (born in 1855). As these selections reveal, Hooker frequently met with resistance in her efforts to mete out maternal guidance

and "governance." Occasionally, she felt overwhelmed
by the responsibility of being a good Christian mother.

43   August 14, 1850

... I am deceiving myself I fear with the hope that she [Mary] will never need another whipping—but I suppose I must keep up courage and firmness enough to administer this most disagreeable form of punishment if necessary.[1] Since her return from Bloomfield, where she troubled Grandma [Hooker] by a peevish obstinacy, I have used the whalebone two or three times with great effect—doubtless it may be equally beneficial for perhaps years longer. That was all Grandma needed—if she had once established her authority in that manner it would have saved many worrying hours I dare say. ...

My prevailing expectation is, that Mary if she lives will prove a very lovely, intelligent, pious woman—[S]he is not precocious that I perceive—but *womanly*—and emminently feminine in her characteristics. It is the easiest thing in the world to influence her by a sense of modesty and propriety and she already for a long time has exhibited her father's and Grandma's *caution* as to personal exposures of any kind.

If I could only be sure of wisdom to train her aright what a treasure might she become to all her friends and dear little Alice—[B]ut alas! [W]ho is sufficient for these things? I think I study over the subject of government enough—but do not seek guidance by prayer and communion with Christ as I ought. Self reliance will be the rock on which I may make ship wreck of my children—and the danger of this, is strengthened by my husband's entire confidence in me, insomuch that he does not in the least assist or advise concerning the children. The Lord grant in mercy that my failures in duty may not be their ruin—I would sooner die this day than lead them away from happiness and heaven by wrong example or neglect.

Feb[ruar]y. 25[,] [1851]

Mary, is just going with me, to see Aunt E. and being very busy in preparing and thinking about the visit she suddenly inquires, "Has Aunt Esther got any children of her own[?]"—"No[.]"—pause—"Is she mar-

---

1. In July of 1849, Isabella had confided to Harriet that she was having great difficulty in deciding how to discipline Mary. Hooker evidently felt that her elder sister was an expert when it came to handling "obstinate, irritable children." See Document 105.

ried[?]"—"No[.]" "Not married yet—and she so old—and you are married when you are so young[?]"—"Yes[.]"—"Why don[']t somebody marry her[?]" "Because, she don[']t want them to[,]" I suppose was my reply—which closed the conversation—[H]ow naturally the idea of marriage as a woman's portion occurs to a little girl—[H]ow much better to foster this idea rationally than to discourage it, as they grow older and from false delicacy or affectation render it almost a forbidden subject till the very hour of destiny arrives.

March 17, 1852

It pains me greatly to make the entry which I now must in Mary's Journal—not so much because she has been so very naughty—but I did so truly mean a long time since never to whip her again and it fairly shocks and mortifies me to think I have done so. There have been such periods of fretfulness, (taking the form often of perverse obstinate dialogues with me,) as have been exceedingly trying to my patience and judgment. Argument and persuasion have only served to lengthen the debate and increase the sullenness—[Y]et there was no real ugliness—but only a sort of discontented unhappy state of mind, which she made no effort to control—[N]either could I stimulate her to make any.

At last I did some weeks ago, tell her I should certainly try the stick on her hands the next fit that occurred and I did so, with considerable effect—but the shock was not powerful enough to last very long. Two or three days since, after bearing a good while and speaking very gently and persuasively I started up, seized the long handled brush and proceeded after the usual fashion of administering regular whippings. She was frightened horribly and tho' half choked, and violently struggling, said— very plainly "I want Alice to go out"—thus showing her sense of shame to be uppermost. I sent Alice out and whipped pretty hard—but the pain was nothing to the mortification I think. The effect has been excellent in every respect—yet I feel mortified every time I think of it—just as I should to have my husband or brother flogged on board ship. I always have entertained the greatest horror of physical punishments administered to *grown* people—and Mary has for a long time seemed to me to belong to that class—I believe I somewhat over-estimate her maturity of character and have allowed myself to be hampered by this in trying to govern her aright.

She can be nothing but a child after all—at seven yrs.—[Y]et there is a sense of shame about her that makes her seem most womanly—and which ought not certainly to be rudely dealt with. I have perhaps too cautiously avoided influencing her by this—lest this weapon should be turned against me, in cases where there was no just ground for its use—and here is a fair specimen of the difficulties under which a parent labors who really studies the characteristics of children, with the sincere purpose of leading them to the highest point of moral attainment. Nothing is easier than to shame a child into a certain sense of conduct or out of another—[B]ut try this often and either the sensibility to shame is soon exhausted or it is morbidly excited—so as to act at improper times and on unsuitable occasions.

My aim has been, leaving this motive almost entirely out [of] the question, to press only love to Christ and to friends and to humanity—reserving fear of punishment for the last—to be used only when all else fails.

Sometimes I feel satisfied with the depth and sincerity of Mary's conscientiousness and am ready to congratulate myself on the success of my efforts. Again I am discouraged and think her remarks which sound so well are only the result of habit and imitation—as she cannot but know very well what will please me and has been well furnished in materials from which to make them. My hopes preponderate however—and generally it is my expectation that she will grow up in habits of love and trust such as are expected usually, only from the mature christian—[C]ertainly my desires and prayers have had no other aim from the hour of her birth. . . .

April 18, 1852

Mary has been very much tired with headaches again for several weeks. She has complained also of pain in the back a good deal and occasionally of pain in the side—[T]hese symptoms, together with her paleness and general debility have filled me anew with apprehensions for her future health if not for her life.

I really knew not what to do—I finally sent her home, some two weeks since, to try change of air and scene. She has rallied wonderfully—so much so that when I went out a week after she left, I found her sitting at the tea table, neatly dressed and with a glow on her cheeks that was perfectly transforming. I could hardly keep my eyes from her face—it was *beautiful* in the highest degree. Yesterday, Papa, was out again and he brings still more favorable accounts of her health and beauty—so that I am again hopeful. Often of late I have easily yielded to the persuasion that her life is to be short and her death premature—and in some aspects the thought has not been painful. To think of her as safe in heaven, shielded from all rude blasts, from which her delicacy will ever make her shrink, is pleasant—[Y]et my soul seems to rest on hers so much that I know not how to sustain myself alone—[S]he seems a part of myself—and to lose her, would be to find myself dismembered.

Towards Alice I feel differently in this—that I desire to live myself to take care of her—to guide and guard—without expecting so much in return—[N]ot but that she is generous—and more affectionately demonstrative than Mary—but somehow I do not *rely* upon her and cannot yet feel that I ever shall. She seems to me more a fancy piece to amuse and please than a solid article for daily use and comfort. As such she seems invaluable—just to see her walk, with a skip between each step is a daily treat—and to feel her soft hands about my face sends a thrill over my whole frame. In this latter respect the children differ as much as in any other—I mean their power of impressing one by their touch—Mary's *hand* has no power at all with me, or with any one—[Y]ou must look into her face—and clear down into her deep spiritual eye to be impressed by her—or you must feel her conscientiousness, her trustworthiness, and good sense. But, let Alice clasp your hand in her little velvet fingers and you are magnetized—and when she springs up into your lap and lays her downy cheek against yours and strokes and fondles and says, "Oh how I *do* love you" you smother her with kisses which will not come half fast enough and think she is the most charming little sprite that ever stole your heart in spite of yourself. . . .

July 26, 1853

. . . I had informed Mary some weeks ago, of the origin of babies and somewhat of their advent—feeling assured that she was learning on the farm somewhat of these matters and preferring to be her instructor myself. She took the explanation with all the gravity and intelligence I anticipated—but she seemed not to observe any thing peculiar in her Aunt Elisa. At last, on Saturday when the doctor came for a preparatory call, I questioned her as to what she suspected to be the object of his coming, and thinking from her answers that she really knew, I told her of the expected baby. Such an expression of *surprised extacy* [sic] I never saw in any human face—"Why I never thought of that—are we going to have a little baby right in this house" etc. etc. I urged entire secresy [sic] and I cannot learn that she breathed a word to any one all that afternoon—though she was full to overflowing. She went into her Aunt's room, while she was still dressed and sitting up—scanned her figure closely and when Robert told his brother with great innocence that he thought she was better now a days and not going to be sick any more,

Mary seemed ready to burst with laughter—but on Aunty's shaking her head at her, she quieted down and Bob was none the wiser for her newly acquired knowledge.

She afterwards asked me many very sensible questions with a womanly interest and gravity that made them generally very easy to answer. She was considerably exercised however about the part which God and man were respectively responsible for in the creation of human beings— and inquired once before Grandma and the nurse whether Aunt Elisa could have a baby just when she wanted or how the matter was adjusted. I satisfied her very easily, by saying No—that people often wished for children, but God did not send them—and sometimes they came oftener than they were desired.

Another day however when we were alone she asked in the same connection and after a similar explanation, "but does'nt [*sic*] Uncle Francis have to do anything about it[?]" Whereupon I was rather evasive than otherwise. . . .

September 8, 1854

. . . The children are in the habit of having long talks with me on various subjects of moment—frequently marriage and domestic life has come up—and they always speak with as much seriousness and sense as an old lady of fifty. It is really amusing to hear them—but I always talk soberly also—not wishing to diminish in the least their freedom with me.

A little time since, in the begining of such a conversation, Alice lay kicking about my bed and said all at once—Oh Ma,—I'm glad you married Pa—because I shouldn[']t love any other father.

Mary seemed absorbed in the contemplation of the distresses attending ill assorted marriages—and finally remarked "It seems a great risk Ma—I should want to marry some one I had known from my childhood—I should like to be engaged a long long time too—and find out every thing about *them*." . . .

I do enjoy these talks—[I]t does seem as if girls who confided everything to a Mother so early and found sympathy and companionship in her, never could prefer to make confidants of other girls—or try to learn from them the mysteries of life—which should be unfolded to them by their own dear Mother first and chiefly.

I may err on the side of too great frankness—may indoctrinate them too early—but I remember so well the pangs of ungratified curiosity in my early days[2]—and the various researches into books and cross questioning of bigger girls, which some of us practiced, that I prefer to tell my children too much rather than too little . . . .

[May] 26, [1855]

Weighs 8 [lbs.] 14 [oz.]

Sunday 26. Eddy grows more sweet and charming every day—[H]e talks and coos every morning and sometimes during the day—[B]ut this last week has taken to sleeping rather unquietly all the time. We really think the lettuce I have eaten every day must be the cause—[H]e has seemed so *drowsy*—just as if under the influence of opium.

He enjoys riding in the big carriage in *any body's* arms, exceedingly—[S]o I take both the children one to drive or whip the horse, the other to hold him and we have fine times riding about to do errands without fatiguing me in the least. I have been obliged to save myself all possible care and fatigue in order to have strength to nurse him and still entertain many fears that I cannot do it through the summer even. I am trying my best however and actually am as lazy and self indulgent as any one need ask. If disturbed at all in the night, more than to nurse him once, I lie as late as I feel like doing in the morning—seldom eating breakfast till *eight* or after and then have some choice bit of beef cooked for me—or eggs—or whatever may tempt the appetite.

Then I ride—or walk round the grounds watching the growth of tree and flower or planting a few seeds—then lie down as long as it is pleasant and occasionally take a few *stitches*—but abjuring sewing, writing and everything fatiguing, all for the sake of the little darling, who needs all I can give him and more too. We feed him with cream and water once a day now—towards night—when my breast feels dragged out, in spite of all my care. There continues to be a singular painful sensation, distinct from sore nipples—as if the cords were straining through the nipple—when he begins to nurse—which wears off, in a few minutes generally—but leaves the breast feeling lame and tired all the time—and often it is stung by sharp darting pains.

June 3, 1855

Weighs 9 [lbs.] 8 [oz.]

Eddy has had a bad state of bowels several days—and one day cried pretty much all the time, save when he was nursing. I lay with him on my

2. Isabella appears to be referring to the fact that her own mother had died when she was only thirteen.

breast by the hour together and was wretchedly fatigued before night. He sends up every day whole volleys of wind and is often in real pain from that cause—[W]e are in trouble to know what is best to do—[M]y health is so feeble it seems as if the milk must be poor—yet he grows more and more fond of nursing and will not *now be denied.* He is even refusing to be fed from a spoon—which he enjoyed from his birth till now—so what can we do?

Sep[tember] 2, 1855

Tonight at the supper table Mary asked "What is a Golden Wedding[?]"—[W]e explained that and the Silver Wedding at twenty five yrs—[F]ather then said we would have such a celebration in eleven years from this time—and added "If we should be alive then and all our three children what a favored life we shall have had—but it is more than probable that some of us will be gone before that time[.]"—Well said Alice with serious cheerfulness—"We shall be in a great deal happier place, if we are[.]"—"So we shall my darling["] said I, putting my arm around her neck—["]and it matters little how soon we go—or who goes first[.]" How could this volume be more appropriately closed, than with this little incident[?]—

[IBH, 1845–55 Journals, SD]

An unsigned article in the Atlantic Monthly *by feminist/abolitionist Thomas Wentworth Higginson entitled "Ought Women to Learn the Alphabet?" prompted the following outburst from Isabella. Writing to her Hartford friend and neighbor, Rachel Burton, the thirty-seven-year-old wife and mother anguished over her own lack of formal education, blasted the unequal treatment accorded her Beecher siblings, and ventured to air her own views on sexual equality.*

44   Jan[uar]y 25, 1859

Dear Rachel

I send you the first Article in the Feby. Atlantic to read forthwith—[I]t has been more than a trumpet call to me this morning, sick and feeble though I was and sure that nothing could rouse me for this day.

What will you say when I tell you, I would rather have written these twelve pages, than any other twelve that ever I read?—[T]he truth must be spoken sometimes and I do say it with all my heart. There's not a vital thought there, but I have had for my own, and spoken it too, in a whisper and in my blundering way and it is only my lack of this very Alphabet that has given this favored mortal (man or woman is it?) such a precedence before the world.

I could have said all this and just as well too, if the boy's training had been mine, physical as well as mental. At fifteen my dear good father (instigated of course by his new wife) came to me and suggested, that I should begin to teach school now and support myself. I, who had never been to school in earnest, for two years together in my whole life—and who had gained such physical vigor as I then had, only thro' a determined preference, for boy's games and out door sports, that added not at all to my general reputation.

Then when one blessed year was granted, in the Female Sem. here at Hartford, what thirst and what supply—[B]ut this was the end— [H]ealth declined through terrible accident first and man's ignorance at last—and there was no brain power left, for reading even, much less study.

At sixteen and a half, just when my brothers began their mental education, mine was finished—except as life's discipline was added with years and that we shared equally. Till twenty three, their father, poor minister as he was could send them to College and Seminary all *six*—cost what it might, but never a daughter cost him a hundred dollars a year, after she was sixteen. I *have* wanted to be the author of Aurora Leigh, but this smaller triumph would suffice me now—[T]here is History, Philosophy, Mathematics (vis demonstration) all here in small compass—and I could add the Theology. . . . Men *might* to be sure have seen, that in the begining woman led the way towards mental acquisition—vis knowledge of good and evil—thus emphatically proclaiming her divine origin and sexual equality, not to say superiority—[B]ut misled by their own appetites they called it alimentiveness [*sic*] or at best curiosity. Well—well— what am I doing and where is my backache[?]—[N]o matter I must take another slip, just to say, that all these bare bones, have stared me in the face for months and years—[I]f I could have only have clothed them with the flesh and drapery of historic literature as this Author has done (he is a man I think, by his gallantry and alas! by his learning) you might have seen something more than a skeleton—[A]s it was, my manikin never walked out of his sarcophagus. . . .

I make no apology for this egotism—you are too kind and just to need any—[B]esides, what's the use of having a friend, if one, being an over-full cup, can't spill over into her neighborly saucer, now and then without reproof.

ever yrs.

I. B. H.

Mr. Gillette has just been in and says that women are superior to men, he thinks when they have equal opportunities. I don[']t—they are cut from the same *batch*—and (this is a new thought to me) the reason they have seemed to have more quickness of perception etc. is that they have been driven to their wits—preternaturally excited—long ages—by this deprivation of all external helps. When physical and mental training are similar, they will rank *with* men,—not *above* them—certainly not below. So, I mean to get a patent for making girls as stupid as boys, founded on above principles.

[IBH to Rachel Burton, SD]

Isabella addressed letters to her family virtually every day after leaving Hartford for Mrs. R. B. Gleason's water cure. This Elmira, New York, health resort was located near the home and church of her brother, the Reverend Thomas K. Beecher. During the five months she spent there, Isabella not only received treatment for gynecological problems and her approaching menopause but also found time to cultivate her mind. When five-year-old Edward came down with whooping cough in June, she sent John detailed instructions from Mrs. Gleason regarding his care. But she continued to resist her husband's pleas that she cut short her stay. However, she did invite John to pay her an intimate visit in the second of these letters. (The Livy Langdon mentioned in Isabella's final letter would later marry the Hookers' Hartford neighbor, Mark Twain.)

45   April 28, [18]60

Dear husband

. . . I have a great mind to copy my items of expense—so religiously kept thus far—just to fill up my sheet—and plague myself in the writing and so incidentally plague you—but I won[']t do it—and moreover I won[']t hate to send for just as much money as I want—because it is all for your sake that I am trying to get well—yours and the [babe's?]—so it's nothing to me what it costs. . . .

. . . I am going to get a Bloomer dress . . . so that I can have it for gardening at home or Mary for walks in the woods. . . .

Hattie's [Harriet Beecher Stowe's] plans are so uncertain—they cannot affect mine at all. I have no doubt that stepping into the home atmosphere of her room—so directly—is what has saved me from homesickness—of which I have hardly had a twinge—and do not expect to in the future. It is such a relief—to have nobody to care for—nothing that *must* be done. I despise undressing and dressing every minute of the day—but still—as there is no hurry about it and some exercise and *health* at the end—I am content. . . .

You should read my letters to sister Mary and the girls about the gardening and the dressmaker—seeing you are father and mother both now, you ought to be in possession of all essential facts. I have acted in this double capacity so long, there is no reason, you should not try it—for a month or two—only you cannot reach the depths of experience in this very short time. . . .

   Love to all from your loving wife.
   [Isabella]

          [IBH to John Hooker, SD]

---

46   June 19, 1860

My dear husband—

. . . To begin with Eddie—I have not allowed myself to be anxious about him or to think of going home on his account—because—I have every reason to think he will get along nicely at this most favorable season—and because although, I should delight to have the care of him, I know it is just what I ought not to have—just what would probably undo, all that has been so well done for me—these two months past—and once more—because I can get home in twenty four hours after a telegram—any day—[I]f it were not for this last consideration I should suffer—of course—but it *ought* to be comforting and it is. . . .

And now for myself—I have evidently not given you the detail of my treatment or you could not suggest the possibility of taking it at home—knowing your fastidiousness in such matters. . . . The neck and mouth of the uterus is (or was) very much enlarged—hard almost as a bony surface—and very red and angry looking—[T]he body of uterus, was also heavy and distended and prolapsed—[B]oth were tender to the touch—

and so engorged as to cause not only the sensation of weight which has been so oppressive to me for years—but the profuse menstruation of the last year—which has been *fearful*—I think even you, to whom I have complained the most of anyone—have no idea, of the utter prostration and pain I have felt at these times—[L]atterly—it has seemed to me that I should lose my reason—from the sympathetic affection of the brain and the sort of despair, as to ever being any better. But then—I have an enormous amount of resolution and energy and the worst being past—I could always under the stimulus of "plenty to do"—rouse myself and go ahead—but I had an increasing conviction that I could not keep on so always—there *would* come a breaking down place—and what would be the end—I could not foresee. So this morning I have asked Mrs. Gleason—what would be the probable result of neglecting the case—or leaving it, in its *present* state—even—stated as moderately as possible. She said—it would not be death—immediately—and if I were younger might be only years of suffering and of conquest like the past—[B]ut considering the crisis of my life [menopause] which is approaching— there was quite a possibility of flowing to death then—or if not that—an almost certainty of from five to ten years—of invalidism, severe and painful—and no certainty of any good health afterward—thro' life. If one enters that period with this enlarged and inflamed condition of the uterus—all that can possibly be done, during the period of change, is to alleviate and keep it from growing worse—[T]here is not the slightest hope of curing while so much functional irritation is going on—and this is the reason she is so anxious to make a thorough cure now—[I]t is the only period when it can be done and it is the best possible preparation for the approaching period of change—As to whether I should lose all that I have already gained by going away now she thinks it quite prob- able I should—a little overdoing, would call back the old symptoms very likely—[H]er experience with other patients has been that she has often consented to their going home too soon. . . . I am sure from my own close observation of Mrs. Gleason that she is in more danger of erring in this way, than the other—[S]he is very sympathetic—knows all the claims upon a wife and mother and so, longs to give a dismission even before her better judgment would allow—[T]hen she is very sensitive to the possible criticism that pecuniary considerations may have weight with her—tho' no one in his senses, who has known her for one week, would ever think of such a thing. Well now as to mode of treatment—the baths which I take are only intended as a soothing accompaniment to the *local* treatment—*that* is the chief and only thing and in that Mrs. Gleason is unrivalled. . . . She gives me treatment twice a week—(watching the effect very closely). [I]t is done by instruments—of course—of which she is perfect mistress—and consists of applications of nitrate of silver—to [the] mouth [of the uterus] [cauterized?] etc—injections into the uterus itself—and various and sundry other things that you cannot comprehend—(tho' I do perfectly)—and that no one but an experienced hand could perform—Of course it would be only absurd to talk about taking such treatment at home—and this is all that I came for or am staying for—[M]ere baths I could and would take at home. The only wonder to me is that I may be cured in so short a time as four months—[T]his has been the accu[mu]lation of years—[T]he prolapse commenced before my marriage—has never been treated but once. . . .

So far as I am concerned—no amount of homesickness, would induce me to leave here—so long as Mrs. Gleason thinks I need the least bit more of treatment—I have such a dread of being a worse invalid than ever—of being useless or bed ridden—a trial to my husband and children—a nervous, fidgety old woman causing gloom in the house instead of sunshine—(and I see very clearly, that I might easily become the latter, judging by my past feelings and the struggles I have already had) that I would rather stay away a year, than *run the risk* of it even—Much as I want to see my dear children and take my share of all the home cares—and comfort you in your feebleness and sustain you, under your pressure of business and care and responsibility—I should still feel it a great disappointment to be called home now—or before the right time comes, for me to go—I should fear, that I could never come back, till it was too late to be of much use—or till I should have to stay away many more, long, weary months. It has seemed to me one of the most marked, of our many remarkable guidances, that I came here, just when I did—and that all things have so far favored my stay. . . .

. . . If I stay into August as I am certain I ought to, (on account of my monthly period coming just the last of July—or first of Aug. and I must have treatment after that, before leaving finally) it would break up these two months most charmingly to have you here a few days—and I *know*—yes certainly know—that we could have such a good time . . . and your health would be so much improved that you would go home—and not think of the small four weeks that must pass, before I should follow you.

. . . In confidence also—and best of all—I asked dear loving Mrs. Gleason—whether I might make you most heartily welcome—and could do so, without detriment to health—and she said—yes—without hesitation—and wished you would come by all means—[S]he would secure our room to us, unmolested and do everything she could to make your visit pleasant.

. . . I thank God every day for sending me here—and for you being able to provide so bountifully for my restoration and my comfort. It would be so hard if we were really poor—then there would be nothing for me but to work on and on—and suffer on, till death came to *our* relief. . . .

> yrs. lovingly and forever
> Isabel

> [IBH to John Hooker, SD]

---

47 June 24, [18]60

My dear husband

. . . I was so relieved, on opening last night's letter . . . to see that there was nothing discouraging about Eddie—I had rather worked myself into feverish state of expectation—in regard to that particular letter—and now it has come, I feel uncommonly lighthearted and jolly in mind— though quite low in point of bodily condition. But this last is nothing—I am more and more convinced, that pain is a wholesome tonic to me—a right down, genuine ache, is a good thing—now and then—and so much better than a weak miserable feeling—centering nowhere—[T]he former is my case today—and I am quite happy under it—[B]esides it has kept me from church this morning—which as Tom [Thomas Beecher] is gone and Mr Nobody is expected to preach, is quite an item of itself.

I am so rejoiced to hear that you give my proposal of coming here a thought. That is quite enough for me and I am greatly contented for the present. I had such a nice invitation for tomorrow. . . . [I]t is funny, how, every where I go—I have to run on the credit of my relations—no where, but at home—can I lay claim to a particle of individuality—to any distinction of goodness, smartness or any thing else whatever. . . .

It becomes more and more evident to me—that I have great power of personal influence—[F]amily name goes a great way no doubt—but there is a magnetism of heart and eye and voice, that is quite individual—[O]h how I wish I might exert this on a broad scale, to sweep people along in the right path—[A]pprobativeness—real love of admiration is as strong perhaps as in the days of childhood and youth—[B]ut benevolence is uppermost, I am quite sure of that—and thank God for the assurance. I truly wish I knew how much one might enjoy of the personal tribute, that follows successful effort—without becoming self-ish—or even self conscious and vainglorious. I try to test myself in various ways—but I have been in such a tread mill of self analysis the last few years—[I]t seems to me, almost better not to know—than to pursue that process much longer. . . . You say truly "What a comfort these letters are"—[D]on't you think I improve in composition too a little considering I write like a steam engine as to speed[?]

> Yrs ever
> I.

[IBH to John Hooker, SD]

---

48   July 15 [and 16], [18]60

My dear husband

Another bright warm sabbath day—and we so much the nearer to our meeting! [T]hat will be a trysting time for us indeed—that meeting in N. York and I shall have my wish to be young once more—and have a *real* lover and be a responsive mistress. Yesterday, I saw and walked round the Cure and over to Tom's new cottage with a tall fair young man—just married to a bright, wilful girl—[H]e offered me his arm over the rough places—and it was no firmer than your arm is or was—and his cheek had the bright red or pink glow, that yours had in those far off days—and he seemed timid—half scared by his new position of husband and fearful of the jokes that were or might be flying about him—[B]ut my heart went out towards him—and I did him reverence—such as I ought to have rendered you in those days, when I was blind—and self seeking—and too inexperienced in judging of human character, to know the pure gold when I found it.

In nothing have I altered more, than in my appreciation of this delicacy—this fineness of mental constitution, which it seems to me, is scarcely compatible with great strength—power of endurance or combativeness—I even find it hard, to conceive of physical strength, in combination with such exquisite mental traits—though the temple ought to be well and firmly built, which invites so divine a spirit. But I do rejoice and wonder every day and increasingly that our union combines all the main elements of a high and noble human character—that we so highly endowed by God each of us, in certain directions, should have been brought together to pour our treasures into each other[']s mind and heart—and grow together into an almost perfect whole. It seems as if we have no excuse for not becoming perfect examples to our children—and all our neighbors—when we so supplement each other and the love of Christ is within and around us both—day and night. . . .

I think this separation has done me good on the whole—by deepening my impressions of your superiorities. . . . I will not imitate you in decrying my pattern—even the physical—but will rather imitate your generous appreciation of those qualities which are quite different from your own—and which seem the higher because they are different.

I see now, that I have failed in reverence for and towards you—and in inculcating this upon the children. . . . I have felt a something bordering on contempt toward feebleness—timidity—caution—however well surrounded by other and balancing qualities and have had an undue admiration of nerve—and muscle—and fortitude and fearlessness. Now—it seems to me, that nothing very exquisite—can be very strong—that, that word implies a physical, material quality which is inconsistent with this species of mental beauty—and one must be contented to be beautiful in whatsoever God has laid out for him—[S]o I admire and reverence in you, somethings [sic] that you are ready to despise—and I despise myself for not having seen and appreciated them earlier. . . .

I wrote so far, at Mr. Langdon's yesterday—having concluded to stay at that hospitable mansion till after tea. I had a very pleasant Sunday of it—[T]hese friends are so really fond of me, for my own sake as well as for Tom's—they have made my stay here more endurable in many little ways. The only daughter, is my roommate for the present—Livy Langdon—[S]he is a sweet young girl of Mary's age—but in very delicate health and I have helped persuade them to place her under Mrs. Gleason's care—[S]he has been living on her nerves instead of her muscles all her life so far—and will not have *anything* left to live upon, pretty soon, unless she is made over. Oh dear—how blind mothers are—and what miserable work they make of educating daughters—the best of them—except—don't you think our daughters are pretty emphatic testimonials to their Mama's wisdom? Tom preached a capital sermon to children yesterday—[H]e does this once every month—and every minister ought to and ought to preach just as he does. He said that every child ought to learn to work with his and her hands—as Paul did in the text—and have a means of support, aside from brain power—a trade—an occupation—whatever might be the chosen business of life afterward—[B]ut I will not go into particulars now—though I will say that he is the only minister that preaches to girls and women—and knows how to illustrate from their lives and habits and occupations—and this is an essential failing in most ministers—as I have always thought. . . .

> ever yrs lovingly,
>
> I.

[IBH to John Hooker, SD]

---

*"Shall Women Vote? A Matrimonial Dialogue" consti-
tutes Isabella's first attempt at a public statement on
women's rights. Here she refutes an editorial that had
attacked the position taken by Henry Ward Beecher
and others who advocated woman suffrage as a means
of reforming politics. Although she sent the manuscript
to T. W. Higginson, who agreed to forward it to the
Atlantic, the article was not published during her lifetime. It was signed "Mrs. John Hooker."*

49   Scene: New York, February 18, 1860
Dramatis Personae: Mr. Smith, Mrs. Smith

Mr.: Did you read this Editorial in the Independent, on woman's voting?

Mrs.: Yes . . . (pause) . . . and I thought the premises excellent but the
conclusions decidedly weak.

Mr.: I don't know about that. It was rather a new idea to me and one
of some force too, that women, by the very fact of their sex and the
sicknesses incidental to it, are unfitted for public life.

Mrs.: To be sure. That is the case, with mothers, who are rearing a
family, but how many there are, like my sister Martha for instance who
have got through with that long ago—children all married and gone, and
she left with nothing under the sun to do.

Mr.: She has a house and a husband to care for. [Y]ou know how she
said she could not possibly leave home and go to Boston the other day to
take care of Rebecca, sick as she was, because Mr. Howard had the
rheumatism and couldn't even get his coat on without her help.

Mrs.: Yes—and I *did* go—leaving all my little children behind and
nobody the worse for it either. [B]ut that is not to the point. . . . [I]f you
take all the single women and all who would be single, if they did not
fear the loneliness and ennui of such a life, all the widows and childless
ones, and then the middle aged mothers who have reared their brood
and started them on their own independent flight . . . there is material

enough I am sure, for a very respectable Congress—respectable in point of character and ability too, as well as numbers. . . . I have been thinking of this very thing lately, in reference to Sister Martha, and others like her. [J]ust see what maturity of thought, real wisdom, there is in her, gained in this most motherly way of discriminating between her own children— adapting influence and government according to character and bringing out a harmonious whole, from so many discordant or at least different elements. What a pity that such a disciplined mind should lie inactive, unfelt almost, in the very ful[l]ness of its power. . . .

Mr.: My, you grow eloquent, my dear—but then you must remember that there are not many women like *your* sister, either in character or situation.

Mrs.: I am not so sure of that. I could mention quite a number in our own circle this moment. . . .

Mr.: Well—suppose they had a call to sit on a jury, for instance[.] [J]urors are town officers you know—chosen by each town or village, as a body to be selected from when occasion requires—and if a man is called he must go—and perhaps sit up all night on a tough case. What would one woman do, among eleven men, shut up by themselves in the Court House, all night long[?]

Mrs.: In the first place, they won[']t sit up all night, under the new regime[.] *[W]omen* know better than to expect pure judgments, according to evidence, from midnight consultations and *manipulations*. [Y]our jurors, in the millenial times now dawning, will go home early, go to bed at nine o'clock, sleep over the knotty points—may be praying a bit over them first, and wake in the morning with revised judgments and stout hearts to maintain them.

Mr.: But women being on a jury, would involve their presence during the very delicate (*you* would say indelicate) matters. What do you say to that?

Mrs.: I say just this, and I am glad you have brought it up—I have wanted to talk over this whole question of modesty and propriety with you, for a long time, for I fear we do not agree here, as well as in most things. My position is . . . that a man is by nature, less fitted to handle "delicate subjects" so called, than a woman. It is just as Mr. Beecher has said in his speech on "Woman's Influence in Politics," in this very same paper. . . , "*Men* think from the physical and passional stand point," and so, it seems to me are very susceptible of contamination, when dealing with subjects exciting to the passions. "*Women*," as he truly says, "think from the stand point of affection and moral sentiment." [C]onsequently, in the same circumstances, they will *impart* a purifying influence, rather than *receive* a taint. [A]nd I do most firmly believe that if there were but one woman on the bench, or among the advocates, or in the jury box, the character of *criminal* trials would be materially changed—and the newspapers would have no chance to report the nauseous matter that the public taste now demands (so they say). I can't tell you, what I have felt on this custom of allowing boys to read, in the classics and elsewhere, things that their sisters mustn't—and so training up men to talk obscenities among themselves that they would shudder to have their wives listen to. And, speaking of jury trials, as illustrative of the whole matter, there is not a discussion of principles or of evidence, under the laws of anatomy, physiology, and so on, that a woman could not enter into with as much ability and fineness of perception as a man. While looking at it from her higher stand point, she would certainly come to closer discriminations and more righteous judgments. . . . I see woman, purified by long ages of suffering, self disciplined in the cloister of home, ready to lead the way to *knowledge* and *purity*—one at last—and man, toiling through the same ages to supply the demands of his senses—burdened by the woman he cannot live without and by their common offspring, made strong, through labor and conflict. *Wisdom*[,] *purity*[,] and *strength*—from this time, these th[r]ee walk hand in hand, with even pace till the great consummation. There you have it—My first speech. I declare, and I feel easier for getting it off. [I]t has lain on my soul, like lead, these months past. . . .

Mr.: . . . [B]ut to come back to the voting, don[']t you see that in most cases, you only duplicate the vote, and so merely add to the labor of counting up[?] [E]very wife would be pretty sure to vote just as her husband does—and daughters with their fathers or brothers.

Mrs.: . . . [H]usband and wife might vote for the same candidate . . . but that is not necessarily the very same candidate the husband would vote for were his wife in her old ignorance and indifference on political matters. She would imitate the wise procedure of a certain young gentleman I knew once—who, having married a spicy young girl, that hated abolitionists more than she did slavery; begged her in the long winter evenings of the first year to read aloud . . . "The Life of Wilberforce . . ." and surreptitiously laid on her table "Jay's View" "Thom and Kimball on West India Emancipation" etc. etc.—till in the course of months she waked up a full blooded Anti Slavery *woman*—and did not at once suspect the influence. That is just the way I would serve you, if I could ever catch you on the wrong side of anything. . . .

Mr.: I do not succumb to flattery, my love. [Y]ou have failed to convince me that homes can spare their mistresses very often, even for the public good. . . .

Mrs.: . . . I don[']t wish to see the homes robbed, any more than you do, and I don't think they will be, when every disability is removed from woman. . . . It is here just as it was years ago, when rights of color were first talked about—and amalgamation was the weighty argument against allowing a black man to vote. I remember how you hooted the idea, that white girls would rush to marry black men, the moment they were admitted to the simple rights of men. And so now, every other woman in town, is not going to Congress, nor the Legislature nor the Court Room just because she is granted the right to vote, and to speak, and to do every other thing that God made her capable of doing. . . .

Mrs.: . . . [B]ut, I put it to you now, on the spot—what rights have you, as an intelligent, moral, and accountable being, that *I* have not? We are peers, before God and man—[Y]ou have said so to me a thousand times, virtually—and all after this is but a question of time and expediency.

Mr.: . . . [Y]ou would vote for universal suffrage—without distinction of color or sex, this minute, if you had the chance.

Mrs.: Yes, I would give an individual vote, certainly. [B]ut if absolute power were in my hands, I would not open the polls to women today— no, nor next year, nor ever, unless public opinion demanded it. I honor too highly the Divine precedent, to do such a thing as that. It has been the one thing hardest for me to learn—this "patience of waiting." [B]ut I see more and more the strength and beauty of this gradual upbuilding— this calling on the ages to work—this doing with our might, and leaving the results with God. . . .

[Manuscript of "Shall Women Vote?
A Matrimonial Dialogue," SD]

II. The Power of Womanhood

5.
Catharine Esther Beecher: "A Power and Station and Influence"

B Y 1830, Catharine Beecher was growing restless. Although the Hartford Female Seminary continued a success, Beecher had been unable to realize her larger goals for the school. Most discouraging was Hartford's refusal to supply an endowment, which would have allowed the seminary to become a boarding institution and funded the position of moral instructor. Perhaps, as Beecher's biographer, Kathryn Kish Sklar, has suggested, parents were reluctant to place their daughters full-time in an all-female community and opposed Beecher's plan "to replace the role of the male clergyman with a female."[1] Catharine felt the blow keenly. She attributed the subsequent decline of the seminary to this cause, noting bitterly that even as they rejected an endowment for her school, Hartford citizens found the money to endow a local college for men.[2]

It was Lyman Beecher who supplied the resolution to Catharine's growing frustrations. In 1826, Lyman had moved from Litchfield, Connecticut, to Boston, where he undertook to drive heresy from the home of the Puritans. Now, at the end of the decade, he began to look westward, to the struggle for the great heartland of the country. As he wrote Catharine in 1830, "The moral destiny of our nation . . . turns on the character of the West, and the competition now is for . . . the rising generation, in which Catholics and infidels have got the start of us."[3] When Lyman was offered the presidency of the Lane Theological Seminary in 1832, Catharine was ready to move to Cincinnati with him. There, in 1833, she established the Western Female Institute, dedicated to moral development as well as to academic and domestic education. She shared the principalship with Harriet—but Catharine's attention was soon drawn to other matters.

Lyman carried with him to the West assumptions about the superiority of Calvinism and the New England way. Catharine shared that regional bias, claiming in her 1836 *Letters on the Difficulties of Religion* (written in Cincinnati) that "the regular habits, the domestic comforts, the intellectual resources, the moral and religious enjoyments of the common people" all marked New England as the model "of the religion of the Bible."[4] She also shared with Lyman a conviction that the values of the Beecher family could—and should—be writ large as the identity of the nation. Yet in Catharine's mind the issues assumed a slightly different shape.

In 1831, just before leaving Hartford, Beecher had published *The Elements of Mental and Moral Philosophy*. There she returned to the religious themes raised in her *Suggestions Regarding Improvements in Education*, now binding morality even more securely to behavior and to the pursuit of "a course of conscious rectitude." God's purpose in creating humans, she wrote, "was *the production of happiness*." Because humans were social beings, "the purest and highest kind of happiness" was found, not in individual pleasure, but in "the mutual relations of minds," in seeking "the *greatest amount of general happiness*, irrespective of [one's] own particular share." That general happiness, Beecher believed, consisted in each person's pursuit of "a perfect and infallible standard of rectitude"—"rules of *neatness*, of *order*, of *regularity*, and of *taste* or *fitness*" found in the Bible. Since "the mind is a free and independent agent . . . influenced by *motives*," those rules—and thus virtue itself— could be *taught*, developed in habits of self-sacrifice and proper social conduct.[5]

This conclusion met a number of Beecher's own needs. First, conceiving of virtue in behavioral terms rather than as a rebirth from a corrupt nature enabled her to understand herself as a moral person, even if she remained unconverted. More particularly, however, defining virtue as learned social behavior allowed Beecher to identify a special mission for women—for female teachers, like herself—in the West. If virtue was achieved through learning the rules of social conduct, then the challenge of the West was not who would convert it, but who would civilize it. And who better suited to that work than female teachers?

Personally, Catharine's assault on the West was a disaster. She had associated her own views with those of her father. Not flattered by the idea that it required *either* saving *or* civilizing, Cincinnati society rejected both Lyman's Calvinism and Catharine's pretensions to cultural superiority. After the abolitionist controversy swept Lane Seminary like a fire storm,[6] their Cincinnati neighbors branded both Beechers interlopers and troublemakers. In 1837, Catharine's school failed.

Yet Catharine's faith in her own ability to determine what was best for

America remained unshaken. In 1837, she published *An Essay on Slavery and Abolitionism*, a response to the efforts of Sarah and Angelina Grimké to enlist women in the abolitionist cause. Averring that she abhorred slavery, Beecher nonetheless denounced abolitionism as unchristian and inappropriate for women.[7] In an early exposition of her concept of female influence, she argued that women's power must never be exerted directly (as active abolitionism would have required), for to do so would associate women with self-interest and deprive them of the high moral ground of self-sacrifice she had envisioned in *Mental and Moral Philosophy*: "Woman is to win every thing by peace and love," she insisted, "by making herself so much respected, esteemed and loved, that to yield to her opinions and to gratify her wishes, will be the free-will offering of the heart." She called on "every female instantly to relinquish the attitude of a partisan, in every matter of clashing interests" and to assume her role as gentle moral exemplar to her nation.[8]

In the *Essay*, too, Catharine returned to the association that had been at the heart of her earlier *Suggestions*—that of teaching with mothering. Having determined that woman's influence was to be confined to "the domestic and social circle," Beecher went on to suggest that, among other reasons for eschewing abolition work, women were needed in more "appropriate" tasks—especially that of educating themselves to work as teachers in the West. Because many Americans still considered education incompatible with "true womanhood," in 1837 Beecher added that "the more intelligent a woman becomes, the more she can appreciate the wisdom of that ordinance that appointed her subordinate station, and the more her taste will conform to the graceful and dignified retirement and submission it involves."[9] Later (in part as a result of her own efforts), Beecher would feel less compelled to defend women's professional training per se; indeed, she would eventually argue that it was in supporting women's education that society showed its true esteem for womanhood.

In discussing the need for teachers in the West, Catharine was preparing for her own next move. A decade before, she had used her concern for education in the newer states to rationalize her decision to leave Hartford. Now that her plans for Cincinnati had failed, she began to contemplate a national organization, drawing on women "without respect to religious or political divisions, to secure the proper education of the women and children of this nation, as the chief ground of hope for its prosperity and safety."[10] Funded by the contributions of women in the East, she would supply New England virtues to the West in the form of New England teachers, prepared by Catharine Beecher herself. In one form or another,[11] this plan would occupy much of Beecher's energy for the next twenty years. Virtually everything she would publish—whatever its stated subject—would include a plea for the importance of preparing women as teachers and an appeal for financial support.

Meanwhile, Catharine began to work out in more detail her argument for the special mission of women as the conduits of civilization and the teachers of morality. In 1841, she published *A Treatise on Domestic Economy, for the Use of Young Ladies at Home, and at School.* An immediate and lasting success, the *Treatise* was reissued fifteen times over the next fifteen years. Its sequel, *Miss Beecher's Domestic Receipt Book,* published in 1846, also went through numerous printings. In 1869, much of the content of these two volumes was presented in expanded form in *The American Woman's Home,* which Catharine published with her sister, Harriet Beecher Stowe.

As well as compendia of useful household information, the *Treatise* and *The American Woman's Home* comprised an extended paean to American womanhood and to woman's special role in determining the character of American society. Those views began, as did the *Treatise* with its dedication to "American Mothers," with the equation of womanhood with motherhood, and of motherhood with the success or failure of society: "The mother writes the character of the future man," Beecher warned, ". . . whose energies may turn for good or for evil the destinies of a nation."[12] Beecher's emphasis on motherhood derived directly from her conclusions in the *Mental and Moral Philosophy.* In that work, she had cautioned that apparently altruistic behavior might in fact spring from essentially selfish motives—"a desire for notoriety, and the praise of men," for example.[13] Such temptations assailed one at every turn in public life, tainting the impulse to true virtue.

In both the *Treatise* and *The American Woman's Home,* Beecher argued that a reliable model of virtue existed only in the privacy and self-sacrifice of the family, and there, only in the role of the mother. Focused constantly on the welfare of others, mothers embodied that selflessness which lay at the heart of true morality: their "great mission is self-denial, in training [the family] members to self-sacrificing labors for the ignorant and weak."[14] As *women,* mothers were unenfranchised, and therefore could not become competitors in the political sphere. As *married* women, they were subordinate in the relations of civic and domestic life. Thus, their position in society and the family set mothers apart from the self-aggrandizement that might underlay the actions of others. To them alone might American society entrust "the formation of the moral and intellectual character" of others.[15]

As she had in the *Essay on Slavery and Abolitionism*, Beecher insisted that the nature of female influence was to be indirect. Like the "drops of heaven," woman would "freshen the earth," "extending over the world those blessed influences, that are to renovate degraded man, and 'clothe all climes with beauty.' " Should women feel a grievance, they had but to express it: "in all cases, in which [women] do feel a concern," Beecher insisted, "their opinions and feelings have a consideration, equal, or even superior, to that of the other sex."[16] Presumably, a grateful society would always listen.

The *Treatise* and *The American Woman's Home* both focused primarily on the family, and on woman as wife and mother. But as Beecher knew all too well, unmarried women, like herself, remained marginal to that definition of womanhood.[17] Indeed, on at least one occasion her unmarried status called into question her credentials for even writing about family life: observing Catharine's progress on the *Treatise*, her cousin Elizabeth Elliot Foote had commented acidly, "If it were not for these maiden ladies instructing the married ones how to keep house and take care of children I don't know what would become of us."[18] Alert to the criticism, Beecher explained in the volume's preface that she had been trained as a young girl "to the care of children, and to the performance of most domestic duties" and had lived "most of her life, in the families of exemplary and accomplished housekeepers."[19] In another respect, Beecher's status as an unmarried women made it appropriate that she should write the book. Like most unmarried women in the antebellum period, she faced recurrent financial hardship: she needed the money. Aware of the numbers of women, like herself, for whom "womanhood" must include money-making, she was determined to expand the rhetoric to fit her own circumstances.

Perhaps for this reason, although Beecher based woman's power on the model of motherhood, she did not recognize as "mothers" only those women who actually bore children. While the *Essay* had focused on the influence of women in families, the *Treatise* also specifically included women in paid employment: "the woman who labors in the schoolroom; the woman who, in her retired chamber, earns, with her needle, the mite to contribute to the intellectual and moral elevation of her country; even the humble domestic. . . ;—each and all . . . are agents in accomplishing the greatest work that ever was committed to human responsibility."[20]

In the *Treatise*, broadening the definition of motherhood remained a minor theme. In 1851, however, in response to the new women's rights movement, which sought protection for women in expanded legal rights, Beecher published *True Remedy for the Wrongs of Woman*. As Harriet observed, it was in *True Remedy* that Catharine's work at last became a "great *whole*."[21] There she fused the two elements of her thinking, creating a domestic utopia based on woman's position in the home but encompassing women's professional work beyond the home. Beecher accomplished this, in part, by explicitly designating "motherhood" a profession, not a biological relationship; specifically, it was the profession of acting "as the conservators of the domestic state, the nurses of the sick, the guardians and developers of the human body in infancy, and the educators of the human mind."[22] In all of its contexts, the work of mothering was undervalued, Beecher insisted, but "the grand source of the heaviest wrong that oppresses our sex is found in the fact that they are so extensively cut off from honorable and rumunerative employ in their professional vocation."[23] What women suffered from most was the general disdain of their work as nurses, domestic servants, and, most especially, teachers. In that "perfected state of society" toward which humanity progressed, Beecher prophesied, "the office now filled by the domestic, the nurse, and the teacher, will become the most honorable"—and, not incidentally, profitable.[24] Although throughout the work Beecher conflated the "mother" and the "teacher," she had made an important modification in the domestic ideal: it was not wives, but teachers, "who really are rendering the most service to society,"[25] and it was by their status that the status of womanhood must be measured.

Beecher pursued this linkage of the domestic female ideal with a new professional female ideal in *The American Woman's Home*, which took as its purpose "to elevate both the honor and the remuneration of all employments that sustain . . . the family state." In this work, Beecher emphasized the increased autonomy for women implicit in her redefinition of motherhood: "The blessed privileges of the family state are not confined to those who rear children of their own." Any woman, married or single, became a mother simply through her ministrations to others— and not necessarily children: "the orphan, the sick, the homeless, and the sinful," husband, brothers, and friends were all potential objects of her aid. Indeed, other than as recipients of women's care, men were virtually expendable in the creation of motherhood, since, "Any woman who can earn a livelihood, as every woman should be trained to do, can take a properly qualified female associate, and institute a family of her own."[26]

Her interest in defining motherhood as a profession helps to account for an interesting inconsistency in Beecher's thought. Although she variously ascribed woman's role as mother to Nature, the principles of democracy, and the tenets of Christianity, she also viewed motherhood as a socially constructed role. In *Mental and Moral Philosophy*, she had concluded that self-sacrifice—the core of motherhood—was itself *learned* behavior. She returned to this theme in her *Educational Reminiscences and Suggestions*, recalling that her father took that delight in child-rearing "which is generally deemed a distinctive element of the woman." Thinking of her parents, she concluded that "much that passes for natural talent is mainly the result of culture."[27] Determined to elevate the importance of trained female teachers as agents of moral development, Beecher would leave to another age the belief that woman's destiny lay entirely in her anatomy.

Beecher had based her argument for female selflessness on women's social subordination and close association with domestic life. But, as she made clear in *True Remedy*, submission did not mean subservience. She was adamant that those women who "write and talk as if the great end and aim of woman was to conform to the will and wishes of husbands" utterly misunderstood the relationship. "The true attitude to be assumed by woman," she insisted, "not only in the domestic but in all our social relations, is that of an intelligent, immortal being, whose interests and rights are *every way* equal in value to that of the other sex."[28] Women were to exercise power; they merely were not to be *perceived* as exercising it. Moreover, far from diminishing woman's role in social affairs, subordination was its base.

In each of these works, Beecher was attempting to shape the social order even as she accepted it, selecting those elements that validated her view of America and of the power of women within it. She was working within two older traditions of womanhood. At the core of her female ideal stood the pious and industrious Puritan wife—her mother—laboring tirelessly for her family's welfare, her every act infused with the strength of her faith. She was "the wise woman [who] buildeth her house."[29]

Associating antebellum women with their Puritan forebears enabled Beecher to enshrine her own regional, religious, and family identity in the national order. Equally important, she was arguing for the importance of women's traditional domestic work in a society that was coming to value the importance of only that work which was paid.[30] The *Treatise* set out immediately to embed housework in the work of creating the democracy and it acknowledged, as fewer and fewer Americans did in the antebellum period, that housework *was* work—difficult, exhausting, and essential. Perhaps this recognition accounts for the manual's popularity with mid-nineteenth-century housewives. But Beecher had another end in mind, as well. From the beginning, she had argued that women's *paid* vocations deserved status and remuneration precisely because they so closely resembled women's *unpaid* work in the family. If housework was unworthy of respect, so too were teaching, nursing, and domestic service. By 1851, Beecher was ready to proclaim domestic science the necessary core of all women's education, whether they worked within their own families or for pay.

But the virtuous Puritan woman had remained largely silent. Especially in matters of religion, she had submitted to the teachings of men. On this point, Beecher turned to the newer rhetoric of "Republican motherhood," which had identified social stability with the home and particularly with the mother. Barred from direct political participation, post-Revolutionary writers had argued, mothers would influence the course of history through the moral development of their children, the future citizens of the nation.[31]

"Republican motherhood" had signaled a shift in the rhetoric of womanhood—from inner piety to outward social behavior. In a democracy, conversion was less important than outward conduct. It also recast woman's work—from household labor to character formation. Although she rejected this bifurcation as incompatible with her elevation of "woman's profession," Beecher claimed much of the content of "Republican motherhood" as her own and refashioned it to suit her ends. She accepted women's exclusion from formal political life, using this to bolster her argument for woman's structural position as the embodiment of the spirit of self-sacrifice. Most especially, she took the association of "mother" with "teacher." For the Puritans, the father had been the conduit of culture, instructing his wife, his children, and his servants in matters religious and social. But the ideal woman of the Revolution had been a teacher, the essential guardian of the values of democracy. Still seeking her own place within the Beecher family tradition, Catharine retained the piety of the Puritan wife but cast it in the Revolutionary mold. The combination resulted in a new, distinctly nineteenth-century, voice—the voice of the female minister.

Throughout, Catharine Beecher was working within a distinctly Protestant framework, seeing in the life of Jesus an example for the ideal social relations of a democracy. In this fusion of religious and secular concerns, Beecher was not unusual. Indeed, in the stir of religious fervor that characterized the second quarter of the nineteenth century, both middle-class and working-class reformers found in Christianity the tenets of a just society. Abolitionists drew on this perfectionist spirit in their opposition to slavery, and utopianists and early labor organizers incorporated the rhetoric of Jesus' egalitarianism in their efforts to overthrow the social and economic inequities of early industrialization.

Beecher's use of the model differed from these groups, however, and reveals a divergence within the impulse of Protestant millennialism during the early nineteenth century. Beecher recoiled from the broad leveling implications of Christianity. Her discomfort with the "promiscuous masses" was particularly evident in the *Treatise*, where she worried that "a mingling of all grades" and the absence of "distinct classes" presaged chaos in the republic.³² Seeking protection against this perceived threat, Beecher attempted to confine rather than to generalize the radical potential of Christ-like "selflessness"—literally, to domesticate it within the walls of the middle-class home, where mothers could exercise their "peculiar responsibility" to channel its manifestations and effects. When Beecher wrote the *Treatise*, this view remained in competition with its more radical counterpart. By 1869, when she and Harriet Beecher Stowe published *The American Woman's Home*, the moment of tension had largely passed. Speaking for the now-dominant middle-class culture, Beecher wrote confidently: "The family state," not the social organism, was "the aptest earthly illustration of the heavenly kingdom, and in it woman is its chief minister."³³ For Beecher, the power of womanhood had become inseparable from the politics of class.

NOTES

1. Kathryn Kish Sklar, *Catharine Beecher: A Study in American Domesticity* (New Haven, Conn.: Yale University Press, 1973), pp. 93–94.

2. Catharine E. Beecher, *Educational Reminiscences and Suggestions* (New York: J. B. Ford, 1874), pp. 65–66, 79–81.

3. Lyman Beecher to Catharine Esther Beecher, July 8, 1830, in Barbara Cross, ed., *The Autobiography of Lyman Beecher*, 2 vols. (Cambridge, Mass.: Harvard University Press, Belknap Press, 1961), 2:167.

4. Catharine E. Beecher, *Letters on the Difficulties of Religion* (Hartford: Belknap and Hamersley, 1836), pp. 16, 20.

5. [Catharine E. Beecher], *The Elements of Mental and Moral Philosophy, Founded upon Experience, Reason, and the Bible* (Hartford: Peter B. Gleason and Co., 1831), pp. 249, 243, 244, 252, 275, 409, 249.

6. For a discussion of the Lane controversy, see Introduction.

7. On Catharine's views of abolitionism, see also Catharine Esther Beecher to "My dear Brethren and Sisteren," Beecher Family Circular Letter, January 24–February 18, 1838, SD. See Document 99.

8. Catharine E. Beecher, *An Essay on Slavery and Abolitionism, with Reference to the Duty of American Females* (Philadelphia: Henry Perkins, 1837), pp. 100–101, 128. See Document 50.

9. CEB *ESA*, pp. 101, 105, 107–8. See Document 50.

10. CEB *ER*, p. 119.

11. Beecher's original plan was that she should combine lecturing and fund-raising in the East with locating and preparing female teachers, while an agent found teaching locations in the West and prepared community support for the women. For a time, Catharine's brother-in-law, Calvin Stowe, acted as her agent (for his response to his business association with Catharine, see Document 35). In 1846, Catharine hired former Vermont governor William Slade to act as secretary and general agent of the Central Committee for Promoting National Education. Unhappy with Slade's independence, Beecher separated herself from the organization and, in 1852, founded the American Woman's Educational Association (AWEA). By this time her specific objectives had changed somewhat. In 1850, Catharine had founded the Milwaukee Female Seminary. A main goal of the AWEA was to try to raise an endowment for the school. The importance of providing educated women to the West as teachers remained a prominent theme in Beecher's efforts throughout, however. See Beecher's discussion of this period of her life in "An Appeal to American Women" in Catharine E. Beecher and Harriet Beecher Stowe, *The American Woman's Home* (New York: J. B. Ford, 1869), pp. 463–70. See Document 75.

12. Catharine E. Beecher, *A Treatise on Domestic Economy, for the Use of Young Ladies at Home, and at School* (Boston: Marsh, Capen, Lyon, and Webb, 1841), p. 13. See Document 51.

13. Beecher, *Mental and Moral Philosophy*, p. 385.

14. *AWH*, p. 19. See Document 53.

15. CEB *TDE*, p. 13. See Document 51.

16. Ibid., pp. 13–14, 9. See Document 51.

17. For a full-scale treatment of the lives of unmarried women in the antebellum period, see Lee Virginia Chambers-Schiller, *Liberty, A Better Husband: Single Women in America—The Generations of 1780–1840* (New Haven, Conn.: Yale University Press, 1984).

18. Elizabeth Elliot Foote to Harriet Foote, January 28 and 29, 1841, SD.

19. CEB *TDE*, p. viii.

20. Ibid., p. 14. See Document 51.

21. Harriet Beecher Stowe to Lyman Beecher and Henry Ward Beecher, September 9, 1851, SML.

22. Catharine E. Beecher, *The True Remedy for the Wrongs of Woman* (Boston: Phillips, Sampson, and Company, 1851), p. 28. See Document 52.

23. Ibid., pp. 32–33. See Document 52.

24. Ibid., pp. 24, 27. See Document 52.

25. Ibid., p. 30. See Document 52.

26. *AWH*, pp. 17, 20. See Document 53.

27. CEB *ER*, pp. 14–15. See Document 5.

28. CEB *TR*, p. 230. See Document 52.

29. *AWH*, p. 23. (See Document 53.) For a fuller discussion of the work and

roles of Puritan women, see Laurel Thatcher Ulrich, *Good Wives: Image and Reality in the Lives of Women in Northern New England, 1650–1750* (New York: Alfred A. Knopf, 1982) and Laurel Thatcher Ulrich, "Vertuous Women Found: New England Ministerial Literature, 1668–1735," *American Quarterly* 28 (Spring 1976): 20–40.

30. See Jeanne Boydston, *Home and Work: Housework, Wages, and the Ideology of Labor in the Early Republic* (New York: Oxford University Press, 1990). On the history of housework in the United States, see also: Dolores Hayden, *The Grand Domestic Revolution: A History of Feminist Designs for American Homes, Neighborhoods, and Cities* (Cambridge, Mass.: MIT Press, 1981); Susan Strasser, *Never Done: A History of American Housework* (New York: Pantheon Books, 1982); and Ruth Schwartz Cowan, *More Work for Mother: The Ironies of Household Technology from the Open Hearth to the Microwave* (New York: Basic Books, 1983).

31. For fuller discussions of Revolutionary ideologies of womanhood, see Linda K. Kerber, *Women of the Republic: Intellect and Ideology in Revolutionary America* (Chapel Hill: The University of North Carolina Press, 1980), and Mary Beth Norton, *Liberty's Daughters: The Revolutionary Experience of American Women, 1750–1800* (Boston: Little, Brown and Co., 1980).

32. CEB *TDE*, p. 17. See Document 51.

33. *AWH*, p. 19. See Document 53.

The Essay on Slavery and Abolitionism *(1837) was written in response to Angelina Emily Grimké's* An Appeal to the Christian Women of the South *(1836) and was explicitly addressed to "Miss A. D. Grimke."[1] The daughter of a Southern slave-owning family, Grimké planned to carry her abolitionist appeal to women in New York City. Beecher, a supporter of recolonization, used the* Essay *not only to attack abolitionism as violent in its methods,[2] and inappropriate for women, but also to develop her concept of female "influence."*

50   My Dear Friend,[3]

Your public address to Christian females at the South has reached me, and I have been urged to aid in circulating it at the North. I have also been informed, that you contemplate a tour, during the ensuing year, for the purpose of exerting your influence to form Abolition Societies among ladies of the non-slave-holding States.

Our acquaintance and friendship give me a claim to your private ear; but there are reasons why it seems more desirable to address you, who now stand before the public as an advocate of Abolition measures, in a more public manner.

The object I have in view, is to present some reasons why it seems unwise and inexpedient for ladies of the non-slave-holding States to unite themselves in Abolition Societies; and thus, at the same time, to exhibit the inexpediency of the course you propose to adopt. . . .

The distinctive peculiarity of the Abolition Society is this: it is a voluntary association in one section of the country, designed to awaken public sentiment against a moral evil existing in another section of the country. . . .

The best way to make a person like a thing which is disagreeable, is to try in some way to make it agreeable. . . . If the friends of the blacks had quietly set themselves to work to increase their intelligence, their usefulness, their respectability, their meekness, gentleness, and benevolence, and then had appealed to the pity, generosity, and christian feelings of

1. The middle initial "D." was an error. Grimké's middle name was Emily.

2. See also Catharine Esther Beecher to "Brethren and Sisteren" (*sic*), Document 99.

3. Grimké had for a time considered enrolling in Beecher's Hartford Female Seminary.

their fellow citizens, a very different result would have appeared. Instead of this, reproaches, rebukes, and sneers, were employed to convince the whites that their prejudices were sinful, and without any just cause. . . . This tended to irritate the whites, and to increase their prejudice against the blacks. . . . Then, on the other hand, the blacks extensively received the Liberator,[4] and learned to imbibe the spirit of its conductor.

They were taught to feel that they were injured and abused, the objects of a guilty and unreasonable prejudice—that they occupied a lower place in society than was right—that they ought to be treated as if they were whites; and in repeated instances, attempts were made by their friends to mingle them with whites, so as to break down the existing distinctions of society. Now, the question is not, whether these things, that were urged by Abolitionists, were true. The thing maintained is, that the method taken by them to remove this prejudice was neither peaceful nor christian in its tendency, but, on the contrary, was calculated . . . to generate anger, pride, and recrimination, on one side, and envy, discontent, and revengeful feelings, on the other. . . .

Take another example. If a prudent and benevolent female[5] had selected almost any village in New England, and commenced a school for coloured females, in a quiet, appropriate, and unostentatious way, the world would never have heard of the case, except to applaud her benevolence. . . . But instead of this, there appeared public advertisements . . . stating that a seminary for the education of young ladies of colour was to be opened in Canterbury, in the state of Connecticut. . . . It was an entire disregard of the prejudices and the proprieties of society, and calculated to stimulate pride, anger, ill-will, contention. . . .

The assertion that Christianity itself has led to strife and contention, is not a safe method of evading this argument. Christianity is a system of *persuasion*, tending, by kind and gentle influences, to make men *willing* to leave off their sins. . . .

4. The newspaper of abolitionist William Lloyd Garrison.

5. Prudence Crandall operated the Canterbury (Connecticut) Female Boarding School. When she admitted a black student, local citizens threatened to withdraw their support and white parents began to remove their daughters. In 1833, Crandall converted the institution to an all-black school. After other forms of harrassment failed, Canterbury citizens secured the passage of a state law prohibiting schools from admitting out-of-state black students or individuals from teaching any black students not living in Connecticut without the consent of local authorities. Crandall was arrested, but Canterbury continued the assault, threatening students, breaking windows, and trying to burn the building down. In 1834, Crandall's school closed.

The preceding are some of the reasons which, on the general view, I would present as opposed to the proposal of forming Abolition Societies; and they apply equally to either sex. There are some others which seem to oppose peculiar objections to the action of females in the way you would urge. . . .

It is Christianity that has given to woman her true place in society. And it is the peculiar trait of Christianity alone that can sustain her therein. "Peace on earth and good will to men" is the character of all the rights and privileges, the influence, and the power of woman. A man may act on society by the collision of intellect, in public debate; he may urge his measures by a sense of shame, by fear and by personal interest; he may coerce by the combination of public sentiment; he may drive by physical force, and he does not outstep the boundaries of his sphere. But all the power, and all the conquests that are lawful to woman, are those only which appeal to the kindly, generous, peaceful and benevolent principles.

Woman is to win every thing by peace and love; by making herself so much respected, esteemed and loved, that to yield to her opinions and to gratify her wishes, will be the free-will offering of the heart. But this is to be all accomplished in the domestic and social circle. There let every woman become so cultivated and refined in intellect . . . so unassuming and unambitious . . . so "gentle and easy to be entreated," as that every heart will repose in her presence; then, the fathers, the husbands, and the sons, will find an influence thrown around them, to which they will yield not only willingly but proudly. . . . But the moment woman begins to feel the promptings of ambition, or the thirst for power, her aegis of defence is gone. All the sacred protection of religion, all the generous promptings of chivalry, all the poetry of romantic gallantry, depend upon woman's retaining her place as dependent and defenceless, and making no claims, and maintaining no right but what are the gifts of honour, rectitude and love.

. . . If these general principles are correct, they are entirely opposed to the plan of arraying females in any Abolition movement; because . . . it brings them forward as partisans in a conflict that has been begun and carried forward by measures that are any thing rather than peaceful in their tendencies; because it draws them forth from their appropriate retirement, to expose themselves to the ungoverned violence of mobs,[6] and to sneers and ridicule in public places; because it leads them into the

6. As when English abolitionist George Thompson had attempted to address the Boston Female Antislavery Society in 1835, Northern abolitionist meetings were frequently threatened with disruption by hostile mobs.

arena of political collision, not as peaceful mediators to hush the opposing elements, but as combatants to cheer up and carry forward the measures of strife.

If it is asked, "May not woman appropriately come forward as a suppliant for a portion of her sex who are bound in cruel bondage?" It is replied, that, the rectitude and propriety of any such measure, depend entirely on its probable results. If petitions[7] from females will operate to exasperate; if they will be deemed obtrusive, indecorous, and unwise, by those to whom they are addressed; . . . if they will be the opening wedge, that will tend eventually to bring females as petitioners and partisans into every political measure that may tend to injure and oppress their sex . . . then it is neither appropriate nor wise, nor right, for a woman to petition for the relief of oppressed females. . . .

In this country, petitions to congress, in reference to the official duties of legislators, seem, IN ALL CASES, to fall entirely without the sphere of female duty. Men are the proper persons to make appeals to the rulers whom they appoint, and if their female friends, by arguments and persuasions, can induce them to petition, all the good that can be done by such measures will be secured. But if females cannot influence their nearest friends, to urge forward a public measure in this way, they surely are out of their place, in attempting to do it themselves.

There are some other considerations, which should make the American females peculiarly sensitive in reference to any measure, which should even *seem* to draw them from their appropriate relations in society.

It is allowed by all reflecting minds, that the safety and happiness of this nation depends upon having the *children* educated, and not only intellectually, but morally and religiously. There are now nearly two millions of children and adults in this country who cannot read, and who have no schools of any kind. To give only a small supply of teachers to these destitute children, who are generally where the population is sparse, will demand *thirty thousand teachers.* . . . Where is this army of teachers to be found? Is it at all probable that the other sex will afford even a moderate portion of this supply? . . . Men will be educators in the college, in the high school, in some of the most honourable and lucrative common schools, but the *children*, the *little children* of this nation must, to a wide extent, be taught by females, or remain untaught. . . . And as

7. By 1837, female abolitionists were organized into antislavery societies across the North and had begun a petition campaign to Congress to end slavery.

the value of education rises in the public mind . . . women will more and more be furnished with those intellectual advantages which they need to fit them for such duties.

The result will be, that America will be distinguished above all other nations, for well-educated females. . . . But if females, as they approach the other sex, in intellectual elevation, begin to claim, or to exercise in any manner, the peculiar prerogatives of that sex, education will prove a doubtful and dangerous blessing. But this will never be the result. For the more intelligent a woman becomes, the more she can appreciate the wisdom of that ordinance that appointed her subordinate station, and the more her taste will conform to the graceful and dignified retirement and submission it involves.

But it may be asked, is there nothing to be done to bring this national sin of slavery to an end? . . .

To this it may be replied, that Christian females may, and can say and do much to bring these evils to an end; and the present is a time and an occasion when it seems most desirable that they should know, and appreciate, and *exercise* the power which they do possess for so desirable an end. . . .

And is there not a peculiar propriety in such an emergency, in looking for the especial agency and assistance of females, who are shut out from the many temptations that assail the other sex,—who are the appointed ministers of all the gentler charities of life,—who are mingled throughout the whole mass of the community,—who dwell in those retirements where only peace and love ought ever to enter,—whose comfort, influence, and dearest blessings, all depend on preserving peace and good will among men?

In the present aspect of affairs among us, when everything seems to be tending to disunion and distraction, it surely has become the duty of every female instantly to relinquish the attitude of a partisan, in every matter of clashing interests, and to assume the office of a mediator, and an advocate of peace. . . .

[CEB *ESA*, pp. 5–6, 8, 26–28, 30–32,
46, 97, 100–109, 128]

Manuals of household advice were popular among early nineteenth-century women, who found themselves in the midst of often confusing transformations in family life and in domestic work. In her Treatise on Domestic Economy for the Use of Young Ladies at Home and at School *(1841), Beecher elaborated the prescriptive potential of that genre, setting detailed information on housework in the context of a highly nationalistic discussion of woman's true mission.*

51 There are some reasons why American women should feel an interest in the support of the democratic institutions of their Country, which it is important that they should consider. The great maxim, which is the basis of all our civil and political institutions, is, that "all men are created equal," and that they are equally entitled to "life, liberty, and the pursuit of happiness."

But it can readily be seen, that this is only another mode of expressing the fundamental principle which the Great Ruler of the Universe has established, as the law of His eternal government. "Thou shalt love thy neighbor as thyself." . . .

The principles of democracy, then, are identical with the principles of Christianity.

But, in order that each individual may pursue and secure the highest degree of happiness within his reach, unimpeded by the selfish interests of others, a system of laws must be established, which sustains certain relations and dependencies in social and civil life. What these relations and their attending obligations shall be, are to be determined, not with reference to the wishes and interests of a few, but solely with reference to the general good. . . .

For this purpose, it is needful that certain relations be sustained, that involve the duties of subordination. There must be the magistrate and the subject, one of whom is the superior, and the other the inferior. There must be the relations of husband and wife, parent and child, teacher and pupil, employer and employed, each involving the relative duties of subordination. The superior in certain particulars is to direct, and the inferior is to yield obedience. . . .

But who shall take the higher, and who the subordinate, stations in social and civil life? This matter, in the case of parents and children, is decided by the Creator. He has given children to the control of parents, as their superiors, and to them they remain subordinate, to a certain age, or so long as they are members of their household. . . .

In most other cases, in a truly democratic state, each individual is allowed to choose for himself, who shall take the position of his superior. No woman is forced to obey any husband but the one she chooses for herself; nor is she obliged to take a husband, if she prefers to remain single. So every domestic, and every artisan or laborer, after passing from parental control, can choose the employer to whom he is to accord obedience, or, if he prefers to relinquish certain advantages, he can remain without taking a subordinate place to any employer.

Each subject, also, has equal power with every other, to decide who shall be his superior as a ruler. The weakest, the poorest, the most illiterate, has the same opportunity to determine this question, as the richest, the most learned, and the most exalted.

And the various privileges that wealth secures, are equally open to all classes. Every man may aim at riches, unimpeded by any law or institution that secures peculiar privileges to a favored class at the expense of another. . . .

The tendencies of democratic institutions, in reference to the rights and interests of the female sex, have been fully developed in the United States; and it is in this aspect, that the subject is one of peculiar interest to American women. In this Country, it is established, both by opinion and by practice, that women have an equal interest in all social and civil concerns; and that no domestic, civil, or political, institution, is right, that sacrifices her interest to promote that of the other sex. But in order to secure her the more firmly in all these privileges, it is decided, that, in the domestic relation, she take a subordinate station, and that, in civil and political concerns, her interests be intrusted to the other sex, without her taking any part in voting, or in making and administering laws. The result of this order of things has been fairly tested, and is thus portrayed by M. De Tocqueville,[8] a writer, who, for intelligence, fidelity, and ability, ranks second to none.

The following extracts present his views.

"There are people in Europe, who, confounding together the different characteristics of the sexes, would make of man and woman, beings not only equal, but alike. They would give to both the same functions, im-

8. The Frenchman Alexis de Tocqueville toured the United States in the early 1830s. His observations, titled *Democracy in America*, were published in 1835. Beecher's extracts are from that work.

pose on both the same duties, and grant to both the same rights. They would mix them in all things,—their business, their occupations, their pleasures. It may readily be conceived, that, by *thus* attempting to make one sex equal to the other, both are degraded; and from so preposterous a medley of the works of Nature, nothing could ever result, but weak men and disorderly women.

"It is not thus that the Americans understand the species of democratic equality, which may be established between the sexes. They admit, that, as Nature has appointed such wide differences between the physical and moral constitutions of man and woman, her manifest design was, to give a distinct employment to their various faculties; and they hold, that improvement does not consist in making beings so dissimilar do pretty nearly the same things, but in getting each of them to fulfill their respective tasks, in the best possible manner. The Americans have applied to the sexes the great principle of political economy, which governs the manufactories of our age, by carefully dividing the duties of man from those of woman. . . .

"In no country has such constant care been taken, as in America, to trace two clearly distinct lines of action for the two sexes, and to make them keep pace one with the other, but in two pathways which are always different. . . .

"If, on the one hand, an American woman cannot escape from the quiet circle of domestic employments, on the other hand, she is never forced to go beyond it. . . ."

It appears, then, that it is in America, alone, that women are raised to an equality with the other sex; and that, both in theory and practice, their interests are regarded as of equal value. They are made subordinate in station, only where a regard to their best interests demands it, while, as if in compensation for this, by custom and courtesy, they are always treated as superiors. Universally, in this Country, through every class of society, precedence is given to woman, in all the comforts, conveniences, and courtesies, of life.

In civil and political affairs, American women take no interest or concern, except so far as they sympathize with their family and personal friends; but in all cases, in which they do feel a concern, their opinions and feelings have a consideration, equal, or even superior, to that of the other sex.

In matters pertaining to the education of their children, in the selection and support of a clergyman, in all benevolent enterprises, and in all questions relating to morals or manners, they have a superior influence.

In all such concerns, it would be impossible to carry a point, contrary to their judgement and feelings; while an enterprise, sustained by them, will seldom fail of success.

If those who are bewailing themselves over the fancied wrongs and injuries of women in this Nation, could only see things as they are, they would know, that, whatever remnants of a barbarous or aristocratic age may remain in our civil institutions, in reference to the interests of women, it is only because they are ignorant of it, or do not use their influence to have them rectified; for it is very certain that there is nothing reasonable which American women would unite in asking, that would not readily be bestowed.

The preceding remarks, then, illustrate the position, that the democratic institutions of this Country are in reality no other than the principles of Christianity carried into operation, and that they tend to place woman in her true position in society, as having equal rights with the other sex; and that, in fact, they have secured to American women a lofty and fortunate position, which, as yet, has been attained by the women of no other nation. . . .

And this is the nation, which the Disposer of events designs shall go forth as the cynosure of nations. . . . To us is committed the grand, the responsible privilege, of exhibiting to the world, the beneficent influences of Christianity, when carried into every social, civil, and political institution. . . .

But the part to be enacted by American women, in this great moral enterprise, is the point to which special attention should here be directed.

The success of democratic institutions, as is conceded by all, depends upon the intellectual and moral character of the mass of the people. If they are intelligent and virtuous, democracy is a blessing; but if they are ignorant and wicked, it is only a curse, and as much more dreadful than any other form of civil government, as a thousand tyrants are more to be dreaded than one. It is equally conceded, that the formation of the moral and intellectual character of the young is committed mainly to the female hand. The mother writes the character of the future man; the sister bends the fibres that hereafter are the forest tree; the wife sways the heart, whose energies may turn for good or for evil the destinies of a nation. Let the women of a country be made virtuous and intelligent, and the men will certainly be the same. The proper education of a man decides the welfare of an individual; but educate a woman, and the interests of a whole family are secured.

If this be so, as none will deny, then to American women, more than to any others on earth, is committed the exalted privilege of extending over the world those blessed influences, that are to renovate degraded man, and "clothe all climes with beauty."

No American woman, then, has any occasion for feeling that hers is an humble or insignificant lot. The value of what an individual accomplishes, is to be estimated by the importance of the enterprise achieved, and not by the particular position of the laborer. The drops of heaven that freshen the earth are each of equal value. . . . The builders of a temple are of equal importance, whether they labor on the foundations, or toil upon the dome.

Thus, also, with those labors that are to be made effectual in the regeneration of the Earth. The woman who is rearing a family of children; the woman who labors in the schoolroom; the woman who, in her retired chamber, earns, with her needle, the mite to contribute for the intellectual and moral elevation of her country; even the humble domestic, whose example and influence may be moulding and forming young minds, while her faithful services sustain a prosperous domestic state;— each and all may be cheered by the consciousness, that they are agents in accomplishing the greatest work that ever was committed to human responsibility. It is the building of a glorious temple, whose base shall be coextensive with the bounds of the earth, whose summit shall pierce the skies, whose splendor shall beam on all lands, and those who hew the lowliest stone, as much as those who carve the highest capital, will be equally honored when its top-stone shall be laid, with new rejoicings of the morning stars, and shoutings of the sons of God.

. . . [A]s it has been shown, that American women have a loftier position, and a more elevated object of enterprise, than the females of any other nation, so it will appear, that they have greater trials and difficulties to overcome, than any other women are called to encounter. . . .

Now, the great portion of American women are the descendants of English progenitors, who, as a nation, are distinguished for systematic housekeeping, and for a great love of order, cleanliness, and comfort. And American women, to a greater or less extent, have inherited similar tastes and habits. But the prosperity and democratic tendencies of this country produce results greatly affecting the comfort of housekeepers, and which the females of monarchical and aristocratic lands are not called to meet. . . .

. . . [H]ow different is the state of things in this country. Every thing is moving and changing. Persons in poverty, are rising to opulence, and persons of wealth, are sinking to poverty. . . . [E]ven in the more stationary portions of the community, there is a mingling of all grades of wealth, intellect, and education. There are no distinct classes, as in aristocratic lands, whose bounds are protected by distinct and impassable lines, but all are thrown into promiscuous masses. . . .

In addition to this, the flow of wealth, among all classes, is constantly increasing the number of those who live in a style demanding much hired service, while the number of those, who are compelled to go to service, is constantly diminishing. Our manufactories, also, are making increased demands for female labor, and offering larger compensation. In consequence of these things, there is such a disproportion between those who wish to hire, and those who are willing to go to domestic service, that, in the non-slaveholding states, were it not for the supply of poverty-stricken foreigners, there would not be one domestic for each family who demands one. And this resort to foreigners, poor as it is, scarcely meets the demand. . . .

The difficulties and sufferings that have accrued to American women, from this cause, are almost incalculable. There is nothing, which so much demands system and regularity, as the affairs of a housekeeper, made up as they are of ten thousand desultory and minute items; and yet, this perpetually fluctuating state of society seems forever to bar any such system and regularity. The anxieties, vexations, perplexities, and even hard labor, that come upon American women, from this state of domestic service, are endless; and many a woman has, in consequence, been disheartened, discouraged, and ruined in health. . . .

No women on earth have a higher sense of their moral and religious responsibilities, or better understand, not only what is demanded of them, as housekeepers, but all the claims that rest upon them as wives, mothers, and members of a social community. An American woman, who is the mistress of a family, feels her obligations, in reference to her influence over her husband, and a still greater responsibility in rearing and educating her children. She feels, too, the claims the moral interests of her domestics have on her watchful care. In social life, she recognises the claims of hospitality, and the demands of friendly visiting. Her responsibility, in reference to the institutions of benevolence and religion, is deeply realized. The regular worship of the Lord's day, and all the various religious and benevolent societies that place so much dependence on female activity, she feels obligated to sustain, by her influence and example. Add to these multiplied responsibilities, the perplexities and evils that have been pointed out, resulting from the fluctuating state of society, and the deficiency of domestic service, and no one can deny that

American women are exposed to a far greater amount of intellectual and moral excitement, than those of any other land. . . .

Having pointed out the peculiar responsibilities of American women, and the peculiar embarrassments they are called to encounter, the following suggestions are offered, as the remedy for these difficulties.

In the first place, the physical and domestic education of daughters should occupy the principal attention of mothers. . . .

And it is to that class of mothers, who have the most means of securing hired service, and who are the most tempted to allow their daughters to grow up with inactive habits, that their country and the world must look for a reformation, in this respect. Whatever ladies in the wealthier classes decide shall be fashionable, will be followed by all the rest; while, if ladies of this class persist in the aristocratic habits, now so common, and bring up their daughters to feel as if labor was degrading and unbecoming, the evils pointed out will never find a remedy. . . .

A second method of promoting the same object, is, to raise the science and practice of domestic economy to its appropriate place, as a regular study in female seminaries. . . . But it is to the mothers in this Country, that the community must look for this change. It cannot be expected, that teachers, who have their attention chiefly absorbed by the intellectual and moral interests of their pupils, should properly realize the importance of this department of education. But if mothers generally become convinced of the importance of this measure, their judgement and wishes will meet the respectful consideration they deserve, and the thing will be done.

The third method for securing a remedy for the evils pointed out, is by means of endowed female institutions, under the care of suitable trustees, who shall secure a proper course of female education. . . .

The endowment of colleges, and of law, medical, and divinity, schools, for the other sex, is designed to secure a thorough and proper education, for those who have the most important duties of society to perform. . . . Liberal and wealthy men contribute funds, and the legislatures of the States also lend assistance, so that every State in this Nation has from one to twenty such endowed institutions . . . to carry forward a superior course of instruction . . . at an expense no greater than is required to send a boy to a common school and pay his board there. . . .

But are not the most responsible of all duties committed to the care of woman? Is it not her profession to take care of mind, body, and soul? and that, too, at the most critical of all periods of existence? And is it not as much a matter of public concern, that she should be properly qualified for her duties, as that ministers, lawyers, and physicians, should be prepared for theirs? And is it not as important to endow institutions that shall make a superior education accessible to all classes, for females, as much as for the other sex? And is it not equally important, that institutions for females be under the supervision of intelligent and responsible trustees, whose duty it shall be to secure a uniform and appropriate education for one sex as much as for the other? It would seem as if every mind must accord an affirmative reply, as soon as the matter is fairly considered. . . .

It is generally assumed, and almost as generally conceded, that women's business and cares are contracted and trivial; and that the proper discharge of her duties demands far less expansion of mind and vigor of intellect, than the pursuits of the other sex. This idea has prevailed, because women, as a mass, have never been educated with reference to their most important duties. . . . The covering of the body, the conveniences of residences, and the gratification of the appetite, have been too much regarded as the sole objects on which her intellectual powers are to be exercised.

But as society gradually shakes off the remnants of barbarism, . . . a truer estimate is formed of woman's duties. . . . Let any man of sense and discernment . . . fully comprehend all her cares, difficulties, and perplexities; and it is probable he would coincide in the opinion, that no statesman, at the head of a nation's affairs, had more frequent calls for wisdom, firmness, tact, discrimination, prudence, and versatility of talent, than such a woman.

She has a husband, whose peculiar tastes and habits she must accomodate; she has children, whose health she must guard, whose physical constitution she must study and develope, whose temper and habits she must regulate, whose principles she must form, whose pursuits she must direct. She has constantly changing domestics, with all varieties of temper and habits, whom she must govern, instruct, and direct; she is required to regulate the finances of the domestic state, and constantly to adapt expenditures to the means and to the relative claims of each department. She has the direction of the kitchen, where ignorance, forgetfulness, and awkwardness are to be so regulated, that the various operations shall each start at the right time, and all be in completeness at the same given hour. She has the claims of society to meet, calls to receive and return, and the duties of hospitality to sustain. She has the poor to relieve; benevolent societies to aid; the schools of her children to inquire and decide about; the care of the sick; the nursing of infancy; and the endless miscellany of odd items constantly recurring in a large family. . . .

[CEB *TDE*, pp. 1–6, 9–10, 12–18,
21, 26–30, 142–44]

The True Remedy for the Wrongs of Woman *(1851)*
was a response to the early stirrings of the women's
rights movement, with its call for woman suffrage.
Making the case for woman's special power as the so-
cial subordinate of man, Beecher offered a utopian vi-
sion of womanhood in the future. In True Remedy, *she*
explicitly tied the status of women to the status of fe-
male teachers, a fundamental expansion of older views
of womanhood that defined women entirely within the
family.

52   Letter III

My Dear Sister:—

The only true method of estimating the wrongs to which such multi-tudes of our sex are victims, is to bring before our minds their future condition in that perfected state of society toward which, we believe, humanity, under the guidance of Christianity, is steadily tending.

When this state is fully attained, every man and every woman will *practically* love their neighbors as themselves, and all the institutions of society will emanate from this spirit. And then all men will employ their time, and wealth, and influence, as heartily for the good of others as for themselves and their own families. Of course, all land-monopolies, and all abuse of capital, and every institution that gives undue advantages to any one class, will be known no more.

When this period arrives, every healthful, mature man will be able to sustain a family; and, saving some few exceptions, every man will have a wife. . . . [W]ith these few exceptions, all matured women will be wives, mothers, and housekeepers.

Then comes the question, "Who, in each of these families, will do the work now done by domestics, nurses, and female teachers?" Of course, men and boys will not be taken for this service from the labor appropri-ate to their sex, for there will be the same increased demand for laborers in all the appropriate business of man.

There will be no resource then but the *daughters* in each family. No doubt, at that period, there will be wonderful labor-saving inventions. The recent discovery by which we foresee how, some day, we may be enabled to kindle our fires, light our lamps, and perform our ablutions, with the same element, is a foreshadowing of the multiplied improve-ments of that coming day.

No doubt, too, there will be many wise methods, in each community, for the *division of labor*, so that those who have a taste and talent for physical employment will have such duties to perform, while gifts that indicate the nurse or the educator will be employed mainly in their appropriate sphere. Still, even then, there will be all the routine of housekeeping, nursing children, the care of the sick, and the education of the young, to be carried forward by the mothers and daughters of each family.

In this state of society, how entirely will many of our present notions and practices be reversed! *Now*, the drone of society who contributes nothing of service to the common good, but who spends the earnings of father or husband, as well as all her own time, in a mere round of self-gratification, is called "the lady," and is looked up to as the leader of society.

But *then*, those few who, having no families of their own, can be induced to lend their aid to others (wages being proportioned to the demand), must necessarily become wealthy, while their good will and favor will be especially valued. Thus, the office now filled by the domestic, the nurse, and the teacher, will become the most honorable, while those who voluntarily contribute no labor for the common good will be regarded as the dregs of society. . . .

Whenever this golden period arrives, *all women will be educated*, and, what is more, they will all be educated *for their profession*, as the conservators of the domestic state, the nurses of the sick, the guardians and developers of the human body in infancy, and the educators of the human mind. In addition to all that discipline and knowledge which tends to enlarge and develop the mental faculties, the science and practice of Domestic Economy will be thoroughly taught to every woman. And all that science which is now confined to the profession of a physician will be confided, in a certain extent, to all women; and, to the full extent, to all who are to act professionally as nurses.

And, above all, everything which tends to perfect a woman for the discharge of her grand office as the educator of mind, will be abundantly bestowed. And in that day every woman will be so profitably and so honorably employed in the appropriate duties of her peculiar profession, that the folly of enticing her into masculine employments will be deemed . . . ridiculous. . . .

With this view of the matter, we are prepared to understand *what are the real wrongs of woman*. They may all be regarded as involved under these general heads: that her profession is dishonored; that she is not educated for her profession; that in a vast majority of cases she is cut off from all employ in her true vocation; and that where it is open to her, she is drawn to it by few of those motives of honor and advantage that stimulate the other sex.

. . . In the most cultivated and influential class of society, to live so as not to perform any family work, and to be totally ignorant of both the science and practice of Domestic Economy, is not only very general, but often is boasted of as the particular claim to the character of "a lady."

Meantime, those who really are rendering the most service to society by performing these labors, are despised as the lowest class. Even the teachers of young children, as the general rule, receive poorer wages than are paid to the higher class of domestics, and are regarded as an inferior caste by those who consider themselves the nobility of society. . . .

But the grand source of the heaviest wrong that oppresses our sex is found in the fact that they are so extensively cut off from honorable and remunerative employ in their professional vocation. This is owing in part to the disgrace which is attached to the performance of the most important services of the family, and in part to the fact that, to a wide extent, men have usurped the most important department of woman's profession, and thus she has been driven to take up the relinquished employments of man.

The *training of the human mind* in the years of *infancy and childhood*—this, it is claimed, is the appropriate and highest vocation of woman. . . .

Letter XVII

My Dear Sister:

. . . On the subject of woman's rights and duties, I regard the Bible view of the case as not only the common-sense aspect, but that it is far *more favorable* to woman's increased influence and high position in social and domestic life than that of those who dissent from it.

What, then, is the *general principle* which the Bible inculcates? It is simply the common-sense rule that where there is *power*, and power that can not be successfully resisted, there men and women both, are to submit without contest. . . .

But there is another side to this subject. For while it is our duty when subject to power not to resist, it is equally taught that whenever this power passes into our hands, we may lawfully *use* it. . . . The general principle . . . is this: If you are not able to resist successfully, or to escape from any power that oppresses you, do not attempt it, but submit without repining, for it is the will of God. But as soon as you have the power, *use it.* . . .

But how is it with man and woman in the relation of the family? If there is anything to which a man has a right, it is his own earnings; and when a woman consents to be supported by him, she can not take away this right. As the general rule, therefore, man must hold the power of *physical strength* and the *power of the purse.* The Bible, then, gives this very wise and common-sense advice: If a woman chooses to put herself into the power of a man by becoming his wife, let her submit to that power and obey her husband. . . .

No woman is under obligations to marry unless she chooses to do so. . . .

. . . [W]hat is the law of the Bible to the husband? In the first place, he is to love his wife as he does himself; that is, he is to regard her wishes, enjoyment, and interests as of the same value as his own. Next, he is to *honor* his wife; and, what is better, he is to honor her *"as the weaker vessel"*—that is, he is to treat her more tenderly and guard her from evil more carefully than he would if she were his equal in position and strength. Thus, he is to give her the precedence of himself in all the enjoyments, comforts, and conveniences, of life. . . .

Neither men nor women, when talking and writing on this subject, have fully recognized what are the *Bible rights* of woman. . . .

And owing to this, some women . . . write and talk as if the great end and aim of woman was to conform to the will and wishes of husbands, to soothe all their ill humors, and to make the most of a bad bargain. . . .

The true attitude to be assumed by woman, not only in the domestic but in all our social relations, is that of an intelligent, immortal being, whose interests and rights are *every way* equal in value to that of the other sex. . . . And every woman is to *claim* this, as the right which God has conferred upon her. . . .

It is my full conviction that there is no *real* social evil to which woman is now subjected which is not fully in her power to remedy.

Is it claimed that there are civil laws which are unjust and unequal, and contrary to the Bible rights of our sex? Let every intelligent woman use her influence with the lawmakers, and in *an acceptable manner*, and these laws would speedily be changed.

Is it claimed that, in social customs, the guilty woman is treated with overbearing cruelty, and the guilty man with shameful leniency? Let all virtuous women decide that they will treat both sexes alike, and the unjust custom will speedily pass away.

Is it claimed that woman is deprived of the means of education, and of honorable and remunerative employ? There is wealth and power enough in the hands of women alone, to rectify all the evils that spring from this source.

Is it claimed that women are excluded from all offices of honor and emolument? Instead of rushing into the political arena to join in the scramble for office, or attempting to wedge into the over-crowded learned professions of man, let woman raise and dignify her own profession, and endow posts of honor and emolument in it, that are suited to the character and duties of her sex. . . .

[CEB *TR*, pp. 24–30, 32–33, 224–32]

By 1869, Catharine Beecher had passed the peak of her career. Perhaps for that reason, The American Woman's Home, *which was based upon two of her earlier works, was published jointly with her now more famous sister, Harriet Beecher Stowe.*

53 I. The Christian Family

It is the aim of this volume to elevate both the honor and the remuneration of all employments that sustain the many difficult and varied duties of the family state, and thus to render each department of woman's profession as much desired and respected as are the most honored professions of men. . . .

The distinctive feature of the family is self-sacrificing labor of the stronger and wiser members to raise the weaker and more ignorant to equal advantages. The father undergoes toil and self-denial to provide a home, and then the mother becomes a self-sacrificing laborer to train its inmates. The useless, troublesome infant is served in the humblest offices; while both parents unite in training it to an equality with themselves in every advantage. Soon the older children become helpers to raise the younger to a level with their own. When any are sick, those who are well become self-sacrificing ministers. When the parents are old and useless, the children become their self-sacrificing servants. . . .

Jesus Christ came . . . to teach by example the self-sacrifice by which the great family of man is to be raised to equality of advantages as children of God. For this end, he "humbled himself" from the highest to the lowest place. . . . And he taught that his kingdom is exactly opposite to that of the world, where all are striving for the highest positions. "Whoso will be great shall be your minister, and whoso will be chiefest shall be servant of all."

The family state then, is the aptest earthly illustration of the heavenly kingdom, and in it woman is its chief minister. Her great mission is self-denial, in training its members to self-sacrificing labors for the ignorant and weak: if not her own children, then the neglected children of her Father in heaven. She is to rear all under her care to lay up treasures, not on earth, but in heaven. All the pleasures of this life end here; but those who train immortal minds are to reap the fruit of their labor through eternal ages.

To man is appointed the out-door labor—to till the earth, dig the mines, toil in the foundries, traverse the ocean, transport merchandise, labor in manufactories, construct houses, conduct civil, municipal, and state affairs, and all the heavy work, which, most of the day, excludes him from the comforts of a home. But the great stimulus to all these toils, implanted in the heart of every true man, is the desire for a home of his own, and the hopes of paternity. . . .

The blessed privileges of the family state are not confined to those who rear children of their own. Any woman who can earn a livelihood, as every woman should be trained to do, can take a properly qualified female associate, and institute a family of her own, receiving to its heavenly influences the orphan, the sick, the homeless, and the sinful, and by motherly devotion train them to follow the self-denying example of Christ. . . .

The maxims and institutions of this world have ever been antagonistic to the teachings and example of Jesus Christ. Men toil for wealth, honor, and power, not as means for raising others to an equality with themselves, but mainly for earthly, selfish advantages. Although . . . children brought up to labor have the fairest chance for a virtuous and prosperous life, and for hope of future eternal blessedness, yet it is the aim of most parents who can do so, to lay up wealth that their children need not labor with the hands as Christ did. . . .

. . . [M]anual labor has been made dishonorable and unrefined by being forced on the ignorant and poor. Especially has the most important of all hand-labor, that which sustains the family, been thus disgraced; so that to nurse young children, and provide the food of a family by labor, is deemed the lowest of all positions in honor and profit, and the last resort of poverty. . . .

. . . It is the earnest desire of the authors of this volume to make plain the falsity of this growing popular feeling, and to show how much happier and more efficient family life will become when it is strengthened, sustained, and adorned by family work.

II. A Christian House

In the Divine Word it is written, "The wise woman buildeth her house." To be "wise," is "to choose the best means for accomplishing the best end." It has been shown that the best end for a woman to seek is the training of God's children for their eternal home, by guiding them to intelligence, virtue, and true happiness. When, therefore, the wise woman seeks a home in which to exercise this ministry, she will aim to secure a house so planned that it will provide in the best manner for health, industry, and economy, those cardinal requisites of domestic enjoyment and success. To aid in this, is the object of the following drawings and descriptions. . . . The aim will be to exhibit modes of economizing labor, time, and expenses, so as to secure health, thrift, and domestic happiness to persons of limited means, in a measure rarely attained even by those who possess wealth.

At the head of this chapter is a sketch of what may be properly called a Christian house; that is, a house contrived for the express purpose of enabling every member of a family to labor with the hands for the common good, and by modes at once healthful, economical, and tasteful.

Of course, much of the instruction conveyed in the following pages is chiefly applicable to the wants and habits of those living either in the country or in such suburban vicinities as give space of ground for healthful outdoor occupation in the family service. . . . The cultivation of flowers to ornament the table and house, of fruits and vegetables for food, of silk and cotton for clothing, and the care of horse, cow, and dairy, can be so divided that each and all of the family, some part of the day, can take exercise in the pure air, under the magnetic and healthful rays of the sun. Every head of a family should seek a soil and climate which will afford such opportunities. Railroads, enabling men toiling in cities to rear families in the country, are on this account a special blessing. . . .

Fig. 12 is an enlarged plan of the kitchen and stove-room. The chimney and stove-room are contrived to ventilate the whole house. . . .

Between the two rooms glazed sliding-doors, passing each other, serve to shut out heat and smells from the kitchen. The sides of the stove-room must be lined with shelves; those on the side by the cellar stairs, to be one foot wide, and eighteen inches apart; on the other side, shelves may be narrower, eight inches wide and nine inches apart. Boxes with lids, to receive stove utensils, must be placed near the stove.

On these shelves, and in the closet and boxes, can be placed every material used for cooking, all the table and cooking utensils, and all the articles used in house work, and yet much spare room will be left. The cook's galley in a steamship has every article and utensil used in cooking

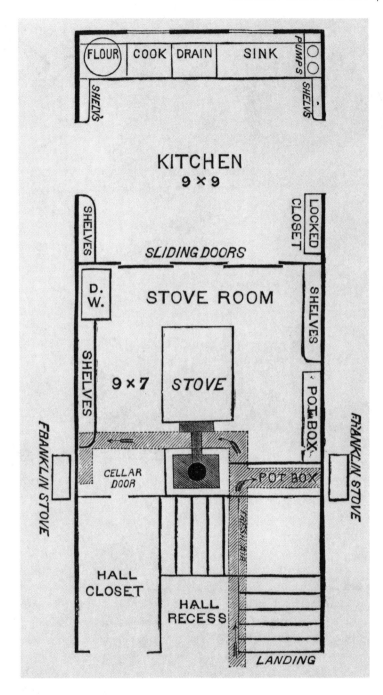

Floor plan of the kitchen.
From the first edition of *The American Woman's Home.*

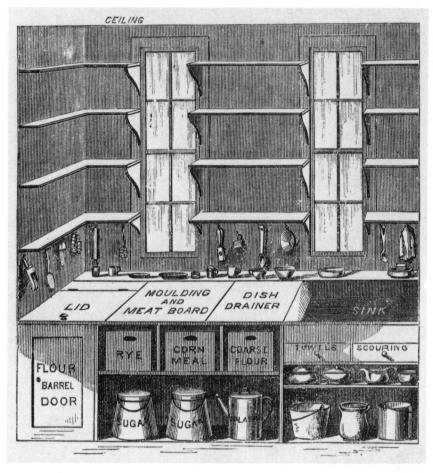

Drawing of the arrangement of the kitchen.
From the first edition of *The American Woman's Home.*

for two hundred persons, in a space not larger than this stove-room, and so arranged that with one or two steps the cook can reach all he uses. . . .

Fig. 13 is an enlarged plan of the sink and cooking-form. Two windows make a better circulation of air in warm weather, by having one open at top and the other at the bottom, while the light is better adjusted for working, in case of weak eyes.

The flour-barrel just fills the closet, which has a door for admission, and a lid to raise when used. Beside it, is the form for cooking, with a moulding-board laid on it; one side used for preparing vegetables and meat, and the other for moulding bread. The sink has two pumps, for well and for rain-water—one having a forcing power to throw water into the reservoir in the garret, which supplies the water-closet and bath-room. On the other side of the sink is the dish-drainer, with a ledge on the edge next the sink, to hold the dishes, and grooves cut to let the water drain into the sink. It has hinges, so that it can either rest on the cook-form or be turned over and cover the sink. Under the sink are shelf-boxes placed on two shelves run into grooves, with other grooves above and below, so that one may move the shelves and increase or diminish the spaces between. The shelf-boxes can be used for scouring-materials, dish-towels, and dish-cloths; also to hold bowls for bits of butter, fats, etc. Under these two shelves is room for two pails, and a jar for soap-grease.

Under the cook-form are shelves and shelf-boxes for unbolted wheat, corn-meal, rye, etc. Beneath these, for white and brown sugar, are wooden can-pails, which are the best articles in which to keep these constant necessities. Beside them is the tin molasses-can with a tight, movable cover, and a cork in the spout. This is much better than a jug for molasses, and also for vinegar and oil, being easier to clean and to handle. Other articles and implements for cooking can be arranged on or under the shelves at the side and front. A small cooking-tray, holding pepper, salt, dredging-box, knife and spoon, should stand close at hand by the stove. . . .

The articles used for setting tables are to be placed on the shelves at the front and side of the sink. Two tumbler-trays, made of pasteboard, covered with varnished fancy papers and divided by wires . . . save many steps in setting and clearing table. Similar trays . . . for knives and forks and spoons, serve the same purpose.

The sink should be three feet long and three inches deep, its width matching the cook-form. . . .

[*AWH*, pp. 17–25, 32–36]

Catharine E. Beecher, at the height
of her career, circa 1848.
Courtesy of Schlesinger Library.

Catharine E. Beecher, circa 1860.
Courtesy of Schlesinger Library.

Catharine E. Beecher, near the end
of her life, circa 1870–75.
Courtesy of Stowe-Day Foundation.

Mary Beecher Perkins, circa
1896–1900.
Courtesy of Stowe-Day Foundation.

Harriet Beecher Stowe and Calvin Stowe in the early 1850s.
Courtesy of Schlesinger Library.

Harriet Beecher Stowe, shortly before the publication of *Uncle Tom's Cabin* (*above, left*), courtesy of Schlesinger Library; Harriet Beecher Stowe in the 1870s (*above, right*) and in the front parlor of her home in Hartford, Connecticut, August 18, 1886, courtesy of Stowe-Day Foundation.

Isabella Beecher Hooker with her son
Edward, March 1863.
Courtesy of Stowe-Day Foundation.

Isabella Beecher Hooker,
circa 1873—in the midst of the
Beecher-Tilton scandal.
Courtesy of Stowe-Day Foundation.

Isabella Beecher Hooker and John Hooker on their
fiftieth wedding anniversary, 1891.
Courtesy of Stowe-Day Foundation.

Three generations: Isabella Beecher Hooker *(center)* with her daughter, Alice Hooker Day *(left)*, and her granddaughter, Katharine Seymour Day *(right)*, circa 1896–1902.
Courtesy of Stowe-Day Foundation.

154

Lyman Beecher and his children, circa 1859. *From left, top row:* Thomas, William, Edward, Charles, Henry; *bottom row:* Isabella, Catharine, Lyman, Mary, Harriet. Missing from the photograph are James Beecher and George Beecher.
Courtesy of Stowe-Day Foundation.

6.
Harriet Beecher Stowe:
"My Heart's Blood"

HARRIET BEECHER STOWE struck one note of unequivocal darkness in a letter filled with the light and shadows of her life. Writing Eliza Cabot Follen in December 1852, the "mother of seven children" mourned the death of "the most beautiful and the most loved" of her children who had been lost to cholera three years earlier. Only then, she said, had she "learned what a poor slave mother may feel when her child is torn away from her." She recalled that her prayer had been "that such anguish might not be suffered in vain."[1] That anguish informed and made powerful Stowe's signal contribution to the antislavery movement. Although the landscape of *Uncle Tom's Cabin* is littered with slavery's victims, none is more charged with significance than the "poor slave mother," none more invested with "anguish." Threatened with separation from her son, the "soft and timid" Eliza cries, "They have sold you! but your mother will save you yet!" Eliza succeeds, but other mothers are unable to prevent the ultimate loss. Told that her infant has been sold, Lucy is silent. "The shot," Stowe informs her readers, "had passed too straight and direct through the heart, for cry or tear." Just as silently, Lucy drowns herself. Having already lost a son and a daughter, Cassy is forced to become the agent of her own grief: "I had made up my mind,—yes, I had. I would never again let a child live to grow up!" She gives her third child laudanum and watches as "he slept to death."[2]

Although Stowe's opposition to slavery was galvanized by the institution's impact upon the family, there were other sources that influenced both her posture and her expression of it in *Uncle Tom's Cabin*. The most immediate was the body of legislation known as the Compromise of 1850, which included the Fugitive Slave Act, a more stringent law mandating the forcible seizure and rendition of slaves who had fled the South. Legally required to provide assistance in the pursuit of slaves, Northerners found themselves more deeply implicated in the institution. Compliance constituted support of slavery, defiance made one subject to fines and imprisonment. Whatever the response, it became less and less tenable to define slavery solely as a Southern institution. Highly publicized incidents in which fugitive slaves were captured in cities such as Boston and returned South made neutrality about slavery all the more difficult.

Enroute to Brunswick, Maine during the spring of 1850, Harriet spent a week with each of three siblings, visiting Mary in Hartford, Henry in Brooklyn, and Edward in Boston at the end of the journey. Already committed abolitionists, Edward and his wife Isabella proved instrumental in rallying Harriet. Denouncing the Compromise then being debated in Congress, Edward and Isabella did nothing to disguise their revulsion at the prospect of the Fugitive Slave Act. Harriet's initial response recalled her behavior during her earlier—and only—exposure to plantation slavery. She listened carefully, and remained silent. After passage of the Compromise of 1850, Edward and Isabella sought to persuade others to join them in opposition. Their different approaches reflected the separate spheres in which their lives were led. In standing before his congregation and excoriating the Compromise, Edward the clergyman addressed the public. Isabella chose the private and more personal letter as her vehicle, but the plea was nonetheless impassioned. To her sister-in-law she wrote: "Hattie, if I could use a pen as you can, I would write something that will make this whole nation feel what an accursed thing slavery is."[3] Stowe's children, with whom she had shared Isabella's letter, recalled that their mother vowed, "I will write something. I will if I live."[4] Eventually, Harriet combined Edward's and Isabella's approaches, offering the public a critique that made her readers confront slavery's deeply personal impact upon the family.

Initially, however, Stowe had little idea what she would actually do. She had never before written a novel, nor had she envisioned undertaking such an enterprise. Nonetheless, her tales and sketches had been appearing in magazines for more than fifteen years, and most recently four of them had been published in Gamaliel Bailey's *National Era*. The antislavery weekly was an obvious vehicle, the tale or sketch an equally obvious approach. In a letter to Bailey on March 9, 1851, Stowe proposed "a story which will be a much longer one than any I have ever written," adding that the "thing may extend through three or four numbers." But if Stowe had not yet decided upon the length of her story, she was most definite about her subject and her reasons for undertaking it. In describing her focus on slavery, she told Bailey that until that year she had "always felt that I had no particular call to meddle with this subject." Nevertheless, she said, "the time is come when even a woman or a child who can speak a word for freedom and humanity is bound to speak." She compared herself to the Carthagenian women who "had cut off their hair for bow-strings to give to the defenders of their country" and declared her willingness to do likewise. Her pen would be the means, her contribution a portrait: "My vocation is simply that of *painter*, and my object will be to hold up in the most lifelike and graphic manner possible Slavery."[5]

As the number of weekly installments mounted beyond the three or four originally envisioned by Stowe, so too did the occasions that Bailey had to tell expectant readers that " 'Uncle Tom's Cabin' reached us at too late an hour for insertion this week." Just as she had done before, the "literary woman" sought to meet the obligations both to her family and to her rapidly increasing public. Still, the demands of domesticity continued uninterrupted and she accorded them more importance than her first novel. Immersed in his professorship at Bowdoin College, Calvin provided little aid. But Catharine was present as well. Having joined the household, the mentor combined forces once again with her former apprentice to establish a small school. Writing to father Lyman and brother Henry two months after her novel began appearing in the pages of the *Era*, Harriet informed them that Catharine "has agreed to give me a year of her time to act conjointly with me."[6] The two sisters also forged a second collaboration designed to provide some relief for the harried author. Although there was a practical division of labor, "conjointly" would again have been an apt description. Essentially, Catharine assumed responsibility for the domestic demands to enable Harriet to pursue the literary. Nonetheless, Catharine had to intervene to insure that the division was maintained. Telling their sister Mary that she had begun sending both husband and wife to Calvin's study at the college, she said of Harriet that "there was no other way to keep her out of family cares and quietly at work." Catharine added, "I am trying to get Uncle Tom out of the way" before the beginning of winter.[7]

But Harriet, Uncle Tom's creator, had miscalculated for a second time. Two days before Catharine sent her letter to Mary, the *National Era* issued the sixteenth of the forty-four chapters published in the weekly. Little Eva had been introduced only two weeks earlier; Eliza's future remained unsettled; and Tom had yet to be sold to Simon Legree. Still, the author had come to recognize that she was indeed engaged in a novel. And Catharine had come to recognize that she should begin to negotiate its publication. Convinced that she should serve as Harriet's intermediary, Catharine offered her sister's novel to the publishers of her own recently issued *True Remedy for the Wrongs of Women*. Despite

Catharine's efforts, the partners of Boston's Phillips, Sampson and Company believed that an antislavery novel, especially one written by a woman, had too limited an appeal. But Jewett and Company, a smaller firm in Boston, informally agreed to publish *Uncle Tom's Cabin*. Shortly before publication on March 15, 1852, the negotiations were concluded and the contract was signed with John P. Jewett. Displeased that the contract gave her sister only 10 percent of the profits, Catharine thought to intervene again, threatening to denounce Jewett in print.[8] However, family members, including Lyman, rallied to dissuade her. Ironically, Phillips, Sampson, and Company bought Jewett's rights two years later. Eager to capitalize on the popularity they had doubted earlier, they urged Stowe to begin another antislavery novel, and she subsequently published *Dred* in 1856.

Advertised by John P. Jewett as "The Greatest Book of Its Kind Ever Issued from the American Press," *Uncle Tom's Cabin* generated a polarized reaction from critics. Depending upon how the "American"—whether a Northerner or a Southerner—defined the "Kind" of book authored by Stowe, the varying responses highlighted the increasing tensions in an already divided nation. The *North American Review* contradicted itself with every breath, first praising the novel as "a work of genius," then demurring that *Uncle Tom's Cabin* "has defects of conception and style, exhibits a want of artistic skill, is often tame and inadequate in description, and is tinctured with methodistic cant," and finally granting that "thought, imagination, feeling, high moral and religious sentiment, and dramatic power shine in every page." Yes, the magazine concluded, there was genius—but "by no means [of] the highest order." If, then, the novel's genius was flawed, the *Review* asked: why had it generated such an impact? Noting the obvious, that Stowe's treatment of slavery was central to *Uncle Tom's Cabin*, the *Review* concluded that its popularity derived from "its foundation in truth."[9]

Putnam's Monthly Magazine, which in contrast considered *Uncle Tom's Cabin* a "nearly perfect work of art," also addressed the issue of its acclaim. Fascinated by its success, the magazine sought to explain why Harriet Beecher Stowe had become "as familiar a name in all parts of the civilized world as that of Homer and Shakespeare." The novel succeeded, *Putnam's* declared, "not because it is a tale of slavery"; rather, it was "the consummate art of the storyteller that has given popularity to Uncle Tom's Cabin and nothing else." Moreover, Stowe's sentiments on slavery, sentiments "obtruded by the author in her own person," constituted the novel's sole defect. Fortunately, however, the interpolations could easily be removed if only Stowe would "permit some judicious friend to run his pen through these excrescences."[10] In an approach that was as facile as it was mistaken, the magazine detached sentiments from subject and regarded the interpolations separately from the narrative, in effect misreading the visionary genius of the novel.

Ironically, the *Southern Literary Messenger* was more perceptive. Not only did its editors recognize that Stowe's passion deeply informed her subject, they also understood that her interpolations infused her narrative. Not surprisingly, however, they found both the substance of the narrative and the technique repugnant. The object of fiction, declared the editors of the *Messenger*, was communication of truth, and they forthwith named *Uncle Tom's Cabin* a "most reprehensible" perversion: "It is a fiction, not for the sake of more effectually communicating truth; but for the purpose of more effectually disseminating a slander." What was truth for one was slander for another. The *Messenger* also disagreed with *Putnam's* explanation for the novel's popularity, stating that "the frenzy of fanaticism and the fever of political intrigue, have all conspired to give a popularity and currency to the work." As "loathesome" as the novel was, the magazine undertook its critique with some hesitation "in consideration of its being the effusion of one of that sex, whose natural position entitles them to all forbearance and courtesy."[11] The *Southern Quarterly Review* had no such qualms. Stowe's "foul imagination," her "malignant bitterness," had produced a novel "whose touch contaminates with its filth." Having exhibited no forbearance and little courtesy, the *Southern Quarterly* spent the next twenty pages mocking characterization, dialogue, and plot. Its conclusion was predictable: "Mrs. Stowe's" portrayal was "revolting at once to decency, truth, and probability."[12]

In its critique of *Uncle Tom's Cabin*, the *Southern Literary Messenger* had declared that Stowe, the woman, had deliberately stepped "beyond the hallowed precincts—the enchanted circle—which encompass her with a halo of divinity."[13] However much the *Messenger* and the "literary woman" disagreed about slavery, both subscribed to the ideology mandating distinctly separate spheres for women and men. But, ironically, it was this very allegiance that had propelled Stowe beyond the hallowed precinct and led to her indictment of practices and values in the worldly arena of males. Precisely because she was a woman with a deep identification with motherhood, Stowe believed it her responsibility to expose slavery's impact upon the family. Through the pages of *Uncle Tom's Cabin*, she wove the threads of an evolving ideology of domesticity that conceived of the wife and mother as the moral and spiritual leader of the home. Exemplar and inculcator of the values that ought to govern public as well as private spheres, the wife and mother defended the sanctity of the family and sought to transform the world beyond. Slavery, however, made a mockery of this idealized conception of woman's role in the family. Marriages could be ended at a moment, mothers could be separated forever from their children. In locating womanhood's greatest power in motherhood, Stowe used her ideology of domesticity to provide the context for her portrayal of slavery's greatest threat: separation of the mother from her child.

In the ninth chapter of the novel, the cherished ideal is set alongside the ugly reality. The idealized portrait of the Birds is juxtaposed against the plight of Eliza and her child. Returning from a session of Ohio's legislature, John Bird enters a "cosey parlor" and removes his boots "preparatory to inserting his feet in a pair of new handsome slippers, which his wife had been working for him while away on his senatorial tour." His wife prepares their tea, "ever and anon mingling admonitory remarks to a number of frolicsome juveniles." This image of an orderly, harmonious, and secure home created and sustained by a mother is in marked contrast to the predicament of a slave mother upon her arrival at the Birds: Eliza "with garments torn and frozen, with one shoe gone, and the stocking torn away from the cut and bleeding foot, was laid back in a deadly swoon upon two chairs." After opening her eyes, the mother's immediate thought is of her child: "O my Harry! Have they got him?"[14]

The same ideology that informs Stowe's portraits of two families demarcates the boundaries of the domains within which wife and husband fulfill their responsibilities. Mary's "husband and children were her entire world, and in these she ruled more by entreaty and persuasion than by command and argument." Hers is also a world distinctly separate from John's, and only rarely does she trouble "her head with what was going on in the house of the state, very wisely considering that she had enough to do to mind her own." However, the passage of legislation requiring that Ohio's residents aid in the search for fugitive slaves leads Mary to cross those boundaries. Astonished both that such a "shameful, wicked, abominable law" could be passed and that her husband could support it, Mary declares, "I'll break it, for one, the first time I get a chance; and I hope I *shall* have a chance, I do!"[15] She stands ready to deny the social and legal basis of male authority. Ironically, she must leave her sphere in order to defend it against the violations of a world that treats human beings as property.

During the ensuing exchange between wife and husband, Stowe employs nineteenth-century premises about differences in the nature of woman and man, aligning Mary with the heart and John with the head.

From the outset, it is readily apparent that the author also aligns herself with the heart as the superior guide. John tells Mary, "We mustn't suffer our feelings to run away with our judgment" and informs her, "It's not a matter of private feeling,—there are great public interests involved." But Mary immediately rejects John's abstract and impersonal defense and forces her husband to confront the issue on more palpable and human terms: "I put it to you, John,—would *you* turn away a poor, shivering, hungry creature from your door, because he was a runaway?" John's position is all the weaker because he rests his defense upon the secular, Mary the sacred. The law, he says, demands that we "put aside our private feelings." Mary dismisses his appeal to authority as "politics" and his "reasoning" as typical of the "way you political folks have of coming round and round a plain right thing." Mary reminds her husband that there is a higher authority requiring their obedience: "I can read my Bible; there I see I must feed the hungry, clothe the naked, and comfort the desolate; and that Bible I mean to follow."[16]

Throughout this matrimonial debate in which Stowe skillfully plays upon her readers' sensibilities, she also demonstrates her conviction that womanhood entails a power different from that wielded by men. Stated succinctly, it is indirect agency, the "entreaty and persuasion" that Stowe has already ascribed to Mary. Armed with intuition as her guide and Scripture as her source, Mary attempts to persuade her husband. It is influence that she wields, and it is the same influence that induces John to open his heart. As Mary tells him, "your heart is better than your head," at least in this matter. However, neither entreaty nor persuasion suffices for Eliza. This mother must challenge the institution that treats her and her son as property and threatens their separation. Yet she too acts upon the principles embedded in her heart and reinforced by Scripture. Having fled with her son, Eliza tells the Birds, "The Lord helped me; nobody knows how much the Lord can help 'em, till they try."[17] Both Mary and Eliza rely upon an authority higher than that mandated by men such as John Bird. Equally significant, they are willing to challenge male authority, be it clothed in a law remanding slaves to their masters or a system shattering the ties of family. By insisting that human beings cannot be treated as chattel and thereby denying the very premise that undergirded slavery, they stand as subversives. Their defiance takes the form of civil disobedience.

Just as Mary and Eliza challenge the social and legal boundaries of their society, so they cross the nineteenth-century barrier separating free from enslaved, white from black. Motherhood, the central element in Stowe's ideology of domesticity, is portrayed as the bond uniting women regardless of condition or race. Providing Eliza and Mary with a solidarity women alone can experience, the meaning and significance of motherhood are illustrated in their relationship. The first exchange between the Birds and Eliza highlights a bond presumed to be immediate and lasting. Turning to Mary rather than John, Eliza pleads for her son and herself, "Do protect us! don't let them get him!" Mary responds that in this home "Nobody shall hurt you." The second and decisive exchange occurs after John's questions have established that Eliza's slave master had been kind, her slave mistress equally so. Why then did she flee? John asks. Turning yet again to Mary, Eliza says, "Have you ever lost a child?" There remains only a final exchange between the mothers, this one unspoken. Shortly before Eliza's departure with her son Harry, Mary prepares a bundle of clothing for Harry that includes the coats, aprons, and stockings of *her* lost child. Asked by her own sons how she can part with them, Mary says, "I give them to a mother more heartbroken and sorrowful than I am; and I hope God will send his blessings with them."[18]

Harriet Beecher Stowe had concluded *Uncle Tom's Cabin* with an impassioned plea that the mothers of the nation—"you, who have learned, by the cradles of your own children, to love and feel for all mankind"—try to intervene against the injustices of slavery.[19] Two years later, she addressed them again in response to another congressional debate on slavery. Stowe's "Appeal to the Women of the Free States" spoke in a litany of questions to the most recent issue: "Are we willing to receive slavery into the free States and territories of the Union? Shall the whole power of these United States go into the hands of slavery?" Obviously not, yet such was possible because the newly proposed legislation entailed repeal of the Missouri Compromise, which had prohibited slavery north of Missouri's southern border. Charging that there was not a "mother among us all, who clasps her child to her breast, who could ever be made to feel it right that that child should be slave," Stowe continued to appeal to the bond that supposedly transcended race or class. She also stated explicitly that which had been implicit in her characterization of Mary and John Bird. Women were indeed different from men. The latter's perceptions might be obscured by "ambition and the love of political power," but God had endowed women with a "knowledge, in those holier feelings, which are peculiar to womanhood, and which guard the sacredness of the family state." In directing her "Appeal" to women, Stowe called upon those excluded from participation in the political process that elected officials and debated legislation. The means she could offer were inevitably fewer and less direct than those available to the enfranchised male. Nonetheless, she exhorted women to fulfill their duty "as mother, wife, sister, or member of society." Denied the exercise of direct political power, a woman was still "bound to give her influence on the right side."[20] Unlike her sister Catharine, Stowe included petitioning Congress within the scope of female "influence." Women's relation to others as mothers, wives, and sisters imposed the obligation, petitions provided the indirect agency. Like so much else in her experience and her prose, the "literary woman's" perception of slavery and antislavery was filtered through the prism of women's responsibilities to those constituting her family. Therein lay the power of womanhood *and* its boundaries.

NOTES

1. Harriet Beecher Stowe to Eliza Cabot Follen, December 16, 1852, Massachusetts Historical Society, Boston, Mass. E. Bruce Kirkham has noted that three other versions of this letter are deposited with Houghton Library, Harvard University; Vassar College Library; and Doctor Williams Library, London, England. See Kirkham's meticulously researched *The Building of Uncle Tom's Cabin* (Knoxville: The University of Tennessee Press, 1977). An excerpt from the letter is printed in Document 55.

2. Harriet Beecher Stowe, *Uncle Tom's Cabin; or Life Among the Lowly,* 2 vols. (Boston: John P. Jewett and Co., 1852), 1:60, 190; 2:210.

3. Isabella Jones Beecher to Harriet Beecher Stowe, undated, in Charles Edward Stowe, *Life of Harriet Beecher Stowe* (Boston: Houghton Mifflin and Co., 1889), p. 145.

4. *LHBS,* p. 145. Stowe's initial challenge appeared shortly before the passage of the Compromise of 1850. Published by *The National Era* in its issue of August 1, 1850, "The Freeman's Dream: A Parable" was the first of her contributions to the antislavery weekly. It is possible that Isabella Jones Beecher was explicitly referring to this story in her letter to Stowe. However, the letter is undated. Stowe also acknowledged the impact of the Fugitive Slave Act in her "Concluding Remarks" to *UTC,* 2:310–22.

5. Harriet Beecher Stowe to Gamaliel Bailey, March 9, 1851, in Forrest Wilson, *Crusader in Crinoline: The Life of Harriet Beecher Stowe* (Westport, Conn.: Greenwood Press, 1972), pp. 259–60.

6. Harriet Beecher Stowe to Lyman and Henry Ward Beecher, September 19, 1851, SML. In a later letter written to Catharine, Harriet detailed the investment each of them had made in the school. See excerpts from both of these letters in Documents 107 and 109.

7. Catharine Beecher to Mary Beecher Perkins, September 27, 1851, SML. See Document 108.

8. The tangled history of the negotiations with John P. Jewett is described in Kirkham's *Building of Uncle Tom's Cabin*, pp. 140–49. Isabella Beecher Hooker and Mary Beecher Perkins both commented on sister Catharine's threatened intervention in private correspondence. See excerpts from their letters in Documents 110 and 111.

9. "Review of *Uncle Tom's Cabin*," *North American Review* 77 (October 1853): 467, 468, 470. Thomas F. Gossett's recent study has persuasively analyzed the popular and scholarly reactions to *Uncle Tom's Cabin* in both the nineteenth and twentieth centuries. See his *Uncle Tom's Cabin and American Culture* (Dallas: Southern Methodist University Press, 1985).

10. "Uncle Tomitudes," *Putnam's Monthly Magazine* 1 (January 1853): 100, 98, 100.

11. "Review of *Uncle Tom's Cabin*," *Southern Literary Messenger* 18 (December 1852): 721, 722, 723, 721.

12. "*Uncle Tom's Cabin*," *Southern Quarterly Review* 23 (January 1853): 81–82, 104.

13. "Review of *Uncle Tom's Cabin*," *Southern Literary Messenger*, p. 722.

14. HBS *UTC*, 1:118, 123, 124. See Document 54. Recent feminist scholarship has demonstrated both the complexity of *Uncle Tom's Cabin* and its centrality to an understanding of nineteenth-century American culture. Scholars have sought as well to extrapolate from the novel Stowe's definition of female power. Basing her analysis almost entirely upon the character of little Eva, Ann Douglas has argued that the novel exemplifies a sentimentalism that left women powerless and legitimated an oppressive status quo. Douglas's interpretation has been countered by Jane Tompkins's emphasis upon Stowe's presentation of a matriarchal ideal in her portrayal of Rachel Halliday and the Quaker settlement. Noting that *Uncle Tom's Cabin* presents a cultural alternative to the marketplace and the masculine values of capitalism, Tompkins has stressed that Stowe portrays the home as the very center of a social and economic order in which distinctively female values are upheld by women and men alike. Building upon Tompkins's innovative analysis, Gillian Brown has suggested that Stowe's opposition to slavery is rooted in the conviction that the institution erases the distinction between the home and marketplace and contaminates the family, whether slave or free. *Uncle Tom's Cabin*, Brown also argues, demands that domestic ideology be reformed and freed from any complicity with the marketplace. Elizabeth Ammons's particularly suggestive interpretation stresses that Stowe transforms a relatively conservative concept of femininity into a fundamental challenge to patriarchy. Feminine, and especially maternal, values are substituted for masculine ones, and mothers become the models for emulation by both sexes. See Ann Douglas, *The Feminization of American Culture* (New York: Alfred A. Knopf, 1977); Jane Tompkins, "Sentimental Power: Uncle Tom's Cabin and the Politics of Literary History," *Glyph* 8: 79–101; Jane Tompkins, *Sensational Designs: The Cultural Work of American Fiction, 1790–1860* (New York: Oxford University Press, 1985), pp. 122–146; Gillian Brown, "Getting in the Kitchen with Dinah:

Domestic Politics in *Uncle Tom's Cabin*," *American Quarterly* 36 (Fall 1984): 503–23; and Elizabeth Ammons, "Heroines in *Uncle Tom's Cabin*," *American Literature* 49 (May 1977): 161–79.

15. HBS *UTC*, 1:120, 119, 121.

16. Ibid., 1:121, 121–22, 121, 122–23, 121.

17. Ibid., 1:131, 126.

18. Ibid., 1:124, 127, 132.

19. Ibid., 2:316.

20. Harriet Beecher Stowe, "An Appeal to the Women of the Free States," *Independent* 6 (February 23, 1854): 57. See Document 56.

Entitled "In Which It Appears That a Senator Is But a Man," the excerpt from chapter 9 of Uncle Tom's Cabin *is set in the home of Senator John Bird, a member of Ohio's legislature, and his wife, Mary. With the unexpected arrival of Eliza, who has fled with her son Harry, John and Mary are forced to confront the implications of both slavery and a recently enacted Fugitive Slave Law. If they obey the law, which the senator has supported, the relationship between mother and child will be severed and both returned to slavery. But the Birds, as presented by Stowe, have another choice: if they engage in civil disobedience, Eliza and Harry can continue the journey that will eventually unite the family and bring them freedom in Canada. Eliza's plea, Mary's position, and the latter's influence upon John constitute basic elements in Stowe's perspective on womanhood's power.*

54   The light of the cheerful fire shone on the rug and carpet of a cosey parlor, and glittered on the sides of the tea-cups and well-brightened tea-pot, as Senator Bird was drawing off his boots, preparatory to inserting his feet in a pair of new handsome slippers, which his wife had been working for him while away on his senatorial tour. Mrs. Bird, looking the very picture of delight, was superintending the arrangements of the table, ever and anon mingling admonitory remarks to a number of frolicsome juveniles, who were effervescing in all those modes of untold gambol and mischief that have astonished mothers ever since the flood.

"Tom, let the door-knob alone,—there's a man! Mary! Mary! don't pull the cat's tail,—poor pussy! Jim, you mustn't climb on that table,—no, no!—You don't know, my dear, what a surprise it is to us all, to see you here to-night!" said she, at last, when she found a space to say something to her husband.

"Yes, yes, I thought I'd just make a run down, spend the night, and have a little comfort at home. I'm tired to death, and my head aches!"

Mrs. Bird cast a glance at the camphor-bottle, which stood in the half-open closet, and appeared to meditate an approach to it, but her husband interposed.

UNCLE TOM'S CABIN;

OR,

LIFE AMONG THE LOWLY.

BY

HARRIET BEECHER STOWE.

VOL. I.

BOSTON:
JOHN P. JEWETT & COMPANY.
CLEVELAND, OHIO:
JEWETT, PROCTOR & WORTHINGTON.
1852.

Frontispiece from the first edition of *Uncle Tom's Cabin*.
Courtesy of Special Collections, Dartmouth College.

"No, no, Mary, no doctoring! a cup of your good hot tea, and some of our good home living, is what I want. It's a tiresome business, this legislating!"

And the senator smiled, as if he rather liked the idea of considering himself a sacrifice to his country.

"Well," said his wife, after the business of the tea-table was getting rather slack, "and what have they been doing in the Senate?"

Now, it was a very unusual thing for gentle little Mrs. Bird ever to trouble her head with what was going on in the house of the state, very wisely considering that she had enough to do to mind her own. Mr. Bird, therefore, opened his eyes in surprise, and said,

"Not very much of importance."

"Well; but is it true that they have been passing a law forbidding people to give meat and drink to those poor colored folks that come along? I heard they were talking of some such law, but I didn't think any Christian legislature would pass it!"

"Why, Mary, you are getting to be a politician, all at once."

"No, nonsense! I wouldn't give a fip for all your politics, generally, but I think this is something downright cruel and unchristian. I hope, my dear, no such law has been passed."

"There has been a law passed forbidding people to help off the slaves that come over from Kentucky, my dear; so much of that thing has been done by these reckless Abolitionists, that our brethren in Kentucky are very strongly excited, and it seems necessary, and no more than Christian and kind, that something should be done by our state to quiet the excitement."

"And what is the law? It don't forbid us to shelter these poor creatures a night, does it, and to give 'em something comfortable to eat, and a few old clothes, and send them quietly about their business?"

"Why, yes, my dear; that would be aiding and abetting, you know."

Mrs. Bird was a timid, blushing little woman, of about four feet in height, and with mild blue eyes, and a peach-blow complexion, and the gentlest, sweetest voice in the world;—as for courage, a moderate-sized cock-turkey had been known to put her to rout at the very first gobble, and a stout house-dog, of moderate capacity, would bring her into subjection merely by a show of his teeth. Her husband and children were her entire world, and in these she ruled more by entreaty and persuasion than by command or argument. There was only one thing that was capable of arousing her, and that provocation came in on the side of her unusually gentle and sympathetic nature;—anything in the shape of cruelty would throw her into a passion, which was the more alarming and inexplicable in proportion to the general softness of her nature. Generally the most indulgent and easy to be entreated of all mothers, still her boys had a very reverent remembrance of a most vehement chastisement she once bestowed on them, because she found them leagued with several graceless boys of the neighborhood, stoning a defenseless kitten.

"I'll tell you what," Master Bill used to say, "I was scared that time. Mother came at me so that I thought she was crazy, and I was whipped and tumbled off to bed, without any supper, before I could get over wondering what had come about; and, after that, I heard mother crying outside the door, which made me feel worse than all the rest. I'll tell you what," he'd say, "we boys never stoned another kitten!"

On the present occasion, Mrs. Bird rose quickly, with very red cheeks, which quite improved her general appearance, and walked up to her husband, with quite a resolute air, and said, in a determined tone,

"Now, John, I want to know if you think such a law as that is right and Christian?"

"You won't shoot me, now, Mary, if I say I do!"

"I never could have thought it of you, John; you didn't vote for it?"

"Even so, my fair politician."

"You ought to be ashamed, John! Poor, homeless, houseless creatures! It's a shameful, wicked, abominable law, and I'll break it, for one, the first time I get a chance; and I hope I *shall* have a chance, I do! Things have got to a pretty pass, if a woman can't give a warm supper and a bed to poor, starving creatures, just because they are slaves, and have been abused and oppressed all their lives, poor things!"

"But Mary, just listen to me. Your feelings are all quite right, dear, and interesting, and I love you for them; but, then, dear, we mustn't suffer our feelings to run away with our judgment; you must consider it's not a matter of private feeling,—there are great public interests involved,—there is such a state of public agitation rising, that we must put aside our private feelings."

"Now, John, I don't know anything about politics, but I can read my Bible; and there I see that I must feed the hungry, clothe the naked, and comfort the desolate; and that Bible I mean to follow."

"But in cases where your doing so would involve a great public evil—"

"Obeying God never brings on public evils. I know it can't. It's always safest, all round, to *do as He* bids us."

"Now listen to me, Mary, and I can state to you a very clear argument, to show—"

"O, nonsense, John! you can talk all night, but you wouldn't do it. I put it to you, John,—would *you* now turn away a poor, shivering, hungry creature from your door, because he was a runaway? *Would* you, now?"

Now, if the truth must be told, our senator had the misfortune to be a man who had a particularly humane and accessible nature, and turning away anybody that was in trouble never had been his forte; and what was worse for him in this particular pinch of the argument was, that his wife knew it, and, of course, was making an assault on rather an indefensible point. So he had recourse to the usual means of gaining time for such cases made and provided; he said "ahem," and coughed several times, took out his pocket-handkerchief, and began to wipe his glasses. Mrs. Bird, seeing the defenseless condition of the enemy's territory, had no more conscience than to push her advantage.

"I should like to see you doing that, John—I really should! Turning a woman out of doors in a snow-storm, for instance; or, may be you'd take her up and put her in jail, wouldn't you? You would make a great hand at that!"

"Of course, it would be a very painful duty," began Mr. Bird, in a moderate tone.

"Duty, John! don't use that word! You know it isn't a duty—it can't be a duty! If folks want to keep their slaves from running away, let 'em treat 'em well,—that's my doctrine. If I had slaves (as I hope I never shall have), I'd risk their wanting to run away from me, or you either, John. I tell you folks don't run away when they are happy; and when they do run, poor creatures! they suffer enough with cold and hunger and fear, without everybody's turning against them; and, law or no law, I never will, so help me God!"

"Mary! Mary! My dear, let me reason with you."

"I hate reasoning, John,—especially on such subjects. There's a way you political folks have of coming round and round a plain right thing; and you don't believe in it yourselves, when it comes to practice. I know *you* well enough, John. You don't believe it's right any more than I do; and you wouldn't do it any sooner than I."

At this critical juncture, old Cudjoe, the black man-of-all-work, put his head in at the door, and wished "Missis would come into the kitchen;" and our senator, tolerably relieved, looked after his little wife with a whimsical mixture of amusement and vexation, and, seating himself in the arm-chair, began to read the papers.

After a moment, his wife's voice was heard at the door, in a quick, earnest tone,—"John! John! I do wish you'd come here, a moment."

He laid down his paper, and went into the kitchen, and started, quite amazed at the sight that presented itself:—A young and slender woman, with garments torn and frozen, with one shoe gone, and the stocking torn away from the cut and bleeding foot, was laid back in a deadly swoon upon two chairs. There was the impress of the despised race on her face, yet none could help feeling its mournful and pathetic beauty, while its stony sharpness, its cold, fixed, deathly aspect, struck a solemn chill over him. He drew his breath short, and stood in silence. His wife, and their only colored domestic, old Aunt Dinah, were busily engaged in restorative measures; while old Cudjoe had got the boy on his knee, and was busy pulling off his shoes and stockings, and chafing his little cold feet.

"Sure, now, if she an't a sight to behold!" said old Dinah, compassionately; "'pears like 't was the heat that made her faint. She was tol'able peart when she cum in, and asked if she couldn't warm herself here a spell; and I was just a askin' her where she cum from, and she fainted right down. Never done much hard work, guess, by the looks of her hands."

"Poor creature!" said Mrs. Bird, compassionately, as the woman slowly unclosed her large, dark eyes, and looked vacantly at her. Suddenly an expression of agony crossed her face, and she sprang up, saying, "O, my Harry! Have they got him?"

The boy, at this, jumped from Cudjoe's knee, and, running to her side, put up his arms. "O, he's here! he's here!" she exclaimed.

"O, ma'am!" said she, wildly, to Mrs. Bird, "do protect us! don't let them get him!"

"Nobody shall hurt you here, poor woman," said Mrs. Bird, encouragingly. "You are safe; don't be afraid."

"God bless you!" said the woman, covering her face and sobbing; while the little boy, seeing her crying, tried to get into her lap.

With many gentle and womanly offices, which none knew better how to render than Mrs. Bird, the poor woman was, in time, rendered more calm. A temporary bed was provided for her on the settle, near the fire; and, after a short time, she fell into a heavy slumber, with the child, who seemed no less weary, soundly sleeping on her arm; for the mother resisted, with nervous anxiety, the kindest attempts to take him from her; and, even in sleep, her arm encircled him with an unrelaxing clasp, as if she could not even then be beguiled of her vigilant hold.

Mr. and Mrs. Bird had gone back to the parlor, where, strange as it may appear, no reference was made, on either side, to the preceding conversation; but Mrs. Bird busied herself with her knitting-work, and Mr. Bird pretended to be reading the paper.

"I wonder who and what she is!" said Mr. Bird, at last, as he laid it down.

"When she wakes up and feels a little rested, we will see," said Mrs. Bird.

"I say, wife!" said Mr. Bird, after musing in silence over his newspaper.

"Well, dear!"

"She couldn't wear one of your gowns, could she, by any letting down, or such matter? She seems to be rather larger than you are."

A quite perceptible smile glimmered on Mrs. Bird's face, as she answered, "We'll see."

Another pause, and Mr. Bird again broke out,

"I say, wife!"

"Well! What now?"

"Why, there's that old bombazin cloak, that you keep on purpose to put over me when I take my afternoon's nap; you might as well give her that,—she needs clothes."

At this instant, Dinah looked in to say that the woman was awake, and wanted to see Missis.

Mr. and Mrs. Bird went into the kitchen, followed by the two eldest boys, the smaller fry having, by this time, been safely disposed of in bed.

The woman was now sitting up on the settle, by the fire. She was looking steadily into the blaze, with a calm, heartbroken expression, very different from her former agitated wildness.

"Did you want me?" said Mrs. Bird, in gentle tones. "I hope you feel better now, poor woman!"

A long-drawn, shivering sigh was the only answer; but she lifted her dark eyes, and fixed them on her with such a forlorn and imploring expression, that the tears came into the little woman's eyes.

"You needn't be afraid of anything; we are friends here, poor woman! Tell me where you came from, and what you want," said she.

"I came from Kentucky," said the woman.

"When?" said Mr. Bird, taking up the interrogatory.

"To-night."

"How did you come?"

"I crossed on the ice."

"Crossed on the ice!" said everyone present.

"Yes," said the woman, slowly, "I did. God helping me, I crossed on the ice; for they were behind me—right behind—and there was no other way!"

"Law, Missis," said Cudjoe, "the ice is all in broken-up blocks, a swinging and a tetering up and down in the water!"

"I know it was—I know it!" said she wildly; "but I did it! I wouldn't have thought I could,—I didn't think I should get over, but I didn't care! I could but die, if I didn't. The Lord helped me; nobody knows how much the Lord can help 'em, till they try," said the woman, with a flashing eye.

"Were you a slave?" said Mr. Bird.

"Yes, sir; I belonged to a man in Kentucky."

"Was he unkind to you?"

"No, sir; he was a good master."

"And was your mistress unkind to you?"

"No, sir—no! my mistress was always good to me."

"What could induce you to leave a good home, then, and run away, and go through such dangers?"

The woman looked up at Mrs. Bird, with a keen, scrutinizing glance, and it did not escape her that she was dressed in deep mourning.

"Ma'am," she said, suddenly, "have you ever lost a child?"

The question was unexpected, and it was a thrust on a new wound; for it was only a month since a darling child of the family had been laid in the grave.

Mr. Bird turned around and walked to the window, and Mrs. Bird burst into tears; but, recovering her voice, she said,

"Why do you ask that? I have lost a little one."

"Then you will feel for me. I have lost two, one after another,—left 'em buried there when I came away; and I had only this one left. I never slept a night without him; he was all I had. He was my comfort and pride, day and night; and, ma'am, they were going to take him away from me,—to *sell* him,—sell him down south, ma'am, to go all alone,—a baby that had never been away from his mother in his life! I couldn't stand it, ma'am. I knew I never should be good for anything, if they did; and when I knew the papers were signed, and he was sold, I took him and came off in the night; and they chased me,—the man that bought him, and some of Mas'r's folks,—and they were coming down right behind me, and I heard 'em. I jumped right on to the ice; and how I got across, I don't know,—but, first I knew, a man was helping me up the bank."

The woman did not sob nor weep. She had gone to a place where tears are dry; but every one around her was, in some way characteristic of themselves, showing signs of hearty sympathy.

The two little boys, after a desperate rummaging in their pockets, in search of those pocket-handkerchiefs which mothers know are never to be found there, had thrown themselves disconsolately into the skirts of their mother's gown, where they were sobbing, and wiping their eyes and noses, to their hearts' content;—Mrs. Bird had her face fairly hidden in her pocket-handkerchief; and old Dinah, with tears streaming down her black, honest face, was ejaculating, "Lord have mercy on us!" with all the fervor of a camp-meeting;—while old Cudjoe, rubbing his eyes very hard with his cuffs, and making a most uncommon variety of wry faces, occasionally responded in the same key, with great fervor. Our senator was a statesman, and of course could not be expected to cry, like other mortals; and so he turned his back to the company, and looked out of the window, and seemed particularly busy in clearing his throat and wiping his spectacle-glasses, occasionally blowing his nose in a manner that was calculated to excite suspicion, had anyone been in a state to observe critically.

"How came you to tell me you had a kind master?" he suddenly exclaimed, gulping down very resolutely some kind of rising in his throat, and turning suddenly round upon the woman.

"Because he *was* a kind master; I'll say that of him, anyway;—and my mistress was kind; but they couldn't help themselves. They were owing money; and there was some way, I can't tell how, that a man had a hold on them, and they were obliged to give him his will. I listened, and heard him telling mistress that, and she begging and pleading for me,—and he told her he couldn't help himself, and that the papers were all drawn;—and then it was I took him and left my home, and came away. I knew 't was no use of my trying to live, if they did it; for 't 'pears like this child is all I have."

"Have you no husband?"

"Yes, but he belongs to another man. His master is real hard to him, and won't let him come to see me, hardly ever; and he's grown harder and harder upon us, and he threatens to sell him down south;—it's like I'll never see *him* again!"

The quiet tone in which the woman pronounced these words might have led a superficial observer to think that she was entirely apathetic; but there was a calm, settled depth of anguish in her large, dark eye, that spoke of something far otherwise.

"And where do you mean to go, my poor woman?" said Mrs. Bird.

"To Canada, if I only knew where that was. Is it very far off, is

Canada?" said she, looking up, with a simple, confiding air, to Mrs.
Bird's face.

"Poor thing!" said Mrs. Bird, involuntarily.

"Is't a very great way off, think?" said the woman, earnestly.

"Much further than you think, poor child!" said Mrs Bird; "but we
will try to think what can be done for you. Here, Dinah, make her up a
bed in your own room, close by the kitchen, and I'll think what to do for
her in the morning. Meanwhile, never fear, poor woman; put your trust
in God; he will protect you."

Mrs. Bird and her husband reentered the parlor. She sat down in her
little rocking-chair before the fire, swaying thoughtfully to and fro. Mr.
Bird strode up and down the room, grumbling to himself, "Pish! pshaw!
confounded awkward business!" At length, striding up to his wife, he
said,

"I say, wife, she'll have to get away from here, this very night. That
fellow will be down on the scent bright and early to-morrow morning; if
't was only the woman, she could lie quiet till it was over; but that little
chap can't be kept still by a troop of horse and foot, I'll warrant me; he'll
bring it all out, popping his head out of some window or door. A pretty
kettle of fish it would be for me, too, to be caught with them both here,
just now! No; they'll have to be got off to-night."

"To-night! How is it possible?—where to?"

"Well, I know pretty well where to," said the senator, beginning to put
on his boots, with a reflective air; and, stopping when his leg was half in,
he embraced his knee with both hands, and seemed to go off in deep
meditation.

"It's a confounded awkward, ugly business," said he, at last, beginning
to tug at his bootstraps again, "and that's a fact!" After one boot was
fairly on, the senator sat with the other in his hand, profoundly studying
the figure of the carpet. "It will have to be done, though, for aught I
see,—hang it all!" and he drew the other boot anxiously on, and looked
out of the window.

Now, little Mrs. Bird was a discreet woman,—a woman who never in
her life said, "I told you so!" and, on the present occasion, though pretty
well aware of the shape her husband's meditations were taking, she very
prudently forbore to meddle with them, only sat very quietly in her chair,
and looked quite ready to hear her liege lord's intentions, when he
should think proper to utter them.

"You see," he said, "there's my old client, Van Trompe, has come over
from Kentucky, and set all his slaves free; and he has bought a place
seven miles up the creek, here, back in the woods, where nobody goes,

unless they go on purpose; and it's a place that isn't found in a hurry. There she'd be safe enough; but the plague of the thing is, nobody could drive a carriage there to-night, but *me*."

"Why not? Cudjoe is an excellent driver."

"Ay, ay, but here it is. The creek has to be crossed twice; and the second crossing is quite dangerous, unless one knows it as I do. I have crossed it a hundred times on horseback, and know exactly the turns to take. And so, you see, there's no help for it. Cudjoe must put in the horses, as quietly as may be, about twelve o'clock, and I'll take her over; and then, to give color to the matter, he must carry me on to the next tavern, to take the stage for Columbus, that comes by about three or four, and so it will look as if I had had the carriage only for that. I shall get into business bright and early in the morning. But I'm still thinking I shall feel rather cheap there, after all that's been said and done; but, hang it, I can't help it!"

"Your heart is better than your head, in this case, John," said the wife, laying her little white hand on his. "Could I ever have loved you, had I not known you better than you know yourself?" And the little woman looked so handsome, with the tears sparkling in her eyes, that the senator thought he must be a decidedly clever fellow, to get such a pretty creature into such a passionate admiration of him; and so, what could he do but walk off soberly, to see about the carriage. At the door, however, he stopped a moment, and then coming back, he said, with some hesitation,

"Mary, I don't know how you'd feel about it, but there's that drawer full of things—of—of—poor little Henry's." So saying, he turned quickly on his heel, and shut the door after him.

His wife opened the little bed-room door adjoining her room, and, taking the candle, set it down on the top of a bureau there; then from a small recess she took a key, and put it thoughtfully in the lock of a drawer, and made a sudden pause, while two boys, who, boy like, had followed close on her heels, stood looking, with silent, significant glances, at their mother. And oh! mother that reads this, has there never been in your house a drawer, or a closet, the opening of which has been to you like the opening again of a little grave? Ah! happy mother that you are, if it has not been so.

Mrs. Bird slowly opened the drawer. There were little coats of many a form and pattern, piles of aprons, and rows of small stockings; and even a pair of little shoes, worn and rubbed at the toes, were peeping from the folds of a paper. There was a toy horse and wagon, a top, a ball,— memorials gathered with many a tear and many a heart-break! She sat down by the drawer, and, leaning her head on her hands over it, wept till the tears fell through her fingers into the drawer; then suddenly raising her head, she began, with nervous haste, selecting the plainest and most substantial articles, and gathering them into a bundle.

"Mamma," said one of the boys, gently touching her arm, "are you going to give away *those* things?"

"My dear boys," she said, softly and earnestly, "if our dear, loving little Henry looks down from heaven, he would be glad to have us do this. I could not find it in my heart to give them away to any common person—to anybody that was happy; but I give them to a mother more heart-broken and sorrowful than I am; and I hope God will send his blessings with them!"

There are in this world blessed souls, whose sorrows all spring up into joys for others; whose earthly hopes, laid in the grave with many tears, are the seed from which spring healing flowers and balm for the desolate and distressed. Among such was the delicate woman who sits there by the lamp, dropping slow tears, while she prepares the memorials of her own lost one for the outcast wanderer.

After a while, Mrs. Bird opened a wardrobe, and, taking from thence a plain, serviceable dress or two, she sat down busily to her work-table, and, with needle, scissors, and thimble, at hand, quietly commenced the "letting down" process which her husband had recommended, and continued busily at it till the old clock in the corner struck twelve, and she heard the low rattling of wheels at the door.

"Mary," said her husband, coming in, with his overcoat in his hand, "you must wake her up now; we must be off."

Mrs. Bird hastily deposited the various articles she had collected in a small plain trunk, and, locking it, desired her husband to see it in the carriage, and then proceeded to call the woman. Soon, arrayed in a cloak, bonnet, and shawl, that had belonged to her benefactress, she appeared at the door with her child in her arms. Mr. Bird hurried her into the carriage, and Mrs. Bird pressed on after her to the carriage steps. Eliza leaned out of the carriage, and put out her hand,—a hand as soft and beautiful as was given in return. She fixed her large, dark eyes, full of earnest meaning, on Mrs. Bird's face, and seemed going to speak. Her lips moved,—she tried once or twice, but there was no sound,—and pointing upward, with a look never to be forgotten, she fell back in the seat, and covered her face. The door was shut, and the carriage drove on.

[HBS *UTC*, 1:118–33]

*In her letter to the poet and abolitionist Eliza Cabot
Follen, Stowe responded to Follen's request that she
comment upon herself and the reasons she had written
her enormously popular novel. Describing how she had
become an "authoress," Stowe highlighted the impact
of her experience as a wife and mother. That same experience deeply informed* Uncle Tom's Cabin *and the
nine other novels Stowe wrote in the next three
decades.*

55   December 16, 1852
My Dear Madam,

I hasten to reply to your letter, the more interesting that I have long
been acquainted with you, and during all the nursery part of my life
made daily use of your poems for my children.

So you want to know what sort of woman I am! Well, if this is any
object, you shall have statistics free of charge. To begin, then, I am a little
bit of a woman,—somewhat more than forty, about as thin and dry as a
pinch of snuff—never very much to look at in my best days and looking
like a used up article now.

I was married when I was twenty-five years old to a man rich in Greek
and Hebrew and Latin and Arabic, and alas, rich in nothing else. . . . But
then I was abundantly furnished with wealth of another sort. I had two
little curly headed twin daughters to begin with and my stock in this line
has gradually increased, till I have been the mother of seven children, the
most beautiful and the most loved of whom lies buried near my Cincinnati residence. It was at his dying bed and at his grave that I learned what
a poor slave mother may feel when her child is torn away from her. In
those depths of sorrow which seemed to me immeasurable, it was my
only prayer to God that such anguish might not be suffered in vain.
There were circumstances about his death of such peculiar bitterness, of
what seemed almost cruel suffering that I felt that I could never be
consoled for it unless this crushing of my own heart might enable me to
work out some great good to others.

I allude to this here because I have often felt that much that is in that
book had its root in the awful scenes and bitter sorrow of that summer. It
has left now, I trust, no trace on my mind except a deep compassion for
the sorrowful, especially for mothers who are separated from their
children.

During these long years of struggling with poverty and sickness and a hot debilitating climate my children grew up around me. The nursery and the kitchen were my principal fields of labor. Then one of my friends pitying my toils copied and sent a number of little sketches from my pen to certain liberally paying "Annuals" with my name. With the first money that I earned in this way I bought a *feather bed*! for as I had married into poverty and without a dowry, and as my husband had only a large library of books, and a great deal of learning—the bed and pillows was thought on the whole the most profitable investment. After that I thought that I had discovered the "Philosopher's Stone," and when a new carpet, or a new mattress, was going to be needed, or when at the close of the year, it began to be clear that my family accounts, like poor Dora's, "wouldn't add up"—then I used to say to my faithful friend and factotum Anna who shared all my joys and sorrows "Now if you will keep the babies and attend to the things in the house for one day I'll write a piece, and then we shall be out of the scrape." And so I became an authoress,—very modest at first, I do assure you, and remonstrating very seriously with the friends who had thought it best to put my name to the pieces by way of getting a reputation. . . .

You ask with regard to the remuneration which I have received for my work here in America. Having been poor all my life, and expecting to be poor to the end of it, the idea of making anything by a book, which I wrote just because I could not help it never occurred to me. It was therefore an agreeable surprise to receive ten thousand dollars as the first fruits of three months sale and presume as much more is now due.

I am now writing a work which will contain, perhaps, an equal amount of matter with "Uncle Tom's Cabin." It will contain all the facts and documents on which that story was founded, and an immense body of facts, reports of trials, legal documents, and testimony of people now living South, which will more than confirm every statement in "Uncle Tom's Cabin." . . .

I suffer exquisitely in writing these things. It may truly be said that I write with my heart's blood. Many times in writing "Uncle Tom's Cabin" I thought my health would fail utterly; but I prayed earnestly that God would help me till I got through, and still I am pressed beyond measure and above strength.

This horror, this nightmare abomination! can it be in my country! It lies like lead on my heart, it shadows my life with sorrow; the more so that I feel, as for my own brothers, for the South, and am pained by every horror I am obliged to write, as one who is forced by some awful oath to disclose in court some family disgrace. Many times I have thought that I must die, and yet I pray God that I may live to see something.

It seems to me so odd and dream-like that so many persons desire to see me, and now I cannot help thinking that they will think, when they do, that God hath chosen "the weak things of this world."

If I live till spring I shall hope to see Shakespeare's grave, and Milton's mulberry tree, and the good land of my fathers—old, old England! May that day come!

Yours affectionately,

H.B. Stowe

[HBS to Eliza Cabot Follen, MHS]

Published in the Independent *on February 23, 1854, Stowe's "Appeal to the Women of the Free States" appeared in the midst of the Congressional debate on the Kansas-Nebraska Bill. Like others who opposed the legislation, her stance was based upon the bill's two key provisions: the principle of "popular sovereignty," which empowered the residents of territories to decide whether they would enter the union with or without slavery, and the explicit repeal of the Missouri Compromise. Eventually passed by Congress, the bill had exactly the effect its proponents, North and South, had sought to avoid, turning Kansas into a virtual battleground and exacerbating sectional controversy.*

56   The Providence of God has brought our nation to a crisis of most solemn interest.

A question be now pending in our national legislature, which is most vitally to affect the temporal and eternal interests, not only of ourselves, but of our children, and our children's children for ages yet unborn. Through our nation, it is to affect the interests of liberty and Christianity throughout the whole world.

Of the woes, the injustice, and the misery of slavery, it is not needful to speak. There is but one feeling and one opinion on this among us all. I do not think there is a mother among us all, who clasps her child to her breast, who could ever be made to feel it right that that child should be a slave; not a mother among us all who would not rather lay that child in its grave.

Nor can I believe that there is a woman so unchristian as to think it right to inflict on her neighbor's child what she would think worse than death were it inflicted on her own. I do not think there is a wife who would think it right *her* husband should be sold to a trader, and worked all his life without rights and without wages. I do not believe there is a husband who would think it right that *his* wife should be considered, by law, the property of another man, and not his own. I do not think there is a father or mother who would believe it right, were they forbidden by law to teach their children to read. I do not believe there is a brother who would think it right to have his sister held as property, with no legal defense for her personal honor, by any man living.

All this is inherent in slavery. It is not the abuse of slavery, but the legal nature of it. And there is not a woman in the United States, when the question is fairly put before her, who thinks these things are right.

However ambition and the love of political power may blind the stronger sex, God has given to woman a deeper and more immovable knowledge, in those holier feelings, which are peculiar to womanhood, and which guard the sacredness of the family state.

But though our hearts have bled over this wrong there have been many things tending to fetter our hands, to perplex our efforts, and to silence our voice. We have been told that to speak of it, was an invasion of the rights of other States. We have been told of promises and of compacts, and the natural expression of feeling has in many cases been restrained by an appeal to those honorable sentiments which respect the keeping of engagements.

The warm beatings of many hearts have been hushed; our yearnings and sympathies have been repressed because we have not known what to do; and many have come to turn a deaf ear to the whole tale of sorrow, because unwilling to harrow up the soul with feeling, where action was supposed to be impossible.

But a time has now come, when the subject is arising under quite another aspect.

The question is not now, shall the wrongs of slavery exist, as they have, on their own territories? But shall we permit them to be extended over all the free territories of the United States? Shall the woes and miseries of slavery be extended over a region of fair, free, unoccupied territory, nearly equal, in extent, to the whole of the free States?

Nor is this all; this is not the last thing that is expected or intended. Should this movement be submitted to in silence, should the North consent to this breach of solemn contract on the part of the South, there yet remains one more step to be apprehended, vis: the legalizing of slavery throughout the free States. By a decision of the Supreme Court in the Lemmon case, it may be declared lawful for slave property to be held in the northern free States. Should this come to pass, it is no more improbable that there may be, four years hence, slave depots in New York city, than it was four years ago, that the South would propose a repeal of the "Missouri Compromise."

Women of the free States! the question is not, shall we remonstrate with slavery on its own soil? but are we willing to receive slavery into the free States and territories of the Union?

Shall the whole power of these United States go into the hands of slavery?

Shall every State in it be thrown open as a slave State? This will be the final result and issue of the question which is now pending. This is the fearful crisis at which we stand. And now, is there anything which the women of a country can do? Oh women of the free States! what did your grave mothers do in the time of our revolutionary struggle? Did not *liberty* in these days feel the strong impulse of woman's heart? . . .

What, then, is the duty of American women at this time? The first duty is for each woman, *for herself* thoroughly to understand the subject, and to feel that as mother, wife, sister, or member of society, she is bound to give her influence on the right side.

In the second place, women can make exertions to get up petitions, in their particular districts, to our national legislature. They can take measures to communicate information in their vicinity. They can employ lecturers to spread the subject before the people of their town or village. They can circulate the speeches of our members in Congress, and in many other ways secure a full understanding of the present position of our country.

Above all, it seems to be necessary and desirable that we should make this subject a matter of earnest prayer. The recent crisis in the history of the world, is one which calls upon all who believe in an Almighty Guardian and Ruler of nations, to betake themselves to his throne. . . .

Let us pray that in the agitation of this question between the North and the South, the war of principle may not become a mere sectional conflict, degenerating into the encounter of physical force. Let us raise our hearts to Him who has the power to restrain the wrath of man, that He will avert these consequences, which our sins as a nation have so justly deserved.

And as far as our social influence extends, let us guard against indiscriminate bitterness and vituperation.

Doubtless, there are noble minds at the South, who do not participate in the machinations of their political leaders, whose sense of honor and justice is outraged by this proposition, equally with our own.

While, then, we seek to sustain the cause of free principle unwaveringly, let us hold it also to be our true office, as women, to moderate the acrimony of political contest, remembering that the slaveholder and the slave are alike our brethren, whom the law of God commands us to love as ourselves.

For the sake of both, for the sake of our dear children, for the sake of our common country, for the sake of outraged and struggling liberty throughout the world, let every woman of America now do her duty.

[*Independent* 6 (February 23, 1854): 57]

7.
Isabella Beecher Hooker:
"The Cause Dearer to Me
Than Any Other in the World"

ISABELLA BEECHER HOOKER'S ability to transform herself from private woman to public reformer was the result of several factors, the most important of which was her evolving belief in the power—and obligations—of womanhood. Indeed, she would entitle her only book, published in the very midst of the Beecher-Tilton scandal, *Womanhood: Its Sanctities and Fidelities*. Hooker's postbellum exchange with the political philosopher John Stuart Mill, included as one of the chapters of her book, reveals that she had begun to locate the power of womanhood in the "sense of motherhood." In turn, she announced motherhood to be the very source of woman's innate moral superiority (a view with which Mill politely but firmly disagreed but which Hooker shared with her sisters Catharine and Harriet). Declaring that "ages of subjection demand ages of exaltation," Isabella insisted that to her conception "a mother is the only being in this world who . . . approximates the divine nature." This superior creative ability, when combined with woman's "more intimate fellowship with the child of her womb during the antenatal period, and the power of sympathy that comes through this," provided her sex with "a moral advantage that man can never have, and for which he has no equivalent or compensation."[1]

Isabella had come to regard woman's spiritual power as compensation for her relative lack of physical strength. Yet she effectively turned the tables on antisuffragists like Catharine when she used this "fact" as part of her justification for women's entry into politics, thereby dismissing Catharine's objection that politics would contaminate women and bring ruin upon both the private and public spheres (a tactic also adopted by Harriet in her 1865 prosuffrage essay, "The Woman Question"). By embracing the bifurcation of male and female qualities while rejecting the ideology of separate spheres with which it was usually associated,

Isabella (and others) radically reinterpreted the meaning of womanhood. This reinterpretation enabled her to present women's agitation for political equality not as an end in itself but as a necessary means of domesticating the public sphere and initiating the rule of spirit over brute force. In the hands of her sex, the ballot would thus become a divine weapon in the struggle against all forms of moral as well as political corruption.

Women's historians usually identify this approach to reform with late nineteenth-century feminism, especially the suffrage movement's attempts to win support from more conservative women's organizations.[2] Yet Hooker's career testifies to the fact that this type of political feminism began much earlier than most studies have suggested. Moreover, in her speeches and writings, Isabella merged demands for social and political equality based on natural rights theory with this revised version of domesticity.

Hooker had argued on the basis of equal rights and justice as well as expediency—albeit with unequal emphasis—in her antebellum essay, "Shall Women Vote?" Significantly, she enthusiastically recommended Harriet Taylor Mill's piece on the "Enfranchisement of Women" in her next prosuffrage article, *A Mother's Letters to a Daughter on Woman Suffrage.* Isabella lavished praise on Harriet Mill's "new gospel of individual responsibility" and explicitly rejected the doctrine of separate sexual spheres, announcing: "I can see no reason for closing any avenue of thought, study, or action to her [woman]. . . . That every young woman should limit her expectation of happiness and her ideas of duty by her possible wifehood and motherhood, is as absurd as that a young man should limit himself after the same fashion." But she did so only after redefining motherhood as the very source and foundation of woman's "political" expertise. Eager to defend women, especially mothers, from the charge that they were unfit—either by nature or education—for voting and "the work of law making," Hooker was apparently unaware of the tension between her belief that womanhood entailed qualities as well as reponsibilities based exclusively on gender and her conception of women as autonomous individuals with differing goals and inalienable rights.[3]

The title and demure epistolary format of this 1868 tract as well as its author's initial willingness to publish it as the anonymous offering of an "affectionate Mother" suggest that Isabella was attempting to reach more politically conservative women. What she sought was a revision of Catharine's definition of woman's true "profession." Isabella's starting point was an outright rejection of Catharine's endorsement of female "influence" as a substitute for political parity. Yet her success in subverting the logic of Catharine's critique of women's social and political equality derived from her ability to retain and reinterpret several of her sister's key tenets, most notably woman's moral and social obligation to educate herself and improve the race.

In differing proportions, the twin themes of woman's destiny as political "savior" of the nation and women's natural rights as citizens would pervade Hooker's most important writings. Even in the closely argued speeches in which she cited constitutional precedent to make the case for equal justice, Isabella made sure to include appeals based on the unique power of womanhood. Hence she attempted to buttress her highly legalistic 1902 argument on United States citizenship by presenting women as natural pacifists and reminding the all-male legislature to "Honor thy father and thy *mother*."[4] It is important to understand that this double-barrelled strategy was the outcome of Isabella's agenda for the moral as well as the political reconstruction of her country (two goals that she considered to be inseparable) rather than a mere rhetorical strategy aimed at two of the main components of her audience, middle-class wives, mothers, and daughters; and male legislators. As Hooker emphatically stated in her 1888 speech before the International Council of Women, she perceived questions of legislation to be questions of morals and therefore considered "true manhood" as well as "true womanhood" to be unattainable while women were politically subordinated. Convinced that the values associated with domesticity could and should reconstruct not only politics but also reality itself (in effect eliminating any pretense that the public and private spheres ought to be morally distinguishable), she concluded this lengthy analysis of women's constitutional right to vote with a discussion of their moral *obligation* to do so.[5]

Although Hooker's notions of morality were undeniably class-bound, her intent was not repressive. The terms in which she conceived of woman's impending power were decidedly nonpatriarchal and noncoercive: "The thunders of Sinai are passed away . . . and we have come to the still small voice of love and tenderness." Rather than aiming to impose her personal beliefs and practices on others by legislative fiat, Isabella viewed women's efforts to reconstruct politics as the catalyst for the coming millenial age during which womanhood, formerly silenced and oppressed, would gain an equal and perhaps even predominant voice in the governance of the world. As she had predicted to John Stuart Mill, "ages of subjection demand ages of exaltation, by way of recompense."[6]

Isabella's commitment to an inclusive and politically aggressive version of "true womanhood" placed her firmly in the camp of the New York wing of the suffrage movement. Angered by what they considered to be a series of betrayals at the hands of abolitionists as well as Republicans, Elizabeth Cady Stanton and Susan B. Anthony had retaliated by airing their grievances in their new journal, *The Revolution*, and then founding an independent organization, the National Woman Suffrage Association (NWSA), in 1869. Their Boston counterparts, who differed with them on matters of morality and style as well as strategy, responded by establishing a competing organization, the American Woman Suffrage Association (AWSA), which was led by Lucy Stone and Henry Blackwell. Following their break with the abolitionists, Stanton and Anthony had begun to lobby in Washington for a federal suffrage amendment, and they attempted to establish a coalition with working women. The Bostonians not only preferred to lobby on a state-by-state basis but made consistent—if only partially successful—efforts to keep the movement clear of all "side issues" and "extraneous entanglements," a pointed rebuke of the New York wing, especially Stanton's campaign for the reform of marriage and divorce laws.[7]

Hooker's refusal to repudiate the "compromising" New Yorkers in 1869, despite repeated warnings about Stanton and Anthony from her close friends in the Stone-Blackwell faction, reflected her tacit agreement with Susan B. Anthony's opinion of the AWSA, which she impatiently described as being "sick unto death with propriety."[8] Isabella pronounced Anthony "a woman of incorruptible integrity" and endorsed a co-worker's description of Stanton as "the truest womanliest woman of us all," courageously embracing them both as "worthy leaders and representatives of the cause dearer to me than any other in the world." Her refusal to be intimidated by gossip concerning Anthony's alleged mismanagement of Kansas campaign funds and Stanton's views on divorce testified to her faith in the purifying and transforming power of womanhood. Rejecting the popular contagion metaphor so crucial to the maintenance of the sexual double standard and the segregation of different "classes" of women, Isabella would later explain that "woman cannot be injured [by] woman—only men are endangered."[9]

As a letter addressed to Anthony from Hooker reveals, this belief was sorely tested in the wake of Victoria Woodhull's unexpected appearance before the Judiciary Committee of the House of Representatives in January 1871. Unlike Stanton, who cautiously advocated changing marriage and divorce laws to protect the rights of women and children but who bridled at the erroneous label of "free lover," Woodhull would delight in shocking lecture audiences by vehemently denouncing marriage as sexual slavery and openly insisting upon the right of women as well as men to experience sexual freedom and satisfaction. Yet in her highly dignified congressional testimony Woodhull provided the NWSA with a new and potentially effective strategy by arguing that the Fourteenth and Fifteenth Amendments protected women's constitutional right to vote as citizens. Had the position Woodhull took in this eloquent speech been upheld by either the legislative or judicial branch of the federal government, no additional amendment to the United States Constitution would have been necessary.[10]

Struck by Victoria's powerful performance, especially her magnetic personal presence, Isabella praised her brain, heart, manners, and conduct profusely to Anthony and others, despite Woodhull's notorious reputation. Announcing that she would "always love" Woodhull and "in private shall work for her redemption if she is ensnared," Isabella drew the line only when her co-worker announced that she planned to run for president. While Hooker was not prepared to support a candidate whose morality was in question, she vowed to Anthony that she would not "denounce her [Woodhull] publicly, however guilty till the time when men guilty of the same crimes are avoided and denounced." Confident that womanhood was now firmly "entrenched in the Capitol, never to be dislodged," Hooker prepared to encourage women all over the nation to register to vote, though she advised Anthony that one test case would suffice as a trial of the Woodhull strategy.[11]

Despite mounting pressure from worried fellow suffragists as well as disapproving friends and relatives, Isabella refused to disassociate herself from Victoria. Along with Stanton, Hooker initially supported Woodhull's subsequent efforts to effect a political coalition between her reform-minded followers in the spiritualist movement, her labor allies in the American branch of the International Workingmen's Association (founded by Karl Marx), and the NWSA. When Woodhull remained determined to run on a third-party ticket, even after the coalition faltered, Isabella confided to Stanton that she viewed these developments as part of God's battle plan, pronouncing the Woodhull candidacy a divine "instrument" for removing the burden of radicalism from the NWSA and healing the split in the suffrage movement. She also reminded Stanton that Woodhull had "sunk a hundred thousand dollars" in the cause "besides enduring tortures of soul innumerable." Women may have "underrated their power" in the past but it was now time to finish the work of reconstruction.[12]

Yet this confident assessment of the movement's immediate prospects for unification and political triumph proved to be much too sanguine. Isabella did not live to see the passage of the Nineteenth Amendment in 1920, which finally guaranteed women the right to vote, though eighteen years after this letter to Stanton was written she did attend the Washington convention during which the two wings of the movement downplayed their differences and merged to form the NAWSA (National American Woman Suffrage Association). By this time, both factions were struggling to recover from the serious damage done to their reputations by years of movement infighting and the adverse publicity generated by the Beecher-Tilton scandal.[13]

What Hooker could not have anticipated was the enduring effect these developments would have on her career as a reformer, her domestic life, and her posthumous reputation. She had fled to Europe in the summer of 1874 in an unsuccessful attempt to avoid the controversy generated by her brother's adultery trial and the bitter resentment against her that arose when she refused to assume his innocence. Profoundly depressed and under great stress, Isabella began to experience visions of her mother in her Paris hotel room. Harriet Porter Beecher offered her daughter unconditional love and acceptance as well as the maternal guidance that Isabella so sorely missed. In the years that followed, Isabella's mother would send "messages" regarding everything from proper clothes and home furnishings to her daughter's political destiny. These messages confirmed Isabella's conversion to spiritualism and eventually resulted in matriarchal visions of herself as a female leader of her country, visions which—when viewed out of their personal and historical context—were subsequently used by scholars to question Isabella's sanity and dismiss her contributions as a reformer.[14]

Yet it was not these compensatory millenial visions that threatened to undermine Isabella's sanity or her political effectiveness. Shortly after returning from Europe, Hooker confessed that she had "not *been able to get into public suffrage work* yet scarcely known why—the hindrance has been entirely from *within*."[15] As her 1876 diary reveals, Isabella was by then experiencing severe inner turmoil as a result of the strained relations between the Hookers and their two conservative sons-in-law, who had almost totally ostracized John and Isabella in the wake of the scandal.[16] These circumstances rendered even more painful the untimely death from tuberculosis of the Hookers' elder daughter Mary in 1886. Three years later Isabella managed to make the difficult reentry onto the national suffrage scene, but her correspondence as well as her intensified involvement with spiritualism testify that she was preoccupied with Mary's death and her enforced separation from her grandchildren, especially Mary's daughter, Kate: "This mother love is such a tremendous thing," she wrote to Alice, "I doubt if there is anything like it . . . and I do hope some day it may find its own and be satisfied." A few months

later she described herself as being fully "absorbed" in Connecticut suffrage work, especially her efforts to organize political science clubs for
women across the state where they could learn that domestic and political economy were twin sisters. The importance of such clubs rested upon
Isabella's belief that the safety of the republic depended upon the quality
of local government. But as she pointedly warned Alice: "masculine wisdom and patriotism cannot be depended upon to protect and educate
even a village community." She went on to cite the rape of a Litchfield
schoolteacher by "a young man of respectable family" as evidence.[17]

In another revealing letter to her sole surviving daughter, this one
written just after she had attended the Washington convention of 1890
during which the movement finally achieved unification, Isabella noted
how impressed she was by the participants' patriotism and statesmanship. In spite of their lack of formal education, women had "gathered
our wisdom and knowledge while caring for our children in the family
or teaching other people[']s children in the schools." This observation
moved Isabella to conclude that she was indeed proud of her sex, adding:
"I am so glad men have had to have mothers as well as fathers. Though
you wouldn't suspect it from history or current literature." Despite all
that had happened, Isabella's fervent belief in "the superior mental and
moral power of womankind"[18] remained unshaken.

NOTES

1. Isabella published her correspondence with Mill in *Womanhood: Its Sanctities and Fidelities* (Boston: Lee and Shepard Publishers, 1873), pp. 33–37. See
Document 57.

2. Although the analogy between housekeeping on a private scale and government, which was conceived of as "enlarged housekeeping," has been identified as
a species of late nineteenth-century Progressive era thought, it was implicit in
Isabella's postbellum writings and suffrage-related correspondence. According to
historian Aileen Kraditor, this analogy provided turn-of-the-century women such
as Florence Kelley and Jane Addams with a justification of and a blueprint for
their entry into politics, settlement work, and other reform-related activities. See
Kraditor's *The Ideas of the Woman Suffrage Movement: 1890–1920* (Garden
City, N.Y.: Anchor Books, 1965), especially pp. 51–55. Anne F. and Andrew M.
Scott discuss the alliance between the suffrage movement and the Women's
Christian Temperance Union under the leadership of Frances Willard in *One Half
the People: The Fight for Woman Suffrage* (New York: J. B. Lippincott and Co.,
1975), pp. 20–22. In their selection of documents as well as in their headnotes,
they lend support to the assumption that the government as enlarged housekeep-

ing argument was primarily associated with the postbellum temperance movement and is therefore a product of late nineteenth-century suffragist thought.
See, for example, their introduction to the remarks of Mrs. Zerelda G. Wallace
before the Senate Judiciary Committee in January of 1880, reprinted in Scott and
Scott, *Fight for Woman Suffrage*, pp. 96–99.

3. Isabella Beecher Hooker, *A Mother's Letters to a Daughter on Woman
Suffrage* (Hartford: Press of Case, Lockwood and Brainard, 1870), pp. 3, 18–19.
See Document 59. This tract of the Connecticut Woman Suffrage Association
was originally published anonymously in *Putnam's Magazine* for November and
December of 1868. In her introduction to *John Stuart Mill and Harriet Taylor
Mill: Essays on Sex Equality* (Chicago: University of Chicago Press, 1970), Alice
S. Rossi effectively discredits the popular misconception that John rather than
Harriet Taylor Mill was the primary author of this article on the "Enfranchisement of Women" for the July 1851 *Westminster Review*. Rossi also notes that,
unlike her husband, Harriet Mill insisted that even married women should seek
employment in order to avoid financial dependence upon men. In *The Subjection of Women* John Stuart Mill would attempt to resolve the inconsistency
in his own position by arguing that although a married woman should have the
"power" to support herself, it was not "a desirable custom" that she should
exercise that power. Rossi, *Essays on Sex Equality*, pp. 41–43, 178–80. Both
essays have been reprinted by Rossi in their entirety.

4. Isabella Beecher Hooker, *An Argument on United States Citizenship Before
the Constitutional Convention of the State of Connecticut, January 1, 1902*
(Hartford: Plimpton, Mfg., printers, 1902), pp. 9–11. See Document 67. Ironi-
cally, the convention refused to grant Hooker the right to be heard on this issue.
Her account of this incident can be found in "The Last of the Beechers," *The
Connecticut Magazine* 9 (May 1905): 298.

5. Isabella Beecher Hooker, *The Constitutional Rights of the Women of the
United States: An Address Before the International Council of Women, Washington, D.C., March 30, 1888* (Hartford: Case, Lockwood and Brainard, 1900), pp.
18–19. See Document 63.

6. IBH W, pp. 35–36. See Document 57.

7. Among the best secondary sources on these internal disputes are the following works: Eleanor Flexner, *Century of Struggle: The Woman's Rights Movement
in the United States*, rev. ed. (Cambridge, Mass.: Harvard University Press, Belknap Press, 1975); Ellen DuBois, *Feminism and Suffrage: The Emergence of an
Independent Movement in America, 1848–1869* (Ithaca, N.Y.: Cornell University Press, 1978); and Scott and Scott, *Fight for Woman Suffrage*. The NWSA's
attempt to form an alliance with working women is chronicled by DuBois on pp.
126–61.

8. Susan B. Anthony to Isabella Beecher Hooker, March 5, 1871, SD.

9. Isabella Beecher Hooker to Mary Rice Livermore, March 15, 1871, SD. See
Document 89. Isabella's generation was not the first to reject the contagion
metaphor, as Carroll Smith-Rosenberg's influential study of antebellum social

purity reformers reveals. See her "Beauty, the Beast and the Militant Woman: A Case Study in Sex Roles and Social Stress in Jacksonian America," *American Quarterly* (October 1971): 562–84. In 1860 Stanton had set off a heated debate when she introduced a series of resolutions on marriage and divorce before the Tenth National Woman's Rights Convention in New York City. Her account of these resolutions and the ensuing debate has been reprinted by Mari Jo and Paul Buhle, eds., in *The Concise History of Woman Suffrage: Selections from the Classic Work of Stanton, Anthony, Gage, and Harper* (Chicago: University of Illinois Press, 1978), pp. 170–89.

10. Isabella Beecher Hooker to Susan B. Anthony, March 11 [and 14], 1871, SD. See Document 61. Woodhull's January 11th testimony has been reprinted by Scott and Scott, *Fight for Woman Suffrage*, pp. 76–80. (They note, however, that Francis Minor was the originator of this line of reasoning.) The full range of Woodhull's social and political thought, including her sexual radicalism, is documented in *The Victoria Woodhull Reader*, ed. Madeline B. Stern (Weston, Mass.: M & S Press, 1974). See especially part 1, "Sociology," and part 2, "Political Theory."

11. Isabella Beecher Hooker to Susan B. Anthony, March 11 [and 14], 1871, SD. See Document 61. Anthony herself was to test this strategy. Her successful attempt to register to vote in the 1872 election led to her subsequent arrest and trial on the charge of "illegal voting." Isabella's discussion of the legal and moral implications of this trial can be found in IBH *CRW*, pp. 13–17. See Document 63.

12. Isabella Beecher Hooker to Elizabeth Cady Stanton, May 12, 1872, SD. See Document 62. Anthony's antagonism toward Woodhull's third party initiative permeates the chapter her biographer devoted to these incidents. See Ida Husted Harper, *The Life and Work of Susan B. Anthony*, 2 vols. (Kansas City: Bowden-Merrill Co., 1899), pp. 383–415.

13. The reunification of the movement as well as the factional rivalry that preceded reunification is ably summarized and analyzed in Scott and Scott, *Fight for Woman Suffrage*, especially pp. 22–23. Unlike many commentators, they perceive the positive as well as the negative effects of the competition between the two wings of the movement, arguing quite correctly that "the rivalry . . . kept both sides alert and active." However, they do not even mention Hooker's contributions to the suffrage movement or her role in the Beecher-Tilton scandal; and they dismiss Woodhull as "beautiful, clever and unprincipled," thus seriously underestimating the importance of her candidacy and the issues she championed. Scott and Scott, *Fight for Woman Suffrage*, pp. 18–19.

14. Isabella Beecher Hooker, 1876 Diary, p. 85, The Connecticut Historical Society, Hartford, Conn. Note: direct quotations from this diary are no longer permitted. The family restricted use of this diary after Kenneth Andrews cited it to ridicule and dismiss Isabella, especially her involvement in spiritualism, in his *Nook Farm: Mark Twain's Hartford Circle* (Cambridge, Mass.: Harvard University Press, 1950), pp. 53–62, 223–24. Andrews regarded feminism in general and

social purity issues in particular with similar condescension. See, for example, his comments on *Womanhood*, pp. 141–43. Subsequent treatments of the Beechers and the Hookers have tended to recycle Andrews's ahistorical approach to spiritualism.

15. Isabella Beecher Hooker to Samuel Bowles, March 26, 1877, SML.

16. Yale's collection of Henry Ward Beecher's papers includes typescripts of the letters Henry wrote to Isabella counseling her to remain silent. Each of these letters was copied by Henry Eugene Burton, one of the Hookers' sons-in-law and brother of their friend, the Reverend Nathaniel Burton. (See Henry Ward Beecher to Isabella Beecher Hooker, April 25, 1872; before November 1, 1872; and November 9, 1872, SML.) While Henry Burton's hostility toward the Hookers, especially Isabella, appears to have been longstanding, it intensified during and after the scandal as a result of his admiration for and loyalty to Henry Ward Beecher. On this matter see Isabella's extract, taken from a copy of her husband's 1878 letter to their other son-in-law, John Calvin Day, in which John Hooker defends his wife's behavior during the scandal. Isabella Beecher Hooker, Memo, February 10, 1884, SD.

17. Isabella Beecher Hooker to Alice Hooker Day, February 5 [and 6], 1889, and May 17, 1889, SD. See Documents 64 and 65. Isabella dated her growing involvement with spiritualism from 1885 in "The Last of the Beechers," p. 298. Regarding the ostracism and its extremely painful effects (about which she understandably remains silent in these autobiographical reminiscences), see Isabella's restricted 1876 Diary at The Connecticut Historical Society, Hartford, Conn.

18. Isabella Beecher Hooker to Alice Hooker Day, February [28], 1890, SD. See Document 66. As this letter reveals, Isabella envied Elizabeth Cady Stanton for having a daughter who would follow in her reform footsteps. A signed copy of "Women Under the Laws of Connecticut," published by Isabella in 1892, was addressed to Alice from her mother, presumably as a gesture of encouragement. See the Stowe-Day Foundation's copy of this article from *The Business Woman's Journal* 4, no. 3 (March 1892): 110.

In her book, Womanhood: Its Sanctities and Fidelities, *Isabella quoted excerpts from Harriet Taylor Mill's 1851 essay on the "Enfranchisement of Women," citing it as a turning point in her own development. She then published the following exchange between herself and John Stuart Mill, who had responded to her praise of his wife in 1869 by sending her an early copy of* The Subjection of Women.

57   H A R T F O R D, Conn., Aug. 9, 1869.

D E A R S I R: Accept my warmest thanks for your book on "The Subjection of Women," which I should have acknowledged earlier but that unusual family cares prevented. And let me thank God, too, for this book. He has inspired you with His own wisdom, and you must have opened wide your heart to the inspiration.

Not only so, but you have condescended, as few men have ever done, to be taught by a woman in the deep things of nature, and have not hesitated to acknowledge her leadership, thereby proclaiming your own most excellent manhood. Some passages in this connection were of overwhelming significance to me. Flesh and blood have not revealed them unto him, I said, but the spirit of a noble woman, even of her who has gone before, that she may beckon him on to her own serene heights.

And this brings me to a point where alone I have any doubt whether you are entirely right. It is as to the comparative endowment of the sexes. It is a question of no practical moment now, perhaps, but is of curious interest in estimating mankind in its dual form. For many years I have contended, privately I mean, that men were, by nature, capable of as high moral excellence as women, and, under the same outward circumstances, would develop the same moralities. But of late I have been impressed more and more with the closer likeness to the divine nature which woman seems to bear, in that she is more sensibly, if not more truly, a creator than man is. Add to this her more intimate fellowship with the child of her womb during the antenatal period, and the power of sympathy that comes through this, and you have given her a moral advantage that man can never have, and for which he has no equivalent nor compensation.

What father can say, "Thou art *my* child," as a mother can?—and through what channels does he count the life-beat of his child as his own? And to my mind there is more sense of power in this sense of motherhood than in all things else; that power we all reach after by virtue of our divine ancestry. To create is to live; to express our own being through another and another is everlasting youth; and to mould, guide, and control this offshoot of our being, itself an independent power,—this is the glory of existence, its very most supreme delight. To my conception a mother is the only being in this world who thus approximates the divine nature. So feeble in the comparison is the father's relation to her child, so lost in her higher and diviner relation, that it is within the experience of many a mother, whether recognized by herself or not, that from the moment of blessed annunciation to heavenly birth, she, like the Virgin of old, has known no father to her child save the Holy Ghost.

If you say that this is no otherwise than it should be,—that ages of subjection demand ages of exaltation, by way of recompense,—I reply, the disadvantage, perhaps I may say the injustice, to man remains the same, is even the greater, since he, after all, has suffered the greater loss, by just so much as the master is always below the slave in point of moral privilege.

I write this out because I, like yourself, have an inordinate love of justice, of perfect equality; and, cleaving the future, I see such honor and power coming to woman as makes me tremble; for with power comes responsibility for the just use of it; and who save He that sees the end from the beginning is competent to this?

Let me thank you again for the book; it will surely help to unseal the lips of many noble women from whom, as you say, the world has yet much to learn. Would that all were as ready to listen as you have ever been.

The thunders of Sinai are passed away, thank God[!] and we have come to the still small voice of love and tenderness. This shall be heard and felt till time shall be no more.

> I am, with sincere regard and esteem,
> Your friend,
> ISABELLA BEECHER HOOKER.

AVIGNON, Sept. 13, 1869.

DEAR MADAM: I beg to acknowledge with many thanks your letter of August 9th.

You have perceived, what I should wish every one who reads my little book to know, that whatever there is in it which shows any unusual insight into nature or life, was learned from women,—from my wife, and subsequently also from her daughter.

What you so justly say respecting the infinitely closer relationship of a child to its mother than to its father, I have learned from the same source to regard as full of important consequences with respect to the future legal position of parents and children. This, however, is a portion of the truth for which the human mind will not, for some time, be sufficiently prepared to make its discussion useful.

But I do not perceive that this close relationship gives any ground for attributing a natural superiority in capacity of moral excellence to women over men. I believe moral excellence to be always the fruit of education and cultivation, and I see no reason to doubt that both sexes are equally capable of that description of cultivation.

But the position of irresponsible power in which men have hitherto lived, is, I need hardly say, most unfavorable to every kind of moral excellence. So far as women have been in possession of irresponsible power, they, too, have by no means escaped its baleful consequences.

With hearty congratulations on the progress of the cause of women in both our countries, and in most other parts of the civilized world,

> I am, dear madam,
> Yours very truly,
> J. S. MILL.

[IBH W, pp. 33–37]

Isabella first met Elizabeth Cady Stanton and Susan B. Anthony while staying at Paulina Wright Davis's home[1] during a Newport, Rhode Island, women's rights convention. In this letter to Caroline Severance, whose sympathies were with the Stone-Blackwell faction of the movement, Hooker attempted to carve out a mediatory role. She closes by mentioning her plans to hold Connecticut's first suffrage convention that fall.

1. Paulina Wright Davis, a longtime friend and ally of Elizabeth Cady Stanton, was then president of the Rhode Island Suffrage Association. Davis's wealth, which appears to have initially attracted Isabella to her, did not render her social activism respectable to the very well-to-do Providence community in which she lived.

58   August 27 [and 29],[1869]

My dear friend.

. . . This is the resumé of my position. Once upon a time I met you and fell in love with you—found to my surprise after the deed was done, that you were a believer in Women's Rights and Theodore Parker[2]—and had actually been a reform speaker. This was the beginning of a knocking away of my prejudices in two directions—I saw clearly that I could heartily fellowship and enjoy one who failed to believe the religious truths most precious to me of all truth—and who violated my ideas of taste and expediency in matters of reform—and all this because she was an honest, fearless womanly woman, full of the spirit of love to all mankind. . . .

More than a year ago I met Mrs. Davis at the Boston Convention.[3] . . . I fell in love with her also, and found after awhile, again to my surprise that she too, a woman as gentle, as intellectual as loveable every way as yourself had been a public speaker and a life long advocate of woman's rights and after meeting her again and again I found to my unspeakable delight that she loved my Savior and *rested on Him*, just as I do. This is the secret of a peculiar fellowship you may have noticed between us and which led you perhaps to ascribe to "taste" a regard that has far deeper foundation. . . .

At last, this twin sister tells me that Mrs. Stanton, who has been a life long friend of hers, is a noble woman, a magnificent woman and the truest womanliest woman of us all—that my prejudices against her would certainly go down under the influence of her presence and conversation. So I hasten to accept an invitation to meet her, (after exchanging with her letters of friendliness and of criticism, in which the latter largely predominated) and I have now spent three days in her company and in the most intense heartsearching debate I ever undertook in my life. I have handled what seem to me her errors, *without gloves* and the result is that I love her also, just as I do you. I have handed in my allegiance to you three women, as worthy leaders and representatives of the cause dearer to me than any other in the world—The past life of all of you justifies my

2. Bostonian Theodore Parker, a Unitarian minister, had once been banned from the pulpit of Boston's First Church because of his controversial theological views. An eloquent public speaker, Parker delivered sermons and lectured on tour on a wide variety of reforms, including temperance, divorce, and abolitionism.

3. This convention was called to found the New England Woman Suffrage Association.

present confidence that you will not fail to represent woman—in her wants, her rights, her dignities, just as she should be represented before the public—and that you differ on some points and will inevitably show to the world that you differ does not and never will impair my confidence in any of you. Only one thing can do that—if either of you becomes jealous or suspicious of the other, or in any way permits herself to injure the other in reputation and fair fame, ascribing bad motives to conduct where good ones might be found, then my confidence in that one must inevitably be lessened—then such an one is in my judgment an unworthy leader of the woman's cause. But so far, I have failed to discover an approach to this jealousy and suspicion in either of you three dear friends—[I]t is rare in my opinion that three men or women can be found, who are of so pure and unselfish a spirit as you three women— and I cannot but see the Lord's hand in it when you are made so prominent in this great movement. Lucy Stone I have not yet met in social life—but I have lent myself to the powers of her oratory and was quick to hand in my allegiance to her as an orator. How she will bear the test of this closer personal contact remains to be seen and I shall never refuse any offered opportunity to make her more intimate acquaintance. At present I have letters from her in regard to Miss Susan B. [Anthony] and letters from the latter in regard to the former and the spirit of love is unmistakenly in the one and not in the other. I can say too, with great truth that both Mrs. Stanton and Miss Anthony *speak* of Mrs. Lucy with tenderness and regard and ascribe her present statements which are so injurious to them to misconceptions on her part brought about by the state of her health rather than to any intentional misrepresentation.

. . . And now as to Susan herself—the one really hoofed and horned demon of this movement to all minds—mine among them. I have studied her day and night for near a week in all. I have taken the testimony of Mrs. Davis who has known her a little for twenty years—but whose taste was offended by personal contact and slight collision years ago so that she shunned an intimacy—and the testimony of Mrs. Stanton who has been by circumstances driven in to the closest intimacy . . . and they are united on this resumé of her character. She is a woman of incorruptible integrity and the thought of guile is not in her heart—[I]n unselfishness and benevolence—(tautology that is) they hardly know her equal—and her energy and executive ability are bounded only by her physical power, which for a human being is immense. Sometimes she fails in judgment according to their standard, which they own may be an imperfect one— but in right intentions never—and as for her faithfulness to her friends and her cause whatever it may be, death alone can interrupt that.

I confess that after studying her carefully now for days—and under the shadow of Mrs. Lucy's repeated letters to me and yours, as well as under the light of these old friends, and after attending a two days Convention in Newport engineered by her in her own fashion . . . after all this, I am obliged to accept the more favorable interpretation of her that prevails here, rather than that of Boston. And just here I want to say that so far as I can judge by my own feeling and by the expression of feeling in others, Lucy has hurt the woman's cause in refusing to accept her husband's name,[4] in just the same way that Susan has by her repeated carelessnesses and indiscretions and Mrs. Stanton by the expression of her too deep (or too superficial I should say) views of the marriage question. . . . I for my part am able to pardon both and all because I believe them all to be honestly striving for the truth and sure to find it and recommend it more or less wherever they go. . . .

. . . [W]e are bound for one port and must virtually take passage on the same ship—at least there is but one line of vessels and we must not think of such a thing as running athwart each other—the overriding vessel is just as likely to go down as the other and deserves to a great deal more. . . . I know you have done all this writing to save me from a misstep—and my heart is sorry that you cannot bring me to your view. The truth is, the more people are mistaken and going in a wrong way, provided they are *good and noble* people, the more I am inclined to keep company with them in the hope of using with them what influence I may have, towards a right way. . . . [W]hen you call me a mediator and ask for work in that direction I go to work—and I find as mediators usually do that we are all *at one*, already—if we only knew it—and so I walk hand in hand with those nearest to me at the moment. . . .

I agree with Mrs. Davis in feeling that I can work with the N. Y. Society and feel at home—still I expect to call our Conn. Conventn unofficially, getting all the private signatures I can—to the call—and organising an independent state Soc. for suffrage. If in time this should desire to become auxiliary to any other it can do so—but I doubt whether we shall care to do this. . . .

. . . I hope to give a reception or Mrs. Stowe will, the day before so as to bring out the fastidious ones to the meeting—but I can't invite half the speakers I would like because I have decided on one day only—three sessions. I can't endure any more and the whole burden of this must

4. Although Lucy Stone had married Henry Blackwell in 1855, she insisted upon retaining her maiden name as a protest against unjust marriage laws, a position with which her husband heartily concurred.

come upon my single shoulders. . . . I am ready to give up my official connection with your Soc. if you all think best and I incline to do so— but at present I shall work on my own hook entirely.

>With much love
>ever yrs
>I. B. Hooker

>[IBH to Caroline Severance, SD]

The following is excerpted from part 1 of A Mother's Letters to a Daughter on Woman Suffrage. *Originally published anonymously in* Putnam's Magazine *(November and December, 1868), the two-part piece was reprinted under Isabella's name as a tract of the Connecticut Woman Suffrage Association, of which she became president.*

59   MY DEAR DAUGHTER:

You ask me what I think of the modesty and sense of a woman who can insist, in these days, that she is not sufficiently cared for in public and in private, and who wishes to add the duties of a politician to those of a mother and housekeeper. . . .

. . . [L]et me begin by asking you the meaning of the word politician. Having consulted your dictionary, you reply, "One who is versed in the science of government and the art of governing." Very well. Now who is thus versed in the science and art of governing, so far as the family is concerned, more than the mother of it? In this country, certainly, the manners, the habits, the laws of a household, are determined in great part by the mother; so much so, that when we see lying and disobedient children, or coarse, untidy and ill-mannered ones, we instinctively make our comments on the mother of that brood, and declare her more or less incompetent to her place.

Now let me suppose her to be one of the competent ones who, like your Aunt E., has helped six stout boys and four of their quick-witted sisters all the way from babyhood up to manhood and womanhood, with a wisdom and gentleness and patience that have been the wonder of all beholders—and let us think of her as sitting down now in her half-forsaken nest, calm, thoughtful, and matured, but fresh in her feeling as ever she was . . . and what wonder if she finds it hard to realize that she is unfitted either by nature or education for the work of law making, on a broader and larger scale than she has ever yet tried.

Her youngest boy, the privileged, saucy one of the crowd, has just attained his majority, we will say, and declaims in her hearing on the incompetence of women to vote—the superiority of the masculine element in politics, and the danger to society if women are not carefully guarded from contact with its rougher elements—and I seem to see her quiet smile and slightly curling lip, while in memory she runs back to the years when said stripling gathered all he knew of laws, country, home, heaven, and earth, at her knee—"and as for soiling contacts, oh! my son, who taught you to avoid these, and first put it into your curly little head, that evil communications corrupt good manners, and that 'a man cannot *touch* pitch, except he be defiled.' "

I have taken the bull by the horns, you perceive in thus taking our mother from her quiet country home and setting her by imagination among the legislators of the land;—but it is just as well, because the practical end of suffrage is, not *eligibility* to office merely, but a larger *use* of this privilege than most women have ever yet dreamed of, much less desired. . . .

And now she is there, we will say, in the legislature of our State—a high-minded, well-bred woman; one who, amid all her cares, has never failed to read the newspapers more or less, and to keep alive her interest in the prosperity of her country, whatever the claims of her numerous family. She is one, too, who has not had the assistance of wealth in doing all this; she is, as you know, straight from the rural districts, a genuine farmer's wife. But she has more leisure now than she once had, and with it there comes a longing for change, for more cultivated society, for recreations and diversions such as her busy hours have seldom afforded her; and just now, by the unanimous vote of her townspeople, she is sent to our glorious old Hub, to spend the winter in considering what the Commonwealth of Massachusetts shall do this year, by legislation, for the public good. . . . Having secured a home not far from the old State House, she seeks the Assembly Room and meets there gentlemen from all parts of the State—farmers, merchants, and mechanics, physicians, teachers and ministers, lawyers and bankers, and they go into debate on such questions as these: Shall our deaf mutes be educated at home, or in the Institution at Hartford, as heretofore? . . . State Prison—shall the discipline be penal merely, or reformatory? the institution self-supporting by a system of rigid tasks, or partially supported by the State? what punishment should be allowed, what religious and moral instruction furnished, and what sanitary regulations enforced? The prohibitory law—has it proved itself adapted to the suppression of intemperance? are its provisions enforced, and why not? . . . The school for juvenile offenders—is that managed judiciously? Here obviously the great aim should be reformation. Is a system of rewards or punishments, or both together, best adapted to that end? Should boys and girls be associated in the same buildings and classes, and for what length of time should they be retained for improvement before sending them out again into society? Endowments for colleges and other educational institutions, supported in whole or in part by the State: Shall these be confined to institutions designed exclusively for men, or shall they be applied equally to the education of both sexes? . . . Prostitution—shall it be licensed as in the old countries, or left to itself, or subjected to severe penalties? Divorces—by whom granted, and for what cause, and upon what conditions? Common schools, and high schools, and the whole system of State education; insane asylums, poor-houses, jails, and many other institutions of modern civilization:—in all these objects, you will perceive, our mother has a deep and intelligent interest, and it is not difficult to imagine the warm, even enthusiastic energy with which she will give herself to the discussion of the questions involved—some of them the highest that can come before a body of legislators.

If you say, There are other State interests with which she is less familiar, I reply, No one legislator is prepared by his previous habits of business and thought, to deal intelligently with all the questions that may come before the House, or is expected to; committees are appointed for specialties, as you know, and composed, or they ought to be, of those whose education and training have fitted them for that special investigation. . . .

And so in all matters pertaining to merchandise and business, which fairly come under state jurisdiction; it is late in the day to assert that women know nothing of these things, and could not learn if they should try. There are too many honest and successful woman-traders, artists, and litterateurs in every city of the land, and too many men dependent in whole or in part upon their earnings, to give a show of color to such assertions. . . .

On the whole, then, my dear, you begin to perceive that my mind receives no shock when I am charged with the crime of desiring to meddle with politics, and to educate my daughters as well as my sons to take an intelligent, and, if need be, an active part in the government of their country; and I am convinced that these sons will not fail ere long to be the first to recognize the propriety and wisdom of such a course on my part. The truth is, that one chief reason why young men oppose the extension of suffrage is, that their sense of true gallantry, their desire to shield and protect, is violated by their *conception* of the probable result of a woman's going to the polls. This is certainly a misconception. Every woman knows in her own heart that she does not hold her purity and delicacy subject to injury by such cause. We know that we have never entered any precinct, however vile and debased, without carrying something of that God-given power of womanhood—of motherhood—with us, which is a greater protection against insult and contamination than all the shields that man can devise. But we ought not to blame men too severely for their reluctance to relinquish this office of protector and guardian, which custom has so long laid upon them as a high duty and privilege.

In the days when physical forces ruled the world, men might naturally offer, and women receive with thankfulness, the protection of a strong arm, and become greatly dependent upon it, without serious harm to either sex; but in the day of moral forces it is quite otherwise. This day has come upon us, however, so silently, so gradually, that we ourselves have scarcely recognized that we are now near its noon-tide: how then can our fathers, brothers, and husbands, be expected to feel its quickening glow and inspiration? . . .

. . . I am persuaded, contrary to the judgment of many earnest advocates of equal suffrage, that women are quite as much responsible for the present condition of affairs as men, and that they, as a body, will be the last to be convinced of their duty in the matter of good citizenship; so I am seriously anxious to make converts to my faith from the young mothers, rather than from any other class. I know, of course, that the power of regulating suffrage now lies wholly with men; that not a single vote can be given, save by them . . . and I am convinced that the indifference, not to say opposition, of their wives, mothers, and sisters, stands in the way of their coming to a right solution of the problem before them, beyond anything and all things else. . . .

I am always your affectionate
Mother.

[IBH *ML*, pp. 3–8]

Evidence that Isabella's tracts and speeches reached
"ordinary" women across the state can be found in this

moving letter from a Norfolk, Connecticut, farmer's wife. (Hooker's reply has not been located and may not have been preserved.)

60   October 24, 1871

Mrs. Hooker or Madam

Excuse the boldness of this communication, as I write to you as to a friend, for you *are* a friend to us all. And without further preliminaries, let me state my case.

I am a farmer's wife—in this little hill-side town, having been here seventeen years. I have no children and have only the dreary routine of household cares to occupy my mind. My husband is an old-fashioned farmer, and plods contentedly on year after year without a mower or reaper, without books or anything to make home pleasant. His amusement is to go to the village store to spend his evenings and rainy days, while I *amuse* myself by mending his old pants, or some other equally agreeable occupation. I have often asked him to allow me to take some child to care for, but this he will not do. It involves expense. Of course, such a man is bitterly opposed to "woman's rights" and loses no opportunity for the usual sneer. I have no money and but few clothes. He forbids my giving anything away, as everything is *his* and nothing mine. In short I am nothing but a housekeeper without wages, doing *all* the work of the family. I have no fondness for this kind of life, but on the contrary have as keen a relish for amusements, concerts, lectures etc. as any woman in the city of Hartford.

Now Mrs. Hooker, please give me a little advice. Is it my duty to spend *all* my life in this way? Would it be wrong for me to go to Hartford this winter for a few weeks or to some other place where people *live*? Have you any friend who would give me a pleasant home, and an opportunity to attend an occasional entertainment in exchange for my services? If you ask what I can do, I reply I can do what women in the country usually do. I can sew, or do anything that is necessary to be done,—can take care of children and teach them, as this was formerly my employment. I must get away from here for a while or go crazy. Perhaps you will say I am *already* deranged.

My husband's father buried his *fourth wife* a few days since. She laid down the burden of life willingly, at sixty-two years of age. He will doubtless marry again soon, as it *costs too much* to hire a housekeeper.

You are my first and *only* confidant in this matter. If this seems worthy of a reply, please address

    Mrs. S. H. Graves.

P.S. I have omitted to say that this husband of mine has bonds[,] stocks, and notes and to these he is wedded.

     S. H. G.

              [Mrs. S. H. Graves to IBH, SD]

Two months after meeting Victoria Woodhull and hearing her unexpected testimony before the House Judiciary Committee, Isabella was still in Washington, D.C., trying to set up a national educational bureau in behalf of woman suffrage. Although she registered her mounting distress regarding the growing controversy over Woodhull, Hooker confidently predicted the political triumph of womanhood in this letter to Susan B. Anthony.

61   March 11 [and 14], 1871

Dear friend Susan.

I have longed to see and talk no less than you. . . . We agree to the dot, in everything and we have been organizing a plan of centralising the feeling and action of women all over the Union that will prove an educational Bureau, just as sure as we live to carry it out. Here it is in brief—to every woman who sends her signature to Pledge and they are coming fifty a day sometimes, we send a printed acknowledgment . . . generally on "Legal Disabilities" for . . . there is nothing like that to rouse indignation and stir to action—(I am so thankful Conn. law is so bad, we could not illustrate tendencies by a revised Code half so well). . . . These women are all so hungry—but of course they must take what we can send and circulate and circulate the one or two tracts till more money pours in. But I like the working of all this immensely—for what poor eager women borrow or pay for out of their scanty means they will read and read and remember and circulate—and in good time the little rills will begin to pour in and make a deep strong current, bearing not only vows and prayers and pledges but gold also—and we at the centre shall have the privilege of sending back for years to come all the blessed teachings of our lives on the whole duty of woman; to herself, her family and her country. To make the songs for a people was well and a power indeed in by gone years—but to write the political tracts and send them to the mothers in their homes, is to preach the gospel to every creature and that is what we may do if we will. . . .

. . . Mrs. W[oodhull] evidently and properly has her own boat to row, her own friends and party to consult and we are pretty sure that she cannot do any more for us specifically. . . . I am keeping quiet however—still praising and defending her though my sisters, all three . . . have nearly crazed me with letters imploring me to have nothing to do with her. . . . [A]nd at last comes a letter from sister Harriet from which I make an extract.[5] . . . Now as this story has a reputable name behind it and comes so nearly direct, I feel bound to give it such attention as I have given to nothing before.[6] . . . I confess that so far from being troubled at having been associated with her publicly here, provided she proves false, . . . I am only too thankful that I was sent here to reap the fruits, with my pure sisters, of her great energy and her political influence. . . . I could make pages of commendation of her brain, her heart, her manners, her conduct from men and women daily observing her—and I have not heard one word of criticism from any who have *seen her for themselves*—and many . . . came away saying . . . "Well if there is one human being that ought to vote it is that woman." I was never so perplexed to form a judgment in my life—and my prevailing belief is in her innocence and purity. I have seldom been so drawn to any woman and I talked earnestly with her many times. I knew she had visions and was inspired by *spiritual* influences she thought—but her inspiration seemed very like my own, a simple relianse [*sic*] on a Heavenly Father—a prayerful reliance on His guidance and cheerful submission to whatever came as being ordered of Him in perfect wisdom and love. I shall always love her—and in private shall work for her redemption if she is ensnared—for I never

5. According to Harriet, a member of Henry Ward Beecher's church had met Victoria Woodhull, whom he described as traveling in the company of a senator, while riding by train to Washington. Once she arrived at her hotel, Woodhull invited Henry's parishioner to visit her room and she proceeded to narrate the history of her private life. Shocked by the "astonishing" freedom of Woodhull's speech, he could only impute impure motives when she invited him to return in the evening. Instead, he left the hotel feeling that "it was no place for him" and warned the senator that she was "not a proper woman for you to be with." To which the senator replied that Woodhull had promised to "bring over" to his side one of his congressional opponents.

6. Here Isabella notes that she has written the gentleman directly to get the facts firsthand.

saw more possible nobilities in a human being than in her. If she is leading souls to death through this wonderful magnetism of hers, of course we shall not invite her to our platform nor make her a leader in any way—*nor vote for her for president in any contingency*—but we will not denounce her publicly, however guilty till the time when men guilty of the same crimes are avoided and denounced. . . .

You will send this I hope to Mrs. Stanton—and if she is in N.Y. soon she will be able to make some examination of this mysterious family—for of Tennie Claflin[7] I hear most dreadful stories—yet she has the face of a sweet innocent child. . . . But whatever comes of these two women and of our connection with them I see clearly that all is intended by God for our special training in this great work of spiritual renovation. Our battle with prejudice and sin is only just begun—and it is because men see at last that we are going to become a power, and whereto we shall exercise our power, that the powers of evil are rallying for a desperate fight. . . .

. . . Oh how plainly I see that women have got to fight for their freedom as hard as men have for theirs. The question of liberty and responsibility *seems* settled in this country and yet it is hardly touched for women—but you and Mrs. Stanton know all this. . . . Mrs. Woodhull wrote a sweet note to Mrs. Griffing. . . . She seemed wild only on one point—and that was her conviction that she was to be President next time and thus *ruler of the whole world*—our country being destined to lead all others—I advised her to keep this to herself and she appeared to after that. . . .

. . . I read the foregoing to Mrs. G.[riffing] and D.[enison][8] and they said Amen with energy and asked me to request you to send the letter not only to Mrs. Stanton but to Lucretia Mott and Mrs. [Martha Coffin] Wright,[9] which I now do—asking them all to remember . . . that it is quite confidential. I should be glad to have it sent to my husband at last,

7. Tennie C. Claflin, otherwise known as Tennessee Claflin, was Victoria Claflin Woodhull's younger sister and her partner in *Woodhull and Claflin's Weekly* as well as Woodhull, Claflin and Company, their New York brokerage firm.

8. Josephine Griffing, corresponding secretary of the NWSA, and Mary Denison, a popular novelist, both resided in Washington at this time. The name of Denison's clergyman husband has been added by Isabella to the printed list of officers of the Central Woman Suffrage Committee which appears on her stationary.

9. Sisters Lucretia Coffin Mott and Martha Coffin Wright had helped Elizabeth Cady Stanton plan the Seneca Falls Convention of 1848 and remained loyal to Stanton and Anthony after the movement split in 1869.

as he is keeping every hasty line I have written as historical matter concerning this remarkable campaign, in which one thing is chiefly to be observed, that there were no chosen leaders, but womanhood gathered itself together and walked into Congress with so firm yet modest a step that no one thought of staying her—and now she is entrenched in the Capitol, never to be dislodged. . . .

Our plan then is to advise women to register, just to get accustomed to the idea, but not to be at the expense and trouble of taking many cases into Court, since one will test the question as well as many.[10] . . . I feel the refreshing streams watering these households already—and a new era already established—enlightened families—pure politics—political economy and domestic, twin sisters—queens in their own right.

And here comes just the letter I asked for from the gentleman concerning Mrs. Wood.[hull] . . . a simple true statement of *facts* no doubt— and thanks be to God the facts are not really damaging—only *his inferences*—and these he might easily make, in honesty almost any man would, but no woman who has seen her would see any necessity for making them. . . .

A letter also from Mrs[.] Woodhull herself . . . she is feeling the persecution bitterly but stands firm.[11] . . . This is a remarkable woman and of a sweetness I have seldom seen—the truth concerning her will make its way even while she lives and the best thing for her and the cause and all

10. The following year Anthony successfully registered to vote in her home state of New York and was subsequently charged with illegal voting. Hooker analyzed the legal and political implications of Anthony's trial in her 1888 speech to the International Council of Women. See Document 63.

11. Isabella quoted Woodhull as writing: "Under all the curses and imprecations which are being heaped upon me, strong though I feel, I need some little kindness . . . from those who I believe comprehend me. When I went to Washtn. entirely upon my own account I did not desire to arouse all the petty fiendishness that has developed itself since then. . . . I must confess to not a little surprise that whatever I have done or may do is at once denounced as imprudent, unwise [etc.] and the endeavor made to stigmatise me as a very improper person. . . . I thought this was a question of *Right* under the *Constitution*. I did not know it was a question of *Antecedents*. Had I, it is quite likely I could have shown as pure a record as they who seek to defame me can. . . . I shall not change my course because those who assume to be better than I desire it. I have a consciousness within which is above all such petty malice, yet it grieves me that there should be anything to interfere with obtaining justice at the earliest possible moment. Some say they would rather never obtain it than that it should come from such a source."

womanhood will be that she keep on speaking her words of truth and soberness in every city in the land.

. . . I could not just now offer even to accompany her, without endangering the health of my husband perhaps his life, for he is feeble and extremely sensitive and unable to sleep under the least excitement—and he has been so harassed by my *three* sisters in N. York and by every friend we have in Hartford on my acct. that he is scarce able to exist. He defends my course everywhere—but in his own heart doubts the wisdom of it and is compelled to trust my judgment against his own. In the circumstances I feel that I have done my part at present in cordially welcoming Mrs. W[oodhull] to our platform . . . and in working with her . . . while she remained in Washtn. . . .

> Love to all. from yr friend
> I. B. Hooker

> [IBH to Susan B. Anthony, SD]

Hooker continued to focus on the advantages—both political and financial—to be gained by fellowship with Woodhull, even after Woodhull alienated Anthony and other members of the NWSA by deciding to run for president on a third-party ticket in the November 1872 election (a decision she publicly announced during the Apollo Hall convention mentioned below). As this letter to Elizabeth Cady Stanton reveals, Isabella perceived this development as part of a Divine plan for delivering womanhood from bondage.

62   May 12, 1872

Dear Lizzie Cady S.

. . . I thought I had fully estimated the cowardice of politicians—therefore the *opportunity* of the present political crisis. But my darling—the women of courage and singleness of purpose know nothing by intuition of the infirmities of male politicians and therefore we (even I) have underrated our power. I tell you we have got the upper hand today—*Now let us keep it.*

Apollo Hall was a success and through it the Suffrage army moves in *three* columns instead *of two*—and each wing is a host. I have never realized the situation before—now I see the whole battlefield as plainly as though in the heavens looking down upon it, from the side of the

Great God Himself, commanding the hosts. Do not smile at my enthusiasm. You know it is not *we* who have brought ourselves out of recent perils. . . . [T]hough Victoria has been a heavy load, God knows she has been and still is His own instrument for working out the deliverance from bondage and He has opened the Red Sea before us who were willing to pass through under her leadership. . . . Read [Henry] Blackwell's words as reported in Tribune about . . . the *Democratic party* *"which had once given the ballot to poor white men"*—and "where all the platforms were before him when he proposed to vote for that [party] which would most advance the cause so dear to him and if he could see any candidate who would give *woman a better chance he would vote for him.*" There you have Boston and New York fully united—our resolutions say just that—and ahead of us both is the true Labor Convention *not waiting* but nominating its own candidates. Now by the absolutely deferential tone of the Press toward Apollo and by the red flags and communistic mottoes there displayed we must recognize the powerful aid that new party brings to suffrage. They will not dare repudiate us, for they want the prestige of our social position and we want the vague shadowy honor that haunts politicians the moment that bloody revolution is threatened by the ignorant, though often good hearted leaders of the oppressed working classes. So we are the binding link between the extremes of respectability and mobocracy and *looking up* still for our guidance we can steadily guide the advancing hosts.

The first thing then is to prepare an address to the Phil. convention. . . . This must rehearse in the briefest possible manner the rise and progress of the Suffrage movement—but must contain your original 18 grievances and [1848 Seneca Falls] declaration. . . .

The main point of the address on which all forces should culminate should be that whatever the *male people* of the *States* may have to say in regard to woman[']s voting—the *people* of the *United States* are not *Males*—are no where recognized as such in Declaration and Constitution. Therefore in this period of reconstruction first preceeding our centennial Anniversary the voice of the *whole* people should be heard in all *National* Counsils [sic]. I tell you, you can make this the grandest bit of eloquent logic that ever came from your pen and may the Lord inspire and guide. . . .

I do wish that our Suffrage friends who think the cause has lost through the advent of Victoria and our advocacy of her would show us where the money and brains and unceasing energy . . . would have come from if she had not been moved to present her *Memorial* and follow it up with the prodigious outlays of the last year and a half. I verily believe she

has sunk a hundred thousand dollars in Woman Suffrage besides enduring tortures of soul innumerable—let us never forget this—let us still
overlook her faults, if she has them, remembering that she is human like
ourselves.

Ever yrs.

I. B. Hooker

[IBH to Elizabeth Cady Stanton, SD]

---

*In this 1888 speech (delivered before the International
Council of Women meeting in Washington, D.C.), Isabella took as her text* The Constitutional Rights of the
Women of the United States. *After arguing that both
the Constitution and the Declaration of Independence,
properly interpreted, guaranteed women the right to
vote as citizens, Hooker explained how the judge's rul-
ing in Susan B. Anthony's 1873 trial for "illegal voting" had forced suffragists to resort to advocating state
and national constitutional amendments.*

63   . . . And now permit me to give you briefly the argument
of woman's right to vote in our state elections as well as national, in
consequence of the fourteenth and fifteenth amendments to the constitution of the United States. It is simply this: Before the war, and reconstruction acts following it, the word "citizen" was not fully defined,
some jurists contending that all persons owing allegiance to the government and protected by it were properly citizens, and others that only
those who were accredited legal voters could properly be called citizens.
Then, when the Republican party desired to enfranchise the black men,
partly for the sake of securing their votes (I do not say that this was the
sole motive) in the next Presidential election, it was not willing to deface
the national constitution by such words as these: "All black men, formerly slaves, are citizens of the United States;" and "No State shall make
or enforce any law which shall abridge the privileges or immunities of
black men;" and again, "The right of black citizens of the United States
to vote shall not be denied or abridged by any State;" and therefore it
was driven to the annunciation of a general principle of citizenship,
applicable to all persons at all times, and this was the principle that "all
persons born or naturalized in the United States and subject to the jurisdiction thereof are citizens of the United States and of the state wherein

212 | *The Power of Womanhood*

they reside." This is a grand assertion, a true one, and one in harmony, as I have already shown, with the spirit and letter of the whole Constitution of the United States and the Declaration of Independence, and, like them, it embraced all women as well as all men, and secured to all women no less than all men their right to vote.

Now, friends, mark these words: "Secure" and "right to vote." Our claim is that the original constitution gave no right to vote to any man or woman, but it simply secured to every man and woman his or her original, natural right to govern himself or herself, except so far as he or she delegates this to others for purposes of social order. And these amendments, following the spirit of the constitution in preamble and articles, declare that all persons are citizens, and recognize the citizen's right to vote. Can anything be plainer then than that a woman, being a "person," is a citizen, and being a "citizen" has the citizen's right to vote?

It was under this conviction that she had a plain right to vote, and therefore a plain duty to vote, that Miss Anthony determined to cast her vote for President and members of Congress at a certain election. And she succeeded in convincing the registrars of her ward and the inspectors of elections that she had this right, insomuch that they registered her name, and the oath of the elector was administered and her ballot was received and counted, and then the United States came down upon her as a criminal and prosecuted her for illegal voting, under a law of Congress passed in 1870 on purpose to enforce the provisions of the fourteenth and fifteenth amendments.

Please notice, now, that formerly each state had charge of its own elections and the United States had no right to interfere with the elections in any state, even though the election was for national officers, but in the eagerness of the Republican party to enforce the amendments which would bring black votes to their aid, they gave a new power to Congress in this section: "Congress shall have the power to enforce this article," viz: "The right of citizens of the United States to vote without denial on account of race, color, or previous condition of servitude." And Congress passed what is called the Enforcement Act of 1870, which is entitled, "An act to enforce *the right of citizens of the United States to vote in the several states of the Union.*" General terms again here you perceive, not an act to enforce the right of *black men* to vote in the several states of the Union, but of *all citizens* of the United States. And the first eighteen clauses of the act are very minute in their provisions for the protection of these black men whose votes were wanted, and then there was a nineteenth clause that was intended solely to hinder white rebel men from voting, who had been disfranchised during the war, and this clause reads thus: "If at any election for representatives or delegates to Congress of the United States any person shall vote without having a lawful right to vote, every such person shall be deemed guilty of a crime, and shall for such a crime be liable to prosecution in any court of the United States of competent jurisdiction, and on conviction thereof shall be punished by a fine not exceeding $500, or by a term of imprisonment not exceeding three years, or both, in the discretion of the court, and shall pay the costs of prosecution."

And under this clause of the Enforcement Act of 1870, which was made expressly to punish white male rebel citizens for voting after they had been disfranchised for rebellion, Judge Hunt condemned Susan B. Anthony for the crime of voting "without having a lawful right to vote." This woman, the blackest of black Republicans, who had, with others like herself, furnished Mr. Sumner[12] with half his ammunition, in the shape of petitions from thousands and thousands of citizens in behalf of the black man—names which it is an enormous task to collect, but without which all appeals to Congress to do justice would have been in vain—this woman, who had violated the infamous fugitive slave law every time by giving the cup of cold water to the panting fugitive and speeding him on his way to free soil in Canada—she, thank God! of all women in this land, was selected by the government of the United States to be prosecuted, dragged from one court to another, harassed during the space of nearly a year, tried at last in another city,[13] and fined for the crime of voting for the President of the United States and members of Congress, under an act entitled "An act to enforce the right of citizens of the United States to vote in the several states of this Union," and under a clause of that act that made it a crime for a rebel to vote, because he had been deprived of his citizen's right to vote by special act of Congress in consequence of his crime of rebellion.

And, friends, do you not know that no citizen can be lawfully dis-

12. Less than a year after he entered the U.S. Senate, Charles Sumner of Massachusetts attempted to pass an amendment emancipating the slaves. Sumner later became a key political ally of the suffragists.

13. In an effort to educate the public about the issues raised by her impending jury trial, Anthony spent months canvassing the citizens of her county. The district attorney, who was clearly aware of Anthony's prowess as a campaigner, accused her of attempting to influence the jury. Twenty-two days before the trial was scheduled to begin, he moved the proceedings to another county. Anthony unsuccessfully appealed the guilty verdict by carrying a petition to Washington, D.C.

franchised either by State or Nation, except for crime or rebellion, and then only by the judgment of his peers? But in this case of Miss Anthony, she was punished, not only as if she had been guilty of crime or rebellion, or both, but she was, so far as the unjust judgment of the court could do it, disfranchised for evermore, and that without the judgment of her peers in a double sense; for she was not only denied the verdict of the male jury sitting there on purpose to render their verdict, but a jury of her peers she could not have, nor can any woman so long as women are denied the right to vote and sit upon a jury. And in the case of Miss Anthony's jury, had they been allowed to render a verdict, it would have been a verdict not of her peers, but of her political superiors, and this would have been true of them however ignorant or uneducated they were; whether black men or white, drunk or sober, every man of them was her *sovereign*, with power not only to make but to administer the laws under which she is compelled to live.

And herein is the degradation of woman to-day, not only that she cannot have a voice in making the laws and choosing officers to execute the laws, but she is compelled to be taxed, fined, imprisoned, hung even, by the verdict always of her political superiors—her male sovereigns, every one of whom is considered competent to legislate for her and to sit in judgment upon her by court and jury now and for evermore. Do you wonder that Miss Anthony declared to Judge Hunt that she should never pay this fine, or that he, apparently cowed. . ., blandly replied: "The court does not order you to stand committed till the fine is paid"? Judge Hunt knew full well that Miss Anthony would go to jail a thousand times before she would pay this unjust fine. And he knew also that the spectacle of this woman in prison for three years under charge of voting "without having a lawful right to vote" would rouse the nation to a sense of woman's political status before the law as nothing else could do; therefore he virtually remitted the fine, and by so doing sealed forever his own condemnation.

Do you ask, why recount this trial and so asperse the character of a learned and otherwise upright judge? I answer, because his decision has become a precedent, and on this account we have been compelled to relinquish, temporarily at least, our high vantage ground of constitutional rights and guarantees, and resort to the advocacy of an amendment to the national and state constitutions, measures alike dishonoring to the constitutions and to the womanhood of the country. . . .

[IBH *CRW*, pp. 13–17]

*Addressed to Isabella's sole surviving daughter, Alice
Hooker Day, these bulletins from the state and national suffrage fronts are punctuated with meditations
upon maternal love, political science, and rape. By this
time, Isabella had endured the recent death—in 1886—
of her eldest child, Mary. (It is Mary and her daughter,
Kate, to whom Isabella refers in the first letter.)*

64   February 5 [and 6], 1889
[Isabella to Alice Hooker Day]
     I wrote you a hasty line from Washtn my dear daughter and now am in
the dear old room once more, facing the dear picture [of Mary] while I
write. I find when I am away I think of that as my precious daughter and
it takes the place of the sweet but pale and sometimes sorrowful face that
always has come to me, lying on her little bed . . . patiently waiting to be
translated. And it is a great comfort. I saw so little of Mary when she was
well and always that heavy cloud of separation from Kate, that I cannot
recall any sweet expression of face except perhaps at the little lunches I
gave in the dining room here after we began housekeeping once more. I
remember how she enjoyed my broiled chicken from the poultry yard—
and can see her face light up with some witty remark that was just on
the way. I am so glad now I had those little gatherings—though I little
dreamed they would be the last. Sometimes now I seem to catch the same
peculiar turn of the head and quiet smile as she talks with friends on the
other side as I feel sure she does, in a genial happy way. . . . [T]his
mother love is such a tremendous thing. I doubt if there is any thing like
it in the heavens above or the earth beneath or the waters under the
earth—and I do hope some day it may find its own and be satisfied—if
not there never will be any heaven for me. . . .
     . . . I tell you Alice the day is not far off when we can begin to work for
our country and leave behind us all this terrible conflict for our right to
work. And it will be none too soon—Olympia Brown[14] has been study-

14. An ordained minister and one-time officer of the NWSA, Olympia Brown
was a close friend and ally of Isabella. She served as pastor of the Universalist
Church in Bridgeport, Connecticut, before moving to Wisconsin in 1878. As this
letter indicates, Brown resorted to nativist rhetoric and tactics in the 1880s.
Although she appears to be endorsing Brown's strategy here, Hooker took a
different tack in her own public writings. She drew an analogy between "native"
American women and foreign-born men in her January 1871 speech before the

ing the census and finds that so large a proportion of *foreign* population are men, (the women coming in small numbers comparatively) and so large of native pop.[ulation] are now women, (the war having killed so many men) the result is that in many States, the foreigner has two votes to the native American's one. It was startling to us when she gave her report on our platform and it was equally startling to the Judiciary Comm. of the House when she made the same assertion and showed the figures. They asked her to pursue her investigation and send the paper to the Comm. and she finds the matter confirmed at every step. This then may be the crank that is to "open the gates as high as the sky and let Queen Ann and her train pass by"—for the native *women* enfranchised will put foreign and native *men* on equal footing as nothing else can. There are other most cheering indications but I have no time to enlarge. . . .

. . . I send you some hair that you can put in a locket for your bracelet or neck and there is nothing like the life there is in hair you know—and I have saved a great deal that used to grace her [Mary's] beautiful head. When the sun shines through the curls in her picture it makes a veritable halo such as no painter has yet given to his saint—you will be surprised and comforted when you see it. . . .

   With love to all
   your fond Mother.

         [IBH to Alice Hooker Day, SD]

---

65   May 17, 1889

Dear Daughter—

 Much as I love you and enjoy your letters I can hardly bring myself to writing you on this last day for mailing, because I am so absorbed in our work. I will enclose your father's Circular to the members of the [Connecticut] Legislature—so you will understand about the two bills yet to be voted on and I will tell you a little about the vote this week on striking

---

House Judiciary Committee in which she argued against disenfranchising the latter. This speech was later published by Isabella as part of *CRW*, pp. 27–30. And, in 1898, she would praise the civic enterprise of foreign-born women in "Are Women Too Ignorant?"—a prosuffrage broadside. See Document 96.

out the word *male* from the Constitution—44 in favor, 90 against—but already the ayes are coming to us and saying "we are of the 44"—and they bring us the reprobates to be converted. The speeches of the opposition were so weak and silly that even Maj. Kinney said to a friend, "if I had to vote according to the *arguments* made today there is but one way I could vote." The [Hartford] Courant has been bitter and vigilant all the way—and is now complacent and rejoicing. But it looks as if some of the noes are ashamed of their advocates and many are willing the women should vote on school matters so we may carry the School Bill and possibly the Temperance Bill—tho' the great fight now a days is from the liquor dealers. In our hearing before the Commitee on Constitutnl Amendmts—which had charge of this Bill on striking out male six were strongly in favor and only two against—and of these two one was a young man who did no[t] attend either of our hearings, and the other was an *Irish saloon keeper*—but even he was so much impressed that he listened to me with his mouth wide open and in the public debate last Tuesday said that Mrs. Hooker was fit to be President of the U.S. but that she was an exception. . . .

. . . I have been to Litchfield, Winsted and South Manchester . . . and formed Clubs at each place for the study of political science and . . . I mean to have such a Club in every town in this State in the course of the year—then in parlor meetings women will be reading and talking about the same things and getting ready to manage town affairs as they should be managed. My first and chief proposition is that if the towns and villages are well cared for in sanitary matters, in schools in jails and poor houses, in temperance regulations and in police then the State is safe—and the States being well regulated the republic is safe and can never be brought low, as other republics have been. But masculine wisdom and patriotism cannot be depended on to protect and educate even a village community as experience has shown—so we must compel women to bear their share of burden and responsibility. At Litchfield lately, a young teacher on her way from school through some woods, was seized by a young man of respectable family and violated twice in same afternoon—being nearly choked to death—so much for our protectors!! . . .

. . . Nook Farm all well—Clemens[15] deeply interested in W. Suff. Thinks it more important than anything else for the good of country and race he tells Lilly—but whether he will give me the $100. I need remains

15. Samuel Clemens (Mark Twain) was Isabella's Nook Farm neighbor.

to be seen. We have given $150. already—and all my time and strength and much of your father's—

Postman here love to all
[Isabella]

[IBH to Alice Hooker Day, SD]

---

66   February [28], 1890

My dear daughter.

I came from Washtn on Monday and was so exhausted by mental strain day and night that I slept in the cars much of the time and so took cold—but Ned has helped me out of the sore throat and gradually I shall get back to life again. . . . I was better in Washington—but the personal consultations, Committee work, and Convention of four days, all coming after the Susan Anthony banquet which lasted till two o'clock, were enough to disable the strongest, so I am rather triumphant than otherwise and feel sure that with the help so constantly and manifestly given me from the spirit world I shall live to do much more work and see its results. . . .

I spoke half an hour Monday evening, without an idea in my head to begin with—I mean I was too tired from the banquet and from Sunday's consultations which lasted long past midnight to think out any plan—so gave myself up to the inspiration of the moment. The result was most gratifying—very many said "it was most refreshing—not a set speech, but so many points, never to be forgotten and such wit and humor! etc"—To tell the truth as nearly as I could recall the scene it seems as if brother Henry[16] had it all his own way—one gesture I remember especially and the house was convulsed with laughter and moved to tears alternately. He has entreated me many times to give myself up to his control—but I have not been quite ready to trust him to speak for a woman's soul—possibly he saw his opportunity and used it so well I shall never be afraid of him again.

But my daughter—I am more than ever impressed with the superior mental and moral power of womankind. In all those four days there was not a weak word uttered from young or old and every phase of patriotism and statesmanship was clearly manifest. No body of men that ever

16. Henry Ward Beecher had died in 1887. Like other avid spiritualists, Isabella considered herself to be in frequent contact with the spirits of deceased friends and relatives.

came together for righteous purposes I verily believe showed as much common sense and uttered it in such elegant language—yet scarce a woman there has had a liberal education and most of us have gathered our wisdom and knowledge while caring for our children in the family or teaching other people[']s children in the schools. Oh I am proud of my sex—I am so glad men have had to have mothers as well as fathers. Though you wouldn't suspect it from history or current literature. . . .

Speaking of Convention Mrs. Stanton gave a magnificent address and then called from the box where I was sitting with her, her daughter Mrs. [Harriet Stanton] Blatch of Basingstoke Eng.[land] and introduced her to the audience—and she spoke for ten minutes with admirable manner and perfect self possession. She is the one whose address I sent you for England and she wishes much to meet you. She has a daughter five yrs. old, is happily married to a well to do Englishman [(]his father a rich brewer who won[']t let him come to this country so long as he lives[)]. Mrs. Stanton sailed with her the day after this and I could almost envy her such a daughter—beautiful and gifted, who will not only take up her work after she is gone but is enthusiastically with her already. She is a college graduate—studied in the School of Oratory and is already a statesman—yet dresses with exquisite taste and looks not over twenty one—and her husband enjoys seeing her devoted to reform work in England of the most radical sort. . . .

Mother

[IBH to Alice Hooker Day, SD]

In January of 1902 Isabella presented the text of An Argument on United States Citizenship *to the Connecticut Constitutional Convention, then meeting in Hartford. She asked the group to amend the state constitution by striking out the word "male" and adding a section guaranteeing that the right to vote and hold office "shall not be denied or abridged on account of sex." Halfway into this speech, which she had privately printed "by the thousand," she shrewdly incorporated the following personal reminiscence of the 1893 Columbian Exposition (held in Chicago) in which she explicitly connects woman suffrage with the cause of world peace. The convention's refusal to give this argument a public or private hearing struck her as "a crush-*

> *ing blow," for it ended her hopes of living to see the*
> *women of her state vote.*[17]

67   . . . During the six months of the Columbian Exposition
I had the honor of serving my country officially as one of the Board of
Lady Managers, and noticing in the papers one morning that Venezuela
was to open her house to visitors at a certain hour that day, and remembering the profound interest with which I have long regarded these
young republics, struggling for existence and looking to us as an example
of free government, I went alone and early and without special authority
. . . and introducing myself to an officer as one of the Board of Lady
Managers who desired an introduction to the commissioners, was at
once made courteously welcome. . . . [T]he ceremonies began by a short
speech in English welcoming the United States and all foreign peoples to
a cordial friendship and to the hospitalities of the occasion. . . . I looked
about me for members of our Commission who should respond to his
cordial greeting, but not one was in sight, nor even one of my own
Board. I whispered to a gentleman standing near and said, "Is it possible
there is to be no response from the United States?" "Apparently not, (he
said). Would you like to say something?" "Indeed I should if no one else
appears," I replied . . . and after a courteous introduction I said, . . .
"Listening to your encomiums upon our country and her form of government I am reminded of what has been the great felicity of my life—for
fifty years I have enjoyed the daily companionship of a gentleman who is
sixth in descent from Thomas Hooker, the founder of the State of Connecticut. This Thomas Hooker, who as a preacher and theologian stands
foremost in the history of the New England church, was also a statesman, and to him is credited the substance and in part the form of the first
written constitution of the world. That became the Bill of Rights of the
state of Connecticut and upon it was framed the Constitution of the
United States, as well as of many states of the Union. And now at last,
having stood the test of two centuries, you gentlemen are making it in
substance your own. One of your number has just given me a copy of it
in Spanish and informs me that it is already being translated into English, and he kindly offers to send me a copy. When he does this I shall
read it with care, for the study of constitutions seems to me the basis for
the study of political economy—the science of government; and if I find
there that you have improved upon our model, I will surely make it
known to our people, and they will doubtless in due time incorporate it

17. "The Last of the Beechers," p. 298.

into our own constitution, for Connecticut wants the best and will be satisfied with nothing less. But speaking for the Board of Lady Managers, who should I think have sent you an official recognition, permit me to say to you there is one meaning to this great Exposition that I trust will not escape your notice—it is this—[']Peace on earth, good will to men.['] This is our woman's motto—this is the text out of which shall come the fraternity of nations that shall endure so long as time shall last. Carry this home to your constituents, gentlemen, let them know through you that the days of war are ended, at least on this continent, and that in the industries of peace shall be our only rivalry." . . . Afterward . . . a member of the Commission . . . said to me:—"I enjoyed your remarks with one exception—this matter of peace. That can never be; it is useless to hope for it." "Why not?" said I. "Because of the nature of man," said he. "I have studied him professionally and scientifically and this business of cutting throats will never cease. I am sure of that." Seeing my look of amazement he said, "I go so far as this even—I believe these death dealing guns will go on to such perfection that whole nations will be swept out of existence—one after another will yield to the stronger, till only one nation is left, and then internal disputes will rage till only two men will be left and when one of these goes down, the other will destroy himself." Looking him steadily in the face I said, "I see your meaning, and from your point of view it may be so, but you have left out one factor of the problem—the women of the race. They seem to have been forgotten in the past, but are now in the ascendent, and we mothers are fast coming to the fixed resolve that we will bring no more sons into the world to cut each other's throats. Where then will fighters come from?" . . .

[IBH, *Argument*, pp. 9–10]

III.   The Politics of Sisterhood

8.

Catharine Esther Beecher: "Her Aegis of Defence"

T HE half-century mark found Catharine Beecher's energies undiminished. She spent most of the 1850s shuttling back and forth between the East and Milwaukee, where she had founded the Milwaukee Female Seminary in 1850. Catharine raised money for the school, designed its programs, and lobbied its trustees for a permanent home for herself near its grounds. She also continued to publish prolifically. In addition to *The True Remedy for the Wrongs of Woman* (1851) and the 1869 *American Woman's Home*, in the last twenty-five years of her life Beecher wrote three books on religion, two on health, and one each on housework and woman suffrage.[1] In 1874, four years before her death, she would publish her autobiographical *Educational Reminiscences and Suggestions*.

At the end of the 1850s, nevertheless, Beecher's active life was drawing to a close. By then, it was clear that her hopes for retiring to her Milwaukee seminary would not be realized. By then, too, Lyman, whose move to Ohio had prompted Catharine's own, had given up his dream of conquering the West and retreated to the East Coast. He died in Brooklyn, New York, in 1863.

Catharine soon followed her family east. In the late 1860s, she lived with Harriet in Hartford, where the two collaborated on *The American Woman's Home* and where Catharine tried unsuccessfully to revive the Hartford Female Seminary. In 1877, she moved to Elmira, New York, to the home of her brother Thomas and his wife, Julia. There, on May 12, 1878, after half a century of public life, Catharine Beecher died. "She has seen father, and mother . . . ," Charles Beecher wrote, "She is 'gathered to her people' in the Significant language of the old old time."[2]

In 1828, Catharine had written to Edward Beecher that she wished she "could catch my *inward woman*, and give her such an inspection and exposition" as her brother was giving his "*inward man*." "[B]ut she is such a restless being that I cannot hold her still long enough to see her true form and outline," she had complained.[3] Her comments proved prophetic. Throughout her adult life, Beecher avoided self-reflection—claiming, as she had to Edward, that she was too deeply "engaged in moulding, correcting, and inspecting the character of *others*" to undertake the same task for herself.[4] Yet Beecher's aversion to introspection appears to have sprung less from the burden of her duties to the outer world than from her ambivalence about the inner one. During her conversion crisis, her "inward woman"—irrepressibly energetic and eager for autonomy—had threatened all that bound her to her family. Thereafter, Beecher shrank from confrontation, and shrank as well from acknowledging openly the ambitions that prompted her career. Never a rebel by choice, she pursued a more circuitous strategy, seeking to define a public persona congenial to the traditions of her parents, and to work from within to expand women's—and her own—power. The decision was critical not only to her life but to the shape of her philosophy, for Beecher's "domesticity" emerged as an ideology strangely at odds with itself: conservative, even repressive, fundamentally bound to Beecher's class and racial interests, it was nonetheless steeped in discontent, critical of the narrow "sphere of usefulness"[5] allotted to females, and constantly subversive of it. It was the politics of a divided self, writ large into the gender ideologies of a developing nation.

Those divisions were apparent in Beecher's relationships with her family. Loyal and deeply committed to the welfare of her siblings, Catharine was also captive to the imperatives of her own personality. Her relationship with Harriet, her closest family ally during her adult years, was marked by this ambiguity of purpose. Twice, in Hartford and in Cincinnati, Catharine had given Harriet a position in her school—and twice she had ended by giving Harriet all the responsibility as well, insisting "that on account of her reputation it would be better to have the public think that she was at the head of it."[6] In 1851, Catharine moved in with Harriet and Calvin, assuming a portion of the domestic responsibilities so that Harriet could be free to complete *Uncle Tom's Cabin.* But Catharine soon grew proprietary about her sister's work, threatening to attack Harriet's publisher in print if he did not revise her contract. The Beecher family was dismayed. "I wrote to Kate," Mary Beecher Perkins reported to Lyman, "stating that H. and Mr[.] Stowe were perfectly satisfied . . . and entreating her by every thing she loved and valued to be still—[.]" But, Mary added, "all we can say passes by her like the idle wind."[7]

Isabella, too, felt the effects of Catharine's self-absorption. In an 1869 letter, she blasted her elder sibling with the accumulated resentments of years, accusing Catharine of being habitually inconsiderate, of creating animosities among family members, and of taking advantage of her siblings' generosity. Especially striking in the letter, given Catharine's prominence as an educator and advocate of domesticity, was Isabella's disclosure that for years she had been hesitant to allow her daughters to associate with their aunt.[8]

As even Isabella recognized, "nothing could be kinder than [Catharine's] motives,"[9] but her inability to transcend her own needs frequently rendered her actions inappropriate to her stated aims and gave her affection a cast of self-interest. Nowhere was this incongruity more apparent than in her 1843 letter of condolence to her sister-in-law Sarah, following George Beecher's death. Observing that she and her sister-in-law had been "united in suffering and sorrow," she deftly remolded Sarah's grief to her own ends, both long-term and immediate. Sarah should work with Catharine on the project of preparing teachers for the West, Catharine advised; but first, if Sarah could "conveniently loan me one hundred dollars," Catharine could afford to revive her own energies by taking the water cure at a northern New York health spa.[10]

Beecher's apparent insensitivity to her sister-in-law's grief deserves a more generous reading in the context of her own life as an unmarried woman, however. Spinsters had few rights—and many dependencies—in antebellum America, and Beecher fought hard to preserve both her independence and her dignity. Only the year before George Beecher's death, a breach between herself and her second stepmother, Lydia Beals Jackson Beecher, had threatened Catharine's welcome at Walnut Hills, the Beecher family home near Cincinnati. Reliant upon periodic assistance from her family and determined to protect "all my rights and privileges" as a Beecher, Catharine responded with a thinly veiled threat to make the trouble public—an unpleasant tactic, surely, but one that may have seemed necessitated by her vulnerability.[11]

Catharine's preoccupation with the circumstances of her own life also shaped her larger vision of American domesticity. She wrote for an audience of white middle-class women much like herself, and she assumed a community of values with her readers. Indeed, as an unmarried, professional woman—and therefore of marginal status—she struggled all the harder to affirm that community. Her domestic advice was directed to the mistress of a prosperous household, or one only temporarily cut off from middle-class resources. Although she was keenly aware of the varieties of labor required of middle-class wives, her catalogues of domestic work failed to encompass the vending, scavenging, and outwork that added to the family responsibilities of poorer women.[12] And while Beecher was clear-sighted about the domestic hardships of trying to maintain genteel respectability in the face of an erratic economy and inadequate help, her caution that the wise woman "will aim to secure a house so planned that it will provide in the best manner for health, industry, and economy"[13] was hollow advice indeed for women whose families had to double or triple up to afford even a single-room cellar.[14]

Beecher did not recognize, in racial, class, religious, or ethnic backgrounds other than her own, the stuff of which American civilization could be made. She deemed Catholicism "a false and slavish" faith and tended to look upon immigrants as ignorant.[15] Although she insisted that all women should be able to support themselves and deplored the effects of factory labor on females, her understanding of working-class life, and of the dynamics of class privilege, remained superficial.[16] In the *Essay on Slavery and Abolitionism*, Beecher suggested that much of the prejudice faced by blacks was of their own making, arguing that slaves needed to remedy defects in "their intelligence, their usefulness, their respectability, their meekness, gentleness, and benevolence" before seeking emancipation.[17] Indeed, despite her frequent affirmations of the power of sisterhood, Beecher appears to have had a poor opinion of women in general. Her 1870 Boston antisuffrage address included a devastating catalogue of female shortcomings.[18] For herself, both personally and professionally, Beecher cultivated women of "piety, education and wealth."[19] When, near the end of her life, she grudgingly conceded some ground to the suffragists, it was only with the hope that, if females must vote, at least the franchise might be limited to women who "*are duly qualified by paying taxes and a certain measure of education.*"[20] Otherwise, she concluded, the only result of enfranchising women "would be a vast increase of the incompetent and dangerous voters."[21]

Beecher sometimes attacked as "unwomanly" those females whose values departed from her vision of female domesticity. Under her pen, for example, utopianist Fanny Wright became "masculine . . . with brazen front and brawny arms"—not really a woman at all, but rather a "thing in the shape of a woman."[22] More generally, however, women whose lives differed significantly from Beecher's were simply invisible in her writings as Beecher appropriated for her own class and race the mantle of "American womanhood." This assertion of cultural hegemony was particularly apparent in her *Essay on Slavery and Abolitionism*. Arguing that women should oppose slavery only indirectly, by quiet persuasion, she asked rhetorically: "And is there not a peculiar propriety in such an emergency, in looking for the especial agency and assistance of females, who are shut out from the many temptations that assail the other sex,—

who are the appointed ministers of all the gentler charities of life."[23] The assumption that females escaped the assaults of the larger world was inaccurate even for most free women. In a tract about slavery, it amounted to a jarring obliviousness to the experiences of slave women themselves. It might have been to Catharine Beecher, rather than to a male heckler at a suffrage convention, that former slave Sojourner Truth bared her strong arm and demanded, "Ar'n't I a woman?"[24]

In the *Essay on Slavery and Abolitionism*, Beecher had argued for "influence," rather than direct action, as the appropriate vehicle for the exercise of female power. Her reliance on "influence" reflected Beecher's psychological rooting in the early nineteenth century. The Connecticut world in which she had spent her formative years was one in which only freemen who were property owners enjoyed suffrage, and many of these did not vote. Between 1800 and 1823, when Catharine opened the Hartford Female Seminary, voting rates in Connecticut gubernatorial elections averaged only 29 percent, peaking in 1819 at 42 percent.[25] Moreover, the model of her father—exhorting, cajoling, persuading his flocks to God—was a model of power exerted through influence rather than through direct agency.

But the rhetoric of "influence" also reflected Beecher's class allegiance, for female influence was a largely elite tradition. Throughout the late eighteenth and early nineteenth centuries, elite women had used their contacts with male relatives and friends to raise money for charitable organizations, to influence government policy, and even to achieve informally legal rights officially denied to them as women.[26] Without such contacts, and without legal rights after marriage to their wages, to their children, or (unless specified in a special legal instrument) to their own property—indeed, in the case of slave women, existing as property—many women discovered that their influence was minor even within the immediate sphere of their daily lives.

In her own experience, Beecher was not without some understanding of the limits of the politics of "influence." Although in the *Essay on Slavery and Abolitionism*, she had categorically denied the propriety of women's petitioning Congress, in her *Educational Reminiscences*, she proudly recalled her anonymous participation in an 1828 petition campaign on behalf of the Cherokee, and in her 1870 "Address on Female Suffrage," she threatened that opponents of suffrage like herself might lobby the federal government with "such an array of petitions and remonstrances . . . as never before entered congressional halls."[27] More to the point, Beecher's own life had shown her that simply asking was not always enough. For forty-five years, she asked the influential men of the various communities in which she lived to provide her with the funds to endow a school for women. Her request was never granted.

Beecher felt that failure. It is one of the ironies of her career that, barely concealed beneath her prescriptions for female domesticity, was a rankling at the limits set to woman's sphere and a bitterness at the social prerogatives of men. As early as 1829 she had complained that while the "three [male] professions of law, divinity, and medicine, present a reasonable prospect of reputation, influence and emolument," teaching, the only profession available to antebellum women, "has been looked upon as . . . a drudgery suited only to inferior minds."[28] It was a complaint to which she returned often—usually in reference to women's status as teachers, but also in discussions of housework, protesting, "It is generally assumed, and almost as generally conceded, that women's business and cares are contracted and trivial; and that the proper discharge of her duties demands far less expansion of mind and vigor of intellect, than the pursuits of the other sex."[29] But Beecher's most uncontrolled attack on males came at midcentury, in the defense of a former student, Delia Bacon.

In the late 1840s, Bacon was rumored to have engaged in an improper flirtation with New Haven minister Alexander MacWhorter. Bacon insisted that MacWhorter, some years her junior, had initiated the relationship and had even proposed marriage, but a clerical court cleared him of all serious wrongdoing. Mortified by the publicity of the trial, Bacon decided not to press the case further. Not so Catharine Beecher, who identified with the social ambiguities of Bacon's position as a capable, ambitious, and unmarried woman. Although Bacon pleaded with Beecher to spare her a "new kind of martyrdom," in 1850 Beecher published *Truth Stranger than Fiction*, a 300-page attack on MacWhorter, Yale University, and the Connecticut Congregational clergy generally. Most of the volume was given over to the details of the scandal and trial, but Beecher made clear in the opening chapter that her quarrel was equally with the sexual double standard that taught women "that a happy marriage is the summit of all earthly felicity"[30] and yet penalized them for pursuing that goal aggressively. She may have been remembering the cool responses which, recurrently, had greeted her own assertiveness.

Beecher did not confine her attack to the male clergy, but included the male medical profession as well. In *Letters to the People on Health and Happiness* (1855), she argued that the confinement of the home and the growing prejudice against manual labor were acting together to ruin women's health. But she added a barely veiled attack on male doctors, whom she characterized as amoral and whom she charged with sexual assaults on female patients. Although she insisted that she did not mean to impugn the ethics of all male practitioners, Beecher ended the book with the assertion that women should claim health care as a natural aspect of their domain as mothers.[31]

Beecher's anger persisted into her later years. In 1860, she returned to her criticisms of the clergy, now explicitly calling upon women to reject those religious teachings that conflicted with their own experience as mothers: "Every well-educated, pious woman of good common sense, who has trained young children, is *better* qualified to interpret the Bible correctly, on all points pertaining to such practical duties, than most theologians."[32] Even in her spirited opposition to woman suffrage in her 1870 address on the subject, she readily granted that suffragists and antisuffragists shared a conviction that American women had been denied "equal advantages" with men and that "multiplied wrongs and suffering have resulted from this injustice."[33]

Yet Beecher never seriously supported woman suffrage. In part, her own class background accounts for this inconsistency. Beyond that, however, was another concern. Present throughout her adult life, but increasingly pronounced in her later years—and certainly helping to explain her willingness to recognize the validity of all-female families—was a fear of the brute force of males and of the social, sexual, and physical vulnerability of women. Only at their own very great peril did women challenge men's power directly. Beecher hinted at this in the *Essay on Slavery and Abolitionism*, in which she argued against women's participation in the abolition movement in part on the grounds of the sanctions certain to be brought against women acting aggressively in the public sphere: "The moment woman begins to feel the promptings of ambition, or the thirst for power," she warned, "her aegis of defence is gone. All the sacred protection of religion, all the generous promptings of chivalry, all the poetry of romantic gallantry, depend on woman's retaining her place as dependent and defenceless, and making no claims."[34] As much as *Truth Stranger than Fiction* stood as a diatribe against the sexual double standard, moreover, it was even more powerful as a sputtering admission of helplessness in the face of male power, experienced as a cataclysm of nature: "like some of those troubled dreams of the sick bed, when the sun seems moving from his centre, and all the heavenly bodies are rushing from their courses in confusion and dismay."[35] However great her fury, what Beecher produced was an image of disability.

Beecher returned to this discussion of male power and female vulnerability in her antisuffrage writings. In her "Appeal to American Women" in 1869, she argued that since "God has given to man the physical power," men would always be in a position to retaliate against women who challenged their authority. She insisted that it was the purest fantasy to imagine that men would forego the use of that power, and she concluded grimly that the suffragists' "methods are not safe."[36] In her 1870 antisuffrage address in Boston, she reminded women again, "As things now are, men have the physical power that can force obedience; in most cases they have the power of the purse, and in all cases, they have the civil power. They cannot be forced by the weaker sex to resign this power." She advised that women "*ask for the thing needed*," rather than press for the ballot.[37]

Her distrust of males as a group illuminates a final irony in Beecher's defense of the family and in her support of female "influence" as an alternative to direct political action. Corrupted by contact with the world beyond the home, male nature itself posed the greatest threat to women and the domestic realms they sought to create. Only to the extent that maleness could be disciplined and restrained could the threat be defused, and womanhood protected and elevated. That end could not be accomplished through large-scale political action, which, Beecher argued, necessarily depended for its success on the willingness of males to grant the justice of the cause. Rather, womanhood could be protected only on a one-to-one basis, in the home. There individual women might civilize individual men, nurturing the "the hopes of paternity" that characterized "every true man" into feelings of commitment and protectiveness.[38] Only in the home could man be made "to labor and suffer to . . . elevate woman for her high calling."[39]

Rather than risk an open confrontation, then, Catharine Beecher chose what she considered to be a safer way—a way available to her as a result of her class position and race: she accepted the gender system as she found it and attempted to expand women's power within it. Her gains for women were considerable: not only did she contribute measurably to the expansion of women's educational opportunities, and to the social acceptability of women in various professions, but she also helped to shape a notion of shared strength and purpose among women that has been resurgent in the contemporary women's movement. At the same time, Beecher's strategy for the empowering of women was fundamentally divisive and defensive—excluding more women than it included, confining women to a single sphere of action even as it aimed to enlarge their choices. In that respect, too, Catharine Beecher's legacy survives into the late twentieth century.

NOTES

1. These included: *Letters to the People on Health and Happiness* (New York: Harper and Brothers, 1855), *Physiology and Calisthenics for School and Families* (New York: Harper and Brothers, 1856), *Common Sense Applied to Religion, or the Bible and the People* (New York: Harper and Brothers, 1856), *An Appeal to the People in Behalf of Their Rights as Authorized Interpreters of the Bible* (New York: Harper and Brothers, 1860), *The Religious Training of Children in the School, the Family, and the Church* (New York: Harper and Brothers, 1864), *Woman Suffrage and Woman's Profession* (Hartford: Brown and Gross, 1871), and *Miss Beecher's Housekeeper and Healthkeeper* (New York: Harper and Brothers, 1873). *Woman Suffrage and Woman's Profession* was reprinted (with few changes) in 1872 as *Woman's Profession as Mother and Educator, with Views in Opposition to Woman Suffrage* (Philadelphia and Boston: George McClean, 1872). In 1850, Beecher had also published *Truth Stranger than Fiction* (New York: printed for the author). In addition, during this period she co-authored two books on housework with Harriet Beecher Stowe.

2. Charles Beecher to Isabella Beecher Hooker, May 19, 1878, SD.

3. Catharine Esther Beecher to Edward Beecher, August 23, 1828, MHCL. See Document 20.

4. Catharine Esther Beecher to Edward Beecher, August 23, 1828, MHCL. See Document 20.

5. Catharine Esther Beecher to Lyman Beecher, February 15, 1823, SD. See Document 13.

6. Sarah L. Dickinson to Catherine M. Forsyth, n.d., AH&G/CSL. The Stowe-Day Foundation has dated their copy of this letter "after 1844." Dickinson was specifically referring to the Western Female Institute in Cincinnati. In Hartford, too, Catharine had taken advantage of Harriet's presence to evade the burdens of the school—especially after her own enthusiasm had begun to flag in light of Hartford's refusal to support an endowment. For example, Catharine had spent much of the winter of 1829–30 in Boston, leaving Harriet (then only eighteen years old) in charge of the seminary.

7. Mary Beecher Perkins to Lyman Beecher, January 22, 1853, SD.

8. Isabella Beecher Hooker to Catharine Esther Beecher, n.d. [before May 9, 1869?], SD. See Document 112.

9. Isabella Beecher Hooker to Catharine Esther Beecher, n.d. [before May 9, 1869?], SD. See Document 112.

10. Catharine Esther Beecher to Sarah Beecher Buckingham, August 20, 1843, SD. See Document 70.

11. Catharine Esther Beecher to Lydia Beals Jackson Beecher, n.d. [c. 1842], SD. See Document 69.

12. See, for example, Jeanne Boydston, *Home and Work: Housework, Wages, and the Ideology of Labor in the Early Republic* (New York: Oxford University Press, 1990), and Christine Stansell, "Women, Children, and the Uses of the

Streets: Class and Gender Conflicts in New York City, 1850–1860," *Feminist Studies* 8, no. 2 (Summer 1982): 309–35.

13. Catharine E. Beecher and Harriet Beecher Stowe, *The American Woman's Home: Principles of Domestic Science* (New York: J. B. Ford, 1869), p. 24. See Document 53.

14. For descriptions of the living conditions of the working classes of mid-nineteenth-century New York, for example, see John H. Griscom, *The Sanitary Condition of the Laboring Population of New York* (New York: Harper and Brothers, 1845; New York: Arno Press, 1970).

15. Catharine Esther Beecher to Sarah Buckingham Beecher, August 20, 1843, SD. See Document 70. For Beecher's attitudes toward immigrants, see for example, "An Appeal to American Women" in *AWH*, especially pp. 466–67. See Document 75.

16. In the *Treatise*, Beecher insisted that "every domestic, and every artisan and laborer" had the option of choosing the conditions of her or his work—this while the country was experiencing the most widespread unemployment of its sixty-year history. See Catharine E. Beecher, *A Treatise on Domestic Economy, for the Use of Young Ladies at Home, and at School* (Boston: Marsh, Capen, Lyon, and Webb, 1841), p. 3. See Document 51.

17. Catharine E. Beecher, *An Essay on Slavery and Abolitionism, with Reference to the Duty of American Females* (Philadelphia: Henry Perkins, 1837), p. 27. See Document 50.

18. Catharine E. Beecher, "An Address on Female Suffrage, Delivered in the Music Hall of Boston, in December, 1870" in *WSWP*, pp. 10–12. See Document 76.

19. Catharine Esther Beecher to Sarah Buckingham Beecher, August 20, 1843, SD. See Document 70.

20. Catharine E. Beecher, *Educational Reminiscences and Suggestions* (New York: J. B. Ford, 1874), p. 201.

21. Catharine E. Beecher, "Address on Female Suffrage," p. 12. See Document 76.

22. Catharine E. Beecher, *Letters on the Difficulties of Religion* (Hartford: Belknap and Hammersley, 1836), p. 23. See Document 68.

23. CEB *ESA*, p. 128. See Document 50.

24. Sojourner Truth was a former slave and supporter of woman suffrage. This famous question was posed during the 1851 Akron, Ohio, women's rights convention. Truth was specifically addressing a man in the audience, but many white females also resisted sharing the podium—and a movement—with black women. Following Deborah Gray White's lead, I have used the spelling "ar'n't," rather than "ain't," because it is the spelling which appears in Truth's own *Narrative of Sojourner Truth, a Bondwoman of Olden Time*. See Deborah Gray White, *Ar'n't I a Woman: Female Slaves in the Plantation South* (New York: W. W. Norton, 1985). For additional information on black women in the nineteenth century, see Jacqueline Jones, *Labor of Love, Labor of Sorrow: Black Women, Work, and the*

Family from Slavery to the Present (New York: Basic Books, 1985), especially pp. 11–151.

25. These numbers are from J. R. Pole, *Political Representation in England and the Origins of the American Republic* (Berkeley and Los Angeles: University of California Press, 1971), pp. 545–48. For an excellent discussion of the changing importance of suffrage over the antebellum period, and of the importance of this change for women, see Lori D. Ginzberg, *Women and the Work of Benevolence: Morality, Politics, and Class in the Nineteenth-Century United States* (New Haven, Conn.: Yale University Press, 1990), especially pp. 98–132.

26. See Ginzberg, *Women and the Work of Benevolence*, pp. 40–53.

27. CEB *ESA*, p. 104 (see Document 50); CEB *ER*, pp. 62–65; Catharine E. Beecher, "Address on Female Suffrage," p. 16 (see Document 76).

28. Catharine E. Beecher, *Suggestions Respecting Improvements in Education, Presented to the Trustees of the Hartford Female Seminary* (Hartford: Packard and Butler, 1829), p. 4. See Document 21.

29. CEB *TDE*, p. 142. See Document 51.

30. CEB *TSF*, p. 9. See Document 71.

31. CEB *LPHH*, p. 186. See Document 72.

32. CEB *Appeal*, p. 355. See Document 73.

33. Catharine E. Beecher, "Address on Female Suffrage," p. 4. See Document 76.

34. CEB *ESA*, pp. 101–2. See Document 50.

35. CEB *TSF*, p. 237.

36. Catharine E. Beecher, "Appeal to American Women" in *AWH*, p. 468. See Document 75.

37. Catharine E. Beecher, "Address on Female Suffrage," pp. 17, 18. See Document 76.

38. *AWH*, p. 19. See Document 53. For a parallel analysis of contemporary views of the importance of the family and of the home, see Andrea Dworkin, *Right-wing Women* (New York: G. P. Putnam Sons, 1978), especially pp. 13–35.

39. Catharine E. Beecher, "An Address to Christian Women of America" in CEB *WSWP*, p. 184. See Document 77.

Putatively a collection of correspondence with friends of varying religious persuasions, Beecher's Letters on the Difficulties of Religion *(1836) was a layperson's guide to theology. Work on the book coincided with the return to America of British reformer Frances Wright, whose support of liberalized divorce laws, birth control, and free love made her anathema to Beecher's emerging idea of womanhood. A discussion of Wright opened the* Letters.

68   . . . As to Fanny Wright, you said you believed her to be honest in her opinions, amiable in her disposition, philanthropic in her efforts, and endowed with rare intellect. Allowing that you are as near right as partisans usually are, in estimating leaders, still I must compliment you by saying, that I believe you have secret *feelings* that would present a very different picture of this strange excrescence of female character.

Every man of sense and refinement, admires a woman *as a woman*; and when she steps out of this character, a thousand things that in their appropriate sphere would be admired, become disgusting and offensive.

The ap[p]ropriate character of a woman demands delicacy of appearance and manners, refinement of sentiment, gentleness of speech, modesty in feeling and action, a shrinking from notoriety and public gaze, a love of dependence, and protection, aversion to all that is coarse and rude, and an instinctive abhorrence of all that tends to indelicacy and impurity, either in principles or actions. These are what are admired and sought for in a woman, and your sex demand and appreciate these qualities, as much as my own. With this standard of feeling and of taste, who can look without disgust and abhorrence upon such an one as Fanny Wright, with her great masculine person, her loud voice, her untasteful attire, going about unprotected, and feeling no need of protection, mingling with men in stormy debate, and standing up with barefaced impudence, to lecture to a public assembly. And what are the topics of her discourse, that in some cases may be a palliation for such indecorum? Nothing better than broad attacks on all those principles that protect the purity, the dignity, and the safety of her sex. There she stands, with brazen front and brawny arms, attacking the safeguards of all that is venerable and sacred in religion, all that is safe and wise in law, all that is pure and lovely in domestic virtue. Her talents only make her the more conspicuous and offensive, her amiable disposition and sincerity, only make her folly and want of common sense the more pitiable, her freedom from private vices, if she is free, only indicates, that without delicacy, and without principles, she has so thrown off all feminine attractions, that freedom from temptation is her only, and shameful palladium. I cannot conceive any thing in the shape of a woman, more intolerably offensive and disgusting. . . .

[CEB *LDR*, pp. 22–23]

> *As an unmarried woman, without a permanent home of her own, Catharine was particularly vulnerable to strains within the Beecher family—even strains that she helped to create. This was evident in her relationship with Lyman's third wife, Lydia Beals Jackson Beecher. Lydia felt that Catharine had been consistently disrespectful of her,*[1] *while Catharine believed that Lydia was trying to exclude her from the Beecher home, Walnut Hills, in Cincinnati.*

69   [c. 1842]

Dear Mother

When I proposed having a woman come to sew for me, your replies were such that I concluded you did not choose to give your consent—Of course, I should not have one come without your consent—The only alternative is for me to go either to Uncle Sam[ue]l[']s[2] or Harriet[']s and have the woman come there.

I cannot take such a step without results that you ought to be able to take into consideration and therefore I write this.

The strong attachment between father and his children and the anxiety he and Isabella's mother[3] always manifested to have Aunt Esther[4] live with him, are so well and so widely known, that it would be impossible to prevent the public from suspecting that Aunt E. and I both stay away

1. See, for example, [Lydia Beals Jackson Beecher to Catharine Esther Beecher], n.d. [c. 1842], SD.

2. Samuel Foote, Roxana Foote Beecher's brother, who was living in Cincinnati.

3. Lyman's second wife, Harriet Porter Beecher.

4. Esther Beecher, Catharine's aunt, also unmarried, who had lived with the Beecher family for many years.

so much from home as we have done the last five years for *some other* reason than father[']s feelings and wishes on the subject.

Since your children have been so much here and Aunt E[.] and I so much away as during the last two or three years there has been an increasing uneasiness and suspiciousness not only in all our family circle but in the public, that something is wrong and that *father* in his declining years has to suffer deprivations which could not be believed to exist with[out] great and deep felt indignation. . . .

I have always said to my mother's family friends in the city and to all my brothers and sisters that I had all my rights and privileges and that there was nothing to prevent my going home when ever I pleased and living comfortably there. . . .

If it were believed that I could not live comfortably at home and have all done for me that is proper I know it would awaken such feelings among my brothers and sisters and my wide circle of friends as would *make the matter public*—and then there would be two parties and no end to the gossip, the lies and the recrimination that would distress and disgrace us all.

It is necessary *for the reputation of the family* that I should live a part of the time at home and that I should be able still to say as I always have said, that "every thing is done for me that ought to be done and that I have nothing to complain of." . . .

I am very sure that there is nothing in my feelings to prevent my enjoyment of your society and friendship and that if I knew anything I could do, (that was not wrong) I would at least try my best to accomplish it, if I thus might relieve your mind of the painful influences that prevent what I so much desire—and which is so indispensable to the happy fulfil[l]ment of the relations which we hold to each other.

With esteem and respect

truly yours

C.E. Beecher

[CEB to Lydia Beals Jackson Beecher, SD]

In The True Remedy for the Wrongs of Woman *(1851),*
*Beecher would declare "*ORGANIZATION*" the*
"grand instrumentality" for securing woman's "true

*vocation."⁵ In this earlier letter, written to his widow
soon after George Beecher's death, she explored the
idea of organizing all-female communities of teachers
to civilize the West. Beecher's deep ambivalence about
Catholicism—a "slavish faith"—is suggested in her
choice of Catholic nunneries as her model.*

70   August 20, 1843
My Dear Sister [Sarah Buckingham Beecher]

... When you took me into the parlour of your house in P[utnam, Ohio] shortly after we arrived there, and told me of your determination to devote your time and interests to the Seminary reared by your mother[']s beneficence, a new light seemed to break into my mind as to *one probable* design of Providence in the blow that had brought us together as mourners.

I thought of the broad and teeming West—where the "great battle" is to be fought that shall decide whether intelligence and virtue shall make her beautiful vales and prairies blossom as the rose—or ignorance[,] vice and anarchy sweep over them the venom of destruction—I thought of her thousand villages and towns, flourishing in every thing but *intellectual and moral culture* and of all that *well educated* women *might* do to accomplish the great work of national education there. I thought of the Catholic communities of nuns I have met—even in Cincinnati—where women of rank and wealth and learning consecrate themselves to the cause of education and come to this land as "lady abbesses"—and "lady patronesses"—with their ten and twenty young lady associates to educate our people in a false and slavish faith—And I mused whether a time might not come when *Protestant* communities would not take some means to employ the piety, education and wealth among American females that now is all but wasted for want of some such resources as the Catholic church provides for women of talents[,] enterprize and piety.— In the Catholic church there is a notch for every one—the poor girl can find her post as a working nun or teacher—The rich and noble have places provided as heads of great establishments where in fact they have a power and station and influence which even ambition might seek. . . .

... I know of *many, many* women of talents, maturity, and enterprize who *could* be gained as female laborers at the west—and some too who have fortunes of [*sic*] their command—But as yet there is no way open for them—and when your determination to devote yourself to the cause of female education was announced, my imagination pictured some future train of operations that perhaps would bring about for *Protestant* woman the means of extensive influence and activity for which many are now looking in vain. . . .

. . . Oh how I should love to join with you in an enterprize like this—to plan for you—to co-operate with you—to contribute my experience and the influence I have gained among the wise and good—to aid you by my cheerful and sanguine hopefulness—and to be aided by your calm judgement and held back by your less hopeful spirit—We are just fitted to work *together* in such an effort . . . but Providence seems to say *no* to my hopes—After I left you I found that I had been *under strong excitement*—and that after this was withdrawn my strength began to fail . . . and for a time I thought I should be obliged to lay by for want of strength[.] But I gradually recruited—yet now am only about as well as I was when I left Cincinnati—I stopped at Saratoga a day and enquired of the resident physician there if such cases of [*sic*] mine were cured there—He says, *yes*—and strongly urged my spending a month there—*Sharon Springs* also—a new watering place near Utica . . . seems to remedy such cases of nervous debility—as are similar to mine—I should try one or both of these, if I had not used up my means and have a great aversion to running in debt when I have no *certain* means of payment.

Still in thinking this matter over, and considering how much I could do for your happiness and usefulness if I were *only well*—I have felt that I should be more willing to put myself under this sort of obligation to you than to any other of my friends—We have been united in suffering and sorrow. . . . The last time I parted with our dear George (a year ago at your house) he told me if I ever was in any want of means to come to him—and had he now been living this application would have been to him and you together. My present resources would just pay my expenses here and my journey back to Cincinnati. . . . Still in these *failing* times I can not be certain of *any* future payments. . . . But you are so situated that the sum I want might be retained longer than the time specified without inconvenience to you—If therefore you can conveniently loan me one hundred dollars I think I shall spend a month or two at one or both of the above Springs[.] At least I shall try both, and stay if either seems to be the healing remedy. There is nothing now of such value to me, and so far as they are concerned in [*sic*] me, to my friends, as my restoration to active usefulness—and money spent for this object is more wisely expended than for anything else I could seek. . . .

> Ever aff[ectionate]ly Yr sister
>
> C—

[CEB to Sarah Buckingham Beecher, SD]

Truth Stranger than Fiction (1850) was an attack on the sexual double standard, provoked by the refusal of the Congregational church to discipline a minister for (as Beecher believed) engaging in an improper relationship with a female. In this excerpt, Beecher criticizes the minister for claiming that the woman had actively sought his attentions. The passage raises the paradox of defining womanhood in terms of marriage while forbidding women from pursuing husbands openly—a dilemma that Beecher's own work helped to sustain.

71 . . . [A]ll the influence and authority obtained by the Protestant clergy over the consciences and conduct of their people, rests solely on *the confidence* felt . . . in the virtue and piety of the ministry. . . .

The strictness and fidelity with which the clergy in New England have fulfilled these obligations, have preserved to the Christian ministry an intelligent and beneficial influence over all classes of their people, unexampled in any other portion of the world.

One of the most interesting developments of this fact is manifested in the confidence, sympathy, and affection that exist between the ministry and the female members of their flock. But all this is entirely dependent on the confidence that exists in the piety, the purity, the honor, and the superior moral and intellectual endowments of their pastor. And just in proportion as this confidence is destroyed, the influence and authority of their minister with them is destroyed. For this reason it is, that ecclesiastical bodies are especially vigilant and vigorous in regard to all delinquencies, touching the purity and the interests of woman. So that the female sex are accustomed to look upon the ministers of Jesus Christ as their special guardians and protectors. . . .

By the constitution of nature, by the ordinance of Providence, by the training of the family and school, by the influence of society, and by the whole current of poetry and literature, woman is educated to feel that a happy marriage is the summit of all earthly felicity. And yet, by a fantasy of custom, it has become one of the most disgraceful of all acts for a woman to acknowledge that she is seeking to attain this felicity. On the contrary, she is trained to all sorts of concealments and subterfuges, to make it appear as if it was a matter to which she is perfectly indifferent. And such is the influence of custom and high cultivation, that the more delicate, refined, and self-respecting a woman becomes, the more acute is the suffering inflicted, by any imputation of her delicacy in this respect.

It is owing to this, that the most stringent rules of honor are maintained in this direction. A man of high honor not only avoids every thing that would tempt a woman to manifest an interest which cannot be returned, but he scrupulously avoids every thing that would involve her in any such suspicion. . . .

In this aspect, there are a few things deemed more dishonorable than for a gentleman to take a course that secures a display of a lady's willingness to receive public attentions, when he has no intentions to fulfill the expectations that may thus be awakened. While in the whole round of poltroonery, if there is any one act that, above all others, is marked as the climax of baseness, it is that a gentleman should tempt a woman to the indecorum of making offers, which nature and custom alike decide that she is only to receive, and then *betray and disgrace her.*

A man of high honor, however innocent he may have been of any act that would tempt to such a result, would as soon cut out his tongue as to make such a disclosure. . . .

[CEB *TSF*, pp. 5–7, 9–11]

Beecher wrote extensively on the subject of health—advocating a simple, preventive regimen much like that recommended by doctors today. The following passages from Letters to the People on Health and Happiness *(1855) touch on recurrent themes in her work—her special concern about the poor health of American women (which she attributed to poor diet, unhealthful conditions in the home, and a lack of exercise) and her distrust of the male medical profession, here accused of sexually assaulting female patients.*

72   My Friends:

Will you let me come to you in your work-shop, or office, or store, or study? and you, my female friends, may I enter your nursery, your parlor, or your kitchen? . . .

I have facts to communicate, that will prove that the American people are pursuing a course, in their own habits and practices, which is destroying health and happiness to an extent that is perfectly appalling. . . .

I think I can show also, that if a plan for *destroying female health*, in all the ways in which it could be most effectively done, were drawn up, it would be exactly the course which is now pursued by a large portion of this nation, especially in the more wealthy classes. . . .

During my extensive tours in all portions of the Free States, I was brought into most intimate communion, not only with my widely-diffused circle of relatives, but with very many of my former pupils who had become wives and mothers. From such, I learned the secret domestic history both of those I visited and of many of their intimate friends. And oh! what heartaches were the result of these years of quiet observation of the experience of my sex in domestic life. How many young hearts have revealed the fact, that what they had been trained to imagine the highest earthly felicity, was but the beginning of care, disappointment, and sorrow, and often led to the extremity of mental and physical suffering. . . .

. . . At last, certain developments led me to take decided measures to obtain some reliable statistics on the subject. During my travels the last year I have sought all practicable methods of obtaining information, and finally adopted this course with most of the married ladies whom I met, either on my journeys or at the various health establishments at which I stopped.

I requested each lady first to write the *initials* of *ten* of the married ladies with whom she was best acquainted in her place of residence. Then she was requested to write at each name, her impressions as to the health of each lady. In this way, during the past year, I obtained statistics from about two hundred different places in almost all the Free States.

Before giving any of these, I will state some facts to show how far they are reliable: In the first place, the *standard of health* among American women is so low that few have a correct idea of *what a healthy woman is*. . . . A woman who has tolerable health finds herself so much above the great mass of her friends in this respect, that she feels herself a prodigy of good health. . . .

MOST RELIABLE STATISTICS.

Milwaukee, Wis. Mrs. A. frequent sick headaches. Mrs. B. very feeble. Mrs. S. well, except chills. Mrs. L. poor health constantly. Mrs. D. subject to frequent headaches. Mrs. B. very poor health. Mrs. C. consumption. Mrs. A. pelvic displacements and weakness. Mrs. H. pelvic disorders and a cough. Mrs. B. always sick. Do not know one perfectly healthy woman in the place.

Essex, Vt. Mrs. S. very feeble. Mrs. D. slender and delicate. Mrs. S. feeble. Mrs. S. not well. Mrs. G. quite feeble. Mrs. C. quite feeble. Mrs. B. quite feeble. Mrs. S. quite slender. Mrs. B. quite feeble. Mrs. F. very feeble. Knows but one perfectly healthy woman in town.

Peru, N.Y. Mrs. C. not healthy. Mrs. H. not healthy. Mrs. E. healthy. Mrs. B. pretty well. Mrs. K. delicate. Mrs. B. not strong and healthy. Mrs. S. healthy and vigorous. Mrs. L. pretty well. Mrs. L. pretty well.

Canton, Penn. Mrs. R. feeble. Mrs. B. bad headaches. Mrs. D. bad headaches. Mrs. V. feeble. Mrs. S. erysipelas. Mrs. K. headaches, but tolerably well. Mrs. R. miserably sick and nervous. Mrs. G. poor health. Mrs. L. invalid. Mrs. C. invalid.

Oberlin, Ohio. Mrs. A. usually well, but subject to neuralgia. Mrs. D. poor health. Mrs. K. well, but subject to nervous headaches. Mrs. M. poor health. Mrs. C. not in good health. Mrs. P. not in good health. Mrs. P. delicate. Mrs. F. not in good health. Mrs. F. not in good health.

Wilmington, Del. Mrs. —, scrofula. Mrs. B. in good health. Mrs. D. delicate. Mrs. H. delicate. Mrs. S. healthy. Mrs. P. healthy. Mrs. G. delicate. Mrs. O. delicate. Mrs. T. very delicate. Mrs. S. headaches.

New Bedford, Mass. Mrs. B. pelvic diseases, and every way out of order. Mrs. J. W. pelvic disorders. Mrs. W. B. well, except in one respect. Mrs. C. sickly. Mrs. C. rather delicate. Mrs. P. not healthy. Mrs. C. unwell at times. Mrs. L. delicate. Mrs. B. subject to spasms. Mrs. H. very feeble. Can not think of but one perfectly healthy woman in the place. . . .[6]

During the later periods of my investigations in regard to health, I became aware, not only of the general decay of the health of my own sex, but of the terrible suffering, both physical and mental, produced by

6. The list continues and includes, under this heading, descriptions of the health of 255 women in twenty-five towns in nine states. Of these, 29 are pronouced healthy and 30 "well," "pretty well," or "tolerably well." The remainder suffered from such ailments as "sick headaches," consumption, pelvic disorder, neuralgia, "liver complaint," scrofula, "spinal complaint," bronchitis, and dyspepsia.

internal organic displacements. . . . And what seemed the more shocking, was the fact that so many patients of this class were young girls.

But when the fact was ascertained that, in multitudes of cases, there was no possible remedy for this appalling evil but . . . *daily mechanical operations, both external and internal,* . . . and that this was in most cases performed with bolted doors and curtained windows, and with no one present but patient and operator, there was a painful apprehension of evils which foreshadowed future revelations. . . .

In my travels I have met persons of both sexes, of the highest cultivation and refinement . . . who freely advocated the doctrine that there was no true marriage but the union of persons who were in love; that such union needed not legal or religious rites, and that it was those only who were held together by such restraints, who, having ceased to love each other, were guilty of adultery in the only proper sense of the word. . . .

Then, again, there are articles on physiology circulated freely, that maintain that the exercise of all the functions of body and mind is *necessary to health*, and that no perfectly-developed man or woman is possible, so long as any of the functions and propensities are held in habitual constraint. . . .

Let us now suppose the case of a physician, neither better nor worse than the majority of that honorable profession. He has read the writings of the semi-infidel school, till he has lost all reverence for the Bible as *authoritative* in faith or practice. Of course he has no guide left but his own feelings and notions. Then he gradually adopts the above views in physiology and social life. . . . Then he daily has all the opportunities indicated. Does any one need more than to hear these facts to know what the not unfrequent results must be? . . .

A terrific feature of these developments has been the *entire helplessness* of my sex, amidst present customs and feelings, as to any *redress* for such wrongs, and the reckless and conscious impunity felt by the wrongdoers on this account. What can a refined, delicate, sensitive woman do when thus insulted? The dreadful fear of *publicity* shuts her lips and restrains every friend. And it would seem . . . as if it was the certainty of this that withdrew restraint, so that the very highest, not only in character but in position, have not escaped. When *such as these* have been thus assailed, who can hope to be safe? . . .

[CEB *LPHH*, pp. 7, 121–22, 124, 135–38]

Beecher's "domesticity" was inseparable from her struggle with Calvinism and her anger at male authority. In An Appeal to the People in Behalf of Their Rights as Authorized Interpreters of the Bible *(1860), she found the doctrine of original sin (the obstacle to her own conversion years earlier) repugnant to the deepest feelings of motherhood and called on women to reject this creation of the "theologians and clergy." Writing to family friend Leonard Bacon in 1862, after she had formally broken with her father's faith by joining the Episcopal Church, Beecher recalled the effect of Calvinism on her own and her siblings' spiritual development.*

73   . . . It is granted by all, that it is to woman more than to man, that is committed the chief business of training the human mind at its most important stage of development. It is granted, also, that in order to success [*sic*] in culture, both physical and mental, it is the first step to understand *the nature* of that which is to be trained and developed. The first question, then, to every woman, in reference to her first duty is, what is *the nature* of the minds given us to train? . . .

. . . She asks of those who are her Lord's messengers for this very end, what is *the nature* of this wonderful and delicate organization? What is the *end* or *purpose* for which it is made? . . .

. . . For the most part . . . she hears that the *ruined nature* of her offspring is such that she can do absolutely nothing to secure any right development. . . . Others tell her that the mind of her child is constructed wrong, and that nothing can be done to secure its right training and development, but in some way to induce its Maker to re-create it. . . .

In this state of the case many sensible mothers and teachers, all over the land, have adopted a course dictated by their own common sense and their experience of the *nature* of mind, as discovered in their attempts to train it. . . . They have in various forms of language taught their little ones after this fashion: "Your heavenly Father made you to be happy and to make others happy. In order to do this, he wishes that you should always have what you like best, except when it would injure you or others. But when what you like best and want the most, is not *best* for you or *best* for others, you must always choose what is *for the best*, and in so doing you act virtuously and please and obey God. And just so far as you do all that is best for yourself and for others, guided by the teachings of Christ, and with the desire and purpose to obey him, you become a virtuous, pious and holy child, and a true Christian.["] . . .

The great principle of Protestantism, in distinction from Catholicism, is, that every person is to be an independent interpreter of the Bible. . . .

But though all Protestants hold this principle theoretically, by far the larger portion . . . go to theologians and pastors for their *opinions*. . . . Thus it is that ecclesiastics control the faith of a large portion of the Protestant churches, as authoritatively as do the pope and priests control that of the Catholic church. . . .

The present time is one in which the women of this country must decide in regard to this same principle and on practical questions of the deepest moment.

It has been shown, that with small exceptions, the Catholic and Protestant theologians and clergy unite in teaching a depravity of *nature* in every human being, involving these questions:

Are we so depraved as to be incapacitated to interpret the Bible[?] . . .

Are children to be trained to believe that all their feelings and actions are "sin and only sin," till they receive a new nature from God, or be taught that whenever they choose what is *right*, with the *intention* to do right, they act virtuously and please God? . . .

It has been stated that many intelligent and pious women in various parts of our country have already quietly assumed their rights as authorized interpreters of the Bible on all these questions, . . . and thus, in fact, have set themselves in opposition to the clergy, except so far as the clergy themselves have come to the same results. . . .

Some of the . . . most strenuous defenders of ecclesiastical infallibility and authority . . . ask with *naive* simplicity, what right has a woman to apply common sense to religion, or to have any opinions except as she is taught them by the church, at the same time sneering at the idea, that "the dear people" are competent to understand and interpret the Bible for themselves.

. . . The ecclesiastical party, more or less, openly claim that the only authorized interpreters of the Bible are the ordained priesthood, or the regenerated church. On the other hand, the people, and women, as that half of the people to whom the training of the human mind is especially committed, maintain that they are ordained to this office by a Higher Power. . . .

Moreover, it is claimed that every well-educated, pious woman of good common sense, who has trained young children, is *better* qualified to interpret the Bible correctly, on all points pertaining to such practical duties, than most theologians possibly can be. . . .

These facts being so, it is believed that ere long the greater portion of the most intelligent and conscientious women in this country ... will perceive that they are bound, not only to assume and exercise the distinctive rights of Protestantism, as authorized interpreters of the Bible, but to *protest*, by word and deed, against all that opposes the exercise of these rights. ...

They will ... protest ... the interference of church officers to examine them or their children in order to ascertain their mode of interpreting the Bible or the any [*sic*] other signs of regeneration, than the expressed desire to unite with the congregation in the worship and ordinances appointed by Christ.

Should such a course as this result in exclusion from the Lord's table, those thus protesting can depart peaceably to some church which could conscientiously receive them on such terms. And if no such church is to be found, they can quietly relinquish the privilege, until such time as it can be enjoyed without a sacrifice of principle and religious liberty. ...

[CEB *Appeal*, pp. 332–34, 352–57]

---

74   April 24, [18]62

Rev. Dr. Bacon,

My Dear Sir:

... Now the Cong[regational] churches in New England *have* shut the little children out of the fold of Christ—They are not in a course of training as *lambs* of the flocks, to *grow* to Christian life by gradual development of the nature God has given them. But instead they are regarded (theoretically at least) as *young wolves* shut out—and not to be taken in till the shepherds have examined and decided that this *nature* is changed. And under this system *childhood piety* is rare—and grows, as it were, in spite of repressing influences. Not one of my father's children had anything of the kind. As soon as we came to understand that no prayers and services of the unregenerate were accepted, we ceased to pray—and tho' most of these children had the very best of materials for religious culture *not one* entered the church till grown up or nearly so.

And all the churches, except the Episcopal, practically adopt this same system. ...

As for me—I have only stepped from my father[']s house into my mother[']s—and I did it by a public act to take with me some lambs that I could not draw into the fold any other way within my reach. . . .

>   Very truly your friend
>   Catharine E. Beecher

>   [CEB to Leonard Bacon, BL]

Beecher's strategy for elevating the status of women (by raising the prestige and remuneration of distinctly female professions) was at odds with the equal rights argument of the suffrage movement. In "An Appeal to American Women" (appended to the 1869 American Woman's Home), she reviewed her career and the present condition of women and defended her goals.

75   My Honored Countrywomen:

It is now over forty years that I have been seeking to elevate the character and condition of our sex, relying, as to earthly aid, chiefly on your counsel and cooperation. I am sorrowful at results that have followed these and similar efforts, and ask your sympathy and aid.

Let me commence with a brief outline of the past. I commenced as an educator in the city of Hartford, Ct. . . . The staid, conservative citizens queried of what use to women were Latin, Geometry, and Algebra. . . . The appeal was then made to benevolent, intelligent women, and by their influence all that was sought was liberally bestowed. . . .

The next attempt was to introduce Domestic Economy as *a science to be studied* in schools for girls. For a while it seemed to succeed; but ere long was crowded out by Political Economy and many other economies, except those most needed to prepare a woman for her difficult and sacred duties.

In the progress of years, it came to pass that the older States teemed with educated women, qualified for no other department of woman's profession but that of a schoolteacher, while the newer States abounded in children without schools.

I again appealed to my countrywomen for help. . . . The funds were bestowed, and thus the services of Governor Slade[7] were secured, and,

---

7. See above, "A Power and Station and Influence," n. 11.

mainly by these agencies, nearly one thousand teachers were provided with schools, chiefly in the West.

Meantime, the intellectual taxation in both private and public schools, the want of proper ventilation in both families and schools, the want of domestic exercise which is so valuable to the feminine constitution, the pernicious modes of dress, and the prevailing neglect of the laws of health, resulted in the general decay of health among women. . . .

Alarmed at the dangerous tendencies of female education, I made another appeal to my sex, which resulted in the organization of the American Woman's Education Association, the object being to establish *endowed* professional schools, in connection with literary institutions, in which woman's profession should be honored and taught as are the professions of men, and where woman should be trained for some self-supporting business. From this effort several institutions of a high literary character have come into existence at the West, but the organization and endowment of the professional schools is yet incomplete from many combining impediments, the chief being a want of appreciation of woman's profession. . . .

Let us now look at the dangers which are impending. And first, in regard to the welfare of the family state, the decay of the female constitution and health has involved such terrific sufferings, in addition to former cares and pains of maternity, that multitudes of both sexes so dread the risks of marriage as either to avoid it, or meet them by methods *always* injurious and often criminal. . . .

Add to these, other influences that are robbing home of its safe and peaceful enjoyments. Of such, the condition of domestic service is not the least. We abound in domestic helpers from foreign shores, but they are to a large extent thriftless, ignorant, and unscrupulous. . . .

Meantime, domestic service—disgraced, on one side, by the stigma of our late slavery, and, on the other, by the influx into our kitchens of the uncleanly and ignorant—is shunned by the self-respecting and well educated, many of whom prefer either a miserable pittance or the career of vice to this fancied degradation. Thus comes the overcrowding in all avenues for woman's work, and the consequent lowering of wages to starvation prices for long protracted toils.

From this comes diseases to the operatives, bequeathed often to their offspring. Factory girls must stand ten hours or more, and consequently in a few years debility and disease ensue, so that they never can rear healthy children, while the foreigners who supplant them in kitchen labor are almost the only strong and healthy women to rear large families. The sewing-machine, hailed as a blessing, has proved a curse to the poor;

for it takes away profits from needlewomen, while employers testify that women who use this machine for steady work, in two years or less become hopelessly diseased and can rear no children. Thus it is that the controlling political majority of New-England is passing from the educated to the children of ignorant foreigners.

Add to these disastrous influences, the teachings of "free love;" the baneful influence of spiritualism, so called; the fascinations of the *demi-monde*; the poverty of thousands of women who, but for desperate temptations, would be pure—all these malign influences are sapping the foundations of the family state.

Meantime, many intelligent and benevolent persons imagine that the grand remedy for the heavy evils that oppress our sex is to introduce woman to political power and office, to make her a party in primary political meetings, in political caucuses, and in the scramble and fight for political offices; thus bringing into this dangerous *melée* the distinctive tempting power of her sex. Who can look at this new danger without dismay?

But it is neither generous nor wise to join in the calumny and ridicule that are directed toward philanthropic and conscientious laborers for the good of our sex, because we fear their methods are not safe. It would be far wiser to show by example a better way.

Let us suppose that our friends have gained the ballot and the powers of office: are there any real beneficent measures for our sex, which they would enforce by law and penalties, that fathers, brothers, and husbands would not grant to a united petition of our sex, or even to a majority of the wise and good? Would these not confer what the wives, mothers, and sisters deemed best for themselves and the children they are to train, very much sooner than they would give power and office to our sex to enforce these advantages by law? Would it not be a wiser thing to *ask* for what we need, before trying so circuitous and dangerous a method? God has given to man the physical power, so that all that woman may gain, either by petitions or by ballot, will be the gift of love or of duty; and the ballot never will be accorded till benevolent and conscientious men are the majority—a millennial point far beyond our present ken. . . .

[CEB, "Appeal to American Women,"
in *AWH*, pp. 463–68]

In an 1872 letter to Leonard Bacon, Beecher reaf-firmed her belief in the "moral power . . . gained by

taking a subordinate place."[8] *But her antisuffrage
speeches suggest that Beecher's opposition to woman
suffrage arose as well from a class-based distrust of
most women and a belief that "domesticity" provided
the best protection against arbitrary male power.*

76   "An Address on Female Suffrage, Delivered in the
          Music Hall of Boston, in December, 1870"

I appear this evening to present the views of that large portion of my
sex who are opposed to such a change of our laws and customs as would
place the responsibility of civil government on woman. . . .

First, let me state the points in which we agree, that we may more
clearly appreciate those in which we differ.

We agree, then, on the general principle, that woman's happiness and
usefulness are equal in value to those of man's, and, consequently, that
she has a right to equal advantages for securing them.

We agree, also, that woman, even in our own age and country, has
never been allowed such equal advantages, and that multiplied wrongs
and suffering have resulted from this injustice.

Finally, we agree that it is the right and the duty of every woman to
employ the power of organization and agitation, in order to gain those
advantages which are given to the one sex, and unjustly withheld from
the other.

My object, in this address, is not to discuss the question of woman's
natural and abstract right to the ballot, nor to point out evils that might
follow the exercise of this power, nor to controvert the opinions of those
advocating woman's suffrage in any particular point.

Instead of this, I propose . . . to present reasons for assuming that it
must be a very long time before woman suffrage can be gained. . . .

The first reason for believing that the gift of the ballot must be long
delayed is, that it is contrary to the customs of Christian people, by
which the cares of civil life, and the out-door and heavy labor which take
a man from home, are given to the stronger sex, and the lighter labor
and care of the family state, to woman. . . .

Those of us who oppose woman suffrage concede that there are occasions in which general laws and customs should yield to temporary
emergencies; as when, in the stress of family sickness, the husband be-

8. Catharine E. Beecher to Dr. Leonard Bacon, March 9, 1872, BL.

comes nurse and cook; or, in the extremities of war, the women plow, sow, and reap; and it were well if every boy and girl were so trained that they could wisely meet such emergencies.

But while this is conceded, the main question is still open, namely, Is there any such emergency in our national history as demands so great a change in our laws and customs as would be involved in placing the responsibilities of civil government on our whole sex? . . .

. . . [A]t the present time, a large majority of American women would regard the gift of the ballot, not as a privilege conferred, but as an act of oppression, forcing them to assume responsibilities belonging to man, for which they are not and can not be qualified; and, consequently, withdrawing attention and interest from the distinctive and more important duties of their sex. For the question is not whether a class of women, who have no family responsibilities, shall take charge of civil government; but it is whether this duty shall be imposed on the whole of our sex. . . .

This perspicuous statement[9] expresses the present views of probably nine tenths of the most intelligent and conscientious women of our country. . . . But let us consider the other classes that would be included in universal woman suffrage.

Next to the more intelligent class represented by this letter-writer, would come a large body of those whose generous *impulses* take the lead, rather than the cool deductions of reason and experience.

It is this class of enthusiasts that would most confidently attempt to conduct the affairs of the state.

Next to these would come the great body of busy and easy women, who, from pliant kindness and confidence, would vote as fathers, brothers, and husbands advised.

Next to these most respectable classes would come the superficial, the unreflecting, and the frolicsome, to serve only as tools for political wire-pullers.

Then would come the lovers of notoriety, the ambitious—the lovers of power—the caterers for public offices, and the seekers for money. Of these, the most unprincipled would employ the distinctive power of their

---

9. Beecher here included a letter from a woman who described herself as representative of "the educated and thoughtful women of the country" and who argued that women's domestic duties and exclusion from "the life of the street, the caucus, and the primary political meetings" necessarily rendered them uninformed voters.

sex in caucuses, in jury-boxes, and in legislative and congressional committees; thus adding another to the many deteriorating influences of political life.

Next would come that vast mass of ignorant women whose consciences and votes would be controlled by a foreign and domestic priesthood.

Lastly would come the most degraded and despised, who would like nothing better than to insult and oppose those who look down upon them with disgust and contempt.

Lead all these classes to the polls, and the result would be a vast increase of the incompetent and dangerous voters. It would, to a still greater extent, place the wealth and intelligence of the nation under those without intelligence, who, for their own advantage, would lavish wealth on useless schemes, and vote away the property of the industrious to support the indolent and vicious. . . .

Another reason for believing that woman suffrage is afar off is the character of the men who appear to favor this change of our political status. . . . [T]hose associated with the highest class of women place a halo of purity, strength, and honor on the brow of the whole sex. . . . It is this . . . class of men who are foremost advocates of woman suffrage, and their estimate of woman's ability to manage civil government is to be taken with considerable though honorable deductions. . . .

. . . Multitudes of women are now quiet and silent because they have little fear of danger in this direction. But should a time come when the woman suffrage party seem near achieving their aim, there would be measures instituted the power of which, as yet, is little known or appreciated. For *they too* would organize all over the nation and summon to their aid both the pulpit and the press. All the Catholic clergy, to a man, would lend their influence against a measure so contrary to the tenets and spirit of a church that enforces subordination and obedience as prime virtues. Not less decided would be the influence of all the Jewish rabbis.

The Protestant clergy, who have ever been . . . the sympathizing friends of woman, would be the last to enforce new and heavy responsibilities on our sex. . . .

Not less decided are the great majority of the conductors of the press; and if an emergency calls for it, by the cooperation of such powerful auxiliaries, we could bring such an array of petitions and remonstrances in bulk and respectable names as never before entered congressional halls. . . .

Another and the final reason for believing female suffrage at a distant future is the proposed circuitous and indirect mode of remedying evils which could be relieved by a much more direct and speedy method. As things now are, men have the physical power that can force obedience; in most cases they have the power of the purse, and in all cases, they have the civil power. They can not be forced by the weaker sex to resign this power. . . . Why should we not rather take the shorter and surer mode and *ask for the thing needed*, instead of the circuitous and uncertain mode involved in the ballot? . . .

> [CEB, "Address on Female Suffrage,"
> in *WSWP*, pp. 3–8, 10–18]

---

77   "An Address to the Christian Women of America"

. . . [T]he Christian woman in the family and in the school is the most complete autocrat that is known, as the care of the helpless little ones, the guidance of their intellect, and the formation of all their habits, are given to her supreme control. Scarcely less is she mistress and autocrat over a husband, whose character, comfort, peace, and prosperity, are all in her power. . . . God has given man the physical power, the power of the purse, and the civil power, and woman must submit with Christian equanimity. . . .

. . . She is a *subordinate* in the family state, just as her father, husband, brother, and sons are subordinates in the civil state. . . . And obedience in the family to "the higher power" held by man, is no more a humiliation than is man's obedience to a civil ruler.

If this be so, then the doctrine of woman's subjugation is established and the opposing doctrine of Stuart Mills[10] and his followers is in direct opposition to the teachings both of common sense and Christianity.

There is a moral power given to woman in the family state much more controlling and abiding than the inferior, physical power conferred on man. And the more men are trained to refinement, honor, and benevolence, the more this moral power of woman is increased. . . .

The general principles to guide both men and women as to the duties of those in a subordinate station, have been made clear by discussions relating to civil government. But the corresponding duties of those invested with power and authority have not been so clearly set forth,

---

10. John Stuart Mill, English philosopher, who argued that women had a "natural right" to legal and civil equality with men.

especially those of the family state. While the duties of subordination, subjection, and obedience, have been abundantly enforced on woman, the corresponding duties of man as head and ruler of the family state have not received equal attention either from the pulpit or the press. . . .

. . . [F]or the most advanced followers of Christ have but just begun to understand the solemn relations and duties of the family state—man the head, protector, and provider—woman the chief educator of immortal minds—man to labor and suffer to train and elevate woman for her high calling. . . .

. . . But it is not true that women are and should be treated as the equals of men in *every* respect. They certainly are not his equals in physical power, which is the final resort in *government* of both the family and the State. . . .

The duty of subordination, though so fundamental and important, is one to which all minds are naturally averse. . . . Especially is this the case with persons of great sensibilities and strong will. It is owing to this that so many women of this class are followers of Stuart Mills' doctrine that a wife is not a subordinate in the family state. . . .

The agitation at the present time in regard to woman's right and wrongs is greatly owing to the fact that, from various causes, large multitudes of women are without the love and protection secured by marriage. . . . A large portion of these women must earn their own independence, while those who are provided with a support are embarrassed by false customs or unjust laws. In regard to the multitudes of women who flock to our cities and to such direful temptations it is often said, why "do they not become servants in families?" Let any woman who has a young daughter ponder this question as one that may reach her own family. Does not almost every woman feel, more or less, the bondage of *caste* and shrink from taking the *lowest place.* . . ?

There are certain customs of society which are based on the assumption that all women are to marry and be supported by husbands, and that all men are to provide for the support of a family. It is on this assumption that, in cases where men and women do the same work and do it equally well, men receive much larger wages than women.

But . . . there are many wrongs, both to married and unmarried women, consequent on the present false and unchristian state of things. . . .

In enumerating the evils that would result. . . , the most prominent is her increased withdrawal from the more humble, but more important offices of the family state. . . .

. . . To open avenues to political place and power for all classes of women would cause these humble labors of the family and school to be still more undervalued and shunned. . . .

[CEB, "An Address to the Christian
Women of America," in *WSWP*,
pp. 179–82, 184, 186,
189–91, 193–94]

---

78   March 9, 1872

My dear Sir [Leonard Bacon]

"My soul is cast down" at the ignorance and mistaken zeal of my poor sister Bell and her coagitators—Can you not lend a helping pen to show what a mercy it is to woman *to have a head* to take the thousand responsibilities of family life—and how much *moral* power is gained by taking a subordinate place—as the Bible and Nature both teach is her true position. . . .

God made woman for her appropriate duties and her health and intellect both will be best developed in these duties. But in these days, young girls, even of the working classes, are giving up housework and running all to brain and nerve, without the balance of the muscular portion so important to healthful womanhood.

The ladies of Boston of the *conservative* sort are planning and discussing, and large donations counting by *millions* are coming—and nobody knows what to do with them.

I think the right training of woman is now the chief problem of the age.

Very truly your friend
Catharine E. Beecher

[CEB to Leonard Bacon, BL]

9.

Harriet Beecher Stowe:
"The Woman Controversy"

In a letter written to Edward Everett Hale, the editor of *Old and New*, Harriet Beecher Stowe offered an illuminating portrait of herself. Telling Hale in April 1869 that she was beginning a novel dealing with contemporary issues, she informed him that she was "to some extent a woman's rights woman, as I am to some extent something of almost everything that goes."[1] Indeed she was. However, the extent to which Stowe supported the postbellum movement's leaders and their demands was determined by her conception of womanhood. During "the woman controversy," as Stowe characterized the debate concerning women's rights that emerged in the wake of the Civil War, she continued to maintain that women had a vital role to play in both the private and the public spheres.[2] Having previously restricted that role to one of "influence," she now sought to extend women's political power through suffrage and to enhance their social and economic position through property rights for married women and increased vocational opportunities for all women confronted with the need to support themselves. Stowe welcomed expanded rights and opportunities for women precisely because she expected that they would empower the wife and mother and elevate her status. Indeed, she envisioned the achievement of women's *rights* as the catalyst for the performance of woman's *duties*.

Stowe's particular challenge to the patriarchial order did not entail fundamental alterations in the social and economic structure. In its broadest application, her ideology of domesticity, in particular her conception of womanhood, appeared to disregard differences based upon race, class, and individual circumstance. Nonetheless, she had been demonstrably sensitive to the plight of enslaved mothers as evidenced by *Uncle Tom's Cabin*. Stowe was also acutely conscious of the legal vulnerability of wives and mothers, regardless of their race or class. In her challenge to the nearly complete legal power accorded husbands, Stowe strongly supported legislative reforms that granted married women rights to their property and guardianship of their children. Just as she had exhorted the mothers, sisters, and daughters of America to try to eradicate the evils of slavery in both her novel and her "Appeal to the Women of the Free States," so she called upon postbellum women, and especially women of her own social stratum, to articulate objectives and provide leadership for the women's rights movement.

During the months immediately preceding the end of the Civil War, Stowe began publishing a series of sketches that directly and succinctly addressed women's status in nineteenth-century America. She sent the initial sketch to James T. Fields, editor of the *Atlantic Monthly*, and proposed that the series be entitled, appropriately, " 'House and Home' papers," adding that she expected "a hundred dollars a number for them." Furthermore, she said to Fields, they could "talk about a book after."[3] He thought the project a "capital idea." Eagerly supervising serialization of the sketches in the pages of the *Atlantic* during 1864, Fields issued them as *House and Home Papers* under the imprint of Ticknor and Fields a year later.[4]

Presented as a dialogue between Stowe's (ironically) male persona, Christopher Crowfield, and members of his family, the sketches highlighted Stowe's ideology of domesticity with its attendant roles for women and men. In the third sketch, she asked rhetorically "What Is a Home?" thereby addressing the central issue that informed the entire series. Ascribing to women the "power to create a HOME," she made the wife and mother responsible for the transformation of the household into an "Eden." Lest her readers wonder if there was any role to be played by a male counterpart, Stowe acknowledged that "man *helps* in this work," but, she pointedly added, "woman leads." Determined to establish female hegemony in the private sphere, Stowe also sought to establish that sphere's importance in the larger world. Not only did she characterize the home as a refuge from the "shifting, changing, selfish world," she also stressed that it was the source for "all heroisms, all inspirations, all great deeds."[5]

Shortly before she submitted her final sketch to Fields, Stowe proposed continuation of the series, proudly telling her editor that "you see whoever can write on home and family matters, on what people think of and are anxious about, and want to hear about[,] has an immense advantage." She informed him that her next series of sketches, to be based upon the same characters, would also allow her a "great freedom and latitude—a capacity for striking anywhere when a topic seems to be on the public mind."[6] Not surprisingly, Stowe considered woman's sphere a timely "topic," and she again made it the basis for the series. Published in the *Atlantic Monthly* during 1865 and 1866, some of her sketches dealt directly with a controversial issue that was most definitely "on the public mind."

Suffrage was the issue that had generated questions and sparked controversy. Should recently emancipated black men be enfranchised? And if they were, should women, white as well as black, be included? Yes, insisted feminists such as Elizabeth Cady Stanton and Susan B. Anthony. In the appropriately titled "The Woman Question: or, What Will You Do With Her?" Stowe agreed with these two leaders, both of whom made natural rights principles integral to their demand for suffrage. Initially basing her defense on the ground that women were individuals with the same rights as men, Stowe nonetheless chose to emphasize that females had special responsibilities. She insisted that the "state" was simply an extended family and insisted that it "can no more afford to dispense with the vote of women in its affairs than a family." The metaphor was revealing. Women were not to be considered primarily as individuals; instead, they were envisioned as wives and mothers whose "instincts of womanhood" would transform the landscape of politics. Whether as voters or elected officials, theirs would be a cleansing influence in which the "cause of good morals, good order, cleanliness, and public health would be a gainer."[7] In one stroke, Stowe had both incorporated suffrage into her ideology of domesticity and had legitimated the former by the latter. She had also undermined the logic of natural rights principles. Only secondarily an individual with rights regardless of gender, the enfranchised woman envisioned by Stowe was the wife and mother whose domain had been extended beyond the four walls of her home.

Just as Stowe had located women's political participation in the context of their role in the family, so she tied their paid employment in the marketplace to the "profession for which they are fitted by physical organization, by their own instincts, and to which they are directed by the pointing and manifest finger of God." Almost as an afterthought, she added that which was already obvious—"and that sphere is *family life*." Having mandated this single profession for all women, Stowe was understandably troubled by the "slow and gradual reaction against household labor in America." Worse yet, the very women whom Stowe envisioned as leaders in the struggle for women's rights seemed to manifest a particular distaste for domestic employments. Certainly Stowe's desire to elevate the status of the wife and mother could not be achieved "if the intelligent and cultivated look down on housework with disdain, if they consider it as degrading, a thing to be shunned by every possible device." The solution offered by Stowe intertwined gender and class in a female system of noblesse oblige. Since "the training and guiding of a family must be recognized as the highest work a woman can perform," Stowe suggested that "domestic economy" become the central component of female education for daughters of the middle class. Once such training was legitimated, household labor would acquire the requisite "dignity in the eyes of our working classes, and young girls who have to earn their own living may no longer feel degraded in engaging in domestic service." Stowe also sought to multiply vocational possibilities for women of her class who had to pursue paid employment. She told her readers that "refined and educated women" should undertake medicine and especially nursing.[8] Teaching, architecture, landscape gardening, and book-keeping were suggested as additional possibilities.

Four years after her sketch had been published by the *Atlantic Monthly* in December 1865, Stowe returned to the issue of women's rights and opportunities in three articles for *Hearth and Home*, an aptly titled weekly that she had agreed to co-edit with Donald Mitchell. Referring generally to the issues involved as comprising the question of "the political position of woman," she claimed that it had become "*the* question of the age."[9] Here Stowe disclosed that her perspective on the postbellum movement was similarly informed by class identification and attendant noblesse oblige. But her support for the movement and its advocates was not in question.

Stowe's second article, which championed legislation granting both rights of property and guardianship of children to married women, called upon the complacent of her own social stratum to stir themselves on behalf of the movement and to give merited recognition to the female reformers for the statutory modifications already achieved. Was it just, she asked her readers, "because *you* have safety, protection, and a happy home, not to care what becomes of women who are less happily situated?" Until recently, she reminded them, English common law had prevailed throughout the nation and still did prevail in many states, and "the position of a married woman, under English common law, is in many respects, precisely similar to that of the negro slave." True, improvements had been made but, she asked again, "Do you know to whom the women of America owe these improvements, where they have been made? They owe them to these reformers often ridiculed as the Woman's Rights party." These reformers, she said, "were women who were living in peace and protection in happy homes, and were moved to take the course they did merely by their reverence for justice, and their feeling for those of their sex less fortunate than themselves." Rather than "coarse and obstreperous women," as they had been labeled in some

quarters, theirs was "the record of a calm, composed, dignified movement, inspired by noble motives, and appealing directly and logically for
its support to the Declaration of Independence." It was they who exem-
plified "what a true woman and true lady should be."[10]

But in the same year that Stowe published her articles in *Hearth and
Home*, the postbellum movement split into two factions. Leaders such as
Stanton, Anthony, and Harriet's sibling, Isabella, aligned themselves with
a more radical and multidimensional feminism. They also aligned themselves with Victoria Woodhull, whose flamboyant behavior deeply offended Stowe. Woodhull's assault upon the institution of marriage also
made Stowe her decided opponent. Nowhere was Stowe's response to
dissension among the supporters of women's rights and to Woodhull's
increased visibility in the movement more apparent than in her novel,
My Wife and I; or, Harry Henderson's History, published in 1871. And
nowhere was her commitment to a particular model of womanhood
more apparent.

In choosing "A Discussion of the Woman Question From All Points"
as the title for the twenty-fourth chapter of *My Wife and I*, Stowe suggested a neutrality that belied her content.[11] Caricaturing Woodhull as
the "tramp" Audacia Dangyereyes, and damning her paper, *Woodhull
and Claflin's Weekly*, as an attack upon "Christianity, marriage, the
family state, and all human laws and standing order," Stowe demonstrated a capacity for vitriol found only in this novel. She had expected
that all leaders of the movement would repudiate the likes of Woodhull,
precisely because they were "ladies of family and position, ladies of real
dignity and delicacy." The refusal of some to do so astonished and infuri-
ated her. Simply, they had violated Stowe's conception of womanhood.
Just as important, they had betrayed the movement on behalf of their
sex. Arguing that tolerance for a Woodhull "cuts the very ground from
under the whole woman movement," the narrator, Harry Henderson,
made explicit the basis upon which Stowe supported suffrage. "The main
argument," he declares, rests upon "that superior delicacy and purity
which women manifest in family life. But if women are going to be less
careful about delicacy and decorum and family purity than men are, the
quagmire of politics, foul enough now, will become putrid."[12]

The degree to which Stowe had been angered by Woodhull and an-
tagonized by trends in the movement was manifest in her portrayal of the
character Ida Van Arsdel. Only two years before the publication of *My
Wife and I*, Stowe had told Sara Parton, "The more I think of it the more
absurd this whole government of men over women looks." Yes, she had
written, "I do believe in Female Suffrage."[13] Nonetheless, the Ida Van

8

Arsdel whom Stowe presented as a model for women engaged in the movement undercut that same belief in the ballot. Says Ida, "I am, on the whole, very well pleased that there is no immediate prospect of the suffrage being granted to women until a generation with superior education and better balanced minds and better habits of consecutive thought shall have grown up among us."[14] As distasteful and disturbing as Stowe found the controversies surrounding Woodhull and the movement, they provided her with an opportunity to lecture her readers on the "woman question." In the chapter that Stowe said examined the issue "from all points," Stowe's particular point was readily apparent.

An equally important source for Stowe's caustic and contemptuous portrayal of Woodhull was less apparent. Already determined to expose Woodhull as a charlatan, Stowe's fury knew no bounds once Woodhull charged that an adulterous relationship existed between Henry Ward Beecher, Stowe's cherished brother, and Elizabeth Tilton, a member of his congregation. The allegation proved to be threatening indeed—both to Henry and to Harriet's relationship with Isabella.

Although Harriet and Isabella had known about the allegation before Woodhull made it public, they were unable to sustain sisterly relations during the ensuing ecclesiastical and civil trials in which Henry proclaimed his innocence. While Isabella was willing to entertain the possibility that the charges had merit, Harriet's deep attachment and loyalty to Henry precluded an impartial examination of the evidence. "I cannot," she wrote to her daughter Eliza, "hear that subject discussed as a *possibility* open for inquiry without such an intense uprising of indignation and scorn and anger as very few have ever seen in me." Precluded as well was forgiveness for a sister who publicly stood by Woodhull. "Aunt Isabella," she told Eliza, has "deeply wounded my sense of all propriety and affection."[15] Shortly before the end of the trials, Harriet adopted a more tolerant stance. In a letter to her friend, Anne Seymour Robinson, she expressed compassion for her "poor wandering sister Bell." The reasons for Harriet's sympathy were telling. Isabella's mistaken behavior had been motivated by a kindred loyalty. Woodhull's supporters had convinced Isabella that it was the "only way to save her brother." Harriet was also optimistic that "a child of so many prayers and such godly parents" would eventually repudiate her alliance with Woodhull.[16] Devoted Christian that she was, Harriet equated prayers with parentage. Nonetheless, one suspects that her optimism was primarily based upon Isabella's lineage. The younger sister would yet show herself to be a Beecher.

It was an appropriate irony that the politics of sisterhood culminated in a family affair. Harriet Beecher Stowe's involvement in "the woman controversy" was governed by her conception of woman's being and place. She sought to establish the hegemony of the wife and mother in the home and the acknowledgement of her moral and spiritual authority in the world. A famous author who felt deeply ambivalent about her status as a public figure, she rendered home and family matters truly world affairs. A devout believer in the sanctity of the family state, she envisioned the transformation of the political state into an extended family. Stowe had made women's rights and woman's sphere indivisible.

NOTES

1. Harriet Beecher Stowe to Edward Everett Hale, April 14, 1869, SD. Stowe's stance on women's rights is the subject of Josephine Donovan's "Harriet Beecher Stowe's Feminism," *American Transcendental Quarterly: A Journal of New England Writers* 47–48 (Summer-Fall 1980): 141–57.

2. Harriet Beecher Stowe to Annie Fields, November 4, 1870, HL. Writing to Fields from Stockbridge, Massachusetts, where she was visiting her daughter Georgiana, who had recently given birth to a son, Stowe wryly told her friend that the solution to the "woman controversy" was simple. All women had to do was "say that they won't take care of the babies till the laws are altered." After "one week of this discipline," men would capitulate: "Only tell us what you want, they would say, and we will do it."

3. Harriet Beecher Stowe to James T. Fields, undated, HL.

4. James T. Fields to Harriet Beecher Stowe, October 29, 1863, HL.

5. Harriet Beecher Stowe, *House and Home Papers* (Boston: Ticknor and Fields, 1865), pp. 56, 77, 56, 76.

6. Harriet Beecher Stowe to James T. Fields, undated, HL.

7. Harriet Beecher Stowe, "The Woman Question: or, What Will You Do with Her?" *Atlantic Monthly* 16 (December 1865): 674. See Document 79. Three decades after it had appeared in the *Atlantic Monthly*, this sketch was published under the title "Woman's Sphere" along with others in the second series in a volume entitled *Household Papers and Stories* (Boston: Houghton, Mifflin and Co., 1896).

8. Stowe, "What Will You Do with Her?" pp. 681, 679, 683, 681, 682, 683, 676.

9. Harriet Beecher Stowe, "The Woman Question," *Hearth and Home*, August 7, 1869, p. 520. Although Stowe's and Mitchell's names both appeared on the masthead beginning with the initial issue of December 26, 1868, Stowe actually did little except contribute articles to *Hearth and Home*. Exactly one year after she had joined Mitchell, Harriet and her half sister Isabella entered into negotia-

tions to become corresponding editors for *The Revolution*. See excerpt from their letter to Susan B. Anthony in Document 81.

10. "The Woman Question," p. 520. The significance of such legislation is persuasively analyzed in Norma Basch, *In the Eyes of the Law: Women, Marriage, and Property in Nineteenth-Century New York* (Ithaca, N.Y.: Cornell University Press, 1982). See also Michael Grossberg, *Governing the Hearth: Law and the Family in Nineteenth-Century America* (Chapel Hill: University of North Carolina Press, 1985).

11. Harriet Beecher Stowe, *My Wife and I; or, Harry Henderson's History* (Boston: Houghton, Mifflin and Co., 1896). The novel was originally serialized in the *Christian Union* during 1870 and 1871 and then published by J. B. Ford and Co. in 1871. See Document 82.

12. HBS *MWI*, pp. 281, 268, 279, 281.

13. Harriet Beecher Stowe to Sara Parton, July 25, 1869, SSC. See Document 80.

14. HBS *MWI*, p. 272.

15. Harriet Beecher Stowe to Eliza Stowe, May 11, 1873, SchL. See Document 84.

16. Harriet Beecher Stowe to Anne Seymour Robinson, May 2, 1875, SD. See Document 86.

Originally appearing in December 1865, "The Woman Question: or, What Will You Do with Her?" was part of a series which Stowe published regularly in the At-lantic Monthly during the 1860s. The sketches, which were later issued in two volumes, were structured as a dialogue between the narrator Christopher Crowfield and members of his family. Included as well was Bob Stephens, who joined the family as the husband of the Crowfields' daughter, Marianne. Consistently, the sub-ject addressed by Crowfield was "Woman's Sphere," as the sketch was titled when published in Household Pa-pers and Stories *three decades later, and just as consis-tently, Crowfield's opinions reflected those of his cre-ator. Later controversies notwithstanding, Stowe continued to espouse the rights and the duties claimed by her persona in this excerpt. However, she would be-come increasingly intolerant of certain "crudities, ab-surdities, and blasphemies" that her foil Stephens had described as characteristic of the entire movement for women's rights. Divisions within the movement, posi-tions adopted by Susan B. Anthony, Elizabeth Cady Stanton, and Isabella Beecher Hooker, and a scandal surrounding her brother Henry all made Stowe less and less confident that women's rights, at least as supported by NWSA under Anthony's and Stanton's leadership, was, as Crowfield had claimed, a "healthful and neces-sary movement of the human race towards progress."*

79 "What do you think of this Woman's Rights Question?" said Bob Stephens. "From some of your remarks, I apprehend that you think there is something in it. I may be wrong, but I must confess that I have looked with disgust on the whole movement. No man reverences women as I do; but I reverence them *as* women. I reverence them for those very things in which their sex differs from ours; but when they come upon our ground, and begin to work and fight after our manner and with our weapons, I regard them as fearful anomalies, neither men nor women. These Women's Rights Conventions appear to me to have ventilated crudities, absurdities, and blasphemies. To hear them talk about men, one would suppose that the two sexes were natural born enemies, and wonders whether they ever had fathers and brothers. One would think, upon their showing, that all men were a set of ruffians, in league against women,—they seeming, at the same time, to forget how on their very platforms the most constant and gallant defenders of their rights are men. Wendell Phillips and Wentworth Higginson have put at the service of the cause masculine training and manly vehemence, and complacently accepted the wholesale abuse of their own sex at the hands of their warrior sisters. One would think, were all they say of female powers true, that our Joan-of-Arcs ought to have disdained to fight under male captains."

"I think," said my wife, "that, in all this talk about the rights of men, and the rights of women, and the rights of children, the world seems to be forgetting what is quite as important, the *duties* of men and women and children. We all hear of our *rights* till we forget our *duties*; and even theology is beginning to concern itself more with what man has a right to expect of his Creator than what the Creator has a right to expect of man."

"You say the truth," said I; "there is danger of just this overaction: and yet rights must be discussed; because, in order to understand the duties, we owe to any class, we must understand their rights. To know our duties to men, women, and children, we must know what the rights of men, women, and children justly are. As, to the 'Woman's Rights movement,' it is not peculiar to America, it is part of a great wave in the incoming tide of modern civilization; the swell is felt no less in Europe, but it combs over and breaks on our American shore, because our great wide beach affords the best play for its waters: and as the ocean waves bring with them kelp, sea-weed, mud, sand, gravel, and even putrefying debris, which lie unsightly on the shore, and yet, on the whole, are healthful and refreshing,—so the Woman's Rights movement, with its conventions, its speech-making, it crudities and eccentricities, is nevertheless a part of a healthful and necessary movement of the human race towards progress. This question of Woman and her Sphere is now, perhaps, the greatest of the age. We have put slavery under foot, and with the downfall of Slavery the only obstacle to the success of our great democratic experiment is overthrown, and there seems no limit to the splendid possibilities which it may open before the human race. . . ."

"Then," said my wife, "you believe that women ought to vote?"

"If the principle on which we founded our government is true, that taxation must not exist without representation, and if women hold property and are taxed, it follows that women should be represented in the

State by their votes, or there is an illogical working of our government."

"But, my dear, don't you think that this will have a bad effect on the female character?"

"Yes," said Bob, "it will make women caucus-holders, political candidates."

"It may make this of some women, just as of some men," said I. "But all men do not take any great interest in politics; it is very difficult to get some of the best of them to do their duty in voting; and the same will be found true among women."

"But, after all," said Bob, "what do you gain? What will a woman's vote be but a duplicate of that of her husband or father, or whatever man happens to be her adviser?"

"That may be true on a variety of questions; but there are subjects on which the vote of women would, I think, be essentially different from that of men. On the subjects of temperance, public morals, and education, I have no doubt that the introduction of the female vote into legislation, in States, counties, and cities, would produce results very different from that of men alone. There are thousands of women who would close grogshops, and stop the traffic in spirits, if they had the legislative power; and it would be well for society, if they had. In fact, I think that a State can no more afford to dispense with the vote of women in its affairs than a family. Imagine a family where the female has no voice in the housekeeping! A State is but a larger family, and there are many of its concerns which equally with those of a private household would be bettered by female supervision."

"But fancy women going to those horrible voting-places! It is more than I can do myself," said Bob.

"But you forget," said I, "that they are horrible and disgusting principally because women never go to them. All places where women are excluded tend downward to barbarism; but the moment she is introduced, there come in with her courtesy, cleanliness, sobriety, and order. When a man can walk up to the ballot-box with his wife or his sister on his arm, voting-places will be far more agreeable than now; and the polls will not be such bear-gardens that refined men will be constantly tempted to omit their political duties there.

"If for nothing else, I would have women vote, that the business of voting may not be so disagreeable and intolerable to men of refinement as it now is; and I sincerely believe that the cause of good morals, good order, cleanliness, and public health would be a gainer, not merely by the added feminine vote, but by the added vote of a great many excellent, but too fastidious men, who are now kept from the polls by the disagreeables they meet there.

"Do you suppose, that, if women had equal representation with men in the municipal laws of New York, its reputation for filth during the last year would have gone so far beyond that of Cologne, or any other city renowned for bad smells? I trow not. I believe that a *lady-mayoress* would have brought a dispensation of brooms and whitewash, and made a terrible searching into dark holes and vile corners, before now. *Female New York*, I have faith to believe, has yet left in her enough of the primary instincts of womanhood to give us a clean healthy city, if female votes had any power to do it."

"But," said Bob, "you forget that voting would bring together all the women of the lower classes."

"Yes; but, thanks to the instincts of your sex, they would come in their Sunday clothes: for where is the woman that hasn't her finery, and will not embrace every chance to show it? Biddy's parasol, and hat with pink ribbons, would necessitate a clean shirt in Pat as much as on Sunday. Voting would become a *fête*, and we should have a population at the polls as well dressed as at church. Such is my belief."

"I do not see," said Bob, "but you go to the full extent with our modern female reformers."

"There are certain neglected truths, which have been held up by these reformers, that are gradually being accepted and infused into the life of modern society; and their recognition will help to solidify and purify democratic institutions. They are,—

"1. The right of every woman to hold independent property.

"2. The right of every woman to receive equal pay with man for work which she does equally well.

"3. The right of any woman to do any work for which, by her natural organization and talent, she is peculiarly adapted.

"Under the first head, our energetic sisters have already, by the help of their gallant male adjutants, reformed the laws of several of our States, so that a married woman is no longer left the unprotected legal slave of any unprincipled, drunken spendthrift who may be her husband,—but, in case of the imbecility or improvidence of the natural head of the family, the wife, if she have the ability, can conduct business, make contracts, earn and retain money for the good of the household; and I am sure no one can say that immense injustice and cruelty are not thereby prevented.

"It is quite easy for women who have the good fortune to have just and magnanimous husbands to say that they feel no interest in such reforms, and that they would willingly trust their property to the man to whom they give themselves; but they should remember that laws are not made for the restraint of the generous and just, but of the dishonest and base. The law which enables a married woman to hold her own property does not forbid her to give it to the man of her heart, if she so pleases; and it does protect many women who otherwise would be reduced to the extremest misery. I once knew an energetic milliner who had her shop attached four times, and a flourishing business broken up in four different cities, because she was tracked from city to city by a worthless spendthrift, who only waited till she had amassed a little property in a new place to swoop down upon and carry it off. It is to be hoped that the time is not distant when every State will give to woman a fair chance to the ownership and use of her own earnings and her own property."

"Well," said Bob, "the most interesting question still remains: What are to be the employments of woman? What ways are there for her to use her talents, to earn her livelihood and support those who are dear to her, when Providence throws that necessity upon her? This is becoming more than ever one of the pressing questions of our age. The war has deprived so many thousands of women of their natural protectors, that everything must be thought of that may possibly open a way for their self-support."

"Well, let us look over the field," said my wife. "What is there for woman?"

"In the first place," said I, "come the professions requiring natural genius,—authorship, painting, sculpture, with the subordinate arts of photographing, coloring, and finishing; but when all is told, these furnish employment to a very limited number,—almost as nothing to the whole. Then there is teaching, which is profitable in its higher branches, and perhaps the very pleasantest of all the callings open to woman; but teaching is at present an overcrowded profession, the applicants everywhere outnumbering the places. Architecture and landscape-gardening are arts every way suited to the genius of woman, and there are enough who have the requisite mechanical skill and mathematical education; and though never yet thought of for the sex, that I know of, I do not despair of seeing those who shall find in this field a profession at once useful and elegant. When women plan dwelling-houses, the vast body of tenements to be let in our cities will wear a more domestic and comfortable air, and will be built more with reference to the real wants of their inmates." . . .

"Then," said my wife, "there is the medical profession."

"Yes," said I. "The world is greatly obliged to Miss Blackwell and other noble pioneers who faced and overcame the obstacles to the attainment of a thorough medical education by females. Thanks to them, a new and lucrative profession is now open to educated women in relieving the distresses of their own sex; and we may hope that in time, through their intervention, the care of the sick may also become the vocation of cultivated, refined, intelligent women instead of being left, as heretofore, to the ignorant and vulgar. The experience of our late war has shown us what women of a high class morally and intellectually can do in this capacity. Why should not this experience inaugurate a new and sacred calling for refined and educated women? Why should not NURSING become a vocation equal in dignity and in general esteem to the medical profession, of which it is the right hand? Why should our dearest hopes, in the hour of their greatest peril, be committed into the hands of Sairey Gamps, when the world has seen Florence Nightingales?"

"Yes, indeed," said my wife; "I can testify, from my own experience, that the sufferings and dangers of the sickbed, for the want of intelligent, educated nursing, have been dreadful. A prejudiced, pig-headed, snuff-taking old woman, narrow-minded and vulgar, and more confident in her own way than seven men that can render a reason, enters your house at just the hour and moment when all your dearest earthly hopes are brought to a crisis. She becomes absolute dictator over your delicate, helpless wife and your frail babe,—the absolute dictator of all in the house. If it be her sovereign will and pleasure to enact all sorts of physiological absurdities in the premises, who shall say her nay? 'She knows her business, she hopes!' . . .

"And yet there are at the same time hundreds and thousands of women wanting the means of support, whose presence in a sick-room would be a benediction. I do trust that Miss Blackwell's band of educated nurses will not be long in coming, and that the number of such may increase till they effect a complete revolution in this vocation. A class of cultivated, well-trained, intelligent nurses would soon elevate the employment of attending on the sick into the noble calling it ought to be, and secure for it its appropriate rewards."

"There is another opening for woman," said I,—"in the world of business. The system of commercial colleges now spreading over our land is a new and a most important development of our times. There that large class of young men who have either no time or no inclination for an extended classical education can learn what will fit them for that active material life which in our broad country needs so many workers. But the most pleasing feature of these institutions is, that the complete course is open to women no less than to men, and women there may acquire that knowledge of book-keeping and accounts, and of the forms and princi-ples of business transactions, which will qualify them for some of the lucrative situations hitherto monopolized by the other sex. And the ex-penses of the course of instruction are so arranged as to come within the scope of very moderate means. A fee of fifty dollars entitles a woman to the benefit of the whole course, and she has the privilege of attending at any hours that may suit her own engagements and convenience."

"Then, again," said my wife, "there are the departments of millinery and dress-making and the various branches of needle-work, which afford employment to thousands of women; there is type-setting, by which many are beginning to get a living; there are the manufactures of cotton, woollen, silk, and the numberless useful articles which employ female hands in their fabrication,—all of them opening avenues by which, with more or less success, a subsistence can be gained."

"Well, really," said Bob, "it would appear, after all, that there are abundance of openings for women. What is the cause of the outcry and distress? How is it that we hear of women starving, driven to vice and crime by want, when so many doors of useful and profitable employment stand open to them?"

"The question would easily be solved," said my wife, "if you could once see the kind and class of women who thus suffer and starve. There may be exceptions, but too large a portion of them are girls and women who *can or will do no earthly thing well,*—and what is worse, are not willing to take the pains to be taught to do anything well." . . .

"I remember," said I, "that the head of the most celebrated dress-making establishment in New York, in reply to the appeals of the needle-women of the city for sympathy and wages, came out with published statements to this effect: that the difficulty lay not in unwillingness of employers to pay what work was worth, but in finding any work worth paying for; that she had many applicants, but among them few who could be of real use to her; that she, in common with everybody in this country who has any kind of serious responsibilities to carry, was con-tinually embarrassed for want of skilled workpeople, who could take and go on with the labor of her various departments without her constant supervision; that out of a hundred girls, there would not be more than five to whom she could give a dress to be made and dismiss it from her mind as something certain to be properly done.

"Let people individually look around their own little sphere and ask themselves if they know any woman really excelling in any *valuable* calling or accomplishment who is suffering for want of work. All of us know seamstresses, dress-makers, nurses, and laundresses, who have made themselves such a reputation, and are so beset and overcrowded with work, that the whole neighborhood is constantly on its knees to them with uplifted hands. The fine seamstress, who can cut and make trousseaus and layettes in elegant perfection, is always engaged six months in advance; the pet dress-maker of a neighborhood must be engaged in May for September, and in September for May; a laundress who sends your clothes home in nice order always has all the work that she can do. Good work in any department is the rarest possible thing in our American life; and it is a fact that the great majority of workers, both in the family and out, do only tolerably well,—not so badly that it actually cannot be borne, yet not so well as to be a source of real, thorough satisfaction. The exceptional worker in every neighborhood, who does things really *well*, can always set her own price, and is always having more offering than she can possibly do.

"The trouble, then, in finding employment for women lies deeper than the purses or consciences of the employers; it lies in the want of education in women: the want of *education*, I say,—meaning by education that which fits a woman for practical and profitable employment in life, and not mere common school learning."

"Yes," said my wife; "for it is a fact that the most troublesome and hopeless persons to provide for are often those who have a good medium education, but no feminine habits, no industry, no practical calculation, no muscular strength, and no knowledge of any one of woman's peculiar duties. In the earlier days of New England, women, as a class, had far fewer opportunities for acquiring learning, yet were far better educated, physically and morally, than now. The high school did not exist; at the common school they learned reading, writing, and arithmetic, and practised spelling; while at home they did the work of the household. They were cheerful, bright, active, ever on the alert, able to do anything, from the harnessing and driving of a horse to the finest embroidery. The daughters of New England in those days looked the world in the face without a fear. They shunned no labor; they were afraid of none; and they could always find their way to a living."

"But although less instructed in school learning," said I, "they showed no deficiency in intellectual acumen. I see no such women, nowadays, as some I remember of that olden time,—women whose strong minds and ever active industry carried on reading and study side by side with household toils." . . .

"And in those days," said my wife, "there lived in our families a class of American domestics, women of good sense and good powers of reflection, who applied this sense and power of reflection to household matters. In the early part of my married life, I myself had American 'help'; and they were not only excellent servants, but trusty and invaluable friends. But now, all this class of applicants for domestic service have disappeared, I scarce know why or how. All I know is, there is no more a Betsey or a Lois, such as used to take domestic cares off my shoulders so completely."

"Good heavens! where are they?" cried Bob. "Where do they hide? I would search through the world after such a prodigy!"

"The fact is," said I, "there has been a slow and gradual reaction against household labor in America. Mothers began to feel that it was a sort of *curse*, to be spared, to their daughters; women began to feel that they were fortunate in proportion as they were able to be entirely clear of family responsibilities. Then Irish labor began to come in, simultaneously with a great advance in female education.

"For a long while nothing was talked of, written of, thought of, in teachers' meetings, conventions, and assemblies, but the neglected state of female education; the whole circle of the arts and sciences was suddenly introduced into our free-school system, from which needle-work as gradually and quietly was suffered to drop out. The girl who attended the primary and high school had so much study imposed on her that she had no time for sewing or housework; and the delighted mother was only too happy to darn her stockings and do the housework alone, that her daughter might rise to a higher plane than she herself had attained to. The daughter, thus educated, had, on coming to womanhood, no solidity of muscle, no manual dexterity, no practice or experience in domestic life; and if she were to seek a livelihood, there remained only teaching, or some feminine trade, or the factory."

"These factories," said my wife, "have been the ruin of hundreds and hundreds of our once healthy farmers' daughters and others from the country. They go there young and unprotected; they live there in great boarding-houses, and associate with a promiscuous crowd, without even such restraints of maternal supervision as they would have in great boarding-schools; their bodies are enfeebled by labor often necessarily carried on in a foul and heated atmosphere; and at the hours when off duty, they are exposed to all the dangers of unwatched intimacy with the other sex.

"Moreover, the factory-girl learns and practices but one thing,—some one mechanical movement, which gives no scope for invention, ingenuity, or any other of the powers called into play by domestic labor; so that she is in reality unfitted in every way for family duties." . . .

"Well," said Bob, "what would you have? What is to be done?"

"In the first place," said I, "I would have it felt by those who are seeking to elevate woman, that the work is to be done, not so much by creating for her new spheres of action as by elevating her conceptions of that domestic vocation to which God and Nature have assigned her. It is all very well to open to her avenues of profit and advancement in the great outer world; but, after all, *to make and keep a home* is, and ever must be, a woman's first glory, her highest aim. No work of art can compare with a perfect home; the training and guiding of a family must be recognized as the highest work a woman can perform; and female education ought to be conducted with special reference to this.

"Men are *trained* to be lawyers, to be physicians, to be mechanics, by long and self-denying study and practice. A man cannot even make shoes merely by going to the high school and learning reading, writing, and mathematics; he cannot be a book-keeper, or a printer, simply from general education.

"Now women have a sphere and profession of their own,—a profession for which they are fitted by physical organization, by their own instincts, and to which they are directed by the pointing and manifest finger of God,—and that sphere is *family life*.

"Duties to the State and to public life they may have; but the public duties of women must bear to their family ones the same relation that family duties of men bear to their public ones.

"The defect in the late efforts to push on female education is, that it has been for her merely general, and that it has left out and excluded all that is professional; and she undertakes the essential duties of womanhood, when they do devolve on her, without any adequate preparation."

"But is it possible for a girl to learn at school the things which fit her for family life?" said Bob.

"Why not?" I replied. "Once it was thought impossible in schools to teach girls geometry, or algebra, or the higher mathematics; it was thought impossible to put them through collegiate courses: but it has been done, and we see it. Women study treatises on political economy in schools; and why should not the study of domestic economy form a part of every school course? . . .

"Why should there not be a professor of domestic economy in every large female school? Why should not this professor give lectures, first on houseplanning and building, illustrated by appropriate apparatus? Why should not the pupils have presented to their inspection models of houses planned with reference to economy, to ease of domestic service, to warmth, to ventilation, and to architectural appearance? Why should not the professor go on to lecture further on house-fixtures, with models of the best mangles, washing-machines, clothes-wringers, ranges, furnaces, and cooking-stoves, together with drawings and apparatus illustrative of domestic hydraulics, showing the best contrivances for bathing-rooms, and the obvious principles of plumbing, so that the pupils may have some idea how to work the machinery of a convenient house when they have it, and to have such conveniences introduced when wanting? If it is thought worthwhile to provide at great expense apparatus for teaching the revolution of Saturn's moons and the precession of the equinoxes, why should there not be some also to teach what it may greatly concern a woman's earthly happiness to know?

"Why should not the professor lecture on home-chemistry, devoting his first lecture to bread-making? and why might not a batch of bread be made and baked and exhibited to the class, together with specimens of morbid anatomy in the bread line,—the sour cotton bread of the baker,—the rough, big-holed bread,—the heavy, fossil bread,—the bitter bread of too much yeast,—and the causes of their defects pointed out? And so with regard to the various articles of food,—why might not chemical lectures be given on all of them, one after another?—In short, it would be easy to trace out a course of lectures on common things to occupy a whole year, and for which the pupils, whenever they come to have homes of their own, will thank the lecturer to the last day of their life.

"Then there is no impossibility in teaching needle-work, the cutting and fitting of dresses, in female schools. . . .

"In the same manner the care and nursing of young children and the tending of the sick may be made the subject of lectures. Every woman ought to have some general principles to guide her with regard to what is to be done in case of the various accidents that may befall either children or grown people, and of their lesser illnesses, and ought to know how to prepare comforts and nourishment for the sick. Hawthorne's satirical remarks upon the contrast between the elegant Zenobia's conversation and the smoky porridge she made for him when he was an invalid might apply to the volunteer cookery of many charming women."

"I think," said Bob, "that your Professor of Domestic Economy would find enough to occupy his pupils."

"In fact," said I, "were domestic economy properly honored and properly taught, in the manner described, it would open a sphere of employment to so many women in the home life, that we should not be obliged to send our women out to California or the Pacific, to put an end to an anxious and aimless life.

"When domestic work is sufficiently honored to be taught as an art and science in our boarding-schools and high schools, then possibly it may acquire also dignity in the eyes of our working classes, and young girls who have to earn their own living may no longer feel degraded in engaging in domestic service. The place of a domestic in a family may become as respectable in their eyes as a place in a factory, in a printing-office, in a dress-making or millinery establishment, or behind the counter of a shop.

"In America there is no class which will confess itself the lower class, and a thing recommended solely for the benefit of any such class finds no one to receive it.

"If the intelligent and cultivated look down on household-work with disdain, if they consider it as degrading, a thing to be shunned by every possible device, they may depend upon it that the influence of such contempt of woman's noble duties will flow downward, producing a like contempt in every class in life.

"Our sovereign princesses learn the doctrine of equality very quickly, and are not going to sacrifice themselves to what is not considered *de bon ton* by the upper classes; and the girl with the laced hat and parasol, without underclothes, who does her best to "shirk" her duties as housemaid, and is looking for marriage as an escape from work, is a fair copy of her mistress who married for much the same reason, who hates housekeeping, and would rather board or do anything else than have the care of a family;—the one is about as respectable as the other.

"When housekeeping becomes an enthusiasm, and its study and practice a fashion, then we shall have in America that class of persons to rely on for help in household labors who are now going to factories, to printing-offices, to every kind of toil, forgetful of the best life and sphere of woman."

[Stowe, "The Woman Question: or, What Will You Do with Her?" *Atlantic Monthly* 16 (December 1865): 672–83]

Stowe's relationship with the recipient of the following letter was long standing: it had begun when Sara Parton had been a student of Harriet's at Catharine's Hartford Female Seminary and, after an interruption of nearly four decades, was continued through correspondence. The "naughty girl" that Stowe remembered from the years in Hartford had chosen the pseudonym

Fanny Fern and become a writer whose popularity nearly rivalled Stowe's.

80   July 25, 1869

My dearly beloved Sara,

... Yes, I do believe in Female Suffrage—The more I think of it the more absurd this whole government of men over women looks—A friend of mine put it rather nicely the other night—I don't much care about voting she said the other day—but I feel as this girl did who was offended when the cake plate was not passed to her.

Why I thought you did not love cake.

But I do like to have the chance of refusing it says she. This agreement of Tom, Dick, and Harry not to pass the cake plate lest we make ourselves sick with cake seems absurd. Dare not trust us with suffrage lest we become unwomanly. Let them try it. Unsexed? I should like to see what could make women other than women and men than men. ...

[Harriet Beecher Stowe]

[HBS to Sara Parton, SSC]

The year before the following letter was written by Harriet and Isabella, Susan B. Anthony and Elizabeth Cady Stanton had founded a feminist paper and named it The Revolution. *Harriet and Isabella tentatively agreed to become corresponding editors but insisted that the periodical's name be changed. Their demand was rejected, and the paper continued without Harriet's participation in that particular* Revolution.

81   [December 1869]

My dear Miss Anthony,

We will give our names as corresponding Editors for your paper for one year and agree to furnish at least six original articles apiece during the year—and also to furnish an original article from some friend which we shall have read (and revised if in our judgment necessary,) every other week—during the year—said articles to take the place of our own contributions on the weeks not covered by them.

We agree to do this without promised compensation—but on the *condition* that you will *change* the *name* of the paper to the *True Republic* or some name equally satisfactory to us—and on the condition that you will pay us *equally* for this service according to your ability, you yourself being sole judge of that ability.

        H.B. Stowe

        I.B. Hooker

                [HBS and IBH to Susan B. Anthony, VCL]

Only two years after Stowe had almost joined forces with Elizabeth Cady Stanton and Susan B. Anthony, she opened her novel, My Wife and I; or Harry Henderson's History, *on an unmistakably sarcastic note. "I trust," her narrator Harry Henderson declared, "that Miss Anthony and Mrs. Stanton, and all the prophetesses of our day, will remark the humility and propriety of my title. It is not I and My Wife—oh no! It is My Wife and I. What am I, and what is my father's house, that I should go before my wife in anything."*

Originally published as a serial in the Christian Union *during 1870 and 1871,* My Wife and I *dealt openly with issues dividing the women's rights movement. In choosing "A Discussion of the Woman Question from All Points" as the title for chapter 24 of* My Wife and I, *Stowe did not mean to suggest that each of the points was equally valid. Just as she had employed dialogue in "The Woman Question: or, What Will You Do with Her," so she returned to this strategy for a conversation in which her point was readily apparent. The participants in the conversation narrated by Harry include the wealthy Mr. Van Arsdel and his daughters Ida and Eva. They, along with Harry's friend, Jim Fellows, are the vehicles for Stowe's unrestrained critique of Victoria Woodhull. An articulate but highly controversial advocate of women's rights, Woodhull became the prototype for Audacia Dangyereyes. Although some historians and literary critics have suggested that the portrayal of Mrs. Cerulean was based upon Woodhull's supporter, Elizabeth Cady Stanton, contemporaries recognized that Harriet's sister Isabella was the more likely model.*

82   The bold intrusion of Miss Audacia Dangyereyes into my apartment had left a most disagreeable impression on my mind. This was not lessened by the reception of her paper, which came to hand in due course of next mail, and which I found to be an exposition of all the wildest principles of modern French communism. It consisted of attacks directed about equally against Christianity, marriage, the family state, and all human laws and standing order, whatsoever. It was much the same kind of writing with which the populace of France was indoctrinated and leavened in the era preceding the first Revolution, and which in time bore fruit in blood. In those days, as now, such doctrines were toyed with in literary salons and aristocratic circles, where their novelty formed an agreeable stimulus in the vapid commonplace of fashionable life. They were then, as now, embraced with enthusiasm by fair illuminati, who fancied that they saw in them a dawn of some millenial glory; and were awakened from their dream, like Madame Roland, at the foot of the guillotine, bowing their heads to death and crying, "O Liberty, what things are done in thy name!"

The principal difference between the writers on the "Emancipated Woman" and those of the French illuminati was that the French prototypes were men and women of elegance, culture, and education; whereas their American imitators, though not wanting in a certain vigor and cleverness, were both coarse in expression, narrow in education, and wholly devoid of common decency in their manner of putting things. It was a paper that a man who reverenced his mother and sisters could scarcely read alone in his own apartments without blushing with indignation and vexation.

Every holy secret of human nature, all those subjects of which the grace and the power consist in their exquisite delicacy and tender refinement, were here handled with coarse fingers. Society assumed the aspect of a pack of breeding animals, and all its laws and institutions were to return to the mere animal basis.

It was particularly annoying to me that this paper, with all its coarseness and grossness, set itself up to be the head leader of Woman's Rights; and to give its harsh clamors as the voice of woman. Neither was I at all satisfied with the manner in which I had been dragooned into taking it, and thus giving my name and money to its circulation. I had actually been bullied into it; because, never having contemplated the possibility of such an existence as a female bully, I had marked out in my mind no suitable course of conduct adequate to the treatment of one. "What *should* I have done?" I said to myself. "What *is* a man to do under such circumstances? Shall he engage in a personal scuffle? Shall he himself vacate his apartment, or shall he call in a policeman?"

The question assumed importance in my eyes, because it was quite possible that, having come once, she might come again; that the same course of conduct might be used to enforce any kind of exaction which she should choose to lay on me. But most of all was I sensitive lest by any means some report of it might get to the Van Arsdels. My trepidation may then be guessed on having the subject at once proposed to me by Mr. Van Arsdel that evening as I was sitting with him and Ida in her study.

"I want to know, Mr. Henderson," he said, "if you are a subscriber for the 'Emancipated Woman,' the new organ of the Woman's Rights party?"

"Now, papa," said Ida, "that is a little unjust! It only professes to be an organ of the party, but it is not recognized by us."

"Have you seen the paper?" said Mr. Van Arsdel to me. Like a true Yankee I avoided the question by asking another.

"Have you subscribed to it, Mr. Van Arsdel?"

"Well, yes," said he, laughing, "I confess I have; and a pretty mess I have made of it. It is not a paper that any decent man ought to have in his house. But the woman came herself into my counting-room and, actually, she badgered me into it; I couldn't get her out. I didn't know what to do with her. I never had a woman go on so with me before. I was flustered, and gave her my five dollars to get rid of her. If she had been a man I'd have knocked her down."

"Oh, papa," said Ida, "I'll tell you what you should have done; you should have called me. She'd have got no money and no subscriptions out of me, nor you either if I'd been there."

"Now, Mr. Henderson, misery loves company; has she been to your room?" said Mr. Van Arsdel.

"I confess she has," said I, "and that I have done just what you did—yielded at once."

"Mr. Henderson, all this sort of proceeding is thoroughly vexatious and disagreeable," said Ida; "and all the more so that it tends directly to injure all women who are trying to be self-supporting and independent. It destroys that delicacy and refinement of feeling which men, and American men especially, cherish toward women, and will make the paths of self-support terribly hard to those who have to tread them. There really is not the slightest reason why a woman should cease to be a woman because she chooses to be independent and pursue a self-supporting career. And claiming a right to dispense with womanly decorums and act like a man is just as ridiculous as it would be for a man to claim the right to wear woman's clothes. Even if we supposed that society were so altered as to give to woman every legal and every social right that man has; and if all the customs of society should allow her to do the utmost that she can for herself, in the way of self-support, still, women will be relatively weaker than men, and there will be the same propriety in their being treated with consideration and delicacy and gentleness that there now is. And the assumptions of these hoydens and bullies have a tendency to destroy that feeling of chivalry and delicacy on the part of men. It is especially annoying and galling to me, because I do propose to myself a path different from that in which young women in my position generally have walked; and such reasoners as Aunt Maria and all the ladies of her circle will not fail to confound Miss Audacia's proceedings and opinions, and mine, as all belonging to the same class. As to the opinions of the paper, it is mainly by the half truths that are in it that it does mischief. If there were not real evils to be corrected, and real mistakes in society, this kind of thing would have no power. As it is, I have no doubt that it will acquire a certain popularity and do immense mischief. I think the elements of mischief and confusion in our republic are gathering as fast as they did in France before the Revolution."

"And," said I, "after all, republics are on trial before the world. Our experiment is not yet two hundred years old, and we have all sorts of clouds and storms gathering—the labor question, the foreign immigration question, the woman question, the monopoly and corporation question, all have grave aspects."

"You see, Mr. Henderson," said Ida, "as to this woman question, the moderate party to which I belong is just at that disadvantage that people always are when there is a party on ahead of them who hold some of their principles and are carrying them to every ridiculous extreme. They have to uphold a truth that is constantly being brought into disrepute and made ridiculous by these ultra advocates. For my part, all I can do is to go quietly on with what I knew was right before. What is right *is* right, and remains right no matter how much ultraists may caricature it."

"Yes, my daughter," said Mr. Van Arsdel, "but what would become of our country if all the women could vote, and people like Miss Audacia Dangyereyes should stump the country as candidates for election?"

"Well, I am sure," said Ida, "we should have very disagreeable times, and a great deal to shock us."

"It is not merely that," said Mr. Van Arsdel; "the influence of such women on young men would be demoralizing."

"When I think of such dangers," said Ida, "I am, on the whole, very well pleased that there is no immediate prospect of the suffrage being granted to women until a generation with superior education and better balanced minds and better habits of consecutive thought shall have grown up among us. I think the gift of the ballot will come at last as the result of a superior culture and education. And I am in no hurry for it before."

"What is all this that you are talking about?" said Eva, who came into the room just at this moment. "Ma and Aunt Maria are in such a state about that paper that papa has just brought home! They say there are most horrid things in it, Mr. Henderson; and they say that it belongs to the party which you, and Ida, and all your progressive people are in."

"It is an excrescence of the party," said I; "a diseased growth; and neither Miss Ida nor I will accept of it as any expression of our opinion, though it does hold some things which we believe."

"Well," said Eva, "I am curious to see it, just because they don't want I should. What can there be in it so very bad?"

"You may as well keep out of it, chick," said her father, caressing her. "And now, I'll tell you, Ida, just what I think; you good women are not fit to govern the world, because you do not know, and you oughtn't to know, the wickedness that you have got to govern. We men have to know all about the rogues, and the sharpers, and the pickpockets, and the bullies; we have to grow hard and sharp, and 'cut our eye-teeth,' as the saying is, so that at last we come to not having much faith in anybody. The rule is, pretty much, not to believe anybody that you meet, and to take for granted that every man that you have dealings with will cheat you if he can. That's bad enough, but when it comes to feeling that every *woman* will cheat you if she can, when women cut their eye-teeth, and get to be sharp, and hard, and tricky, as men are, then I say, Look out for yourself, and deliver me from having anything to do with them."

"Why, really!" said Eva, "papa is getting to be quite an orator. I never heard him talk so much before. Papa, why don't you go on to the platform at the next Woman's Rights Convention, and give them a good blast?"

"Oh, I'll let them alone," said Mr. Van Arsdel; "I don't want to be mixed up with them, and I don't want my girls to be, either. Now, I do not object to what Ida is doing, and going to do. I think there is real sense in that, although mother and Aunt Maria feel so dreadfully about it. I like to see a woman have pluck, and set herself to be good for something in the world. And I don't see why there shouldn't be women doctors; it is just the thing there ought to be. But I don't go for all this hurrah and hullaballoo, and pitching women head-first into politics, and sending them to legislatures, and making them candidates for Congress, and for the Presidency, and nobody knows what else."

"Well," said I, "why not a woman President as well as a woman Queen of England?"

"Because," said he, "look at the difference. The woman Queen in England comes to it quietly; she is born to it, and there is no fuss about it. But whoever is set up to be President of the United States is just set up to have his character torn off from his back in shreds, and to be mauled, pummeled, and covered with dirt by every filthy paper all over the country. And no woman that was not willing to be draggled through every kennel, and slopped into every dirty pail of water, like an old mop, would ever consent to run as a candidate. Why, it's an ordeal that kills a man. It killed General Harrison, and killed old Zack. And what sort of brazen tramp of a woman would it be that could stand it, and come out of it without being killed? Would it be any kind of a woman that we should want to see at the head of our government? I tell you, it's quite another thing to be President of a democratic republic from what it is to be hereditary Queen."

"Good for you, papa!" said Eva, clapping her hands. "Why, how you go on! I never did hear such eloquence. No, Ida, set your mind at rest, you sha'n't be run for President of the United States. You are a great deal too good for that."

"Now," said Mr. Van Arsdel, "there's your friend, Mrs. Cerulean, tackled me the other night, and made a convert of me, she said. Bless me! she's a handsome woman, and I like to hear her talk. And if we didn't live in the world we do, and things weren't in any respect what they are, nothing would be nicer than to let her govern the world. But in the great rough round of business she's nothing but a pretty baby after all,— nothing else in the world. We let such women convert us, because we like to have them around. It amuses us, and don't hurt them. But you can't let your baby play with matches and gunpowder, if it wants to ever so much. Women are famous for setting things a-going that they don't know anything about. And then, when the explosion comes, they don't know what did it, and run screaming to the men."

"As to Mrs. Cerulean," said Eva, "I never saw anybody that had such a perfectly happy opinion of herself as she has. She always thinks that she understands everything by intuition. I believe in my heart that she'd walk into the engine-room of the largest steamship that ever was navigated, and turn out the chief engineer and take his place, if he'd let her. She'd navigate by woman's God-given instincts, as she calls them."

"And so she'd keep on till she'd blown up the ship," said Mr. Van Arsdel.

"Well," said I, "one fact is to be admitted, that men, having always governed the world, must by this time have acquired a good deal of traditional knowledge of the science of government, and of human nature, which women can't learn by intuition in a minute." . . .

"Yes," said Ida, "I think that an immediate rush into politics of such women as we have now, without experience or knowledge of political economy of affairs, would be, as Eva says, just like women's undertaking to manage the machinery of a large steamer by feminine instincts. I hope never to see women in public life till we have had a generation of women who have some practical familiarity with the great subjects which are to be considered, about which now the best instructed women know comparatively nothing. The question which mainly interests me at present is a humanitarian one. It's an absolute fact that a great portion of womankind have their own living to get; and they do it now, as a general rule, with many of the laws and institutions of society against them. The reason of this is, that all these laws and institutions have been made by men, without any consent or concurrence of theirs. Now, as women are different from men, and have altogether a different class of feelings and wants and necessities, it certainly is right and proper that they should have some share in making the laws with which they are to be governed. It is true that the laws have been made by fathers and brothers and husbands; but no man, however near, ever comprehends fully the necessities and feelings of women. And it seems to me that a State where all the laws are made by men, without women, is just like a family that is managed entirely by fathers and brothers, without any concurrence of mothers and sisters. That's my testimony, and my view of the matter."
. . .

At this moment our conversation was interrupted by the entrance of Jim Fellows. He seemed quite out of breath and excited, and had no sooner passed the compliments of the evening than he began.

"Well," said he, "Hal, I have just come from the Police Court, where there's a precious row. Our friend 'Dacia Dangyereyes is up for blackmailing and swindling; and there's a terrible wash of dirty linen going on. I was just in time to get the very earliest notes for our paper."

"Good!" said Mr. Van Arsdel. "I hope the creature is caught at last."

"Never believe that," said Jim. "She has as many lives as a cat. They never'll get a hold on her. She'll talk 'em all round."

"Disgusting!" said Ida.

"Ah!" said Jim, "it's part of the world as it goes. She'll come off with flying colors, doubtless, and her cock's-feathers will be flaunting all the merrier for it."

"How horribly disagreeable," said Eva, "to have such women around. It makes one ashamed of one's sex."

"I think," said Ida, "there is not sufficient resemblance to a real woman in her to make much trouble on her account. She is an amphibious animal, belonging to a transition period of human society."

"Well," said Jim, "if you'll believe it, Mrs. Cerulean and two or three of the ladies of her set are actually going to invite 'Dacia to their salon, and patronize her."

"Impossible!" said Ida, flushing crimson; "it *cannot* be!"

"Oh, you don't know Mrs. Cerulean," said Jim; "'Dacia called on her with her newspaper, and conducted herself in a most sweet and winning manner, and cast herself at her feet for patronage; and Mrs. Cerulean, regarding her through those glory spectacles which she usually wears, took her up immediately as a promising candidate for the latter day. Mrs. Cerulean don't see anything in 'Dacia's paper that, properly interpreted, need make any trouble; because, you see, as she says, *everything ought to be love*, everywhere, above and below, under and over, up and down, top and side and bottom, ought to be *love*, LOVE. And then when there's general all-overness and all-thoroughness, and an entire mixed-up-ativeness, then the infinite will come down into the finite, and the finite will overflow into the infinite, and, in short, Miss 'Dacia's cock's-feathers will sail right straight up into heaven, and we shall see her cheek by jowl with the angel Gabriel, promenading the streets of the new Jerusalem. That's the programme. Meanwhile, 'Dacia's delighted. She hadn't the remotest idea of being an angel, or anything of the sort; but since good judges have told her she is, she takes it all very contentedly."

"Oh," said Ida, "it really can't be true, Mr. Fellows; it really is impossible that such ladies as Mrs. Cerulean's set—ladies of family and position, ladies of real dignity and delicacy—are going to indorse the principles of that paper; principles which go to the immediate dissolution of civilized society." . . .

"[And]," said Eva, "how can they bear the scandal of this disgraceful trial? This certainly will open their eyes."

"Oh," said Jim, "you will see, Mrs. Cerulean will adhere all the closer for this. It's persecution, and virtue in all ages has been persecuted; therefore, all who are persecuted are virtuous. Don't you see the logical consistency? And then, don't the Bible say, 'Blessed are ye when men persecute you, and say all manner of evil against you'?"

"It don't appear to me," said Ida, "that she can so far go against all common sense."

"*Common* sense!" said Jim; "Mrs. Cerulean and her clique have long since risen above anything like common sense; all their sense is of the most uncommon kind, and relates to a region somewhere up in the clouds, where everything is made to match. They live in an imaginary world, and reason with imaginary reasons, and see people through imaginary spectacles, and have glorious times all the while." . . .

"But the fact is," said Mr. Van Arsdel, "Mrs. Cerulean is a respectable woman, of respectable family, and this girl is a tramp; that's what she is; and it is absolutely impossible that Mrs. Cerulean can know what she is about."

"Well, I delicately suggested some such thing to Mrs. Cerulean," said Jim; "but bless me! the way she set me down! Says she, 'Do you men ever inquire into the character of people that you unite with to carry your purposes? You join with anybody that will help you, without regard to antecedents!' "

"She don't speak the truth," said Mr. Van Arsdel. "We men are very particular about the record of those we join with to carry our purposes. You wouldn't find a board of bankers taking a man that had a record for swindling, or a man that edited a paper arguing against all rights of property. Doctors won't admit a man among them who has the record of a quack or a malpractitioner. Clergymen won't admit a man among them who has a record of licentiousness or infidel sentiments. And if women will admit women in utter disregard of their record of chastity or their lax principles as to the family, they act on lower principles than any body of men."

"Besides," said I, "that kind of tolerance cuts the very ground from under the whole woman movement; for the main argument for proposing it was to introduce into politics that superior delicacy and purity which women manifest in family life. But if women are going to be less careful about delicacy and decorum and family purity than men are, the quagmire of politics, foul enough now, will become putrid."

"Oh, come," said Eva, "the subject does get too dreadful; I can't bear to think of it, and I move that we have a game of whist, and put an end to it. Come, now, do let's sit down sociably, and have something agreeable."

[HBS *MWI*, pp. 268–83]

> *In private correspondence with members of her family, Stowe had no need to disguise as Audacia Dangyereyes the woman whom she had caricatured in* My Wife and I. *Stowe's contempt for Victoria Woodhull turned to outrage after the latter charged that America's most prominent minister had been involved in an adulterous affair with a member of his congregation. The minister was Stowe's beloved brother, Henry, whose alleged liaison with Elizabeth Tilton led to a series of highly publicized trials which titillated Victorian America. The scandal also threatened the bonds of sisterhood between Harriet and Isabella. In the following letters to her twin daughters Hattie and Eliza, Harriet likened Woodhull and her sister Tennie C. Caflin to "witches" and castigated Isabella for her refusal to disavow them.*

83   December 19, 1872

My Dear girls

Those vile women 'jailbirds' had the impudence to undertake to advertise that they were going to give a lecture in [Boston's] Music Hall. It has roused such an indignation among the citizens that I am told the whole thing is to be stopped. It appears that lectures cannot be given without a license of the city government which was not to be forthcoming. The impudence of those witches is incredible! Say nothing however till you hear it from others. I have been privately advised of the movement.

Your ever affectionate Mother

[HBS to Hattie and Eliza Stowe, SchL]

84   May 11, 1873

My Dear Eliza,

. . . I am glad you went ahead and got into pleasant relations with Mary and Eugene [Isabella's daughter and son-in-law] and your Aunt Isabella before I came. They have so deeply wounded my sense of all propriety and affection in the course they took about my brother that for me it would have been impossible to do it, but I am glad you could and did, and I think it will be easier for me to meet them since you have— Your aunt is like many monomaniacs all right if the wrong string is not jarred but I fear that seeing me will jar it. I am not a person who takes offense easily—it is very difficult to offend me—but there are things which strike my *very life* and these accusations against my brother are among them. I cannot hear that subject discussed as a *possibility* open for inquiry without such an intense uprising of indignation and scorn and anger as very few have ever seen in me in these late years—but if ever I should hear those who ought to know better maundering out insinuations and doubts about him I think there will be the eruption of a volcano that has for years been supposed to be extinct—they will see *what* I am—when thoroughly roused.

Nevertheless, I long for peace and quietness—and I trust they will all have the good taste and good sense to accept the [stricture?] which [illegible] society has passed upon this subject.

[Harriet Beecher Stowe]

[HBS to Eliza Stowe, SchL]

Although Harriet and Calvin had made their home in Hartford, Connecticut, after Calvin's retirement from teaching in 1864, they began to spend nearly half the year in Mandarin, Florida, during the 1870s. Because Henry's civil trial coincided with the period spent in Florida, Mary Beecher Perkins, who eventually supported Henry, kept Harriet informed. Anne Seymour Robinson, a member of one of Hartford's prominent families, also wrote to Harriet about both Henry and Isabella. Excerpts from Harriet's letters to Mary and Anne show that the intensity of her loyalty to Henry continued undiminished. But Harriet did become less hostile toward Isabella.

85 January 25, 1875

Dear Mary,

Thank God you are in this camp at last. It is like times of Indian warfare women and children must go inside the stockade.

It will help you to get this to be in sight and hearing of Henry. Do write me at least once a week all the scraps of news you get by being on the spot. I don't think God ever permitted the Devil to hatch a worse plot than this—but God's ways have long reaches and he permits many things. . . .

Your afft sister

H

February 28, 1875

Dear Mary,

You are a good soul to keep writing for you know our distress and our anxiety. . . .

This testimony of Tilton's is an outrage on human decency that I should think must shake the faith of a block and I wonder any lawyer that hoped for a reputation for decency could advise him to give it.

Well, the more the better *nobody* can believe that—They might believe something less but anything like *that* is a nightmare creation of insanity and unnatural lust and indecency. I now believe that all the things which Eunice [Henry's wife] got from Mother Morris [Elizabeth Tilton's mother] about this creature's atrocities and indecencies are strictly true.

To think that Henry who never would listen to an indelicate word, who has kept all this nauseous thing out of his mind being obliged to sit in open court and have this foulness dribbled out before him.

It seems as if it was permitted to him to await drinking the cup to the most nauseous dregs. If he can pity and forgive *now* he does it with his eyes open and with full conscience of what he forgives.

> "Raging waves of the sea—
> foaming out their own shame"
> is all I can think of—. . . .
> Your afft sister
> H

[HBS to Mary Beecher Perkins, SchL]

---

86   May 2, 1875

Dear Mrs. Robinson,

Your kind note was a source of great comfort to me. To feel that we have the prayers[,] the faith and sympathy of such as you is to me encouragement which makes up for all the pain of the scandal. Henry's long cross examination is over and what evil have they found in him? Every inch of his life has been put under a microscope and examined and what evil hath he done? What can anybody allege but over trust in a false friend and a generous chivalrous unselfish effort to shield what the true gentleman always thinks sacred, the weakness of a woman. Mr. Evarts[1] remarked "The fact is the only difficulty is that Mr. Beecher is so much

---

1. William Maxwell Evarts was Henry Ward Beecher's lawyer.

better than common men that it is hard to make people understand it[."]
. . .

The wonderful peace and serenity and unshaken calmness with which Henry has been carried through this trial is a confirmation of our faith in God. Tho he allows the trial he sustains under it and we learn at last rather to glory in infirmity that the power of Christ may rest upon us.

My poor wandering sister Bell—my heart is sad for her. Every disclosure this trial makes of those wretched people the Woodhulls and 'omne genus' fills me with pain for her. They got an ascendancy over her by producing conviction thro that apology that they wrung from Henry and which they showed to Mrs. Stanton—they *fixed* it in her mind that Henry had indeed fallen and they used it as an argument with her to show that the marriage laws ought to be given up since so *great* a man could not get along under them without falling. It was promised her that if Henry would only come out boldly and avow such a course and justify it there would be an immediate rush to his standard of all the emancipated. In the letter which Bell sent to Henry when she urged this course was a postscript by S. B. Anthony saying in so many words—that the *needs* of a nature so large as his were evident, and, that the *only* sin he had committed was living in a false marriage and they hoped he would come out and confess that and show from his own experience from Sunday to Sunday and from day to day the evil of the present system of marriage.—I don't think they would have got Bell over, for she made strong resistance at first if they had not produced a conviction on her mind that the only way to save her brother was to attack the laws of marriage.

I think from what Mr. Chamberlin[2] says that there was a revulsion beginning with her conviction of Henry's innocence and that she was as she declared herself unsettled on the whole subject which I hope means that she is coming back. If only she had a sensible husband she might now be brought right but John ministers to the very poorest and weakest part of her nature. But I am sure a child of so many prayers and such godly parents cannot be left in the snares of Satan and I pray daily for her deliverance. . . .

> Your loving friend
> HBS

> [HBS to Anne Seymour Robinson, SD]

2. Franklin Chamberlin was a Nook Farm neighbor of Isabella and John Hooker.

10.

Isabella Beecher Hooker:
"The Lips of Women Are
Being Unsealed"

WHEN she paused to reminisce at the age of eighty-three, Isabella Beecher Hooker credited her official entrance into the suffrage sisterhood to the influence and example of Elizabeth Cady Stanton and Susan B. Anthony. "Sitting at the feet" of both women in the summer of 1869, Hooker had vowed to share their "obloquy" as well as their work.[1] She soon came to envision her own mediatory efforts on their behalf as a divinely sanctioned means of fulfilling her Beecher legacy. Yet as she ventured first into the postbellum women's rights movement and later into spiritualism, Isabella detached herself from her Calvinist heritage with a remarkable ease that contrasted sharply with her sister Catharine's protracted and painful struggle. For Isabella, faith in the political power of womanhood became a substitute for organized religion. This faith went hand in hand with her fervent belief in the moral imperative of sexual solidarity among women. Indeed, in describing and justifying both goals, Hooker frequently made use of religious terminology and Biblical analogies. Yet ironically, her commitment to these ideals not only caused her to fail in her attempts to mediate between the two wings of the suffrage movement but also alienated her from her own sisters, thus illustrating the complex politics of sisterhood.

Isabella had been staying with Harriet in New York City, helping her edit *Lady Byron Vindicated*, when John Hooker suggested in a series of letters that his wife should seek financing from wealthy ladies in order to set herself up as a preacher to women. Recognizing the advantages that might accrue to both the family and the movement if Isabella could bring Catharine and especially Harriet into the suffrage fold, John also encouraged his wife to introduce her sisters to Susan B. Anthony, whom Isabella had met just a few weeks earlier. He wanted the Beecher sisters to discuss the possibility of contributing regularly to Anthony's journal, *The Revo-*

lution: "What wd be better would be for her [Harriet] to be an associate editor perhaps with you. . . . Put her up to writing a powerful novel on the woman question and publish it in a serial in the Revolution . . . and the publication in book form afterwards wd pay her finely."² Isabella and Harriet promptly offered themselves as associate editors and Anthony was sorely tempted. But when Anthony balked at their demand that she rechristen her journal to suit their notions of propriety,³ only Isabella would agree to serve as a contributor.

Hooker also attempted to secure the support of her famous half sisters in the fall of 1869 as part of her efforts to effect a lasting truce between Boston and New York suffragists. She organized Hartford's first suffrage convention, persuaded Harriet and Calvin Stowe to serve as vice presidents of the Connecticut Woman Suffrage Association (launched during the convention), and even managed to seat Stanton on the same platform as her detractors.⁴ When Isabella's Boston friend Caroline Severance as well as her brother Henry Ward Beecher repeated charges made by Lucy Stone and others against the character and views of Stanton and Anthony and the alleged immorality of *The Revolution*,⁵ Hooker became even more determined to defend the New Yorkers from what she considered to be malicious gossip or misunderstanding. Confessing that Stanton's reputed views on marriage and divorce were "far more trying to meet than anything Susan says or does," Hooker asked Stanton to clarify her position so that she could describe it accurately to friends and family members.⁶

Isabella took it upon herself to defend her brother Henry against charges that he, too, supported free love in her first contribution to *The Revolution* for December 1869. In the process, she began to articulate her opposition to the sexual double standard and her views on female solidarity. She opened "The McFarland-Richardson Tragedy" by reminding her readers that all the facts had not been available to her brother and O. B. Frothingham when the two ministers agreed to officiate at the deathbed marriage of Albert Richardson and Abby Sage McFarland. (Daniel McFarland, her former husband, had shot Richardson in a jealous rage. Although McFarland was tried and found innocent by reason of insanity, he was awarded custody of their child.) Hooker went on to urge her sex to feel sympathy and compassion for the newly widowed Abby Richardson "in this hour of her deepest agony," regardless of whether she turned out to be innocent or guilty of "unfaithfulness to her womanhood and motherhood." Calling for a single standard of judgment, Isabella insisted that readers should apply "the same rule to the husband who treats lightly his obligations to conjugal duty and to the woman who tempts him from the path of virtue, that we would to the wife and her tempter." The nature of Hooker's outspoken objections to the sexual double standard became clear when she added: "We do not by this mean that the standard of social morals should be lowered to meet the case of man, but we do mean that men should be judged by precisely the same standard women now are, and that in every effort to conserve and purify the family state there should be no mitigation of sentence on behalf of the erring husband and father that is not accorded to the erring wife and mother."[7]

By publicly joining in the campaign against the double standard, which tacitly legitimized male sexual license (while penalizing women on the basis of mere accusation alone), Isabella was following in the footsteps of her more famous half sisters. Both Catharine and Harriet had already proven willing (and even eager) to endure severe public censure and condemnation for their respective exposés of male sexual misconduct. Whether the guilty party was a prestigious member of the Yale faculty (as in the case of the MacWhorter trial and Catharine's *Truth Stranger than Fiction*) or a lionized romantic poet (as in the case of Harriet's *Lady Byron Vindicated*), the Beecher sisters had shattered the conspiracy of silence that perpetuated the double standard as part of their campaign to defend the reputations of other women. Isabella's refusal to disassociate herself from Stanton, Anthony, and Victoria Woodhull and her sexual solidarity with these three controversial suffragists— maintained even in the face of Woodhull's subsequent charge that Henry Ward Beecher practiced free love in private while publicly condemning it—must be understood as both an extension and a revision of this sisterly tradition. Isabella sympathized with her "notorious" co-workers and stood by them in part because they alone appeared to embody and insist upon the full social and political power of womanhood at a time when their Boston counterparts seemed to be as concerned with transforming suffrage into a safely "respectable" reform as they were with winning the vote.

At the same time, the nature of Hooker's sustained alignment with the more radical members of the movement suggests that she was paradoxically emulating her sisters' courage and independence by attempting to escape the limitations of their example and their more conservative version of feminism. By her willingness to ignore the question of "antecedents" and acknowledge Victoria Woodhull as both a "born" leader and a "sister" spirit, Isabella was implicitly breaking with Catharine and Harriet over the issues of middle-class respectability and female propriety. The Reverend Phebe Hanaford, a suffragist and longtime Beecher family friend, forced Hooker to confront the full implications of her stance when she adamantly refused to let Isabella speak at her New Haven church because of her fellowship with "the notorious mistress of Col. Blood's affections." As Hanaford bluntly put the case: "For you, personally, we have great admiration and respect. . . . New Haven reverences the Beecher blood in you, and until now no woman in the State would have received a warmer welcome than yourself, but I fear your influence is wrecked by this unholy alliance. . . . If you wish my pulpit to repudiate the claims of that 'darling Queen' [Woodhull] to your allegiance, and to state that you place yourself fairly on the Christian platform of the Am. Wom. Suf. Association, then, it may be attained." In yet another forcefully worded warning to Hooker, Hanaford could not restrain herself from exclaiming that "every drop of the Beecher blood in your veins ought to cry out against her life of shameful disregard of propriety." Noting that Woodhull did not "rank" with Hooker "in morals, in intellect, in social position, or in any thing," Hanaford simply could not understand why Isabella would accept her leadership. "If Mrs. Woodhull was a *real* lady," Hanaford insisted, ". . . she would refuse to hold office. . . . A repentent Magdalen I can accept as a co-laborer—even in office and before the world—but a woman who 'glories in her shame'— *never!*"[8]

The struggle between the NWSA and the AWSA thus intersected with what amounted to a tacit rivalry among no less than four of the Beecher siblings, for Henry Ward Beecher had agreed to serve as president of the Boston wing in late 1869. By mid-1870, with the question of who was entitled to lead and influence the movement very much on her mind, Harriet decided to write prosuffrage articles for Henry's religious paper instead of *The Revolution*. As she confided to her brother: "Our paper has got to hold strong firm decided ground and do a work on this subject unless we wish the great work of our day to be done by Christian unbelievers and as I know how many women won[']t *read* an article on this subject I have baited my trap first with a [serialized] novel of high life." Although the phrase "unbelievers" certainly did not refer to Isabella, Harriet did ridicule her half sister[9] while viciously caricaturing Victoria Woodhull in her subsequent novel on the "woman question," *My Wife and I*. Both the serial and the book version helped fuel the intensifying public outcry against Woodhull's character, behavior, and antecedents referred to with such evident distress by Isabella in her correspondence with fellow suffragists such as Sarah Burger Stearns and Mary Rice Livermore.[10]

This novel also contributed to the mounting pressure then being brought to bear on Isabella by all three of her sisters and virtually every friend of the Hookers in Hartford. By the spring of 1871, Catharine, Mary, and Harriet had taken it upon themselves to investigate Woodhull's Ohio roots and were beginning to "harass" John in an effort to warn and wean Isabella away from her new co-worker.[11] Woodhull, who naturally resented these attempts to isolate, intimidate, and silence her, had already hinted that she could and would retaliate if such attacks continued by identifying secret free lovers in high places. Ignoring this pointed threat (which she may not have realized was being aimed at her own brother), Catharine characteristically persisted in "attacking Mrs. W's private character *infamously* so as to keep people from going out to hear her." Noting that Woodhull "will have a jam next time and last week had a good house on a stormy night," Isabella recognized that Catharine's tactics were already backfiring. Yet, as she complained to Anna Savery, she felt "driven to death." Having "foes in your own household" was dreadful, Hooker confessed, "if you can escape that you can live." But in her next breath Isabella summoned the courage to remind Savery that "we have got to fight for freedom of speech for woman just as if the battle for men had not been fought and the victory won."[12]

Isabella's bold defense of women's right to free speech, whatever their "antecedents," completed her break with the tradition of her elder sisters Catharine and Harriet. Hooker's principled stance, sustained even in the face of Woodhull's subsequent denunciation of Henry Ward Beecher, constitutes one of her most important contributions as a reformer and demonstrates her insightful grasp of the politics of sisterhood. Although Hooker made it clear to Woodhull herself that she did not share her free love views and confided to Savery and others that she found some of Woodhull's messages "unwise and unchristian," her staunch defense of Woodhull's right to advocate such a decidedly unpopular doctrine demonstrated a tolerance exceptional for a Beecher. Ironically, in order to defend Victoria personally, Isabella had first to reconstruct Woodhull's unconventional private life, bringing it into closer conformity with her own model of womanhood: she insisted that rather than exemplifying immorality, Woodhull embodied a standard of benevolence "unapproachable to most of us."[13]

Nevertheless, Isabella's conspicuous lack of self-righteousness as well as her sexual solidarity with a woman from different class and religious origins invite comparison with the middle-class British reformer Josephine Butler, whose ability to identify with working-class women accused of being prostitutes prompted her unprecedented agitation against the Contagious Diseases Acts. Like Butler and her followers, Isabella was among those who opposed the Acts—which called for the physical inspection of women but not men—on the grounds that they constituted an attempt by the state to legitimize prostitution and codify the sexual double standard.[14] Hooker made her opposition public when she devoted the longest chapter in *Womanhood: Its Sanctities and Fidelities* to Butler and her repeal campaign. Recent attempts to legalize prostitution in several American cities had convinced her that it was time to mount Anglo-American resistance to this serious threat to womanhood. Although the need for sexual solidarity across class lines was Isabella's overt theme and goal, the strangely hybrid composition of this chapter suggests that she was preoccupied by and struggling with the issue of free speech for women—especially for those "respectable" women of her own class. After a very brief introduction in which she spoke in the first person, Isabella's voice virtually disappeared as she proceeded to string together a series of long excerpts from the testimony and articles of British repealers, most of them professional men. Equally significant was the fact that Hooker began by reproducing letters that defended Butler's motives as well as her character and eulogized her as a Christian martyr for enduring public scrutiny and criticism. Only then did Isabella present the legal and moral arguments against the Acts themselves.[15]

Published during the Beecher-Tilton scandal, the book as a whole testified to Hooker's conviction that women had the right and obligation to speak out publicly—without Victorian circumlocution—on *any* topic, however "delicate." Abortion and sex education were two such issues; and Isabella's determination to broach them in her opening chapter on "Motherhood" should be viewed in the same context as her willingness to acknowledge the possibility that her clergyman brother might be guilty of adultery and her decision to stand by the woman who brought the charges against him. As Isabella triumphantly announced in her letter to Mary Rice Livermore: "The lips of women are being unsealed."[16]

It was Hooker's courageous advocacy of woman's right to think and speak for herself that alienated her from most of her Beecher siblings, her two sons-in-law, and virtually the entire Nook Farm community in Hartford. It also came close to ruining her relationship with her unusually supportive husband. John Hooker's correspondence with his wife during the scandal years reveals that even though he thoroughly disapproved of her fellowship with Woodhull, he deserves some of the credit for Isabella's clarity of vision on the question of Henry's alleged adultery. While he shared in his wife's desire to believe Henry innocent, John examined each new development with a keen legal eye and refused to avert his gaze when the mounting evidence pointed not only to Henry's guilt but also to his complicity in Woodhull's arrest on trumped up obscenity charges.[17] Bolstered by her husband's ongoing analysis of the case, Isabella repeatedly offered to help Henry confess publicly and thereby save what was left of his integrity and reputation. When Henry's direct efforts to silence his sister failed, one of their Beecher siblings attempted to discredit Isabella by circulating the rumor that she was insane and authoring a public statement alleging that Isabella acknowledged having "wronged" her brother. With his wife in Europe and unable to defend herself, John confronted Harriet, whom he suspected of initiating this "horrible attack." Stowe denied responsibility but joined Mary Beecher Perkins in expressing outrage against their half sister. Mary also informed John that Isabella would not be received into their homes or welcomed back into the community unless she stopped "all intercourse with Mrs. Stanton and Miss Anthony and all that set," though Harriet was not ready to make that "an indispensable condition."[18]

John continued to believe that Henry had an obligation to resign if he was guilty, confessing that the entire case struck him as "an utter mockery of justice" in light of the radically different treatment he and other members of the legal establishment regularly meted out to males of different class and ethnic backgrounds. As he confided to Isabella with evident disgust: "We are frequently sending to State's Prison some drunken Irishman, who, in a wretched hovel, has committed adultery with some drunken woman." Yet the members of Plymouth Church were eagerly preparing to celebrate Henry Ward Beecher's twenty-fifth year as their minister, despite his inability to explain damaging evidence and self-incriminating statements.[19]

John's aggressive defense of his wife's conduct in the face of the harsh criticism leveled at her by family members as well as friends and members of the press is characteristic of his own high integrity and courage, especially when one remembers that he could have joined those who defended his brother-in-law not on the assumption that such a respected clergyman was incapable of committing adultery but on the grounds that such behavior constituted a minor indiscretion at worst on the part of a man of Henry's appetites, influence, and benevolence. What both Hookers objected to most was not the sexual misconduct per se but Henry's hypocrisy and the differential treatment accorded women accused of similar crimes, most notably Elizabeth Tilton herself.[20]

Yet John's behind-the-scenes attempts to silence his wife on the subject of Woodhull and free love demonstrate that even he was not ready to endorse fully woman's right to free speech. Indeed, he repeatedly chided her in private for not letting him do all the talking and later cited the incident as evidence of her chronic lack of good judgment. John's manifest lack of confidence in Isabella angered and depressed her, eventually touching off a remarkable exchange that she recorded in her 1878 diary. The overt expression of anger, especially anger directed toward a husband, was virtually a taboo emotion for a "respectable" middle-class wife like Isabella. Unable to express her keen resentment openly during this extended argument, Isabella fell back on intervention from the spirit of her recently deceased sister, Catharine, who proceeded to criticize John's attitude towards his wife. Sensing that Catharine might have gone too far, Isabella found herself rebelling against her sister's well-intentioned "dictation and interference." Yet Isabella went on to invoke the male example of Jesus repudiating his mother, conspicuously casting herself in the role of the savior and John as the female appendage. Even Divine precedent did not suffice, however, for Isabella's handwriting itself altered suddenly as she began to accept "dictation" from the Hookers' mutual friend, Samuel Bowles. "Bowles's" smaller and more angular handwriting dominated the remainder of the page as the deceased editor of the *Springfield Republican*, himself a supporter of woman suffrage, urged John Hooker to be more tolerant instead of yielding to his "obstinate" masculine nature.[21]

By accepting "dictation" from both of these sources Isabella was attempting to deflect responsibility for her temporarily hostile feelings toward her husband. Casting herself once again in the role of mediator, she sought to modify the outspoken and somewhat harsh "messages" coming from "the other side." Isabella's recourse to a masculine persona and voice in her efforts to defend her right to speak and act as an individual constitutes an eloquent comment on the sexual politics of her class. If Isabella's temporary reliance upon male spiritual reinforcement to resolve her differences with her feminist husband poignantly dramatizes the limited power of womanhood, the effects of the scandal on her reputation and Woodhull's career dramatize the limits of sisterhood. Financially ruined, Victoria Woodhull lapsed into near total public silence for many years under the weight of the legal machinery brought to bear on her immediately following her exposure of Henry Ward Beecher.[22] The extremely painful social ostracism imposed on Isabella Beecher Hooker by her family and neighbors in the wake of the scandal were intended to have a similar effect. As Catharine Beecher had warned, women could not make direct assaults on social and political inequality without suffering severe repercussions, including public and private retaliation.

Isabella's faith that the ballot would eliminate these and other restrictions placed on nineteenth-century women rested on two highly questionable assumptions—both evident in her 1898 broadside, "Are Women Too Ignorant?" She never doubted that women, once enfranchised, would act in concert as "responsible" voters. By responsible voting Hooker meant that women would join ranks with men when it came to eradicating "intemperance and licentiousness, poverty and starvation." In her effort to rebut those who opposed woman suffrage on the grounds that it would only "double the ignorant vote," Isabella cited working-class and black women's benevolent associations and clubs as well as the large numbers of women pursuing higher education as evidence that women from every rank and walk of life wanted to vote and were actively preparing themselves for this civic responsibility.[23] Embedded in this argument was the problematic assumption that womanhood constituted a virtual class unto itself. This assumption blinded Hooker to the realities of conflict among women of differing racial, economic, and ethnic backgrounds. Ironically, Hooker's own experience made it clear that women from the same race, class, and even, at times, from the same family did not automatically share the same political goals and moral priorities. Nor did women who shared the same political goals necessarily agree on questions of social morality, as the tensions between the two wings of the movement and the racism of the predominantly white woman suffrage movement[24] so forcefully attest.

Equally questionable was Hooker's assumption that men would voluntarily join forces with enfranchised women to abolish the sexual double standard in all its forms—political, social, and economic. Yet by equating social and economic morality with political morality and insisting that all men as well as all women could *and should* adhere to this definition, Isabella succeeded in pushing her sisters' visions of domesticity and their belief in the power of womanhood to the very limits.

NOTES

1. Isabella Beecher Hooker, "The Last of the Beechers: Memories on My Eighty-Third Birthday," *The Connecticut Magazine* 9 (May 1905): 295.

2. John Hooker to Isabella Beecher Hooker, November 30, 1869; [December 2], 1869; and November 18, 1869, SD.

3. Harriet Beecher Stowe and Isabella Beecher Hooker to Susan B. Anthony, [December], [1869], VCL. See Document 81. The Beecher sisters also requested compensation from *The Revolution*. In spite of a serious shortage of funds, Anthony had confided to Paulina Wright Davis: "... if *Cash will bring Mrs.*

Stowe to The Rev with her *deepest holiest woman, wife and mother Soul strug-gle*—clothed in her *inimitable story garb*—then *it is cash that must be*—Mrs. Stowe—even—has never *yet given to the world her very best*—for she nor any other woman can, until she *writes direct* out of *her own soul[']s* experiences." Susan B. Anthony to Paulina Wright Davis, July or August, 1869, SD.

4. John Hooker prepared and presented the convention resolutions. A brief account of Isabella's Hartford convention can be found in Elizabeth Cady Stan-ton, Susan B. Anthony, and Matilda Joslyn Gage, eds., *The History of Woman Suffrage* (New York: Fowler & Welles, 1881), 3: 321–24. For Stanton's humor-ous reaction to Isabella's preoccupation with propriety, see Elizabeth Cady Stan-ton to Isabella Beecher Hooker, September 23, 1869, SD.

5. In addition to Severance, Henry Brown Blackwell and William Lloyd Garri-son were among those Bostonians who attempted to warn Hooker away from the NWSA. See, for example, Caroline Severance to Isabella Beecher Hooker, c. August 17, 1869; Henry B. Blackwell to Isabella Beecher Hooker, December 1, 1869; and William Lloyd Garrison to Isabella Beecher Hooker, November 12, 1869, SD. Evidence of Henry Ward Beecher's involvement in this rumor mill can be found in John Hooker's correspondence with his wife. When John remarked in early 1870 that Henry "seems unaccountably ready to believe slanders for one who is compelled perpetually to defend himself against them," he was referring to attacks made against Henry himself as an alleged supporter of free love be-cause of his controversial role in the McFarland-Richardson scandal (discussed below). John Hooker to Isabella Beecher Hooker, January 5, 1870, SD.

6. Isabella Beecher Hooker to Susan Howard, January 2, 1870, SD; emphasis added. See Document 87. It was John Hooker who advised Isabella to send Stanton's article on divorce to Susan Howard in Brooklyn so that she could read it to Henry Ward Beecher. For his own part, John confessed that he did not "fancy" Stanton "at all" at this point: "She is a bold and strong thinker, but she has not a refined nature." However, he found her to be "a pure woman" without "a particle of the sensuality that we generally regard as incident to 'free-lovism' about her." John Hooker to Isabella Beecher Hooker, January 5, 1870, SD.

7. Isabella Beecher Hooker, "The McFarland-Richardson Tragedy," *The Revo-lution*, December 16, 1869, pp. 376–77. *The Woman's Journal* published editori-als on the same incident, but with a different emphasis. See, for example, Henry Blackwell's article of June 4, 1870.

8. Reverend Phebe Hanaford to Isabella Beecher Hooker, September 13, 1871, and August 9, 1871, SD. Hooker would complain bitterly about such "Connecti-cut phariseeism" in her letter to Anna Savery. See Document 90. For a much more positive assessment of Woodhull, see Martha Coffin Wright's 1871–72 correspondence with her husband, David, and her daughter, Ellen Wright Garri-son. Describing a Washington suffrage convention and subsequent testimony before the House Judiciary Committee by Internationals and members of the Labor Reform Party as well as by suffragists, Wright noted that Woodhull, who gave "an excellent speech," was well received. She also observed that "Mrs.

Hooker we all liked—she was full of enthusiasm and there is so much real force behind the Beecher self esteem that she commands respect. She's quite free from any arrogance of manner and the 'I am holier than thou' of her Church—liberal and generous to a surprising degree." Martha Coffin Wright to David Wright, January 15, 1872, SSC. Susan Boone of the Sophia Smith Collection was especially helpful in identifying materials from the Garrison Family Papers that related to Woodhull and the scandal.

9. Harriet Beecher Stowe to Henry Ward Beecher, June 21, 1870, SML. Stowe's dilletantish suffrage leader, Mrs. Cerulean, was recognized by many suffragists to be a highly satirical portrait of Isabella. See, for example, Ellen Garrison's letter to her mother, Martha Coffin Wright, in which she writes: "I have been very much interested in reading 'My Wife and I[.]' [I]t is not at all stupid in point of narrative, tho' her position is weak enough on the woman question. Mrs. Woodhull is so exaggerated that she loses nothing, and Mrs. Stowe gains nothing by the caricature. . . . The supposed copy of Mrs. Hooker has extremely little to do." Ellen Garrison to Mother [Martha Coffin Wright], February 3, 1872, SSC.

10. Isabella Beecher Hooker to Sarah Burger Stearns, [Spring 1871], and Isabella Beecher Hooker to Mary Rice Livermore, March 15, 1871, SD. See Documents 88 and 89.

11. Isabella Beecher Hooker to Susan B. Anthony, March 11 [and 14], 1871, SD. See Document 61. Martha Coffin Wright was among those suffragists who admired Hooker's solidarity with Woodhull, as she confided to her daughter: "I think it is beautiful of Mrs. Hooker to brave all that she does from her own family and others in standing by her [Woodhull]." Martha Coffin Wright to Ellen Garrison, June 20, 1871, SSC.

12. Isabella Beecher Hooker to Anna Savery, November 12 [and 18], 1871, SD. See Document 90.

13. Isabella Beecher Hooker to Victoria Woodhull, July 28, [1872], and Isabella Beecher Hooker to Anna Savery, November 12 [and 18], 1871, SD. See Documents 91 and 90.

14. For an excellent analysis of Butler and the repeal campaign, see Judith Walkowitz, *Prostitution and Victorian Society: Women, Class, and the State* (New York: Cambridge University Press, 1980), especially pp. 67–147.

15. Isabella Beecher Hooker, *Womanhood: Its Sanctities and Fidelities* (Boston: Lee and Shepard Publishers, 1873), pp. 38–105.

16. IBH W, pp. 7–27. See Document 92. Isabella Beecher Hooker to Mary Rice Livermore, March 15, 1871, SD. See Document 89. On nineteenth-century feminists' response to abortion, see Linda Gordon, *Woman's Body, Woman's Right: A Social History of Birth Control in America* (New York: Penguin Books, 1975), pp. 95–115, especially pp. 108–9.

17. See, for example, John Hooker to Isabella Beecher Hooker, November 24 and 25, 1872, SD.

18. John Hooker to Isabella Beecher Hooker, September 23, 1874; September

25, 1874; and October 15, 1874, SD. John Hooker's September 25th letter includes an extract from a statement made by Stowe to him concerning this matter. For her part, Stowe suggested that George Beecher, the invalid son of her brother Edward, was the source of the statement against Isabella, a charge that George firmly denied when questioned by John.

19. John Hooker to Isabella Beecher Hooker, October 31 [and November 1], 1872, SD.

20. Elizabeth Tilton initially denied the charge of adultery but changed her story on several occasions during the scandal. Not long after Henry Ward Beecher was officially exonerated, she issued a public confession. Plymouth Church, which had supported their minister during the scandal and raised his salary to help offset his legal expenses, promptly excommunicated her. Regarding the differential treatment accorded to women, especially Elizabeth Tilton, Isabella complained to her daughter Alice that men defended their sexual passion "as righteous and God sent," yet they "lose all confidence in womanhood when a woman here and there betrays her similar nature and gives herself soul and body to the man she adores." Isabella Beecher Hooker to Alice Hooker Day, c. 1874, SD. It is interesting to note that Stanton analyzed the scandal in economic as well as sexual terms, explaining to Isabella that "the Christian Union—Ford and Co—who publish the Life of Christ [Beecher's biography] and Plymouth Church had too much money at stake to see B. [Henry Ward] sacrificed," so "the 'lie' as they called it was to be saddled upon us women." Stanton went on to charge that "the outrageous persecution of Mrs. Woodhull in our courts shows money and power behind" and concluded: "I have been crucified in this matter as much as you. . . . But through it all I see one thing, we must stand by each other. Women must be as true to women as men are to men." Elizabeth Cady Stanton to Isabella Beecher Hooker, November 3, 1873, SD.

21. Isabella Beecher Hooker, 1878 Diary, entries of September 27, 1878, and November 19, 1878, SD. See Document 95.

22. The seven months of litigation that followed Victoria's and Tennessee's arrest on obscenity charges damaged Victoria's health as well as her popularity on the lecture circuit. By the late 1870s, she had divorced Colonel Blood and moved to England, where she eventually married a wealthy banker and resumed her involvement in reform activities.

23. Isabella Beecher Hooker, "Are Women Too Ignorant?" *The Woman's Journal* 7, no.5 (September 1898). See Document 96.

24. Racism within the women's rights movement is discussed in Rosalyn Terborg-Penn, "Discrimination Against Afro-American Women in the Woman's Movement, 1830–1920," in Sharon Harley and Rosalyn Terborg-Penn, eds., *The Afro-American Woman: Struggles and Images* (Port Washington, N.Y.: National University Publications, 1978), pp. 17–27.

*Writing to Susan Howard, a Brooklyn family friend,
Isabella announced that she intended to contribute to
The Revolution despite Susan B. Anthony's unwillingness to change her paper's name.[1] This letter also reveals that the epithet "free lover" was being used as a
tactical weapon in the struggle for control of the suffrage movement prior to Victoria Woodhull's entrance
upon the national scene. ("Mr. Garrison" is William
Lloyd Garrison, who had become famous as an abolitionist editor and leader. Garrison, who also supported
women's rights, sided with the American wing of the
movement, which had just elected Henry Ward Beecher
as its president.)*

87   January 2, 1870

Dear Susie

... In the first place let me say for your comforting that the plan for
changing [the] name of the Revolution has failed—chiefly because, Miss
A.[nthony] was advised so strongly against it by publishers and other
gentlemen friends. I was not willing she should do it, simply to secure us
[Harriet and Isabella] as Editors (Corresponding and Assistant). That
would lay upon us a responsibility and anxiety in making the new thing
go, that we were not able to assume—so I also advised her not to change
and we remain simply contributors, according to our own pleasure and
under no pledge whatever. My intention is to do for the paper all that I
should have done, but I feel immensely relieved to be under no pledge
and free from official responsibility. But as to the general principle that I
should avoid all connection with that paper and refuse to write for it
because the views of its Editor and Publisher are in some respects not
quite my own, I cannot adopt it. Nor do I think it can be reasonably
defended. When brother Henry [Ward Beecher] was invited to preach in
Theodore Parker's assembly, I thought it one of the grandest opportunities of his life and should have been pained and surprised had he refused
it. But here is my opportunity to preach Christ and his dear gospel of
freedom and responsibility to five thousand people every week if I
please—and I am urged to do it, with no limitations of any kind. ...

... But now we come to Mrs. Stanton and her peculiar views—which
are far more trying to meet than anything Susan says or does, because

1. See the joint 1869 letter from Stowe and Hooker to Anthony, Document 81.

the subject is so difficult to handle—and out of that difficulty comes many a misunderstanding because of the unwillingness of all parties to speak plainly and without circumlocution. . . . She [Stanton], I think has written and spoken from the promptings of a great, loving, motherly heart and it is plain that she has always had the interests of children in mind even more than parents—and out of the desire to protect them from the wretched inheritances they too often receive from uncongenial and discordant parents she has come to look upon easy divorce as a blessing and a necessity. But to say that she ever advocated this, as a means of *personal gratification* to woman or man is simply to insult her in my opinion—and yet that is what free love means if it means anything—and my indignation is aroused every time I hear this word used so loosely as it is coming to be.

This whole question of divorce and the proper relation and duties of husband and wife is the most profound that has ever come before the civilised world—it is up now and will not disappear from the public eye till it has been thoroughly probed and when it is finally and rightfully settled we may begin to look for the millenium—but not before. Meantime the good and faithful ones—Christ's own children will differ and differ and dispute and grow hot and angry and anathematise each other, just as they did about slavery—and out of it all will come emancipation not only of women but of hosts of little children—who will some day rise up to call blessed some of the early apostles who have suffered crucifixion as it were on their behalf. My rule then is—to watch the *life* and *conduct* of reformers—and where that is satisfactory, to listen to their opinions with respectful attention—to overthrow them in fair argument if I can—and to treat them uniformly with friendly courtesy. So long as a woman is faithful to every family duty—is just, tender and truthful I honor her in my heart and will listen to her words patiently—and when she adds to this a life of heroic service in the cause of truth and righteousness as Mrs. Stanton has done and is attacked by enemies I will stand by her, at any cost—and however injudicious at times may be her utterances.

When I see as I do now from Mr[.] Garrison's own conversation and letters what a man of prejudice—of passion of bad judgment he is and always must have been, I realise anew how patient and tolerant reformers should be of each other—the very stuff that makes them reformers, will make them persecutors also if they are not always on their guard. . . .

. . . [F]or depend upon it wherever the work is most efficently prosecuted there will these old workers be found till the end comes—and the more they are accused of their associates the greater odium will the whole cause have to carry—since they are identified with it. It is like leaving foreigners without the ballot and thinking you have settled the question of their harmfulness to the country. They are here and disfranchisement will not annihilate them—but fraternising will educate and gradually make them an integral part of the body politic. . . .

. . . I only wish my dear brother [Henry] could be persuaded to hear some of these things—not because I wish to wean him from his new alliance and friendships—but because he could be much more useful to them and to the whole cause by understanding the counter currents. . . .

. . . Oh Susie—*few men* know what this battle means—but many women, wives and mothers know and *feel* it all—feel it for their sisters if not for themselves—I am one of these and I stagger under the weight of my load.

> yrs. in love,
> I.B.H.

> [IBH to Susan Howard, SD]

Isabella preserved the following "Extract" from her letter to fellow suffragist Sarah Burger Stearns of Minnesota in which she distinguished "free love" from "free lust" and attempted to disassociate both herself and Victoria Woodhull from the latter. Calling for Christian tolerance and sexual solidarity, Hooker shrewdly analyzed the press's attacks on Woodhull and its false accusations against the suffragists in the context of the upcoming presidential election.

88 [Spring 1871]
[Isabella to Sarah Burger Stearns]
. . . And now as to your letter to the Press. The spirit of it is so gentle and charitable I would be glad to see it in print even though it does the greatest injustice not only to Mrs. Woodhull but to those of [us] who refuse to denounce her at the bidding of a hostile Press. You misconstrue our motives and so far as I can see have failed to grasp the idea that was central in the life and work of our Savior—vis—that the business of all pure souls in the world was to call not the righteous but sinners to repentence [sic]—and to that end they must associate on terms of human *sympathy*, not condescension, with wrong doers—and especially must

rejoice over the beginnings of good in them and keep them on in all their work for good ends.

The whole New Testament is luminous with this idea of fraternising with sinners in all their righteous work and full of denunciations of the "I am holier than thou" spirit—of the casting out the mote and forgetting the beam—in short of all forms of Pharaseeism. I have read and prayed over this subject ever since I came from Washtn. having been compelled as it were to go alone to my God, all human friends being timid or harshly critical—and in the stories of the Samaritan woman by the well—of the woman taken in adultery and of Mary Magdalene I have found the mind and heart of the Lord in this matter and am no more sorrowing but rejoicing to be counted worthy to suffer reproach with Him and for any of His dear children. . . .

So much in brief for us who walked in at the door which Mrs. Woodhull opened at Washtn. last winter and were able to organise a great work of national education and have ever since refused to turn upon her with indignation or contempt as unworthy to be a fellow worker with us in the suffrage movement. And all this I mean in case she were the very depraved and deceitful woman so many believe her to be. . . . I think I know that she is striving to put down lust and exalt love—that her motives are exalted and her life pure and her whole nature spiritual in an uncommon degree. I think she is mistaken in some of her theories, but sincerely searching for the truth and so far her life has been surprisingly elevated considering her surroundings and temptations.

That she was married to Col. Blood and divorced[2] and that they are still living as husband and wife must be I suppose simply a protest on their parts against *human* laws of marriage and divorce which seem to them unjust and demoralizing, but in no wise do I understand her to disown or depreciate the *divine* ordinance of marriage and I think she approves a life of chastity beyond the common standard. However I do not understand all her views—and have had no time to ask her concerning them—nor to study these new social theories. To my mind the suffrage must come first and then when women are responsible for the laws

---

2. Not surprisingly, Isabella was somewhat confused about the facts. Actually, Victoria Claflin had married Dr. Canning Woodhull in 1853 when she was only fifteen. Although Victoria subsequently divorced the alcoholic physician in order to marry Colonel James Harvey Blood in 1866, she retained Woodhull's name and permitted her ailing and impoverished former husband to remain part of her household. On this last point, see Isabella Beecher Hooker to Anna Savery, Document 90.

and are sitting in council with men upon them they will together look into the relation of government to marriage and divorce and come at last together to better judgments than either sex could make *alone*. Certain it is that all our legislation touching the sexes is sadly defective—and no cry of free love will keep me from thoroughly investigating the whole subject when the time comes, and considering the theories of all thinker[s] and writer[s] who in the least command respect. I believe fully that one man and one woman should stick close to each other through troubles and sorrows of all sorts and give themselves to their children and the world with utter unselfishness, and that unchastity and sensuality—are as possible in marriage as out of it—in fact that the ideal of marriage is scarcely yet approached and that many jealous souls who are crying out against Mrs. W.[oodhull] are in the sight of their Heavenly Father less spiritually minded than she and full of all carnalities. . . . The [New York] Tribune knows and so does every editor and reporter and reader that neither you nor I nor one of the prominent workers for suffrage believes in free lust (and the trouble with Mrs. W is she uses it with a meaning of her own different from this hateful one as she will some day explain I hope)—but they know as well that if they can frighten us into disavowing any sympathy with such a powerful woman as Mrs. W is proving both because of her own brain and *heart* and because of her command of money (a thing we have never had in our ranks before)—and because of the influence of her paper [*Woodhull and Claflin's Weekly*] among *spiritualists* (a very large and increasingly influential class) and among business men and politicians, then they have dealt a severe blow at the whole suffrage movement and set it back years. Especially they know that at just this crisis of the Pres.[idential] election we may through the need of great parties in closely contested elections establish a precedent by action of congress in receiving some member elected by votes of women, in some State favorable to their admission as voters. This is the cause of all the hue and cry and the bitterness—the devilishness of false accusation and so on. Now if we seemed even to hear the storm we should be lost I think, and on my part—I keep my eyes on the North star and sail for port with all my might and if I stopped for a moment to listen to what enemies in persuit [*sic*] thought of my sailing, as my moral character, or what crew I had on board *or* passengers, they would certainly gain on me—they couldn't sink my ship to be sure—because *truth* never goes down—but they could do me and this blessed Ship great harm and give us a long weary voyage—so I do not look or listen, nor do any of us whom you have named. . . . My friend—women must learn to stand by each other—not submitting to the dictation of men in this matter, heretofore they have sneered at us for not doing this and called us cowards, and faithless ones, with great reason[.] [L]et us follow our convictions of duty and love our sisters and pardon their short comings even as we have our brothers in the past and work with both for all good causes—but not put bad men or women into political offices if we can possibly avoid it[.] [A]t least we will in the words of our Pledge, "make the purity and integrity of candidates for public office the first test of fitness." Leaders in a reform are self-made and God-made— not *elected* by *fellow workers*, and we must not confound working with them thus with voting for them as political rulers. . . .

. . . Let me quote to you in closing your own words—"It is the work of a great soul to bear calumny with calmness," and subscribe myself your very sincere and loving friend.

Isabella B. Hooker

[IBH to Sarah Burger Stearns, SD]

Isabella's perception that some men feared women's impending political power in general and Woodhull's political effectiveness in particular also figures prominently in this letter to Mary Rice Livermore, a leader of the AWSA. Announcing that "the lips of women are being unsealed," Hooker defended Victoria Woodhull's right to be heard and reiterated her own intention to "stand by all suspected women" as if they were her "sisters."

89 March 15, 1871

My dear Mrs. Livermore

. . . The truth is my dear friend, I came to the determination about a year ago, never to allow any *man* however excellent to interpret any woman for me . . . I made a silent vow . . . that without wholesale condemnation of man, but with prayer that his eyes might be opened to see himself as he is in the sight of God, and woman as she is I would stand by all suspected women as if they were my own sisters—and when they were proved guilty I would stand by harder than ever—since no man could with safety to himself do this, but all women could. Woman cannot be injured [by] woman—only men are endangered—to them a vile woman is indeed the spark to the tinder, to us she is a sister for whom God has made us accountable. And this is the battle we are set to fight in the very outset of our last campaign—indeed the reason it is any campaign at all, is that men perceive at last that the little white symbol of power is coming into our hands and begin to realize what we shall do with it. It is by no accident that the question of licensing prostitution appears just now when our Constitutional right to the suffrage is about to be acknowledged—but a God sent conjunction—for women are nearly unanimous on the one matter and are simply becoming impatient for an opportunity to vote upon it. If you could have been here [Washington] these two months! . . . [L]et me assure you that Mrs. Woodhull stands in a most enviable position in this city today—and she is there because she . . . worked for womanhood twelve hours out of the twenty four with such quiet dignity and sweetness that not one person who has seen her in private and talked with her for five minutes and I verily believe not one who heard her great speech (for it is truly great—I never saw an audience of fourteen hundred, many standing, listen as this did to a bare legal argument in my life) has wished to utter a word against her or been able to do it. It is a great comfort to me thus to believe in her innocence—(not that she is not mistaken sometimes and inexperienced always in work of reform—not that I like her paper [*Woodhull and Claflin's Weekly*] entirely)—but I am sure that if it were otherwise it would be my duty to stick close to her, to follow her great legal argumt. with my moral one, whenever occasion offered—to combat her errors by my truth if necessary—to vindicate her right to be heard, tested, followed or rejected on the same ground that men are. It is *secret* friendship and association with the impure that is dangerous—not a public advocacy of a righteous cause, on the same platform—[M]en believe this and practice accordingly, and so far they are right and we women must do the same—but when it comes to voting, then let us stand by our pledge that we will "make the personal purity and integrity of candidates for public office the first test of fitness"—am I not right in this? . . .

. . . The lips of women are being unsealed as Mr[.] Mill prophesied—all over the world—and the day of judgment and of purity draws nigh. . . .

   With sincere love—ever yrs.

   I. B. Hooker

          [IBH to Mary Rice Livermore, SD]

By the time Hooker wrote the following letter to Western journalist Anna Savery, Woodhull was beginning to
warn that she would expose secret free lovers in high
places if the vicious attacks upon her character and
"antecedents" did not subside. Here, after disclosing
the personal factors that led Victoria to embrace her
doctrine of free love, Isabella explained why she continued to regard this mysterious "fore runner" as a
"prophetess" and a spiritual "sister," even though
Catharine Beecher had become one of Woodhull's most
vociferous detractors.

90   Nov[ember] 12 [and 18,] [18]71
Dear Friend

. . . As to what Mrs. Woodhull means by that threat[3] I do not know
and I have no time to ask. I have never talked with her on the social
question fifteen minutes and I will not. My ground is that she alone of all
the women in the U. States [is] succeeding in getting a hearing and a
report out of a dead Congress—a Congress that told Mrs. Stanton and
me last winter that they had *no time* to attend to such a question even if
they thought it worthy of consideration—to which Susan Anthony well
replied—"if we had *votes* gentlemen the time would be forthcoming and
ever at hand." . . . [W]hen the day arrived for her [Woodhull's] Hearing
before the Judiciary Comm. of the House I adjourned our Convention
which was called to meet that same morning and went with many others
to hear what she would say—having been introduced to her the day
before and having had two hours conversation with her which impressed
me not only favorably towards her as a woman—but impressed me profoundly and in a manner I could never describe with the conviction that
she was heaven sent for the rescue of woman from her pit of subjection.
She has ever since appeared to me as then—as a womanly woman, yet

3. Isabella is here referring to a public statement in the May 22, 1871, edition
of the *New York World* in which Woodhull turned the tables on her accusors by
accusing them of hypocrisy. After alluding to but *not* naming two public men,
both highly respected, and charging that one lived "in concubinage" with the
other's wife, she threatened to publish an analysis of their lives. On this point see
Robert Shaplen's *Free Love and Heavenly Sinners* (New York: Alfred A. Knopf,
1954), pp. 123–24.

less a woman than an embodiment of pure thought, soul and reason—a prophetess, full of visions and messages to the people which it would be wo[e] unto her to refrain from proclaiming, even though martyrdom were sure to follow. At the same time, some of her messages seem to me unwise and unchristian according to the Bible standard which I reverence and adopt—but never has her motive or general drift of thought seemed other than the purest and highest I can conceive. She is an idealist—a visionary perhaps—but she is without consciousness of self and absolutely without selfishness. Her standard of benevolence is unapproachable to most of us—and yet *she has lived up to it* in the case of her first husband [Canning Woodhull] and though all the world should condemn and thrust at her, she will care for that man as a mother for her wayward child till the Heavenly Father takes him away from her pure guardianship to a higher one above. She and Col. Blood have always kept him near to his children when not insane that they might help to win him to virtue—and this idiot son[4] is so lovely in his temper and gentleness that he appeals to the tenderness of all who see him—he is not only without reason, but his teeth have never grown and all in consequence of his father's [Woodhull's] vices—of which he informed her within a few weeks after their marriage—demanding that she should love and care for him just as if otherwise.

Now my position is that it would be my duty to work with this woman for suffrage—or temperance—or against legalising houses of prostitution even if she were a brothel keeper and I think the Lord Jesus set himself as an ensample [*sic*] in this respect with a firmness not to be mistaken or misconstrued—But knowing her to be the very strange, yet noble and pure woman she is I would no sooner deny her as my Sister and fellow worker than I would deny the Lord himself—and I believe that she is one of those little ones of whom He said if one should offend, it were better that a mill stone were hung about his neck and he were cast into the depths of the sea. That private note of mine was the outpouring of an admiration I could no longer repress. . . . I said this woman is a born Queen and I owe her the allegiance of my heart—so I wrote just as I felt and it was printed by a *man* without her knowledge and I could not explain without bringing new doubts and discredit upon her, so I have

4. Colonel Blood was Woodhull's second husband. Her first marriage had produced two children: a daughter, Zula Maud, and a son, Byron, who appears to have been handicapped. This fact may explain Victoria's involvement with the late nineteenth-century eugenics movement.

kept silent, though I have suffered agonies so to speak, (through the mortification to my husband and children) at the misconstructions that have been put upon that sisterly confidence. I have come to composure again however and am willing to wait for her and myself the judgment of the future—and a not very distant one either. She is a mystery to me— but so is every *fore runner* to the people of his or her day and for one I am determined to keep my eyes and ears and heart open to any woman who thinks she has a word from above to deliver unto the nations . . . (oh how beautifully Mrs. Woodhull speaks . . . in her address on the rights of the children). . . .

I am driven beyond description with National and State work—and the strain on my feeling in this Woodhull matter has nearly killed me. You at the west can have no conception of Connecticut phariseeism and bigotry nor of what I have suffered in consequence. The sleepless nights of my husband have nearly driven me frantic—but day is dawning and we both shall live through it. He does not agree with me quite about Mrs. W.[oodhull] having never seen her and felt her power—but he stands by me like a man and that makes it all the harder for me. . . .

. . . I am driven to death—and just now my sister Catharine is attacking Mrs. W[oodhull]'s private character *infamously* so as to keep people from going out to hear her—the result is she will have a jam next time and last week had a good house in a stormy night. But it is dreadful this having foes in your own household—if you can escape that you can live. I hope your husband stands by you—surely he must and he is a host. We have got to fight for freedom of speech for woman just as if the battle for men had not been fought and the victory won. I am glad I can have a personal enthusiasm for this woman or it seems as if I should have gone under—nothing can shake me now—and the end is near—so courage good souls—they that be for us are more than they that be against.

> Ever yrs. faithfully
> [Isabella Beecher Hooker]
>
> > [IBH to Anna Savery, SD]

There were limitations, however, to Hooker's endorsement of the social views of her "born Queen," as she makes clear in this letter to Woodhull herself. Although she agreed that women should be freed from "the bondage of law and public opinion," Isabella rejected Victoria's endorsement of free love and clung to her own belief in "ideal marriage" and the coming of "the true monogamy."

91   July 28, [1872]

Dear Friend.

... Whenever I can help you to make men and women better and happier command me—for the rest I am so absorbed in this great work of regeneration and so completely satisfied with the love of my husband and children I have neither time nor inclination to try experiments in friendship. And lest you should misunderstand my position on the question of Social Freedom let me state it briefly here.

Human law should not attempt to regulate marriage—this is a sacrament of souls, owing allegiance to God and their own consciences only. But the ideal marriage is between two only and all departures from this ideal are to be tolerated only because of the infirmity of human nature, which is slow to realise its blessed ultimate. Hence in the near future, woman, released from the bondage of law and public opinion will hold herself sacred to love and motherhood and by degrees will through liberty, teach man to hold himself sacred to love and fatherhood, and the harmonious and blessed family will spring from the life union of these two. But there will be many failures by the way and for a time I greatly fear, men will take new license from this doctrine of liberty propounded by the most spiritual of women.

It is only when the new regime shall have become thoroughly established, in which there will be no more disgrace to a woman in leaving a man's companionship for reasons sufficient unto herself, than in changing a church communion, that the beneficent results of freedom will begin to appear. Then the weak or vicious soul who now roves carelessly from flower to flower sucking poisonous sweets, secure of a peaceful retreat, tender housing and nursing year in and year out whatever may betide, will know that his house may be left unto him desolate any day, and that to ensure fidelity he must practice it.

This is the good time coming for which I labor and for which I wait in the patience of hope, and nothing else: for I firmly believe that it is written in the Constitution of our material and spiritual nature that they *twain* shall be one flesh, and no more—and what God hath joined together no man can put asunder in the long run—so let liberty prevail and out of it will come the true monogamy.

I am very sincerely
your friend
Isabella B. Hooker

[IBH to Victoria Woodhull, SD]

"Motherhood" had originally been written in 1867 as a rebuttal to "Fashionable Murder," an article (in the Boston Congregationalist*) by the Rev. Dr. Todd which held wives, but not husbands, responsible for the "crime of foeticide" (abortion). However, Isabella's response—which endorsed family limitation and advocated sex education for children, especially boys—was rejected by the editor. Six years later, in the very midst of the Beecher-Tilton scandal, she presented it as the opening chapter of her book on* Womanhood. *Isabella prefaced this candid discussion of sexual relations and social morality with an extended defense of her right— as both a mother and a grandmother—to speak out publicly on such "delicate" subjects in "plain language."*

92   April 20th, 1867.

REV. JOHN TODD, D. D.

DEAR SIR: I have just read in the Congregationalist of April 19th your impressive words in condemnation of mothers who criminally relieve themselves of unwelcome offspring, and my mother's heart stirs me to immediate reply. . . .

You have spoken of two great laws of our race that came with transgression—excessive labor for man, suffering and subjection for woman; and it is certainly true that mankind are to this day greatly under the power of these laws. It is no less true, however, that both men and women have all along been rightfully striving to ameliorate their condition in these respects, and to come into a condition of perfect liberty of choice, even the liberty wherewith Christ doth make us free.

That some women have mistaken the way to this personal freedom, and been led into deadly sin and into the fearful suffering which inevitably follows the serious transgression of even physical law, is true, perhaps to the extent you have stated, and such need warning; and I, for one, cannot but rejoice when the sin and danger of their evil ways are plainly set before them; but I rejoice also in the whole truth, and the fair statement of a vital question, and in this respect your article seems to me very defective.

There is a difficulty back of the one stated, which lies in the nature of *mankind* as different from that of *womankind*; and until this difficulty is met, or, at least, considered, no true understanding of the duty of parents to offspring can be expected or hoped for.

I think it is a perfectly fair statement of the case as between men and women the whole world over, that it is not in any great degree desire for offspring on his part that draws the husband to the wife in the closer relations of married life, while on the part of the wife the love of the offspring mingles largely as an impelling motive with the love of her husband; and it is scarcely an exaggeration to say that, so far in the history of our race, the unreasoning and inordinate indulgence of animal passion on the part of the man, and affectionate submission on the part of the woman, have had more to do with the continuance of the race than paternal or maternal instinct, or considerations of any other sort whatever.

That, as a general rule, women are feebly endowed with this passion, and that men are by nature and training (or by lack of it, perhaps) overstocked, will not be denied by any one who has given any thought to the subject; and those who have looked into its depths must have come to the conclusion long ago, I think, that herein lies one of the great mysteries of our being and of God's moral government. That the perpetuation of our race demanded instincts strong as death, we may allow; but why their pressure should be all on one side, so to speak, and the reciprocal impulse so feeble, in this lies the mystery; for granting to woman greater pleasure in mere sexual indulgence than usually comes to her by largest allowance, it is safe to say that, in nine cases out of ten, maternity, with its early pains and later cares, greatly lessens her power of enjoyment, and for the larger part of her married life she is either positively distressed by the apparently necessary demands of her husband upon her, and irresponsive to them, or kept to a cheerful response by a self-abnegation and regard for his comfort, not to say fear of his moral aberration, which is a positive drain upon her health and strength. I think in saying this that I speak the mind of all thoughtful married women of the present day, of whatever station in life; and I am much mistaken if thousands would not in their hearts thank the first man or woman who should give utterance to this sentiment in a manner that would not shock the delicacy of the one sex, nor excite the enmity of the other.

Is it not time, then, that these vital questions, which do, in fact, under-lie all social moralities, were examined and discussed under all the light which science and religion can impart, and be handled by mothers as well as by fathers, and more especially by the former, since they chiefly are the watchful observers and guardians of those young days when right habits and beliefs may be taught to children of both sexes?

And now permit me to say that a great part of the physical and moral deterioration of the present day arises, . . . from the fact that children are not conceived in the desire for them, and out of the pure lives of their fathers, as well as their mothers; and that far worse misfortunes might befall our race than decreasing families, so long as children are born to such an inheritance as too many young men of the present day are likely to transmit. And this I speak, not from a desire to blame them, so much as to call the attention of mothers to their own neglect in the matter of training these faulty sons.

Let us suppose, now, these boys living closely with their mothers in most familiar intimacy up to their very manhood; and how easy for the latter, if only their lips might be unsealed by the removal of all false notions of delicacy, to instruct these sons from whom they hope so much, not only in the physiology of their own bodies, but also in the constitutional differences between themselves and the mothers who bore them, as representatives of all other women!

To my conception, one generation of *instructed* mothers would do more for the renovation of the race than all other human agencies com-bined; and it is an instruction of the *head* they need, rather than of the *heart*. The doctrine of responsibility has been ground into Christian mothers beyond what they are able to bear, . . . because their throbbing hearts, so joined to the children of their womb during the long months of hidden and dreamy expectation, have laid this burden upon them al-ready; and sore experience has taught them how much easier it is to mould the child of their love in thought than in deed. And herein lies, in great part at least, the desire to escape children on the part of both parents,—for it is not wives alone who are seeking how they may lessen care and trouble; the problem how to bring up a family to comfort and honor in these days of sore temptation, besets young people of both sexes, and, joined with the difficulty of mere maintenance, leads husbands to encourage, if not to instigate, such practices as shall save them from excessive toil without denying them the fullest personal gratification.

But our instructed mother will have taught her son very early in life (how early this can be done with wonderful success few realize) that in his body lies the quickening power which shall assist in giving life to the darling child of whom he may one day become the father, and that by so much as he regulates his own body and spirit according to the laws which God has made manifest, he may hope to endow this child with the qualities of an angel, and that by failing to do this he may transmit an inheritance which shall bring anguish to the little one and send curses back upon himself. . . .

And by her own life and needs may she still more impress upon him the self-restraints that he must practice before she can desire that any other mother should commit her daughter to his keeping. She will . . . teach him the physical and moral nature of woman, and in so doing she will have enshrined herself in his heart forever; for there is a power of imagination and conception in the minds of little children which grows sadly dim with years, and the mother who fails to show herself in all the depths of her motherhood to her boy has lost her one golden opportunity in life; her daughter may learn for herself by sad or happy experience, but her son can never truly behold his mother, nor the whole order of beings whom she represents, unless he is called to her in his extreme youth, and before any other human being has planted an image of womanhood in his imaginative mind. . . .

. . . [H]ow easily might this mother have added to her early instruction some special words as to the manner of husband he should prove himself to be! "Children are an heritage of the Lord, my son; blessed is he that hath his quiver full of them; but then, my dear, beware of filling your quiver too quickly and with careless workmanship. If you would have sons that shall speak with the enemy in the gates, remember that their mother must not be overtasked in body nor in spirit. She can neither endow nor rear beyond a certain limit, and in the very excess of your young love, you may easily incapacitate her for both exertions. You will find need for self-restraints that are rarely practiced in these days, though I seem to see a divine intimation of their necessity in that old Jewish law whose moral and sanitary regulations have fallen into a neglect and disrepute unfavorable to the welfare of mankind. Under these a wife was held sacredly apart from her husband for near the half of every month, and this was not only the period of her physical debility and recuperation, but also that of her more probable maternity,[5] so that there could be no plainer exhibition of the thought and will of God in the matter of generation than is here made manifest." . . .

Under such guidance as this, would there be need, think you, of the warnings of your article? and without it may we ever hope for a truly godly seed to inhabit this earth? . . .

You have spoken of ministers' families illustrating by their size the piety of the parents; but it does seem to me the quality of offspring is far better testimony than the quantity . . . I have sometimes thought that many of them [ministers] are just as uninstructed in and just as indifferent to the true theory of the relation of husband and wife, and parent and child, as many of those who make no pretensions to godliness or humanity.

At all events I have heard of one New England minister, the father of many children, whose word to his daughter on her approaching marriage was, "You must instruct your husband, my dear, that he do [*sic*] not allow you to have children too often. If I had known what I now know earlier in life, your mother, of blessed memory, might be living to this day. The drain upon her vitality, in giving birth to all those children, and the incessant care of them through many years of poverty and trial, were more than human strength could endure, and disease coming to her at last, she sank under it, with no power to rally.". . .

By this do I feel encouraged to suggest to all young parents that there is a more excellent way of bringing happiness to their households than by seeking to escape the suffering and care, the toil and privation, that children may bring. You should desire children beyond all mere earthly possessions; they pay their own way, and you cannot afford to live without them; your whole life will be chilled if you wilfully [*sic*] shut out these sunbeams. But you must not invite these little ones to your homes any oftener than you can provide for them in body and in spirit, and for the health and strength of the mothers who are to bear them. . . .

. . . From these faithful souls, made pure by denials of the flesh, shall come, some day, a happy race of children. . . .

With sincere respect,
A MOTHER.

[IBH W, pp. 7–8, 10–19, 22–27]

5. Drawing a false analogy between animals and humans, midcentury medical opinion had incorrectly identified menstruation as the portion of the monthly cycle during which women were most likely to conceive.

In 1874 Isabella fled to Europe with her husband and son in an effort to find relief from the public reverbera-tion and private repercussions generated by her role in the Beecher-Tilton scandal and her brother's ensuing trials, both ecclesiastical and civil. After John Hooker returned alone to Hartford, they carried on a volumi-nous correspondence in which they searched for the truth concerning Henry in light of each new develop-ment. John's letter describing his efforts to defend his wife to her sisters Harriet and Mary, both of whom considered Henry Ward Beecher's innocence to be be-yond any reasonable doubt, prompted the following anguished reply from Isabella (then in Paris).

93   Oct[ober] 15, 1874

My dearest.

I wrote you six sheets . . . in reply to yours . . . and really hoped that it might be the last painfully long letter I should have to write on this subject. But last evening your letter about the talk with my sisters arrived and the whole thing was revived and my heart sunk within me *at first* but fortunately I was just going to hear the great Patti sing in "The Hugenots" and I determined to lend myself to the music and gain time for reflection, and this was not all that I gained—for under the influence of that wonderful composition . . . my soul was strengthened and com-forted and there came to me a great peace, under these new complica-tions, and a voice sounding in my ears, all night as it were, gentle yet strong seemed to say "Be thou faithful unto death and I will give to thee a crown of life." It is strange that this letter and this music should have found each other—for the whole plot of the opera is founded upon the massacre of St. Bartholemew and the trials of religious faith incident to that dreadful time . . . and that plainly was a story of the triumph of the soul over all the ills of life in view of the great rewards of the future. . . .

This then is my present decision—in case sister Harriet writes me on the matter I will answer her letter as best I am able and send it to you, keeping a copy myself, and will authorise [sic] you to send it [to] her, or to keep it back until you can communicate further with me about it. . . .

I have already written you that the expression "and of course is over-whelmingly wretched in feeling that she [Isabella] has so wronged him [Henry] for the last years," though in one sense quite true really conveys a most false impression. . . . But I could not under the light of recent developments correct that statement without discovering how painfully discouraging to my new hopes concerning my dear brother are the second statements of Tilton and Moulton, neither of which I had seen when talking with the Chamberlins.[6] . . . Mrs. Woodhull asserted that I had known my brother's conduct for a *long time* and then followed an intimation that I did not materially disapprove it, but *held her own views in regard to it.* This was very trying to me to submit to in silence—but if I explained it would appear in the first place that I did know and believe the story, or *a* story of his wrong doing, and secondly it would appear that Mrs. W.[oodhull] who had been suffering unjustly because of her suffrage views held in common with myself and many others, and who was now in prison and despoiled of all her goods, on acct. of my brother, had not correctly stated my precise position toward my brother, but had, trusting to my clemency perhaps, committed me to her own views on the social question. . . . I would not in the circumstances add a feather's weight to the burden that persecuted woman was already carrying, although I considered the statement that I had known this thing for a *long time* and *to approve it*, incorrect and an unjustifiable statement. . . . I was not overwhelmingly wretched in feeling that I had "so wronged him [Henry] for the last years"—[O]n the contrary a great part of my manifest wretchedness was because *he had so wronged me* by misleading me in every conceivable manner till I was compelled to condemn him from his own utterances both written and oral. This feeling was so strong, so overpowering with me that it materially qualified the joy I felt on being convinced by internal evidence that Henry's statement was substantially true: and I remember that Mr. C.[hamberlin] expostulated with me on observing this and thought that I ought to forget all sense of personal injury in rejoicing over the innocence of my brother—and this I tried most faithfully to do, and my letters to you at that time and up to the time when Moulton's second statement appeared will testify that I did believe Henry innocent in regard to Mrs. Tilton and rejoiced over it with all my heart. And they will show also that when this matter was finally settled and his innocence fully established before the world I should feel that he [Henry] had a serious account to settle with me personally. Since that time and after reading Moulton's second statement my letters will

6. Frank Moulton attempted to mediate between his mutual friends, Theodore Tilton and Henry Ward Beecher, only to have his own character and motives attacked by Beecher and his supporters. The Chamberlins were equally unsuccessful in their efforts to serve as mediators among the Beechers and the Hookers, as the following letter suggests.

show that my worst fears concerning my brother were revived by the new letters and evidence then brought forward, and though I still clung to a hope founded on Henry's statement and on the horrible increase of condemnation if that were not true, yet this was quenched almost entirely by Tilton's second statement and the very remarkable letters there contained both from Mrs. Tilton and Henry: there are coincidences of views between these two, and similar mental and spiritual conditions that to my mind are overwhelming evidence against the truthfulness of the later assertions of each. I have then nothing left but his [Henry's] word and his oath, and her [Mrs. Tilton's] word under oath as it were and to these I do still cling with the agony of a last hope, and God only knows what that agony is.

It has seemed to me many times that our friends who have been able to believe my dear brother innocent these months and years can have no conception of the suffering we have been called to endure who could not indulge this belief—yet they uniformly look upon themselves as the greatest sufferers. As for Henry, he surely may take unto himself the words of Peter if he is innocent and find great comfort in them—"But if when ye do well and suffer for it ye take it patiently this is acceptable with God—for *even hereunto were ye called*—because Christ also suffered for us—who did no sin, neither was guile found in his mouth—who when he was reviled, reviled not again, when he suffered he threatened not, but committed himself to him that judgeth righteously."

[Isabella Beecher Hooker]

[IBH to John Hooker, SD]

In a subsequent letter to Mary Porter Chamberlin, a Nook Farm neighbor who was serving as an intermediary between Isabella and her Beecher siblings, Hooker reiterated her desire to believe in Henry's innocence yet steadfastly defended Woodhull's right to expose him if he were guilty. But she worried openly about the scandal's impact on herself and John.

94   November 5, 1874

My dear Mrs. Chamberlin,

In a recent letter from my husband he says the C's [Chamberlins] report you "as speaking very strongly against Mrs. Woodhull, stating that you should refuse to meet her if she called on you, and quote Ned

[Hooker] as saying that she would not come in[7] if his arm were strong enough to keep her out." I am very sorry that I did not explain to you in so many words my reasons for speaking thus—for owing to the difference of opinion between us, concerning Mrs. Woodhull, they conveyed to you a decidedly wrong impression. Will you permit me to explain exactly my state of mind at that time[?] I beg you not to repeat to any one what I said, and if you have already done so, to qualify it by what I now say.

My opinion of Mrs. Woodhull is, what it has been for two years past—indeed from the end of the first year after I became acquainted with her at Washington, I have not seen any reason to change the judgment that I formed of her at about that time—and up to that time I was holding my judgment in reserve rather than otherwise—at least I was ready to have my *very* favorable first impressions modified by further acquaintance and by the testimony of others concerning her. When therefore I read my brother's statement and was rejoiced to see internal evidence of his innocence and of his truthfulness, I . . . seized the first opportunity to tell you of my joy—(though you will remember I am sure that I seemed very sad over my brother's treatment of me from first to last, and when looking at the question from that point of view could see *no* light). Just then some one mentioned to us, that Mrs. Woodhull was now in Paris and it became necessary to decide what course we should take if we chanced to meet her there, or if she should call to see me (which she might feel warranted in doing, from our past relations, and from our being strangers in a foreign land, but which I remember saying privately to Ned, I thought after all, she would have too much delicacy to do)—and I decided that out of regard to my brother I ought to avoid her, since my being seen with her on friendly terms would in the present excitement be heralded all over the country to his detriment and as a proof that I still believed the story. But I do assure you that I had no sense of irritation against her because of her being the *mouth-piece* of the charges against my brother—(and she ought never to be accused of anything beyond this)—on the contrary, I have always thought and still do think that, *on the evidence before her, she was fully justified in an exposé.* I told my brother the same, and added that so long as women were *slain by the mere breath of suspicion against their chastity,* I would never help to conceal the wrong doings of a man, though he were my own brother or son. I would not become his first accuser but when he was accused by trustworthy testimony I would not defend him—and the higher his station and influence the less would I try to shield him.

7. To their Paris hotel room.

Can you not see dear friend, that under the circumstances I might have wished to avoid meeting Mrs. W.[oodhull] and even have seemed excited at the thought of it, without dreaming that you would think of me as speaking against her? My mind was occupied with my brother solely, and I was thinking of the best way of maintaining my new convictions concerning his innocence—and it did not occur to me to say, as I now see I ought to have done, "I do not blame Mrs. Woodhull for her course in the matter, but I cannot see her at present without pain, nor be seen with her, without compromising my brother's reputation which now I am only too glad to defend.["]

. . . Is it not plain that the internal evidence of my brother's truthfulness contained in his statement might very properly affect me when it would fail to carry conviction to her, or to anyone not intimately acquainted with him? I see by the papers that many ministers even, are no longer in doubt, but painfully convinced of his guilt.

I write this dear friend, to save my dear husband from further conversation on the subject, as I see clearly that he must be diverted or his health will give way utterly. Will you not talk of other things when you meet, and do not think of replying to this—for I also am trying to think of other things. . . .

> I am always your sincere friend.
> Isabella B. Hooker.
>
> [IBH to Mary Porter Chamberlin, SD]

Evidence that the scandal took its toll on the Hooker marriage can be found in Isabella's 1878 diary. In the first passage we find her meditating upon her strained relationship with John, who openly expressed a lack of confidence in her judgment as well as skepticism regarding the "testimony" and guidance she was now receiving regularly from the spirits of deceased friends and relatives (especially her mother). The second entry records a highly revealing incident, ostensibly touched off by John's disapproval of Isabella's decision to send a youthful looking photograph of herself to one of her young female admirers (on the grounds that it made her look like "one of these dancing girls"). When she chose to disregard his preferences, an angry exchange occurred during which Isabella began by likening John

*to her overbearing sister Catharine but ended up by ac-
cepting reinforcement from her sister in the form of a
"dictation" from Catharine's recently departed spirit.
In the concluding passages of this remarkable entry
(not included below but reproduced on page 328),
Isabella's characteristic handwriting altered drastically:
the narrative shifted in midsentence from the first to
the third person as the spirit of "friend Bowles"[8] began
to "dictate." Samual Bowles warned John not to "mo-
lest" Isabella with "your unreasonable criticism (she
would have me write unreasonable where I should
have used a harsher term)" and urged him not to yield
to his "lower" masculine nature, rechristened "obstinacy," "combativeness," and "muleishness" on the
other side.*

95   September 27, 1878

. . . And all my life is so troubled now—*full to harassment*—but I
should not care for this, only give thanks, if I felt sure I was not a
dreamer—but a truly inspired soul. My husband's lack of confidence in
me is a steady drawback to my happiness—he leans on me to the extent
of my capacity to bear—pities me because I am bound to such a "worthless husband"—insists that I am fitted for positions of immense scope,
yet will not trust me to write a note—or hire a horse, and still has a
vague conviction that many of our troubles about Woodhull and Henry
might have been avoided if I had only followed his counsel when present,
and not dared to think my own thoughts or speak my own words, while
he was absent. I am so tired of being patient with him—(the conflict is
that I love him so tenderly and feel so keenly his disabilities which are of
the flesh entirely, and cloud his beautiful spirit)—so hungry for full companionship with some one, and with him most of all. . . .

November 19, 1878

. . . [T]his morning while arranging my hair . . . John said gently "Are
you settled about sending that picture?["] and I said "yes—perfectly." J:
"I can't bear to have it go—and it does seem as if you ought to regard my
feelings somewhat in the matter." I: "No—I have done too much of that

8. Founder, publisher, and editor of the *Springfield* (Massachusetts) *Republican,* Bowles had died earlier in the year. He was a close friend of both Hookers
and a supporter of woman suffrage.

in the past—and it is ended now—you have trespassed on my individuality just as sister Catharine on her friends, and it has been as bad for you as for me—worse in fact, for the discipline was good for me up to a certain point, (and perhaps this is why so good a man was permitted to do really unjust things—this occurs to me now in passing—perhaps it was the only way in which I could learn to be all things to all men and especially *all women*—who are continually under a subjection hateful to them after they become thinking beings, and injurious to their mates always)—but it has cultivated a wil[l]fullness in you—that you will have to get over in the next life, and it will be easier to begin here—sister C.[atharine] finds it so, and she advises you to begin at once, or you will have a hard time getting yourself right, as she does."

J: "On the contrary, I think the great mistake of my life is that I have been too yielding to you—I have given up more than you and where I ought to have stood my ground."

I: "I am sorry to hear you say that John—very sorry, because you know it is not the exact truth—that is not what you said to John Day [husband of their daughter Alice]."

J: "Well—I ought not to have said what I did—in defense of you, I stretched a point."

I: "You lied then." J: "Yes—I think [I] have sometimes—it has been almost necessary in your defense—but it is your conduct that has created the necessity"—(this last line his idea, but not exact words)—[I:] "I want you to say this to Ned [their son]—I want him to hear it from your own lips."

I: "And the lying is worse than the trespassing, bad as that is—and this strengthens what I said of your moral deterioration—(I ought to have added—deceit always attends cowardice)—this is what made me seem so cross to you yesterday—it was hardly I, it was sister C.[atharine]—she was vehemently angry with you, for your treatment of me all these years—she would have used harder words if I would have permitted, but I remonstrated in spirit with her, and toned her down—but she spoke the truth, when she made me say [']you have ridden me as Balaam the ass (not that you think of me at all as an ass, I interpolated)—but it was the ass who saw the angel, and not Balaam—and all these years you have wished to guide me by the bridle, with a bit in my mouth, and have felt perfectly competent to do so, but this is all over now—the future must be different, and you must begin to understand it.[' "] . . .

. . . I am writing this down not for self [con]gratulation, but for retrospection and analysis. And this is the way the whole thing lies in my mind. John mistakes fastidiousness of taste, for reason and judgment and confuses love of approbation with prudence and wise caution—his mental tendencies are wholly *subjective*—while mine are wholly *objective*—hence in a critical place (or one that he makes critical sometimes when there is really hardly a shadow of a reason for doing so) he puts me in the focus of a magnifying glass of intense power, concentrates the eyes of all the world upon me, and says "see what a figure you cut." Whereas I, intent upon carrying a measure, and then taking [an] undignified breathing spell—forget the world has eyes and knowing that I am chaste and pure and unselfish, don[']t care if it has, nor how it scans either my strength or my weakness. And he treats himself in the same way—he is savage upon his supposed physical defects—and underestimates the power of his exquisite Spiritual nature, which is all there is of him to me—and it is this which holds me to him as to no other man I have ever seen. In his essence he is pure spirit, and loveable "beyond compare"—but, oh, how he has and does worry me with his "fuss and fidgets"—that is what sister C.[atharine] wanted to say, when I put my hand on her mouth—and I begin to feel that I must rebel and settle this matter of dictation and interference once for all. I feel just now, as if I knew just how Jesus felt when his dear and lovely mother came to him with suggestions—"Woman what have I to do with thee[?]"—[I]t was not that he would not willingly be guided by her now as in his boyish days—but those times are past—["]I must be about my Father's business."

If we look at the lives of all men reformers, from Abraham down to present time, they had marked peculiarities to say the least—individualities they really were, which history calls faith, genius, magnetism, eloquence and so on—and women reformers cannot escape the first misjudgments of the world if they would win the later verdict. . . .[9]

[IBH 1878 Diary, SD]

"Are Women Too Ignorant?" was issued as an Equal Suffrage Leaflet in 1898 by the Boston Woman's Journal, *the organ of the AWSA (which had merged eight years earlier with the New York wing to form the NAWSA). Citing the proliferation of women's clubs*

9. Isabella's handwriting begins to alter here, as the photographic reproduction of this paragraph and the remainder of this page demonstrates. See p. 328.

Page from Isabella Beecker Hooker's 1878 Diary

Page from Isabella Beecher Hooker's 1878 Diary, excerpt from entry of
November 19.
Courtesy of Stowe-Day Foundation.

and societies and the influx of women into higher edu-
cation as evidence that her "sisters" of all classes,
races, religious backgrounds, and ethnic origins were
actively preparing for the suffrage, Isabella countered
the charge that enfranchising women would only dou-
ble the "ignorant" vote.

96 An excellent young woman, who believes fully in the true democracy that can only be had when women as well as men are responsible voters, said to me lately: "But women are so ignorant on public affairs, it does seem as if they ought to be educated before they are allowed to vote. It is dreadful to double the ignorant vote; and, besides, women might be bribed just as men are." To this I replied: "First, as to bribery, there would not be money enough to go around when you double the constituency. Second, and if there were, you couldn't *find* the women. They are all either at home, taking care of their children and working for their husbands, or at work in shops and private families, and not loafing in the streets and hanging around saloons as men are and it will be years and years before they could get into the Legislatures if they wanted to. Third, and when found, they will know too much to be bribed." Here is a specimen:

Some years ago, a young Catholic woman who had served in our family a long time as a cook, asked me if I would attend one of her club meetings some evening, and give them a little talk. She had, it seems, been a member some time, but I had not heard of it before. I asked her about the club, and she handed me a little book, entitled "Constitution and Rules of the Ladies' Benevolent Society, Hartford, Conn., Organized August, 1887—Constitution Revised, 1891."

I went to a meeting in our City Mission Hall, a large and charming room which the club rented by the year. I found some two hundred women attending to the usual business, under the leadership of the president, a woman of forty perhaps, who showed herself an excellent parliamentarian, though her occupation was that of tailoress, and she went to work in a shop at 8 A.M., taking her lunch and returning home at 6 P.M. I made them a little talk, to the effect that, when our brothers of the republic should condescend to admit women to their counsels and the ballot-box, they would be astonished at the help they would receive from such women as themselves, and, until that time came, I saw little reason to hope that intemperance and licentiousness, poverty and starvation, would cease to afflict the body-politic. So I begged them to go on with their good work, and wait patiently for the day of recognition. I found there were no restrictions in regard to religion, occupation, or nationality; only good character was requisite for membership. The main sections of the Constitution and By-Laws might serve as a model for the other societies which are being formed in towns and villages all over our country. The membership is now over four hundred, and there is no diminution of interest at the end of the eleven years of the club's existence.

So much for the education that the so-called lower classes are giving themselves. There are many similar clubs, I find, in our own little city; and only last winter I was invited to speak at a Fair given by a society of colored women of Hartford, who were working for the purpose of founding a State home for aged colored people of both sexes. Now, add to this the education that society women are giving themselves in the innumerable literary, scientific, and political clubs of the whole country, and what becomes of the fear of doubling the ignorant vote? . . . [10]

Add to this the number of women now studying the higher branches (including always political economy) in our high schools, normal schools, and colleges, many of whom will become teachers in our public schools. On this point we have the testimony of no less a person than Prof. Harris, National Commissioner of Education at Washington. On my writing him for accurate information as to the number of women compared with men who are now students at these institutions, he wrote me as follows:

I find, on making the actual calculation, that the women in secondary and higher education, added together, number 287,162, and the men number 235,296, equal to 54.9% of the former, and 45.1% of the latter. This, you see, is almost exactly 55% women to 45% men for the entire education higher than the elementary schools.

And President Capen, of Tufts College, said in a recent address: "Our colleges have doubled in numbers within ten years, and the number of women who are getting ready for college is astonishing. When all the women now preparing for college are educated and begin studying the social questions of their time, what may we not hope for in the solution of the difficulties that now confront us?"

Let us take courage, dear sisters, and not allow ourselves to be deluded

---

10. Here Hooker enthusiastically cited a statistical report on "Women's Clubs and Societies" which described the "secret benevolent associations" of various ethnic groups, including Jewish and Irish women.

by the fear that we are not sufficiently educated to take part in public affairs. Responsibility is all the education we need to-day, and when put to the test we shall not be found wanting.

[Isabella Beecher Hooker, "Are Women Too Ignorant?"]

This letter to Clara B. Colby, a younger suffragist who had participated in the merger between Boston and New York, testifies to Hooker's sense that she had not received adequate recognition for her efforts from the leaders of the unified suffrage movement. The eighty-one-year-old Isabella, who would die of a cerebral hemorrhage just four years later, continued to serve as president of the Connecticut Woman Suffrage Association until 1905.

97   Feb[ruary] 16, 1903

Dear Mrs. Colby

Your kind letter touched me greatly—but I could not reply at once because I was in bed with grip—and still am there—but can write a few lines to say that in a day or two I will gather some material to send you. But my main object in writing is to tell you confidentially how it comforts my heart to know that in Washtn. where for so many years I helped to carry on our National Convention I am not forgotten. The truth is ever since the World[']s Fair at Chicago I have been often ignored and never treated with the old time courtesy and appreciation of the value of my devoted service. I was the only officer of our Society who was a Lady Manager—I spent the whole six months at Chicago—largely at my own expense—[(]for we were only paid while the board was in session), yet when the National [NAWSA] met later on Lucy Anthony [*sic*] was called on and gave the report of the whole Lady Manager business and I was never asked to say a word officially—and was really snubbed the whole time instead of being congratulated and honored. I am going to send you clippings from Chicago papers that seemed to me extravagant at the time—but when I said so to ladies in the hotel they said—"That is just the way you appeared to us."

And to this day it has never been suggested that my name should appear with Mrs[.] Stanton's and Miss Anthony's as Honorary Pres[iden]ts although in the earlier days I carried the Convention for them one year when they dared not have their names used because of Boston. [A]nd for several years I went to W.[ashington] every winter—and spent months at my own expense in hard work—and never cost the Society anything. But this is only to show you how it comforts me to be remembered by the old guard at Washtn.

This is all I can write today—sitting up in bed—
　　　　Faithfully
　　　　I.B.H.

　　　　　　　　　　　　　　　　　[IBH to Clara B. Colby, HL]

IV. Conversations among Ourselves

II.

Conversations among Ourselves

LIKE other educated nineteenth-century families, the Beechers relied on correspondence both to maintain close affectional ties and to keep each other current on their views and daily lives. The letters among Catharine, Mary, Harriet, and Isabella are especially rich in detail. Full of information on family comings and goings, and on the successes and frustrations by which each woman measured her life, the letters are particularly valuable as chronicles of the shifting relationships of four sisters. They show women with great and constant caring for one another—now teasing, now gently scolding, now rushing in with aid and solace. Yet the letters make clear that sisterhood did not always come easily to the Beecher women: Harriet found Catharine overbearing, Mary wished Isabella would lead a more retired life, Isabella envied Harriet's fame, Catharine thought Isabella ungrateful. The common ground was difficult to find. Catharine may have captured the promise—and the limits—of sisterhood when she wrote to Isabella in 1869: "I believe all of you are as good and sisterly as ever I could be." In many ways an affirmation of faith, her comment was at the same time an acknowledgment of boundaries. If "as sisterly as ever I could be" was as much as the Beechers, who were united by so much, could hope for from each other, how much more complicated for nineteenth-century American women generally, separated by the chasms of class and race, to find that shared experience.

Scattered from Connecticut to Ohio, in the 1830s the Beechers often kept in touch through "circular" letters—each member writing a paragraph or two and then sending the entire letter on to the next stop until the news had gone full circle. The following excerpts were written from Cincinnati. The first, dated soon af-

ter Harriet's marriage to Calvin Stowe, reveals the lighter side of sisterhood. In the second, Catharine discusses abolition, one of the subjects that had already begun to create strains within the family.

98   May 14 [1836]
[Harriet]:

I suppose you have all heard that Kate and I have been pitted against each other in the newspapers as to who should have Mr[.] Stowe to husband—but I desire to do all people to wit that he married *me.* Whether he married her too or not is no concern of mine—he doesn't seem to remember whether he did or not—

[Catharine]:

I am flourishing in more respects than one—for besides flourishing with a new book and flourishing with Harriet's husband, I am flourishing in health and spirits and [sister] Mary [Beecher Perkins] is doing finely and has presented me with a fine daughter yclept [named] Catharine Beecher—so that my domestic comforts greatly abound. . . .

[HBS and CEB to other members of the Beecher family, SD]

---

99   January 24–February 18, 1838
My dear Brethren and Sisteren [*sic*]—

. . . I have yet to wait for light before I can see that Abolitionism and all that help it along are not doing more harm than good—retarding the prospect of a *speedy* ending of it—and making more and more probable the result of a *dangerous and bloody* issue to what might have been accomplished by safer and gentler means. It is a question that time only can settle and each and all of us must make up our minds to agree to let others think we are in the wrong and doing mischief, without getting into a[?] and [?] . . . Mr. Stowe every once in a while gets into a great wrath about slavery and then he thinks Abolitionism better than nothing—but in his calmer moods he wishes they had never touched the thing and expects they will end it with force and disunion and all sorts of mischief—Harriet sometimes talks quite *Abolitiony* at me and I suppose quite *Anti* to the other side—As to *freedom of speech* and all that matter I never saw less of it than since the Abolitionists have begun to take care of it. . . . *I am as afraid of them as the dogs*—because I expect to have a sound licking from some quarter if I dare to say all I think and feel about the matter in their hearing or knowledge and my hand trembles to write as I have, knowing that it is going into the headquarters of that concern—

. . . Best love to you all from your
aff[ection]ate sister
C
[CEB to other members of the Beecher family, SD]

Not long after the untimely death of her mother in 1835, Isabella was sent from Cincinnati to Hartford so that she could live with her elder sister, Mary Beecher Perkins. The two sisters came to depend upon each other's companionship, and Mary was pleased when seventeen-year-old "Isabel" became engaged to John Hooker, a law clerk in the firm of her attorney husband. Mary addressed the following two letters to her half sister shortly after learning that Isabella, who was then visiting with Lyman and Catharine in Cincinnati, had announced her engagement. Mary's allusion to her sister's "blue feelings" in the second letter was a reference to the anxiety and perhaps even depression with which Isabella faced her impending marriage. (The "mother" referred to at the close of the second letter is Lyman Beecher's third wife, Lydia Beals Jackson Beecher, whom he had married one year after the death of Isabella's mother.)

100   August 31, 1839
[Mary to Isabella]

Your letter dear Isabel with Catharine's P.S. was recd yesterday noon with much joy. . . .

. . . My dear sister I do hope and trust you will not fail to write often and long to me, we know not how long this privilege may be permitted, one of us may be called to our heavenly home. I always live with the feeling that my life is very uncertain—we know not what is before us, but while we are spared, "let us love one another with true hearts fervently[.]" [W]rite as soon as you get this and remember that every thing is interesting that concerns you or other friends[.]

with much affection
yours Mary

October 12, 1839

Dear Isabel

After waiting with much impatience for your letter and often threaten-ing Mr[.] P.[erkins] with my displeasure if he came without one, at last it came to my great delight. I think I feel quite *lover like* about your let-ters[.] I don[']t believe Mr[.] H.[ooker] is more impatient to get one, but what a naughty girl you are to have the *blues* so dreadfully. I think a young lady who weighs 129 lb[.] must not consider herself very much of an invalid, if you are not ethereal in your person you must be so in mind or you will lose all chance of being an *angel*. I don[']t believe an angel ever weighed 129 lb[.] [Y]ou are exceedingly ingenious I allow in the art of tormenting one's self, but I trust with father and Cate and Harriet to talk with you will be helped out of the slough of despond before you sink very deep—

. . . I have heard a rumor that Mr[.] Stowe is invited to the Presidency of Middlebury College, is it true? and if true does he think of accepting— if it were not for father I should hope to see him over the mountains next summer, I think he leaves his heart here, I mean he loves New England best after all but I don[']t think Harriet does, *the hussey.*

. . . I wish I could look in upon you. [Y]ou must write all about at home, about your self—are your blue feelings about Mr. H.[ooker]? What are you going to do this winter—what do you wear and just as tho' you were sitting by me and answering questions[.]. . .

. . . You must try to learn all you can about domestic affairs while with so good a teacher as mother[.] Give much love to all and believe me dear sister with

much affection yours
Mary F. P.

[MBP to Isabella Beecher, SD]

In 1839, prior to his and Isabella's marriage, John Hooker contemplated a career change—from the study of law to preparation for the ministry. In true Beecher fashion, various members of Isabella's family involved themselves in the decision, offering confident and con-flicting advice.

101   Nov[ember] 27, 1839
Dear Brother John
    . . . One other consideration. Bell is formed by nature to *take the lead*—she will every year learn more and more of her power *to influence others*—since she has been home with father and learned his plans of influence in his parish—she has unconsciously and without any worry or responsibility been extending a great influence. Father has been greatly perplexed by fashionable amusements among his young people. She has come among them and can do and will do more than father or any one else could do to stay the evil. . . . She is growing fast in piety—in power of intellect—in power of controlling other minds. What will you find for her to do[?] . . . I do not want to see a woman of her talents and power put out of her place as *a leader*. She is formed for a minister[']s wife as much as you are for a minister. . . .
    If you decide to be a lawyer I shall not be very much disappointed or troubled for tho' I shall think you and Bell will in consequence be less useful and of course less happy, still I shall esteem it as the will of God that so it should be. . . .
                I am truly and affly yrs
                Catharine

                                    [CEB to John Hooker, SD]

102   November 29, 1839
Dear Isabella
    Yesterday Mr[.] Hooker spent most of the day with us and we discussed the question of his changing his profession in its length and breadth. . . . [F]rom all I saw and heard it was very evident to my mind that if he changes, it will be to *please you* and not from a conviction that he is called of God to enter the sacred office. . . . I know him better than father or Catharine does, and perhaps as well as you do. . . . It seems to me that you are all running wild on this subject—pray bring common sense to bear and take some view of society and its various wants and claims besides the ministerial view. . . . Dear Sister I have left the subject of your health last tho not least in my view. You look only on the bright side of the picture and so does father and Catharine. [I]f I tho't you would *ever* have strength and health I would not say a word—but I do not believe you *will ever* be a strong and healthy woman. [Y]ou may be comfortably well, so that you can attend to the duties of your family, educate your children and be very useful and happy if you do not have

duties and responsibilities hanging about you that you have no strength to perform. [T]hink of your own dear mother[,] as well qualified by education and piety as you, and with a better prospect of health, after marriage her health gave way, her spirits sunk, and she was ever mourning that she was so useless as she appeared to herself to be. I do not believe if she were living she would advise the change . . . I think it would be *utter madness* for you to marry a minister and I wonder at Father and Catharine and Harriet that they should think of such a thing when your health is in such a state. I am sure the *indications* of Providence are very strong that *you* ought not to be a *minister['s] wife*. . . .

. . . I have given you a preachment but do *think well*. I wish you were here[.] I know you don[']t—but if Kate [Catharine] sets herself to make Hooker a minister I greatly fear she will succeed[.] [S]he is never afraid of consequences and always thinks things will be just as she wishes them to be. Write to me as soon as you get this and oh that you could relieve my mind of the anxieties I feel for you[.]

> Yours most sincerely
> Mary

> [MBP to Isabella Beecher, SD]

The special closeness Mary Beecher Perkins shared with Isabella, seventeen years her junior, is apparent in the following letters. Mary, who devoted herself entirely to her family, wrote about the cares of the household and advised Isabella, who would marry in August 1841, that her domestic responsibilities should take precedence over any public involvement.

103   November 21, 1840

Dear Isabel

. . . I need not tell you my dear sister how much I have missed you for every step I take and almost every tho't I think brings your image before me and nothing but the hope of your restoration to health would reconcile me to your continued absence. . . . [H]ow I should like to see you my fastidious sister arrayed in your *red flannel*! pride must have a fall, and I think yours will be pretty well used up by the time you get home. Write me every few days how you get along for we are all full of anxiety to hear. We have had no cook now, for ten days and I have got up and got breakfast with [Mary Beecher Perkins' daughter] Emeline's help and several days have done all the other cooking Hannah coming in when she could and Aunt Esther giving all the assistance she could, but I don[']t like it, I must say, this being cook and lady too is rather too difficult—my back is most broken and my poor hands full of cuts and burns and so black, bah!

 . . . good night my dear sis—

ever yours Mary F.P.

[MBP to Isabella Beecher, SD]

---

104 January 13, 1841

Dear Isabella

I cannot express the pleasure I felt when your letter arrived with the cheering news of your improved health and spirits. We were at dinner when Mr. P.[erkins] handed me the letter and there was quite a shout of joy—the children all exclaiming "I wish she would come home[.]" I hope you will let *nothing* interfere with your perfect recovery—. . . . [I]t is your *first duty* to take care of your health[.] [A]void excitment, for it is always bad for you—do not go too much to meetings, the more interesting they are to you the more injurious they will be in your present state of health. I have long had to practise this self denial, and I could not perform any of my duties if I gave way to my feelings and allowed myself to attend meetings and become as much interested as I easily could. [T]his is a novel doctrine to preach but I believe it is the true one for such excitable beings as you and I are. [W]hen we get to heaven, we can indulge our feelings without restraint, unfettered by these frail bodies which here so chain us to the earth and we must be content to wait till then. . . .

 . . . I have got my sewing pretty much done and have a very good cook and little girl so that if we all continue well I hope to have a month or two of leisure[.] My cook had been here but two or three weeks when a *gentleman* of her acquaintance requested leave to "keep company with her" and soon the matter was all settled and they are to be married in April—I really think Cupid and Hymen have a spite against me for they spirit off every good girl I get. . . . So much on the chapter of Helps—

 . . . good bye dear sis—write often and come home as soon as you can— M—

[MBP to Isabella Beecher, SD]

When Isabella addressed the following letter to her sister, then in Cincinnati, she was aware that Harriet and her children had been exposed to the cholera then raging in the city. What Isabella could not have known when she expressed envy of her sister's spiritual contentment was that Harriet's beloved baby Charley had died in the epidemic only eight days earlier. (See Harriet's letters to Calvin of June 29 and July 26, 1849, excerpted in Documents 38 and 39.)

105   July 31, 1849

My dear Sister Harriet

You can hardly imagine how much I longed to sit down and write you a few lines of sympathy and love. . . . But the wave of daily care and responsibility has driven me before it—just as you have so long been driven,—and sometimes has nigh overwhelmed me, soul and body together, so that I have been content to barely live through such long days and rest each weary night—

Not that we have sickness or peculiar trouble—or anything save a large family for young folks—and two meddlesome, little bodies to look after from *early morn to dewy eve*—and in addition, company of one sort or another most of the time. Indeed, when I enumerate my many comforts and blessings (foremost among which I count, the best Protestant Irishwoman that ever gladdened a young housekeeper's door) I am conscious of wanting nothing but *strength* to enjoy them—-and patience to endure little trials.

After all I do want still more—the *faith* which looks within the vail [*sic*]—that want is my great trouble—the being careful for many things, my great sin—The Lord has been very kind to you my dear sister in lifting you above the world in spirit, tho' pressed down and sorrowful oft through the flesh. And no gift from a Father's hand can equal this—the most satisfying, consoling, delightful token of adoption—

In the midst of sorrow and death, you are happier than I—or than any of my acquaintance—in days of cheerful prosperity and health then, how rich must be your experience—unless, indeed, afflictions and apprehension call out the sentiments of piety and submission, as they always do with me, in a peculiar manner. . . .

I wish I could . . . talk over my little Mary with you—and gather something from your experience in obstinate, irritable children, as I do think Mary is very much like Georgy [Georgiana Stowe] as I remember her here. . . . I do wish I could write out all her character for you in the hope of receiving some hints, that would materially assist me in remodeling it. . . . [B]ut I will not tax you or myself further tonight—you have enough to do I think of [*sic*] in your own little nest. . . . How I should love to have you all here in my healthy, delightful home . . . only my poor head I fear which is none of the strongest at best, would utterly fail me in such a crisis—confusion, noise of children and extra care completely upset me—altho' my health is much better than formerly. . . .

Caty Perkins [Mary Beecher Perkins's daughter] is spending two weeks with us. [I]t is quite a pleasure to see how she improves and ripens—she is now very lovely and pleasing—full of friendly offices to the children and desirous of being generally useful. I should like a daughter of her age—well trained, to my hand—right well—have you any such to furnish? . . . I could send a world of love to you . . . all if my sheet would hold it. I have only room to bid you good night. . . . May the power of the Highest overshadow you now and ever—

> yr. affec. sister
> Belle

> [IBH to Harriet Beecher Stowe, SchL]

Seven months after she had left Cincinnati and settled the family in Brunswick, Maine, where Calvin had accepted a position at Bowdoin College, Harriet described herself and her children to Isabella. Born the previous July, Charles Edward, "the reigning baby," bore the name of the infant who had perished in the epidemic a year earlier. Harriet's and Calvin's other sons and daughters were now fourteen, twelve, ten, and seven.

106   [November 1850]
My dear Sister

I don't know whether I owe you a letter or not, but I think of you a great deal and so this Saturday evening as I am disappointed in getting the book I intended to read aloud I will devote the time that creates to you—Thus my baby has heard me and is waking up and proclaiming by loud cries his ambitions to use any spare time I may have—

Well he is asleep again—but now the evening wanes—I am sitting by my round table with the children all about—Henry painting—Hattie and

Eliza reading David Copperfield Anna [Harriet's servant who had accompanied her from Cincinnati] sewing and the baby in his crib. Now for a picture of this same called ala Dickens "the reigning baby." He is the very image of the lost one—so much so as almost to make me feel sad—he is only something fairer—and I think him lovely. . . .

I want you to write me Bell—I think so much of all my brothers and sisters and long for their society so much when I am where it is practicable to get it. I do hope next summer that you and Mary [Beecher Perkins] will come down and see us. Tell me all about your situation—how you are arranged—what you do and how your time passes.

Yours affectionately

H. Stowe

[HBS to Isabella Beecher Hooker, SchL]

In her letter written to Lyman and Henry Ward, Harriet lauded Catharine's recently published True Remedy for the Wrongs of Women. *Harriet also informed her father and brother that her elder sister had agreed to "give me a year of her time." The two sisters operated a boarding school for Beecher family children described in Catharine's letter to Mary. She and Harriet hoped that the enterprise would finance needed repairs to the Stowe's house in Brunswick. The profits and losses of the school later became a point of dispute between the two sisters. Catharine also managed the household, while Harriet completed* Uncle Tom's Cabin, *then being serialized in the* National Era. *Issued in two volumes, the novel was published in March of 1852.*

107   [September 19, 1851]

Dear Father and Henry,

I am going to write to you with relation to Catharine's affairs—as they have now become in a measure interwoven with mine. She has agreed to give me a year of her time to act conjointly with me in taking a class of our young relations and carrying on their education with that of my own children. It is a care that I should not think it right to assume without her—and that I cannot support without her—and it is my desire that the enterprise which she has left in the hands of others may now receive such a support from the public and our family who are a powerful part of it as to render it unnecessary for her to return to labor in that sphere. I hope you have both read Catharine's last book. If you have not—I beg you will not let another day pass without reading it as an act of justice to yourselves [and] to the public. Until I read it I had no proper appreciation of her character [and] motives of action for this eight or ten years past.—I considered her strange, nervous, visionary and to a certain extent unstable—I see now that she has been busy for eight years about *one thing*—a thing first conceived upon a sick bed when she was so sick and frail that most women would have felt that all they could hope for was to lie still and be nursed for the rest of their lives—then she conceived this plan of educating our country by means of its women and this she has steadily pursued in weariness and painfulness in journeys in peril of life and health—in watching and in prayer. A system so extensive carried on by means of correspondence all over the country—dependent on an immense number of influences and agents from Maine to Georgia and from Massachusetts to Iowa *of course* would include *failures in particular parts*—and when one of these have [*sic*] occurred, many not seeing that they were only small parts of the great *whole* which was all the while moving on, have supposed that she was constantly attempting and constantly failing. . . .

Catharine has earned and spent for the cause nearly five thousand dollars—and she has worked as yet almost *against* even her own family for hitherto you know that we have not had full confidence in her plans—but the time has come when in my judgment there is ground and full ground for such confidence and when to neglect them any longer would be unwise and inexcusable. . . .

Furthermore this thing has *got to go*—and it will go either in your hands and under your influence or it will go by the aid of such men as Horace Mann,[1] Horace Greeley[2] and all that modern reform party who all stand waiting for the moment when Catharine will come out on their side to carry up the building with shoutings of "grace, grace" unto it. The great educational movement she has projected if you fail to uphold it will be instantly referred to them and *go* with acclamation but it will take the impress of their sentiments, not of yours and which is best judge ye—I tell you that while you are lukewarm and full of other

1. Horace Mann, antebellum America's most prominent educational reformer, concentrated his efforts in Massachusetts. There he sought to increase support for public education and improve the professional training of teachers.

2. Horace Greeley, editor of the *New York Tribune*, used his paper to promote virtually every prevalent reform, including education.

things they meet Catharine with the warmest of zeal with offers of time, money, influence—everything—They are noble men—noble minded, noble hearted, energetic and yet I would rather they came into the movement as accessories than as leaders that thus they might have their sentiments modified by *you*—for they need it. . . .

I beg therefore—first that you will give Cate[']s book a careful reading, and rectify your own sentiments as I have mine and see just what she has been doing and then do what you can to help this Milwaukee enterprise which is just now the turning point of the whole affair. . . .

> Yours affectionately,
> H. B. Stowe
>
> [HBS to Lyman and Henry Ward Beecher, SML]

---

108   Sept[ember] 27, 1851

Dear Sister Mary,

Not a line from you or Emily and Harriet thinks it very strange. I write now at her request to tell you some things which need to be taken into consideration and she wants you to send this to Uncle Sam[ue]l and Henry as soon as you have read it.

This is a very cold house, in a bitter *cold* climate tho' *dry and steady*. We find we cannot make the children comfortable except by a furnace which will cost $150. We must make partitions and fixtures costing some $30—We must get bed[,] bedding[,] table[,] furniture etc for *five* more in the family. . . . A new carpet is indispensable. . . . Wood and coal and provisions to be laid in all demand ready money. In these circumstances we need to have each pupil bring $50 to begin with. . . . We shall need to receive the rest of the payment [$170] quarterly as we go along.

Now you know how [Calvin] Stowe has a monomania about *running in debt* and his mother is as bad and the only way I could make them comfortable was by *taking all the risk myself* and agreeing to foot all the bills that were not met by the salary and income from the pupils. . . .

The old lady has concluded to spend the winter in Natick—no remarks—

I am trying to get Uncle Tom out of the way. At 8 o[']clock we are thro' with breakfast and prayers and then we send Mr[.] Stowe and Harriet both to *his room in the college.* There was no other way to keep her out of family care and quietly at work and since this plan is adopted she goes ahead finely. I hope it will be finished before the children come. . . .

    With love to all
    Yours affect[ionate]ly
    Catharine

        [CEB to Mary Beecher Perkins, SML]

---

109   [early 1852]

Dear Sister Katy

You were not far from wrong in supposing that I should look on this subject in some different light from what you do. . . .

In the first place then I appreciate the kind interest which led you make the *offer* of assisting me in this plan but you must recollect that it did not come at my solicitation but arose from yourself,—that I had at the time very serious doubts of your ability to carry it through—and stated them often and fully—I told you often and often, if you felt the least hesitation to draw back before we committed ourselves by taking anybody. As it has resulted therefore—I feel very differently from what I should if I had originated the plan and persuaded you into it.

You seem to say that you have made great sacrifices and suffered very much this winter and that I am taking all the profit—I do not consider that there will be *any* profit—but that *pecuniarly* it will be a heavy expenditure—and I should be glad if it does not involve me inextricably in debt. On Christmas I collected all the debts—I paid out every cent that I dared of salary—I got a hundred dollars from Mr. Stowe and took two hundred of my own and still there are heavy bills lying unpaid. Your mode of running up estimates is not accurate—it is easy to lump matters together and say thus and so and thus and so, and *about* this is the result, but when every little item is collected written down and added—the results are very different. My greatest hope in view of all I know of our bills is *not* to come out in debt, beyond our ability to meet. . . .

The outgoes therefore of this campaign of ten months are

Furniture and preparations	158
Coal	58
Your board	32
Girls board	160
	398

. . . My estimates of the matter is that I shall pay out for this concern $200 beyond what I receive—

There is about [$]100 worth of furniture—which will remain with me—But it is furniture the greater part of it which is made necessary only by the establishment and which tho it will be pleasant to have[—], I should not have bought except for it and shall not use often my family is smaller. . . .

I and you undertook what we did from the best of motives—and I trust that in some more important respects than can be estimated by figures of arithmetic the best of results will follow. If god will give us the souls of these children as I trust in time he will, I shall not thro eternity regret this winter—I would not forego this knowledge that I have gained of God's protecting power and ability to support the soul *for anything that could be given me.*

As respects our accounts mutually I do not suppose that you want anything more than an assurance that I am acting right—The matter of that $15 can be easily disposed of—As the sons of Heth said to Abraham

What is that between me and thee?—

> Yours affectionately
> H. Stowe

> [HBS to Catharine Beecher, SchL]

While visiting with the Stowes in Brunswick, Maine, shortly after the publication of Uncle Tom's Cabin, *Isabella wrote her husband John about Catharine's unwelcome efforts to renegotiate Harriet's contract with her publisher, John P. Jewett. Isabella concludes this letter by comparing herself to her sister "Hatty."*

110   June 26 [and 27,] [18]52

[Isabella to John Hooker]

Your very pleasant letter, my dearest husband, reached me yesterday but it served to deepen rather than relieve the homesickness which has tried to haunt me ever since I came here. Somehow I am more drawn homeward than ever tonight—every thing seems strange and confused here and I long to be at rest, you know where. . . .

. . . Mr. Perkins [Mary's husband] came today to spend Sunday—that's the way *he* does and folks call him a pattern husband!!—For my part, you may do as you like about coming and I shall think you in any case better than six like him. No man who witholds confidence from his wife can lay any claim to being a good husband—he lacks the first element. . . .

Poor sister Cate has taken up the matter of Hatty's bargain with the Publishers and is determined to make a fuss about it—tho' Mr. Stowe did the business in his own way and is perfectly satisfied now. Cate is making herself half sick about it—calls Jewett a scoundrel and with her usual pertinacity says she will make the matter public unless they adopt her view of the case. What a pity that she will meddle so—she is so anxious that Hatty shd. have the means of educating her three million children she won[']t rest till she has made trouble somewhere.

Hatty thinks and knows that tis Jewett's efforts and outlays, that have secured so large a sale—she has been behind the curtain and knows where the puffs come from etc—and she says he has lost southern trade before, for publishing A. Sy. [anti-slavery] works and being an abolitionist and she is glad to have him rewarded. She will get [$]20[,]ooo ultimately without doubt to say nothing of future works.

At first I was melancholy—on seeing the evidences of genius all around me here—my own littleness fairly stared me in the face—but I am calming down considerably and begin to think my bump of order and housekeeping capacity are worth something in this working, matter of fact world—and am at least quite a set off to all this fancy and genius. You must try to be comforted by my lack of brilliancy by remembering that I should not be half so good a *wife* and mother probably as I am now—one cannot do or be forty things at once. I can only remain what I have always been[,] a loved and loving wife. . . .

. . . I have spent most of the time this afternoon talking with sister Hatty—altho' I had previously devoted it to you. The only way is however to accept opportunities as they offer—otherwise you may never find them. In some respects Hatty's experience is like mine—but she has reached an assurance of faith and hope for which I yet sigh. One great trouble with me is a want of simplicity of character—I am so forever *conscious*—those people who forget themselves are my delight—but how can one be made over to such a model? . . .

No more now from yr. loving wife. . . .

[IBH to John Hooker, SD]

Catharine's determination to discredit Harriet's publisher, John P. Jewett, provided the impetus for Mary's letter to their father Lyman. Fearful that Catharine would publish something as controversial as Truth Stranger than Fiction, *members of the family joined forces to restrain the eldest daughter. Apparently, they succeeded—Catharine continued to rail about Jewett but did so only in private correspondence.*

111   Jan[uary] 22, [18]53

Dear father—

I wrote to Kate soon after I got home—telling her how feeble Harriet was—and how tried you were by her unauthorized interference in Harriet's business—stating that H. and Mr[.] Stowe were perfectly satisfied and had made the same bargain for this book now writing—and entreating her to everything she loved and valued to be still—I wrote kindly but as emphatically as I could—you see by the enclosed how it has availed, all we can say passes by her like the idle wind—I wish you would write to me and tell me what you have written to her since I saw you—What do you think she is going to do? Is she writing another book after the manner of "Fact [*sic*] Stranger than Fiction"[?] I strongly suspect that she is—but how can we find out—It will be horrible to have this matter brot out with her version and fly all over the country—She is very mysterious—but evidently is preparing some exposure of what she considers an enormous wickedness. . . .

Your afft daughter
Mary F.P.

[MBP to Lyman Beecher, SD]

Like other siblings, the Beecher sisters often disagreed. In the following exchange, Isabella took Catharine to task for being inconsiderate and a family troublemaker. The elder sister responded by reminding Isabella that she had herself in younger days provided a home for various of her siblings—including Isabella. Ironically, only a couple of years later, during the Beecher-Tilton scandal, it would be Isabella who would be accused of violating "the family circle."

112 [before May 9, 1869?]

My dear Sister—

. . . Some weeks ago you sent me a line saying you would be here on such a day to attend a committee meeting—and you did not enquire whether my house was full and your coming would be an inconvenience in any way, nor did you write in season for me to send any reply whatever. . . . Now it seems to me all this was an incivility and an unkindness . . . No friend ever ventures to come down upon another friend for a month's hospitality until he has first learned, what the mind of his host is in the matter and whether his house as well as his heart is ready to receive him. . . . Just so with brothers and sisters . . . and the more loving they are, the more considerate do they become of the convenience and comfort of their beloved. . . .

And this is not all—you have always been principled against laying up from your earnings against a day of sickness and old age—and though often remonstrated with on the subject, you have persisted in giving away to benevolent objects whatever surplus funds you might have. . . . I argued the whole case with you, years ago in our parlor—I said . . . that if we and all other christians followed your rule, there would be no homes for the needy to fly to, when their days of feebleness came, no prosperous friends to share with them of their abundance. . . .

There is one other reason why I am far less happy to receive you into my family that [*sic*] I wish to be—and that is—because your principles, lead you to make use of what you unavoidably see and hear in the family circle to the serious injury of the family among the families of mutual friends. Not that you ever intend this in the remotest degree—nothing could be kinder than your motives—but in fact, you have repeatedly and over and over again, discovered to cousins for instance differences and unfriendlinesses between them that they never thought of and which never existed save in your imagination. . . . Now when my children were young and very susceptible I felt bound to guard them . . . and therefore I have failed to invite you here as often as you might naturally have expected I would. This danger has now passed however—they are old enough and have been so instructed in your peculiarities that they and all of us can well afford to do our part toward making your declining years comfortable and happy. . . .

It is my opinion however, that you would be far happier, to select a good boarding place—in this city, Mrs[.] Kellogg's for instance and gather there all your treasures, calling it home—the home of your old age; then, whenever your affectionate heart goes out to your brothers and sisters and friends in real longings for their society, you can send them messages to this effect and learn when most conveniently they can give you welcome and for how long a time. In this way and this alone you manifest a true regard for their happiness as well as your own—and by this, you escape the imputation of merely making a convenience of your friends. . . .

> yr affec sister
> Belle

[IBH to Catharine Beecher, SD]

---

113   [May 9, 1869?]

Dear Sister Bell

I sympathize with you in your many cares, as chief manager of a large family and do not wish to add to them any more than I can help. I am waiting for *proof sheets* to use which will not come till the 25th—Then I mean to go to the Kelloggs—tho' I can not have my room there, till after Thanksgiving.—

A truly *christian home* is not complete without aged or infirm members—who are preserved in life that the young may be *trained* to reverence grey hairs and tenderly to care for the feeble and infirm—In no other way can they follow Christ's command "Bear ye one another's burdens."

When my work is done and I am worn out this will be my remaining mission and I hope to meet its responsibilities with cheerfulness and patience.

When I had a home of my own, my sisters always found a welcome and I aided them to an education and means of support. I think you for some months had gratuitous board and tuition in my family years ago. I believe all of you are as good and sisterly as ever I could be and I know many other friends that would rejoice to contribute to sustain my declining years.

The "bread cast on the waters will surely return—and the Lord is my Shepherd I shall not want[.]"

Today I am suffering from *too long a walk*—so that my nerves are trembling and shakey—And so I comfort myself with these words.

I love you and trust you as one anxious to do right in all things.

> Your affectionate
> Sister Catharine

[CEB to Isabella Beecher Hooker, SD]

When Catharine was seventy-seven, she retired to the home of her brother Thomas and his wife Julia in Elmira, New York. Although Catharine's relationships with her family had not always been easy, Julia welcomed her, saying "I think there are worse afflictions than the care of an old Christian woman who has at least tried to do good all her life."³ Catharine herself was restless. Nonetheless, Harriet told her sister that she ought to confine her energies to the small circle of relatives and friends in Elmira and leave "the government of the world" to others.

114   [n.d.]

My dear Sister

I am relieved and glad to think of you at home at last with Brother Tom. Too many years have passed over your head for you to be wandering like a trunk without a label.

As to your want of "something to do"—that depends on how you are to take it. . . . Towards the close of life we all must learn the lesson to retire gracefully and to accept the fact that we can no more be leaders. It was most painful to Father when he ceased to have calls to preach—and when he felt himself as well able as ever—but the world did not think so.

But our Lord has so arranged it that the smallest deed . . . loses not its reward. Old people cannot be actors but they can be sympathizers—they can by their own serenity and cheerfulness make life pleasant and cheerful around them. Your thoughts on the wails and woes of the world sometimes seem to me like the discouragement of one night candle in reflecting on the darkness of the world. The care of lighting the world does not depend on that candle. Its only duty is to blaze away cheerily in the small circle where the master puts it. Now you have more talents for making life *agreeable* than most women of your age. You have an [illegible] vein of humor[,] you are good natured and cheerful. You play quite well on the piano and tho your singing is not like a young persons, it is still so hearty as to be agreeable. You can crochet tidies or knit mittens[,] visit and cheer some sick people at the [water] cure and make life

3. Julia Jones Beecher to Olivia Langdon, April 28, 1877, SD.

brighter around you. Meanwhile the government of the world will not be going on a whit worse that *you* are not doing it. . . .

[No ending]

[HBS to Catharine Beecher, SchL]

Catharine Beecher suffered a stroke on the night of May 7, 1878. This letter to Mary, probably completed on the day of the attack, was included among various packets for "Brothers and Sisters" found in Catharine's desk. As the letter makes clear, Catharine knew her life was nearly over and was largely resigned. And yet the energy that had driven her for seventy-eight years burned on. Ever like her father, who had said that he "would enlist again in a moment"⁴ if given a choice between heaven and his work, Catharine found it hard to let go of life and yearned to the end for "something to do." She died on May 12, 1878.

115   April 29, 1878

Dear Sister Mary

I *pine* to see you but as that cannot be, let me hear from you as soon as you get this and tell me all about yourself and your children.

I have just been arranging my papers and letters and find so much of our early life. I long to talk it all over with you. I seem to have "finished the work my Father gave me to do," and now I want to *go to Him*, and also to my earthly father that loved us so tenderly and thus enabled us to better understand "Our Father in Heaven" and His love and care. One of your letters to me was when you were with a baby at father's in Boston and one of his letters was written to me to take care of your health.

One of my papers is our first Catalogue at Hartford in 1826. Of the 25 Hartford girls contemporary with Fanny Strong, twenty are still living. When and where shall we all meet again?

What do you hear from Harriet? I wish we three could meet somewhere this Summer, but I doubt if I can bear the journey both ways, as I suppose this is my house till I depart to the Heavenly Home. Tom and Julia [Beecher] are very kind, and I have all needed comforts. But I am

4. *Autobiography*, 2:414.

longing to depart. If I could find *something to do for others* I could be more easily resigned. XXX—. . . .

Dear Sister Mary.

Yours of May 5 is received. I am not well—have lost appetite—feel as if I was soon to go home to father, mother, Aunt Esther[,] brother George, and best of all to our dear Lord and Savior.

I found this—(a long yellow stained letter to Mr. Boardman in 1836 on perfectionism on which this note was written among old papers and send it for you and Harriet when you meet, and *I shall perhaps be with you the other side of the thin veil*[)].

If I pass away here I want you and Harriet to receive and divide what I leave. Tom and Julia if I die here will know. They have been very good and kind and will be to the end. I shall direct this to them to open when I am gone.

God bless and keep you till we meet in Heaven.

> your affectionate sister
> Catharine.

> [CEB to Mary Beecher Perkins, SD]

Despite their estrangement during the Beecher-Tilton scandal, Harriet and Isabella eventually reestablished sisterly relations. Harriet's letter was written during her husband's final illness. Calvin died on August 6, 1886, exactly a decade before his wife's death. (Edward, who served as the Stowes' physician, was Isabella's youngest child.)

116   January 22, 1885

Dear Belle

I think more of my brothers and sisters than I ever have done before and have written to all and got replies from all but Henry. Your letter is a comfort to me—Yesterday I asked Edward where you were and sent a message to you—I send the autograph you ask for from my poems—It is quite appropriate to the cold frozen season now that keeps me close in doors. Mr[.] Stowe sinks gradually from week to week. Edward thinks he may last months. His mind is clear and he is free from pain. We have the best of nurses and in short we have *all* under the circumstances we could ask for. I can scarcely believe when I see Ed's manly form and face that he came from that little white delicate baby I once knew. He is a son to be proud of.

> Your loving Sister
> Hatty

> [HBS to Isabella Beecher Hooker, SD]

In her last letter to Isabella, Harriet recalled the days of her childhood spent at the home of her maternal grandmother, Roxana Ward Foote, and her aunt, Harriet Foote, in Nutplains, Connecticut. Harriet also drew upon those days in her final novel, Poganuc People, *basing her portrayal of Aunt Debby Kittery upon Harriet Foote.*

117   August 14, 1889

My precious Sister

Having read your note *four times*, the next thing is to answer it. I *do wish* I could have been with you in your pleasant visit at Nutplains, where some of the most joyous days of my childhood were spent. All the things that you mentioned *I have done* over and over again when I was a wild free young girl. I *never got tired* of doing them. The room I slept in for the most part, was the *first right hand room* as you get to the top of the front stairs—the second was the spare chamber for company, where many long remembered pleasant people lodged. . . . The room directly facing the head of the stairs was Aunt Harriet's and Grandma's. [I]t had two large comfortable beds for them—I have slept with Aunt Harriet in her bed and *enjoyed* it as she always kept one so nice and warm. Then there was the colored woman Dinah was a great friend of mine and we had many frolics and capers together—she told me lots of stories and made herself very entertaining. Then there was the grave yard on Sandy Hill, the other side of the river where I often walked—I wonder if it is there now. It had a nice picket fence all round it then with a gate so I could easily get in and read the inscriptions on the grave stones. . . .

Well dear sister I see by my shortening paper that it is time for me to close. When you come back no one will welcome you more warmly than

> Your loving sister Hatty

> [HBS to Isabella Beecher Hooker, SD]

By the time Isabella died in 1907, she had outlived all
of her Beecher siblings. On the occasion of her eighty-
third birthday, Isabella would be asked to reminisce in
print about her early years as one of Lyman Beecher's
eleven children and her subsequent career as a reformer. Appropriately enough, she chose to entitle this
article for The Connecticut Magazine "The Last of the
Beechers." However, in this letter to her friend and co-
worker, Olympia Brown, Isabella responds to a query
concerning Charlotte Perkins Gilman (1860–1935), her
grandniece. In works such as Women and Economics,
"The Yellow Wallpaper," and Herland, Gilman advocated the professionalization of housework and
childcare as a means of improving women's economic
status, exposed the sexual politics of the medical treatment of women, and offered a vision of a matriarchal
utopia. Notwithstanding Hooker's remarks to Brown
concerning Gilman's unorthodox personal "history"
and "peculiarities," it was Gilman—ironically the
granddaughter of Mary Beecher Perkins—who carried
the Beecher sisters' legacy into the twentieth century.

118   April 25, 1901
Dear Friend

I am sorry you have wanted a letter from me—I have not answered one
of the 140 letters now in my desk except by a newspaper such as I sent
you—(beside the book and calendar)[.] And beside these I sent a card
like sample to 50 persons who had sent beautiful flowers—some of them
in pots.—[T]his means a great deal of head work and heart work—for
the newspapers amounted to over 200 sent by post—and I have a large
correspondence beside. But now will try to answer your good letters.

As to suffrage work I agree with you entirely—but cannot write about
it now. I would like to copy yr letter and send to the Convention—
without any name[,] but can[']t get time and fear it would not be wise.
For our State nothing will avail but a permanent organizer on a good
salary—to form Clubs and mother them—and as I cannot have this
helper I shall not try to do much—but wait for time to drag old Con-
nect[icut] into line. If you had staid here we might have done something—but I am absolutely alone—the few workers being without money
or influence—and not a single speaker in the State.

As to Mrs[.] Perkins Gilman she is all right—a noble woman of large gifts who has had a history that can[']t be put into print. She is my grand niece[.] Her father was Frederic Perkins[,] son of my sister Mary Perkins. She was divorced from Mr. Stetson for reasons satisfactory to them and they are warmly attached to each other and to their daughter—who now lives with her mother in the home of Mr[.] Gilman—a New York lawyer. He is her own cousin—the son of Catherine Perkins[,] sister of Fred. And the families are intimate. But I doubt if she can do much but write books—[T]he world will not pardon peculiarities—and you may not be able to carry her without injuring your own usefulness.

I do not know her address—but a letter sent her enclosed in an envelope addressed to Mrs[.] John C. Day 28 Fifth Av. New York would reach her—as Mrs[.] Day is my daughter and would take pleasure in serving you. I shall be in N.Y. about middle of May and shall see Mrs[.] Gilman and can tell her all about you—but I would rather not urge her to anything and I have an impression she is giving up lecturing.

. . . I take magazines and newspapers coming to $75. a year in order to keep intelligent on public affairs—and my head is tired all the time—but it seems my duty to do as much as this. I shall be 80 next Feby.—but I am going to Rochester next month to Convention of The National Municipal League and hope to get in a few words on Woman in Municipal Governmt—this is our Bill in Legislature this year. Good bye for this time.

I am faithfully and affectionately yrs.
        Isabella B. Hooker

                [IBH to Olympia Brown, SchL]

Index